Jungian
Psychoanalysis

GW00777568

Jungian Psychoanalysis

WORKING IN THE SPIRIT OF
C.G. JUNG

Edited by
Murray Stein

OPEN COURT
Chicago and La Salle, Illinois

To order books from Open Court, call 1-800-815-2280 or visit www.opencourtbooks.com.

Open Court Publishing Company is a division of Carus Publishing Company.

Printed and bound in the United States of America.

Library of Congress Cataloging-in-Publication Data

Jungian psychoanalysis : working in the spirit of C.G. Jung / edited by Murray Stein.
     p. cm.
   Includes bibliographical references and index.
   ISBN 978-0-8126-9668-4 (trade pbk. : alk. paper) 1. Psychoanalysis.
2. Jung, C.G. (Carl Gustav), 1875-1961. I. Stein, Murray, 1943-
   BF173.J85J887 2010
   150.19'54—dc22

                             2010017043

CONTENTS

FOREWORD

Thomas B. Kirsch

The history of analytical psychology can be dated from the year 1912 when Jung first used the phrase in his book, *Wandlungen und Symbole der Libido* (later titled *Symbols of Transformation* in the *Collected Works*). At that time, Jung was still president of the International Psychoanalytic Association (IPA), and although in deep conflict with Freud was still considered a Freudian psychoanalyst. It was in the second half of this book that Jung first began to write about dream and myth as symbols of the collective psyche in a manner that led him away from Freud and infantile sexuality. He resigned from the IPA in 1914 and went through a serious and disorienting process of transformation, which he called "Confrontation with the Unconscious" in his autobiographical work, *Memories, Dreams, Reflections*. This period lasted until approximately 1918 (Jung 1961, ch. 6).

When Jung emerged from this inner crisis, analytical psychology was born as a separate but related discipline from psychoanalysis. Because of his basically introverted nature and what he had seen as a publicly and politically active Freudian, Jung was not interested in organizing a professional association around himself. However, because of his increasingly well known writings and many lectures in Switzerland and abroad, individuals from all over the world sought him out for analysis and consultation. This included a particularly significant contingent of people from both England and the United States. Jung began a series of English-speaking seminars in 1921 that were to last until 1939. A combination of analysis with Jung and/or one of his close assistants, mainly Toni Wolff, attendance at seminars, plus a letter from Jung were the basic requirements to establish one as a Jungian analyst. Hence, already prior to World War II there were Jungian analysts in Switzerland, England, the United States, Germany, France, Italy, and other countries. Small professional groups of analysts formed in Zurich, London, New York, and Berlin.

In these cities, too, Analytical Psychology Clubs existed in which both analysts and analysands were accepted for membership. The first of these had its initial meeting in Zurich on February 26, 1916. Its purpose was to provide a meeting place where those interested in archetypal symbolism and amplifying dream imagery could study specific symbols and hear lectures on related topics. Jung also wanted to see what the effect would be of having a group of analyzed people congregate together and how they would interact. Prior to World War II, there was some interest in forming a training institute in Zurich to be named after Jung, but such activities were interrupted by the war and were not renewed again until it ended. A collateral effect of the war was to disperse many of the Jewish Jungian analysts who have lived and worked in Europe to other parts of the world. Erich and Julia Neumann settled in Tel Aviv, James and Hilde Kirsch landed in Los Angeles, Ernst Bernhard fled to Rome, Gerhard and Hella Adler became influential members in London, and the list goes on. The above mentioned became founders of Jungian groups in their newly adopted countries.

After much prodding, Jung acquiesced and an institute named after him was founded in Zurich in 1947. Its goal was to train people in the theoretical and practical aspects of analytical psychology and Jungian analysis, and to that end it offered course work in clinical psychiatry, anthropology, mythology, comparative religion, fairy tales, and several other related fields. The C.G. Jung Institute of Zurich opened in 1948, and for the next twenty years it functioned as the world's leading training center for Jungian analysts. Other training programs were formed in London, New York, Los Angeles, and San Francisco, but in terms of courses and number of trainees Zurich was the main center. London soon became a strong second in importance.

At the time of Jung's eightieth birthday in 1955, the International Association for Analytical Psychology (IAAP) was founded in Zurich to offer an organization structure for the growing number of Jungian analysts internationally and to formally establish the profession as an international entity. One of its primary missions was stated as convening international congresses every three years for the purpose of sharing theoretical and clinical perspectives, offering new ideas, and continuing the development of the field. The first such congress was held in Zurich in August 1958. Some 120 analysts from around the world attended, and Jung himself was present at the opening night and the banquet. Papers amplifying archetypal themes dominated the program. Attendance was strictly limited to analysts only.

The second congress, again held in Zurich, took place in 1962. Jung had died in the interim. A sharp underlying conflict, which had already been present at the first congress, surfaced between the Zurich and London groups. The London Jungians had been deeply influenced by Melanie Klein, Donald Winnicott, Wilford Bion, and other Freudian psychoanalysts, and they had modified the classical Zurich ways of working with patients by utilizing the couch, increasing frequency of sessions to four times a week, and placing primary emphasis on analyzing transference and the impact of childhood development on adult psychological functioning. These modifications were a stark contrast to the approach that Jung himself had utilized and that the majority of Jungians worldwide continued to use in their practices, where they sat face-to-face with their patients, placed strong emphasis on dream interpretation and less on transference, and required a frequency of once or twice a week. For the next twenty years the conflict between London and Zurich dominated the congresses as well the field as a whole. The primary energy of analytical psychology gravitated between these two centers. First-generation Jungians who had analyzed with Jung presented their individual versions of the classical method by amplifying archetypal dream images, whereas the London school presented patients who showed early developmental problems with seemingly more severe psychopathology. In the beginning the contrast was quite marked.

By the mid-1980s, Freudian psychoanalysis had undergone a number of significant developments and shifts, including the appearance of the self psychology of Heinz Kohut and the Relational movement headed by Stephen Mitchell and Jessica Benjamin. In the Jungian world, analysts were paying more careful attention to boundary issues between patients and analysts, a wider variety of clinical issues became evident, and the distance between the London (developmental) and Zurich (classical) schools lessened. In the United States, there was a sharp increase of new analysts, and consequently the American voice was added as an important influence in the world of analytical psychology. International congresses were held in the United States in 1980 (San Francisco) and 1992 (Chicago), which at the beginning of the IAAP was not thought to be possible.

Psychoanalysis, which had its peak authority in mid-century and the decade beyond, began to lose some of its luster. Candidates were no longer lining up to become psychoanalysts. New developments in psychopharmacology promised instant relief from emotional difficulties, and analysis of any sort was no longer considered the gold standard of treatment for emotional disorders. During this same period, analytical psychology continued to grow and develop at a steady pace in the United States, England and Europe, and by 1989 there were 2000 accredited Jungian analysts within the IAAP. The major Western European countries had all developed national groups, which were growing in size. Although the main Jungian centers tended to be in the capital cities of these countries, satellite institutes were forming in the other major cities of each country. Some countries like Italy had two national societies due to political and theoretical differences, and England had four societies, all located in London. By 1989, most of the first generation of analysts, who had worked with Jung or Freud, were no longer active or had died, and relations between Freudian and Jungian psychoanalysts began to become more possible. The old feud that had raged in the first generation on both sides lessened, although even today it can flare up, especially in New York and Los Angeles where there is a large percentage of Jewish psychoanalysts. Jung's professional and cultural activities during the 1930s in relation to Germany continue to present a stumbling block for many professionals who otherwise might be interested in his work. To this day, rumors persist about Jung being a Nazi and actively anti-Semitic. Jung's relationship to the political situation in Europe at that time is complex, and discussions of it have rarely taken into account the nuances that must be addressed in order to understand his position accurately. Many of Jung's Jewish students have attempted to explain his position during the 1930s, but their clarifications have not dispelled the issue (Kirsch 1982 and 1983; Samuels 1993). A forthcoming book of correspondence between Jung and James Kirsch will provide new primary documentation of Jung's position during the 1930s.

The year 1989 was important for the world and also for analytical psychology. The Berlin Wall fell, and the collapse of communism in Eastern Europe and Russia brought about many changes in those countries. Individuals from throughout Eastern Europe and Russia began to show a strong interest in learning more about analytical psychology. Previously, due to the restrictions placed on them by the communist system, these people had little actual knowledge of the history of psychoanalysis and analytical psychology in the West. The conflicts and developments within psychoanalysis, which we in the West had lived with and knew so well, were almost entirely unknown to them. Contact between the countries of Eastern Europe and the West grew rapidly, and a serious problem arose about how to train people interested in becoming Jungian psychoanalysts. The main question was how to arrange for them to obtain personal analysis and supervision. Books and theoretical seminars could more easily be provided. As it happened, a couple of Jungian analysts moved to Moscow for a period of time and were able to provide analysis and supervision, but for the most part either analysts would travel from the West for short periods of time (one to two weeks), or else students from these countries would arrange to travel to Germany or Zurich for analysis.

One specific example should be mentioned because the scope of the project was and continues to be so immense. Under the leadership of Jan Wiener and Catherine Crowther from London (SAP), money was raised from the IAAP, British foundations, and through large-scale benefits to provide regular supervision and shuttle analysis with people identified as suitable candidates for training in St. Petersburg and Moscow. Some twenty Jungian psychoanalysts from the four U.K. groups volunteered to travel to Russia on a regular basis and provide analysis, supervision, and seminars to the analysts in training. At the 2007 IAAP Congress in Cape Town, South Africa, a Russian society of Jungian psychoanalysts with eighteen members was accepted. This is a remarkable achievement in a relatively short time (about seven years). Individuals from other countries formerly behind the Iron Curtain have been able to obtain individual membership in the IAAP, but in none of the other countries has a sufficient number of candidates finished their training to form a society as yet.

The spread of analytical psychology since the 1970s has been worldwide, in fact. Professional Jungian groups have developed in Venezuela, Chile, Uruguay, and Brazil in South America, in South Africa, in Korea, Japan, Australia, and New Zealand. Each of these has gone on to form an official IAAP training society. The growth of interest in analytical psychology has truly become global.

What does the world of analytical psychology look like currently? Although one can find foci of interest in analytical psychology in many countries, there have been definite shifts in influence. Analytical psychology began with Jung in Zurich, and during Jung's lifetime and until his death in 1961 Zurich was looked upon as a kind of Jungian Mecca and the premier place to train. London, with its alternative view of analytical psychology and emphasis on developmental issues and transference, also has been a major training center. The United States has never had a national Jungian association, but instead there exist numerous local societies with slightly differing approaches to Jung's work. An informal Council of North American Societies of Jungian Analysts (CNASJA), founded in 1978 and made up of delegates from each of the North American societies, meets on a yearly basis. The Council has made recommendations on many issues, but it has had no legal authority to enforce decisions.

Almost all Western European countries have a national association and in many countries, such as Italy, Belgium, and the UK, there is more than one national society. Eastern Europe is slowly developing national professional groups. The areas of most rapid growth include South America and Asia, where there is much interest but few Jungian psychoanalysts at this time. In China sandplay, which developed out of Jung's circle in Zurich, is a major interest of psychologists. A similar situation holds true for other Asian countries. The IAAP, as the international organization accrediting Jungian professional societies and individual psychoanalysts, continues to be led by Western Europeans and Americans. The voice of other regions is growing in volume but has not yet reached a critical point.

The complex development of analytical psychology has been shaped by many factors. Jung's two forays into leadership roles in professional psychoanalytic and psychotherapeutic organizations, as president of the IPA and of the International Medical Psychotherapy Society, turned out badly for him personally and for his followers professionally. After these efforts, he did not highly value organizational life, and so professional associations were slow to develop around him even when the need and demand became great. Another important factor was that the Freud/Jung conflict influenced many psychotherapists against Jung, especially while the Freudian model had so much influence in the professional world. Jung's relations with Germans during the Nazi period kept many Jewish psychotherapists from even considering his work. Finally, Jung's interest in the nonrational and in subjects like synchronicity has fascinated many people and turned off others.

From the point of view of this author, who has been in the field for over forty years, it appears that Jung's point of view and that of analytical psychology in general has greater relevance today than ever before. When one looks at the many religious and cultural conflicts around the world, it appears that analytical psychology could have an important role to play. Jung's writings on the spiritual crises of his day are still relevant for contemporary society. Today we no longer have a direct link to Jung, but with his written works and those of many people who have come after him, plus our professional trainings in so many different countries and cultures, we continue to develop the field in creative new ways. This book, *Jungian Psychoanalysis*, is a prime example of that development.

REFERENCES

Jung, C.G. 1961. *Memories, dreams, reflections.* New York: Vintage Books.
Kirsch, James. 1982. C.G. Jung and the Jews: The real story. *Journal of Psychology and Judaism* 6, 2.
———. 1983. Reconsidering Jung's so-called anti-Semitism. In *The arms of the windmill: Essays in Analytical Psychology in honor of Werner H. Engel*, ed. Joan Carson, 5–27. Baltimore: Lucas.
Kirsch, Thomas B. 2000. *The Jungians.* London: Routledge.
Lammers, A., ed. In press. *Correspondence between C.G. Jung and James Kirsch.* New York: Routledge/Brunner.
Samuels, Andrew. 1993. *The political psyche.* London: Routledge.

THOMAS B. KIRSCH, M.D., is a training analyst at the C.G. Jung Institute of San Francisco and a past president of the IAAP. He is the author of *The Jungians* and of numerous papers on the history of analytical psychology.

EDITOR'S PREFACE

I have reserved a table for dinner.
Your name, please.
Carl Jung.
Do you mean you're the famous "Freud, Adler, Jung"?
No, just Jung.

An apocryphal story, but one that says a lot.

Jung differentiated himself from Freud and Adler, two other pioneers of psychoanalysis, and founded a distinctive branch of depth psychology (or medical psychology, as it was called in the early days) called analytical psychology. This school's physical and spiritual home was Zurich, Switzerland. The theoretical and clinical points of difference among the three founding figures, especially the differences between Jung and Freud, have been widely discussed in many publications and biographies. Here I will only remark that in the first and second generations Jungians marked the lines separating themselves from the others with broad pen and heavy ink as the differences in fundamental perspectives and practices were emphasized in order to differentiate the field from its surrounding milieu. More recently the emphasis among contemporary Jungian authors has shifted to perspectives of convergence and dialogue. This may be taken as a sign of maturation in the field. There is less anxiety about identity.

The clinical practitioners in the school that took form around Jung have variously called themselves analytical psychologists, Jungian analysts, and Jungian psychotherapists. In more recent years they have increasingly recognized their historic, if not untroubled, kinship with the greater family of psychoanalysis and have taken to naming themselves Jungian psychoanalysts. Hence the title of this book.

Jungian psychoanalysis is the contemporary name for the clinical application of analytical psychology.

From the very beginning, the people who surrounded Jung and assisted in the development of the school he founded in Zurich came from many parts of the world. A strong international presence therefore has characterized analytical psychology from the outset and continues so to this day. In addition, the people who first took up the practice of analytical psychology were by no means all medically trained. As a consequence, so-called lay analysis was part of the professional make-up of the school throughout its history, and in recent years the large majority of Jungian psychoanalysts have nonmedical backgrounds. Jung himself, while originally educated as a psychiatrist, had interests so broad that he soon saw the limitations of confining the practice of analysis to medical professionals. Collaboration among a multitude of disciplines has been a part of the theory and practice of analytical psychology throughout its history. This spirit continues to be strongly in evidence today.

The articles in the present volume reflect the changes that have taken place in the field during the past decade and a half and after the passing of the second generation, many of whom had known and worked with Jung personally in the 1930s and 1940s. As a statement from the field, this book is, I believe, quite fully representative of the many strands of thought and of the rich diversity of approaches and thinking that today constitute the complex tapestry of Jungian analytical writing and thinking. The reader will find a prevailing interweave, perhaps today approaching the point of seamless integration, of the well known classical, developmental, and archetypal branches of analytical psychology as well as of an impressive array of borrowings from modern psychoanalytic thinkers beyond the boundaries of analytical psychology whose ideas and insights are by no means inspired by Jungian sources but whose views are increasingly regarded as convergent and compatible.

Nevertheless, at the center of contemporary Jungian psychoanalytic thinking there remains, as ever, the towering figure of C.G. Jung. His published works, however variously construed they may be by later authors, continue to occupy the privileged position of key reference point. The twenty volumes of Jung's *Collected Works*, along with the several published volumes of letters, the now well edited and published seminars that he gave in Zurich and abroad, and several other collections of incidental writings form the accepted foundation for theorizing and reflecting on Jungian practice. Jung's seminal intuition of the psyche as evolving, changing, and goal-seeking—in other words, individuating—remains the core perception around which everything else is constructed. It was his long and careful articulation of the unconscious as purposive and of the total psyche as oriented by the self, which guides and governs the lived processes of psychological life, that constitutes the key inspiration behind the work of the thousands (by now) of writings by most other thinkers in this field.

These ideas continue to guide recent contributions to Jungian psychoanalytic thought as much as they did the first two generations of Jungians, and they are plainly in evidence in the articles of this volume. Jung's view of the psyche is that it is not fundamentally flawed and pathological (that is, destined to play out an invariably tragic story) but rather oriented toward lifelong development that may or may not be only partially or relatively fully realized. By no means does this mean that psychopathology is ignored. As many of the articles in this volume will amply testify, pathology no doubt corrupts and interrupts the processes of individuation at all stages of life, but the psyche seeks to overcome its illnesses in various ways, and this individuating self is what the Jungian psychoanalyst looks for, allies with, and uses to foster and encourage the processes of change and growth in consciousness. The analyst tries to follow and facilitate a natural emergence of the self in the psyche rather than imposing a program for improvement in ego functioning or surgically removing pathological structures through incisive interpretations. Generally, Jungian psychoanalysis is seen as a collaborative effort at reflection, and dialogue rather than one-sided dogmatic interpretation is the rule.

To work "in the spirit of Jung" means, if anything, to work with the whole self in mind. As this gets spelled out in this volume, the reader will see that this has principally to do with engagement in a dialectical play between conscious and unconscious and between the two persons taking part in the analytic process. Gradually this dialectic builds toward a sense of wholeness in personal and archetypal terms. The end result of a Jungian psychoanalysis—granting for the moment the possibility of "success" in this endeavor—is not principally "better functioning" or "improved coping skills," nor is it a greater emotional sense of wellbeing, happiness, or self-worth, although these are certainly worthy by-products not to be discounted. The primary sought-for result is awareness of personal life patterns of coherence and direction that are rooted deeply in the psyche as a whole, that is, in the self. One gains as well a wide perspective on how one belongs to one's personal, cultural, and historical context. Personal and cultural complexes and archetypal images rise to the surface of consciousness and merge with ego consciousness to form an image of self that is much greater than it had been before analysis began.

How is this type of consciousness brought into being? Jungian psychoanalysts employ a number of methods that are aimed toward accomplishing this result, as the reader will discover in many of the articles. The sought-after change agent that must be introduced into the psychic matrix is implied in the notion of "coming into contact with the unconscious" or "developing a transcendent function," phrases that are familiar in traditional Jungian literature and that are embedded in many of the articles in this volume as well. The point is not to create a permanent state of all-inclusive consciousness in the individual undertaking analysis, but to catch glimpses of something like that and to develop the freedom to think and feel in the most inclusive and imaginative ways possible. This means working through fears, inhibitions, and defenses of all kinds, especially the unconscious primitive forms. It calls for passing through painful memories and realizations about oneself and others and digesting the bitterness of such recollections and insights. The analyst presses for developing the capacity to see oneself from behind, as it were, to overhear oneself as though one were an interlocutor to oneself, and to offer a welcoming hand to new ideas, images, and self-representations, whatever they may be, as they emerge in the course of analysis.

The methods for bringing about this type of consciousness are designed to open up the mind and to interpret what one finds there. In Jungian psychoanalysis, this exploration takes place in the space created between two persons who are dedicated to the exploration of psychic reality. The analyst may follow several routes for delving into the hidden world of the unconscious (dreams, fantasies, active imagination, complex discharges, transference) and additionally several methods for gathering these insights and fixing them in memory and consciousness (interpretation, sandplay, art-making, body movement). The intention is to build up an identity based on the whole self. The technical term for this expanded image is the transcendent function.

What about infancy, childhood, adolescence, young adulthood? Freudians have traditionally focused heavily on these early stages of life, while Jungians have been more known for addressing issues pertaining to the second half of life. As the reader of these articles will find, however, Jungian psychoanalysts today pay a surprising amount of attention to early development as well. Individuation in the second half of life, which follows a circular rather than a linear path, is heavily dependent on successful passages through the developmental phases in the first half. From a Jungian perspective, the early stages are preparatory for the later, and a major reason for working analytically and therapeutically with children, adolescents, and young adults is to maximize their chances for gaining maturity later on. The pathologies engendered by early trauma, by insufficient bonding and attachment, and by failure of separation from parents and family of origin all lead to a second half of life that is stagnant, defensive, and threatened by steady decline of resourcefulness, resiliency, and creativity. If the fruits of maturity and individuation are greater consciousness and deeper compassion toward oneself and others—in short, wisdom and transcendence—the failure to individuate results in resentment, isolation, and spiritual poverty.

Most Jungian psychoanalysts in practice today are people well advanced into the second half of life. I have not conducted a careful survey, but from my years a president of the International Association for Analytical Psychology I know a great number of them in many parts of the world, and I would estimate their average age today to be in the mid-to-late fifties. They are people who are, if not invariably wise, at least in possession of a good deal of life experience and careful training in the art and craft of analysis. My impression is that for the most part they are dedicated to continuing their personal work toward individuation and honing their skills as professional analysts. At the same time, I do not underestimate the potential for shadow enactments well into old age. Professional societies of analysts have assumed the obligation for watching over their members where ethics are concerned, and many societies are finding it wise to institute requirements for ongoing supervision (or intervision) and continuing education for all of their members no matter how senior. A number of articles cover these matters.

The authors included in this volume have been trained and work in a wide variety of cultural settings. This assembly of voices is international and speaks from six continents. The book reflects the international character of Jungian psychoanalysis and its many perspectives. As Thomas Kirsch explains in the foreword, the field of analytical psychology has expanded considerably from its origins in Switzerland. Jungian psychoanalysts are active today in all the countries of Western Europe and also now in many countries of Eastern Europe as well; throughout the Americas; also in Australia, Asia, and Africa. At the present time, they play a significant role in mental health professions worldwide and increasingly teach in academic institutions. In recent years, Jungians have also taken up extensive consideration of modern developments in other psychoanalytic schools and of contemporary scientific research. What the articles in this volume demonstrate is that these assimilations from outside the field of analytical psychology have enriched but not overshadowed the core ideas and perspectives that Jung expounded in his voluminous writings. If anything, the work of Jung looms larger today than it did forty years ago, in large part because so many of the recent developments in the fields of modern psychoanalysis and neuroscience appear to be affirming and supporting the key principles that he put forward in the first half of the twentieth century.

When I invited the authors in this volume to make their specific contributions, I encouraged them to speak in their own voices, to express their own thinking and feeling as it applies to the topics they are writing about, and to be courageous and creative in expanding upon their own particular visions and convictions. The result, I am happy to say, is a lively collection of distinctive essays rather than a dry textbook of received opinion and references. It might be too much to claim that this is the authoritative text in the field of Jungian psychoanalysis at this time, but it is doubtless as close to such as one will find. I hope the reader will find the essays contained here, singly and as a conglomerate, informative and stimulating.

—MURRAY STEIN

PART ONE

GOALS

Introduction to GOALS
Murray Stein

It is difficult to speak about the goals of analysis in a general and all encompassing way. Each case is different and calls for specific considerations. The Jungian psychoanalyst is trained to look at each analysand as an individual with a unique history and quite specific challenges. The outcome of analysis is therefore in each case different and treatment must be tailored to the individual. One size does not fit all. That said, however, there are some general perspectives that apply to many if not all cases, just as in medicine there are no two cases alike and yet treatment of a heart condition in one case is not so different from treatment in a similar case. Some generalizations can be made as long as one keeps in mind the special uniqueness of each individual soul.

The chapters in this section are principally designed around a model offered by Jung in a paper entitled "Problems of Modern Psychotherapy" (in CW 16), where he outlined four stages of psychotherapeutic treatment: confession, elucidation, education, and transformation. Stanton Marlan's chapter, "Facing the Shadow," takes up the first of these and expands on the concept of confession as a matter of raising the shadow figures and energies of the psyche into consciousness and integrating them. Patricia Vesey-McGrew unpacks the meaning of elucidation in her chapter, "Getting on Top of Thought and Behavior Patterns." This extends the range of consciousness from shadow content and dynamics to emotional and behavioral patterns in general, in order to form a grasp on the personal complexes that control these patterns unconsciously. Thomas Singer, in the chapter he writes with Catherine Kaplinsky entitled "The Cultural Complex in Analysis," lays out the theory of cultural complexes and thereby deepens and broadens the discussion of raising the operation of complexes into consciousness to include content derived from the analysand's cultural background. The goal of analysis, as it is conceptualized in these articles, is to step out of the bipolar dynamics of the autonomous complexes in order to clear consciousness and free a person from the automatic emotional responses engendered by them.

Josephine Evetts-Secker follows up on these reflections with a chapter on "Initiating a Psychological Education" in analysis. This is a cognitive piece in

Jungian psychoanalysis, having the objective of helping the analysand to gain a personal understanding about psychological functioning. In the long run, a full Jungian psychoanalysis is very much an educational experience. The more an analysand understands the dreams, fantasies, thoughts, emotional reactions, and interpersonal dynamics that make up the bulk of psychological life, the better chance there is to form an individual and satisfying attitude toward life in general as it continues during and after analysis.

The most defining goal of Jungian psychoanalysis has traditionally been discussed as transformation of the personality. This means a deeper than merely cognitive change in the analysand's attitudes toward self, others, and the world. Diane Cousineau Brutsche engages this topic in her chapter, "Instigating Transformation," and Joseph Cambray continues the theme in his article, "Emergence and the Self." Jung's main contribution to the psychoanalytic tradition as a whole, it could be said, revolves around his understanding of transformation. These two articles offer a contemporary account of it.

Taken together, the chapters in this section express both the variety and the coherence of how Jungian psychoanalysts reflect upon the goals of analytic treatment today. They weave and blend both traditional and contemporary Jungian perspectives as well as much assimilation from other schools of modern psychoanalysis.

1

FACING THE SHADOW

Stanton Marlan

The Sun and its shadow complete the work.

—MICHAEL MAIER, *Atalanta Fugiens*, 278

Jung's notion of the shadow is an important contribution to the theory and practice of depth psychology and psychoanalysis. The way the shadow has been understood has naturally developed in the context of each writer's orientation within the field, sometimes emphasizing its classical, developmental, and/or archetypal place and meaning within an overall conception of psychic life and view of analysis. As older categories begin to blur, thinking within the field continues to differentiate and thought deepens.

In this essay, I will not precisely trace the history of the concept in Jung's work or within the field in general beyond what is necessary for my reflections, nor provide a summary of the Jungian literature on the shadow. Such information is widely available from many sources. My intention here is to look at the shadow as a living psychological phenomenon that continues to have more to teach us about the psyche.

Facing the shadow is one of the more important goals of Jungian psychoanalysis. In earlier editions of his book, *Jungian Analysis*, Murray Stein described the aims and goals of Jungian analysis as "coming to terms with the unconscious" (Stein 1995, 38). Facing the shadow is a key aspect of this overall work. Stein notes that coming to terms with the shadow means "calling into question the illusions one clings to most dearly about oneself, which have been used to shore up self-esteem and to maintain a sense of personal identity" (Stein 1995, 40). Facing the shadow and confronting one's illusions are understandably painful moments in analysis.

In the most general sense, one might define the shadow as referring to the darkness of the unconscious, to what is rejected by consciousness, both positive and negative contents as well as to that which has not yet or perhaps will never become conscious. Turning toward this darkness means facing the unacceptable, undesirable, and underdeveloped parts of ourselves, the crippled, blind, cruel, ugly, inferior, inflated, and sometimes vile, as well as discovering the potentials for further development of which we are unaware. For Jung, our attempt to fit in with our families and with historical and cultural values result in the personality developing what he called a persona, a mask through which adaptation is facilitated, but a nevertheless necessary structure of relationship.

In order to adapt, those aspects of the larger personality deemed unacceptable are often denied, repressed, and split off from the developing personality. As a result, they can become tortured, wounded, maimed, and can recede into the dark where ultimately they may be killed and buried. Other potentials of the self that have never been conscious may likewise be resisted and never come into conscious relationship with the personality. This dynamic process helps to form that part of the psyche Jung called the shadow. In spite of its banishment to a nether world, the shadow continues to play a dynamic role in our psychological life.

Jung explored the way in which the shadow emerges into awareness, often through irrational eruptions that impede consciousness. The shadow's trickster-like behavior acts as if it had a mind of its own, sending conscious life into a retrograde movement, where something other than the personal will seems to hold sway. The shadow appears as well in dreams, projections, transferences, and countertransferences and, while on the one hand resisting consciousness, on the other seems to be pursuing it by seeking confrontation, challenge and threat, often leaving the person terrified and retreating from contact. Angst about the shadow is not surprising. Some current dream images of patients reveal the shadow emerging in the form of primitive disembodied voices and spirits, wounded animals, impervious cold-blooded prehistoric and mythical beasts, stalkers, murderers, and sexual perverts. In addition, patients' dreams have presented images of disgusting beer-drinking alcoholics, down-and-out gamblers, heavily made-up unattractive women, men with outrageously bad taste, dull-witted jerks, and paralyzed figures locked into frozen rages. Deep emotion has often accompanied images such as those of severe and at times incurable illness, as well as scarred, disfigured, and sometimes dead infants and children haunting graves and burial grounds.

Jacques Lacan once noted that "psychoanalysis involves allowing the analysand to elaborate the unconscious knowledge that is in him not in the form of depth, but in the form of a cancer" (Lacan, in Fink 2007, 74). Facing such horrific images is indeed like facing a cancer not necessarily manifested physically but psychically proliferating and often leading to narcissistic mortification, humiliation, despair, and depression. In the face of such images, rational order can be shaken. Opening our psychic life to such images can be wounding and destabilizing, and there is a natural and understandable resistance to doing so.

I wrote about the most difficult and darkest images of the shadow in *The Black Sun* (Marlan 2005). *Sol niger* is the quintessential image of primordial shadow, and in its blacker than black dimension it resists assimilation. Facing it is one of the most difficult tasks for analysis and is often not possible.

Poems written about the Tantric goddess Kali attempt to capture this over-whelming dimension of psychic life. May Sarton, in her poem "The Invocation of Kali," describes her as a "built-in destroyer," a "savage goddess;" "She keeps us from being what we long to be;" "We may hold her like a lunatic, but it is she held down, who bloodies with her claws" (Sarton 1971, 19–24). Sarton continues her poem by speaking of Kali as "what we fear most and have not dared to face," and Swami Vivekananda likewise describes the impact of facing this goddess:

> The stars are blotted out,
> Clouds are covering clouds . . .
> The flash of lurid light
> Reveals on every side
> A thousand, thousand shades
> Of Death begrimed and black—
> Scattering plagues and sorrows . . .
>
> (VIVEKANANDA, in Mookerjee 1988, 108)

It is hard to imagine facing a shadow figure as potent as the goddess described in these images, and yet the poet Sarton speaks of staying "open-eyed, in this terrible place" and Vivekananda of hugging "the form of Death" and dancing "in destruction's dance." As if addressing the goddess, he invites her in with the words, "Come, Mother, Come!" (Mookerjee 1988, 108).

In these powerful poems, the poets give us a hint about facing this aspect of the primordial shadow. It is difficult to translate this into analytic principles, but clearly the hard work of facing the shadow and of analysis is in part learning to turn toward the painful, unpleasant and at times horrifying figures of the psyche, and thus toward the unacceptable aspects of the self. The deepest recesses of the archetypal shadow may be unredeemable, and we may need to let go of salvationist hopes or be driven to do so, but not all shadow figures are as horrifying as *Sol niger* and Kali. These images remind us that life can be tragic and that the unconscious is not invariably benevolent.

There are limits to what analysis can accomplish, and this is sobering to our overzealous expectations. In such instances, the analyst may be called upon to sit with the analysand in and through loss, grief, despair and the tragic experiences of life, and be company on the ship of death and in silence be witness to the limits of analysis and to the hopes and dreams of the human soul. And yet, there will be moments when the "death" we face may turn out to be a symbolic one, heralding an alchemical process of *mortificatio* and *putrefactio*, which can lead to renewal and the opening to a deepened symbolic life.

Stein has noted that "persons in analysis are asked explicitly or implicitly to stay receptive to the unconscious—to the less rational, more ambiguous, and often mysterious side of the personality" (Stein 1995, 39). It is important that the analyst as well is prepared to venture into the darkest recesses of the shadow as a participant and guide with the capacity to sit still, stay present, accompany, and facilitate facing the darkest aspects of psychic life. In so doing, the shadow figures may show themselves to compensate or complement a one-sided conscious position, and facing them can lead to a more integrated personality. Still, the question remains: how to face such figures?

Not all shadow images are horrific, but nevertheless they remain difficult to face. Hillman speaks of the broken, ruined, weak, sick, inferior, and socially unacceptable parts of ourselves (Hillman 1991). For him, curing these shadow images requires love. He asks: "How far can our love extend to the broken and ruined parts of ourselves, the disgusting and perverse? How much charity and compassion have we for our own weakness and sickness? How far can we . . . allow a place for everyone?" (Hillman 1991, 242). Because the shadow can be socially unacceptable and even *evil*, it is important that it is carried by us, which means that we do not project our unacceptable parts on to others and or act them out. This is an ethical responsibility.

The importance of refraining from creating scapegoats loaded down with our own evils is particularly urgent in today's world situation. This was one of the main concerns of Erich Neumann, who considered the shadow a moral and ethical issue of prime importance (Neumann 1969). For Neumann, facing the shadow and integrating the psychic opposites can lead to the development of a supra-ordinate unity. Carrying Jung's ideas further into the ethical dimension, Neumann found a basic tendency in the psyche that he called centroversion—a dynamic aspect of the self that can enlarge and balance the personality. For Hillman as well, a moral stance toward the shadow is essential and cannot be abandoned, but this is not enough: "At one moment something else must break through" (Hillman 1991, 242–43). Facing the shadow and its cure requires a conjunction of seeming opposites, a confrontation, and a paradoxical union of two incommensurables: "the moral recognition that these parts of me are burdensome and intolerable and must change, and the loving laughing acceptance which takes them just as they are. . . . [One] both judges harshly and joins gladly." Each position holds "one side of the truth" (Hillman 1991, 243). Hillman gives an example from the Jewish mystical tradition of the Chassidim, where "deep moral piety is coupled with astounding delight in life" (Hillman 1991, 243).

To achieve such an attitude requires considerable psychological development, but it still seems almost impossible to imagine taking delight in the deeply heinous and virulent aspects of the shadow. How can we participate in the implications of perversity, with Nazi images of the Holocaust, and with the terrorist shadow? Could Job join gladly with the dark side of God, which according to Jung required a moral transformation and Job's personal outrage? Yet, while feeling judgments are essential to ethical life, moral outrage can also be inflated, too rational and one-sided, that one can miss seeing into the paradoxical and transformational aspects of such horrific images. Therefore, without more fully understanding the psychological implication of such images, we are left with only black or white possibilities.

For Hillman, the traditional psychoanalytic position of the Freudian school was too rational and did not do justice to the psyche. According to him, Freud "did not see fully enough that each image and each experience had a prospective as well as a reductive aspect, a positive as well as a negative side . . . [or] see clearly enough the paradox that rotten garbage is also fertilizer, that childishness is also childlikeness, that polymorphous perversity is also joy and physical liberty . . ." (Hillman 1991, 243). These paradoxical images require the positions of both Freudian and Jungian psychoanalyses and, according to him, are not two specific and conflicting positions; rather, the reductive and prospective aspects of the shadow must be seen together in the paradoxes of symbolic life.

Jungian psychoanalysis carries both reductive and prospective vectors within itself. Jung took for granted the psychoanalytic view, which relies on a series of energetic and developmental notions, including adaptation, resistance, denial, suppression, repression, conflict formation, splitting, projection, the return of the repressed, and so on. In addition to those, he contributed a series of his own conceptual perspectives, mythopoetic and archetypal insights that emerged from his experience of himself and his patients. His choice of the experience-near term "shadow" reflects this contribution and was based on the notion that the unconscious tends to personify itself, as in dreams. Such personifications "show the most striking connections with the poetic, religious, or mythological formulations . . ." (Jung 1939/1968, para. 516). Later in life Jung deepened this notion in his alchemical work. These personifications, when faced, can point in the most surprising directions.

One difficulty in thinking about Jung's idea of the shadow is that he relied on both modes of discourse, and the two styles of thought are often imagined as diametrically opposed. Yet they engender a complexity of personal and archetypal, scientific and mythical, causal-reductive and teleological perspectives. Lambert has described these opposites linguistically in terms of the distinction between the language of the intellect and the language of imagination (Lambert 1981). Samuels has noted that "the goal of having a model in which both languages play a part may be difficult to achieve" (Samuels 1985, 6) and yet, I believe, this is the aim of Jungian analysis. It is most often the case that these two orientations, directed thinking and imagining, play a role in all Jungian orientations, but that one or the other becomes privileged and reduces the other to a secondary position, consciously or unconsciously. In short, these two languages may be said to shadow one another, perhaps by necessity.

The philosopher Paul Ricoeur addressed a similar concern with regard to Freudian analysis. In his book *Freud and Philosophy*, Ricoeur speaks of the possibility of carrying and engendering opposed interpretations, each of which is self-consistent, into relation with one another. He describes these orientations as hermeneutic strategies: one turned toward the "revival of archaic meanings belonging to the infancy of mankind, the other toward the emergence of figures that anticipate our spiritual adventure" (Ricoeur 1970, 496). For Ricoeur, what psychoanalysis "calls overdetermination cannot be understood apart from a dialectic between [these] two functions, which are thought to be opposed to one another but which symbols coordinate into a concrete unity" (ibid., 490). I believe Jung was seeking this same unity in his understanding of a symbolic life.

For both Ricoeur and Jung, concrete symbols carry both functions and link these orientations which both oppose and yet are grounded in one another. "Such symbols both disguise and reveal. While they conceal the aims of our instincts, they disclose the process of self consciousness" (Ricoeur, 497). Living in relation to such symbols and images requires a continuing dialectic between thought and imagination, between what Jung called fantasy and directed thinking (Jung 1956, para. 39) and between what is conscious and unconscious. Ultimately, for Ricoeur it is philosophical and conceptual thought that is able to rise above the shadow to a privileged position. However, from a Jungian perspective, there is a danger in theories becoming too removed from their unconscious base and from life.

Theories, too, cast a shadow, and Jung struggled with this issue:

> Conscious and unconscious do not make a whole when one of them is suppressed and injured by the other. If they must contend, let it be a fair fight with equal rights on both sides. Both are aspects of life. Consciousness should defend its reason and protect itself, and the chaotic life of the unconscious should be given the chance of having its way too—as much of it as we can stand. This means open conflict and open collaboration at once . . . It is the old game of hammer and anvil: between them the patient iron is forged into an indestructible whole, an "individual." (Jung 1939/1968, para. 522)

For Jung, the prospect of rising above images and symbols into the conceptual abstractions of science, philosophy and religion was questionable. He sought instead to bind together and maintain the tensions of psyche life in a way that produced a paradoxical and transcendent but still concrete possibility. This meant staying closely connected to the shadow and imaginal life and not leaving the unconscious or shadow behind. For Jung, it was important to think and theorize but also to 'dream the dream onward' while at the same time not believing naively in the literalism of the unconscious.

According to Jung, the technical languages of philosophy, science, and theology could easily turn one-sided, pressing other modes of discourse into the shadow. This is a position taken up and elaborated by Hillman, who argues for the importance of a language not unlike that of the alchemists in which images do not disappear into concepts (Hillman 1980). To be clear, Hillman is not proposing that we abandon our concepts, just that we do not use them one-sidedly in a way that always translates fantasy thinking into directed thinking. When this happens, "our concepts extend their grasp over concretely vivid images by abstracting (literally, 'drawing away') their matter" (ibid., 125).

One of Jung's main, and perhaps most important, contributions is his use of personification, in which he retains the imagistic quality of thought. As a result, emphasis on the concrete imagery of the shadow has been an important contribution of the Jungian and Archetypal approach. For Hillman, as for Jung, the founding of the psyche upon images and personifications "rather than upon concepts borrowed from the sciences or philosophy [means that] even Jung's metapsychology remains psychology" (Hillman 1975, 22). According to Hillman, Jung never deserts the psyche in search of explanatory principles outside of its own imaginal world. I believe this is what Edinger also meant when he noted, "As Jung studied alchemy he found that this luxuriant network of images was, indeed, the psyche's 'own water' which could be used to understand the complex contents of the psyche" (Edinger 1985, 1).

For Jung, Edinger, and Hillman, the fundamental facts of psyche's existence are fantasy images; for them, image *is* psyche. In the pursuit of privileging this aspect of Jung's heritage, Hillman deconstructs Jung's famous distinction between archetype per se and archetypal images. Archetype per se is disregarded. For some analysts this casts a theoretical shadow of its own.

Kenneth Newman is representative of this latter position. He argues that privileging the image, as is the case to some extent with Jung and even more so with Hillman, neglects an important aspect of the scientific imagination. For Newman, there is a psychic hole within the image, "a shadow of the shadow," where the a-imaginal is found, and "psyche has the capacity to access . . . that which eludes any image because it is outside the sensorium of man" (Newman 1993, 38), but not outside of his imagination. For Newman, "the imagination can see through and beyond what the eye sees . . ." (ibid.). Giving recognition to the realm of the a-imaginal is important and is the reason why the scientific imagination comes into being. He notes that science is "not an instance where nominalism and rational explanation are squeezing out soul, but a realm outside of soul" (ibid, 41). Rather, the reverse is the case:

> Anima-zation or feminine soulizing creates its own lacuna, which eclipses other worlds. And in that umbra, which we have called the shadow of the shadow, we find the animus and masculine soulizing. Scientific thinking is a manifestation of masculine eros relating to the a-sensorial and a-imaginal, by virtue of no longer being image bound, for not all things imaginary are imaginal. (ibid.)

Neil Micklem is likewise concerned about knowledge of what is beyond sense and image. However, instead of imagining access to this a-imaginal world through science, he turns to religion, and particularly to the paradoxical teachings of Meister Eckhart. Opening oneself to the a-imaginal is opening to a transpersonal world of divinity, which requires detachment, emptiness, and "switching off from the senses and ridding ourselves of images in order to gain not the image, but the real thing" (Micklem 1993, 120).

Newman's "science" and Micklem's "religion" find resonance with the masculine Eros of Wolfgang Giegerich, who has also critiqued Jung and Hillman for granting fundamental priority to images. In his book *The Soul's Logical Life*, Giegerich turns to philosophy, particularly the philosophy of Hegel, for inspiration. Like Newman, Giegerich argues that thinking has been undervalued and underdeveloped under the weight of images in Jung's and Hillman's psychology. Giegerich's work turns from the imaginal to the logical.

While Newman, Micklem, and Giegerich see a shadow side to privileging images as the basis for psychic life, each of them thinks about the a-imaginal in his own way. Nevertheless, they agree that a theoretical or metaphysical shadow is cast when the primary focus is on images. Jung's Kantian influence lead him to be more cautious about making what he considered to be metaphysical statements about the real, at least within the realms of philosophy and religion. His orientation remained psychological, and this was why his focus on images was fundamental.

From my perspective, it is important to continue to struggle with the relationship of concept and image without subjugating one to the other, without letting one or the other fall into the shadow. Newman's focus on the a-imaginal as a hole in the image might be seen as part of the dynamic property of images themselves, as a place where thought can reach out beyond psyche. But if thinking becomes disconnected from the subtle body of the image, masculine eros can degenerate into its animus-laden shadow. For me, the hole in the image can also be imagined as an axis point to the unimaginal void, the place where images are both deconstructed and reanimated and where the subtle body announces a mysterious and paradoxical view of images beyond pictures or representations. In this sense, the shadow of the image intimately belongs to it. What most critics of archetypal psychology have failed to note is that for Hillman, too, not everything archetypal can be contained by the psyche "since they manifest as well in physical, social, linguistic, aesthetic and spiritual modes" (Hillman 1983/2004, 13).

Jung ultimately saw in alchemy that the work of facing the shadow was a paradoxical union of opposites at the core of psychological and alchemical work. In the chapter, "The Paradoxa," in his late work, *Mysterium Coniunctionis*, Jung speaks of the importance of the opposites to the alchemists and how they attempted "to visualize the opposites together but to express them in the same breath" (Jung 1955-56/1963, para. 36). In this spirit, I began this article with an epigraph from Michael Maier's *Atalanta Fugiens*: "The Sun and its shadow complete the work." In this vision, the sun and its shadow are intimately linked and reflect the archetypal and cosmic structures in which consciousness and shadow are eternally at play. This great conjunction suggests the alchemical lapis and the Philosophers' Stone, where the *prima materia of the shadow and the illuminated goal of the opus are mysteriously bound together.* For the alchemically oriented analyst, the shadow is not only the beginning of the work, it is the end as well.

REFERENCES

Edinger, Edward. 1985. *Anatomy of the psyche.* La Salle: Open Court.
De Jong, H.M.E. 1969. *Michael Maier's* Atalanta Fugiens: *Sources of an alchemical book of emblems.* Leiden: E. J. Brill.

Fink, Bruce. 2007. *Fundamentals of psychoanalytic technique: A Lacanian approach for practitioners*. New York: W. W. Norton and Co.

Giegerich, Wolfgang. 1998. *The soul's logical life*. Frankfurt: Peter Lang.

Hillman, James. 1978. The therapeutic value of alchemical language. *Dragonflies* 1: 118–26.

———. 1983/2004. *Archetypal psychology*. Putnam, CT: Spring Publications, Inc.

———. 1991. The cure of the shadow. In *Meeting the shadow: The hidden power of the dark side of human nature*, ed. Connie Zweig and Jeremiah Abrams, 242–43. New York: G. P. Putnam's Sons.

Jung, C.G. 1939/1968. Conscious, unconscious, and individuation. In CW 9i.

———. 1955-56/1963. *Mysterium coniunctionis*. CW 14.

———. 1956. *Symbols of transformation*. CW 5.

Lambert, Kenneth. 1981. *Analysis, repair and indivi*duation. London: Academic Press.

Marlan, Stanton. 2005. *The black sun: the alchemy and art of darkness*. College Station: Texas A&M Press.

Micklem, Neil. 1993. The shadow of wholeness. *Harvest: journal for Jungian studies* 39: 114–24.

Mookerjee, Ajit. 1988. *Kali the feminine force*. NY: Destiny Books.

Neumann, Erich. 1969. *Depth psychology and a new ethic*. New York: G.P. Putnam & Sons.

Newman, Kenneth D. 1993. Science: the shadow of the shadow. *Harvest: Journal for Jungian Studies* 39: 37–42.

Ricoeur, Paul. 1970. *Freud and philosophy: an essay on interpretation*. New Haven and London: Yale University Press.

Samuels, Andrew. 1985. *Jung and the post-Jungians*. London and New York: Tavistock/Routledge.

Sarton, May. 1971. *A grain of mustard seed*. NY: WW Norton & Co.

Stein, Murray, ed. 1995. *Jungian analysis*. La Salle: Open Court.

STANTON MARLAN , Ph.D., ABPP, LP is a training and supervising analyst with the Inter-Regional Society of Jungian Analysts and has a private practice in Pittsburgh, Pennsylvania. He is adjunct Clinical Professor of Psychology at Duquesne University and holds Diplomates in both clinical psychology and psychoanalysis from the American Board of Professional Psychology. He is the author of *The Black Sun: The Alchemy and Art of Darkness*.

2

GETTING ON TOP OF THOUGHT AND BEHAVIOR PATTERNS

Patricia Vesey-McGrew

Quite often when working with analysands, I am reminded of the story of Sisyphus, King of Corinth. A cunning and deceitful trickster, his hubris duped him into believing that he, a mortal human, could outwit Zeus, ruler of the pantheon. This vengeful god banished him to Hades, where Sisyphus was condemned to forever push a great stone up a hill only to have it repeatedly roll back down on him. At a phenomenological level, our clients are frequently stymied by critical negative thoughts, illusory beliefs about others' motives and actions, and repeated reactive behaviors that might seem in retrospect to be irrational. Despite their belief that they have overcome, outwitted, or depotentiated their troubling internal demons, they nonetheless, like Sisyphus, often feel they have pushed this rock up the hill many times before, only to feel its crushing weight return. Are they/we condemned to be perpetually frustrated by forces that while known and frequently understood seem beyond the control of the ego? The answer to the question, like the solution to the dilemma, is paradoxical. It is both yes and no.

THE NATURE OF COMPLEXES

Jung's unique structural understanding of the psyche was one of his most significant contributions to the field of depth psychology. It was while conducting his word-association experiments at the Burghölzli Klinik in Zurich that he began to solidify his initial speculations about the nature of complexes and their fundamental position in the individual personality. It was shortly thereafter that he delivered his inspired paper outlining the significance of these independent, self-governing personalities, or splinter psyches, as the basic structural components of psychic life. The autonomous nature of the complex placed it outside the control of consciousness and caused the ego to be vulnerable to frequent disruption (Jung 1911/1973, para. 1352).

Jung viewed the complex as an unconscious phenomenon, yet allowed that there were times when the contents of a complex might have been conscious and then repressed. He perceived the complex to be affect-laden and surrounding a core image, which he referred to as archetypal. Here he differed with psychoanalytic theory, which attributes emotion to ego activity. Jung determined that the ego is the recipient of the emotional charge, which occurs when a complex is constellated (or activated in the unconscious), not the originator of the affect.

While positing the "aetiology of the origin of complex to be a trauma, emotional shock . . . or a moral conflict which ultimately derives from the apparent impossibility of affirming the whole of one's nature" (Jung 1934/1969, para. 204), he also acknowledged "complexes are not entirely morbid by nature but are characteristic expressions of the psyche, irrespective of whether this psyche is differentiated or primitive. . . . Complexes are in truth the living units of the unconscious psyche" (Jung 1934/1969, para. 209–10). Complexes, thus, are often experienced as both blessing and curse. As the basic structural components of the personal psyche they enlarge, add depth and richness to the personality. However, they frequently thwart the intentions of the ego, often causing illusory perceptions, problematic thoughts and behaviors and, not infrequently, intense suffering. Not only do we all have complexes, in fact it is far more often the case that our complexes have us (Jung 1934/1969, para. 200).

Significant advances have been made in how we currently understand the structure of complexes and their dynamic behavior patterns. These fresh perspectives require not only a shift in our awareness at the operational level but also a reassessment and reimagining of the optimal ways in which we work with our clients to resolve, or at the very least minimize, the disruptions created by the activation of powerful complex systems. This discovery of new territory, even in a very familiar world, encourages innovation and creativity in how we approach and manage complexes in the analytic setting.

Less then a decade after Jung's death, John Perry made the astute observation that "the entire psyche is structured not only in complexes, but in their bipolar systems or arrangements; the occurrence of an emotion requires the interplay of two complexes, and habitual emotions belong to habitual pairs" (Perry 1970, 9). He posits that in this dyadic configuration one pole of the pair tends to be ego-aligned and the other pole often projected on an external object. We might examine the workings of this alliance by observing a person in whom the victim/perpetrator dyad has been constellated through some wounding event. Our client might perceive himself or herself as a victim, or that image might lie just below the level of consciousness and become evident in the transference. The incident need not be grossly disturbing to activate the bipolar constellation. Because there can be no wounded subject without a victimizer/aggressor, when the ego is aligned or, in some cases, identified with the victim pole of the complex dyad, then the aggressive, perpetrator energy will be experienced as ego-dystonic and will be projected onto an object outside itself, or experienced internally (that is, in dreams or irrational thoughts) as an attacking object.

Occasionally, a person whose ego tends to be aligned with power and/or aggressive energy will serve as an adequate 'hook' for that projection. However, the suitable object for the projection is not always or necessarily one that is ego-aligned with the opposite pole. This affect-object invariably is "seen through the veil of illusion, colored by the meaning the unconscious ascribes to it" (Perry 1970, 4). It will also follow that when this complex dyad is activated, our client's ego could align itself with the perpetrator pole, a less frequent occurrence. If there is a consistent ego alignment with either pole then a one-sided attitude toward life develops, which Jung believed led to neurosis (Jung 1946/1966, para. 452). The continued repetition of identification with one pole and subsequent projection of the other may result in serious pathological conditions. In this complex configuration, the presentation of the analysand as victim or aggressor may be as subtle as a whisper in a crowded room, or as blatant as a red cape at a bullfight. The determining factor frequently is connected to the level of energy (valence) that has attached itself to the complexes and/or the ability of the ego to tolerate and integrate the chaotic onslaught that often accompanies complex eruptions.

COMPLEX VALENCE AND EGO INTEGRATION

The valence level of individual complexes can be dynamically altered in a number of ways. Valence levels are increased through accretions resulting from situations that have an affinity with an already present complex energy, and decreased by means of ego metabolism and integration. A higher valence increases the tendency for ego disruption and makes ego integration more problematic. However, a high valence level allows us also to imagine that a specific complex has been present for a considerable amount of time in the psyche. Thus, when a new client presents with strongly victimized affect, it is usually safe to assume (unless recently there has been a major traumatic experience) that the current situation is a repetition of an initial wounding that has consistently gathered energy unto itself.

Unconscious identifications with a psychic image, at the core of a complex, can be manifest in an unobtrusive or very dramatic manner. An illustration of this is an encounter that happened a number of years ago at a group practice where I saw some of my analysands. A new client, an academic at a local university, who had remarked at our initial meeting that she had little tolerance for status or titles (which I presumed was a complex indicator) phoned seeking to speak with me. Since I was with a client, she left a message with the office manager. When an hour passed and I had not returned her call, she phoned again and insisted that the manager interrupt my session so she could speak with me for "just a minute." When the manager refused to do so, she yelled into the phone, "Don't you know who I am? I am Dr. —— of —— University!" Then she angrily slammed down the phone, totally unconscious, I assumed, of her strong identification with her role and position. The minute one consciously says, "I am this" or "I am that" whatever is incompatible with "this" or "that" enters the realm of the unconscious, attaching itself to complex energy that is already present. This repressed image, which is ego-dystonic, readily lends itself to outward projection or unconscious acting out. In the above-mentioned situation both were true. My client saw herself as egalitarian and collegial, a "woman interested in finer things: books, music, art." She also projected upon her colleagues a type of shallowness in which she believed their sole goal was to be affiliated with prestigious people, and, to experience themselves as important and powerful. These projections are common enough. However, they assume a malignant quality in the refusal or inability of the ego to imagine them as part of the personal psyche. The more powerful the need for a certain specific identity the darker becomes the unseen and unacknowledged fragments of the personality.

Expanding on Perry's premise regarding the bipolar nature of complex delineation, Sandner and Beebe (1982 and 1995) developed an approach that details the nature of complex configurations in pathological situations, emphasizing the splitting that occurs in both ego-aligned and ego-projected complexes.

Frequently, the analysand's ego vacillated between the two poles of the ego-aligned complexes with virtually no consciousness of the degree to which she was overtaken by the complex energy. In discussing the above-mentioned incident, she pointed out that the office manager was "uneducated and lacked sophistication"; that she needed only a couple of minutes of my time and it was imperative that I speak with her soon, as she had to change her appointment. Initially, her sense of entitlement and her aggressive attitude were unrecognized by her ego consciousness. We had a long difficult road ahead, as these complex dynamics made regular appearances both within and outside the analytic setting.

The hallmark of complex eruptions is the repetitive nature of their occurrence. Complex dyads with a significant energic valence can repeatedly thwart ego functioning. Perry used the psychoanalytic term "repetition compulsion" in describing the continued disruption of the ego by autonomous complexes. He noted that this process afforded the ego the opportunity to encounter repeatedly those parts of the psyche that were ego-dystonic with the goal that ego integration might occur (Perry 1970, 5). Yet, integration by the ego requires more than a purely cognitive understanding. Effecting structural change minimally requires that the heretofore unconscious complex and the "I" of ego are experienced concurrently as different energy states.

REPETITION AND PARADOX

However, the optimal resolution of repetitive ego disruption is facilitated by the simultaneous, paradoxical experience of something deeply familiar combined with something totally new in the analytic field. Interpretation facilitates and at times effects change in complex dynamics. Sandner and Beebe (1995) discuss the importance of both the timing of interpretations and the stability of the analyst in facilitating the integration of "split ego-aligned" complexes. Nevertheless, as is implied by them, it is the experience in the analytic situation that is often key. Complexes are not abstractions. Insight into the nature of the complex combined with a new phenomenological occurrence is crucial in effecting a shift at the structural level. Psychoanalyst Theodore Jacobs, when addressing the issue of therapeutic change, notes: "Understanding and insight, however, are only part of the process of change. . . . Also important is experience: the patient's lived experience with the analyst, which along with insight, has the effect of altering fixed positions, fixed views and fixed automatic responses" (Jacobs 2002, 18). Stephen Mitchell opines that for this level of change to occur "[T]he analyst at all times is both an (or many) old object and a (or many) possible new object" (Mitchell 2002, 83). These intricate dynamics require the analyst to assume a significant responsibility for facilitating the depotentiating of complex energy. This process frequently involves the concurrent experience of what Jung categorized as stages two (elucidation) and four (transformation) in analysis. We might also imagine this process as similar to his understanding of the transcendent function, although expanding the concept to allow for the analyst's own personal psyche to be included in the configuration of the newly emergent system. "The radical nature of this formulation in 1916 resides in its sweeping synthetic approach. It is not reducible to making the unconscious conscious but is a search for the means of engaging with unconscious processes that allow mutual influence (conscious and unconscious) upon one another" (Cambray and Carter 2004, 121).

The late psychoanalyst Paul Russell, while never referencing Jung, espoused a psychological attitude in dealing with problematic, repetitive thought and behavior patterns that was very closely aligned with Jung's synthetic approach. "The only entry that can be made into the relatively airtight older system is through paradox. . . . It could be thought of teleologically, as a stimulus, a goad to the mind to expand the containing framework of understanding" (Russell 1998, 15). This is accomplished when the safety of the analytic relationship allows for the analysand to experience concurrently detachment and loss in the presence of containment and attachment. This will not happen if the analyst is waiting for the patient to work through the transference. The patient needs the therapist to be equally in touch with very dissonant pieces of reality that have not yet come together. And, there can be no real treatment process that does not include some piece of therapy for the therapist (Russell 1998, 16–17).

It is through this dynamic of the analyst containing and allowing for a paradoxical space, in which things are neither consistent nor complete, that also facilitates the analysand's ability to hold the paradox within himself. "Engaging and sustaining the paradox blows the old system apart, just enough for some new organization to emerge" (Mitchell 1998, 55). Thus, the analyst must hold simultaneously (without projecting) the conflicting affect-laden psychic material, which has been constellated in her personal psyche by the analysand, as well as the projected images experienced by her as originating in the psyche of the patient if change is to occur. When the paradox can be contained and held by both analyst and analysand, the potential for liberation is significant. A clinical example might best serve to illustrate this.

A cleric in his mid-thirties on the advice of his graduate school mentor came to see me with the major complaint of not being able to remember people who clearly were connected to him, not intimate connections, but more casual acquaintances and professional colleagues. He would recognize the person as someone he knew but not be able to remember the name or the nature of the connection. A thorough physiological assessment by his physician revealed no organic disease process.

At the initial meeting he offered in great detail the tragic account of the genocidal massacre that he had witnessed and escaped five years prior in his native country in Eastern Europe. The rendering was remarkably free of affect, which gradually became more available to him during subsequent amplifications. Initially, I assumed the memory loss was strongly tied to this profound traumatic experience. However, as the work progressed, significant losses, heretofore unacknowledged, came to the forefront and greatly enlarged the total picture of the inner psychic landscape. A dream provided the impetus for him to discuss what was unthinkable and long repressed.

I am at a place that is like the university where I studied. I am a soldier and we have set up an ambush to surprise the enemies. I make a mistake. I wanted to take a picture of those enemies.

We became the target. One of the enemies is standing behind me. He is a member of my religious community. He shoots me. I believe this is the end. I walk out and another community member is there. He weeps. I tell him to go and tell the rest of the group what has happened.

We spent many hours with this dream. For the first time, he typed pages of associations: first, to the cleric who shot him and then some details about the one who wept. He also included a page of amplifications on the camera. He had never discussed with anyone the pain he experienced when his application to be an officer in the army was denied, mainly due to his ethnic background. Becoming a cleric afforded him a lateral degree of respectability but required an attitudinal shift. Prior to the dream, his awareness of the traits that he shared with the enemy who shot him (a shadow figure) resided in a grey, liminal space. These characteristics included significant racial and ethnic biases (that bordered on revulsion), dishonesty, controlling, aggressive behavior, envy and significant issues with authority. He explained that he had tried to be a "good boy" for much of his life and to hide from his family and his religious group everything that was inconsistent with the image he wished to preserve, not only for others, but also for himself. When discussing the camera, he wrote that it "helped to remember things and that it is much easier to talk about something if one has its picture that will be shown."

A network of interrelated bipolar complexes was constellated in this situation. They were: oppressor/oppressed, insider/outsider, spiritual authority/rebellious puer. The dream helped to facilitate his experiencing to varying degrees both poles of the complex dyads. He saw how easy it had been to observe the oppressor dynamic in others. While we never denied the horror of his trauma, we did create space for his own murderous impulses to be palpably present in the analytic container.

My responses covered a broad gamut. I felt deep compassion for his suffering and immense horror at the atrocities visited upon his people. There was sadness for his loss of an army career and respect for the soldier energy within him. Surprisingly, there was a feeling of relief at all his tales of rebellious deeds. His ethnic background afforded him the privilege of being a member of the minority ruling class. This insider status was radically overturned when the civil war began. He not only became an outsider, but his new position forced him to leave his homeland in order to save his life. He was angry that what he deemed an inferior class had become the new elitist rulers. This specific response activated some of my own long-standing complex material, and I found myself experiencing anger and distaste for his attitude, feelings which stood in direct opposition to my empathy and deep sadness for his losses.

Unbidden, unanticipated, Eros entered this place of both paradox and possibility. His arrival paralleled his nocturnal visits with Psyche. My analysand was shocked that he should have desire for someone who was not only much older but who also seemed so radically different from himself. I experienced Eros's presence as the strong, containing energy that facilitated our ability to hold, combine, and metabolize contradicting feelings. Out of this mixture a new structure emerged. This required, as in the dream, a sacrifice of the former position of the ego. This client, in remembering and getting a picture of the enemy within, began to recognize people again. He viewed them with a much less critical eye. He also discovered that he could experience himself as both a wartime soldier and a spiritual cleric. Within the year, he finished his degree and returned to his homeland. As for me, among other changes, the boundaries between insider/outsider became very blurred and totally arbitrary.

Sisyphus and the Here-and-Now

Clearly what is missing in the Greek myth that introduced this chapter is the image of the analyst. Sisyphus suffers the repetitive, demoralizing task in relative isolation. If we were there, our initial reaction might be deep empathy for his painful situation. Certainly, we would try to facilitate his understanding of how this all came about: his relationship to Zeus, his leadership style, choices he has made and the unconscious components of those decisions. And when he had some insight into the internal forces that play a great role in his plight, we might even imagine with him ways to approach those powerful energies.

If, however, we allow his predicament to penetrate our own repetitive rock-pushing and then are able to tolerate all the disparate, paradoxical reactions that this will generate, we might open the door to a new arrangement for both of us. Our complexes are the structural components of our personal psyche; they will not disappear. Nevertheless, their structural make-up, amount and level of ego disruption, and intrapsychic affiliations can, and hopefully, do transform. Thus, the rock and hill remain, but the picture is radically changed.

REFERENCES

Alschuler, Lawrence R. 2006. *The psychopolitics of liberation: Political consciousness from a Jungian perspective*. New York: Palgrave Macmillan.

Bovensiepen, Gustav. 2006. Attachment-dissociation network: Some thoughts about a modern complex theory. *Journal of Analytical Psychology* 51, 3: 451–66.

Cambray, Joseph, and Linda Carter. 2004. Analytic methods revisited. In *Analytical psychology: Contemporary perspectives in Jungian analysis*, ed. Joseph Cambray and Linda Carter, 116–48. New York: Brunner-Routledge.

Hogenson, George B. 2004. Archetypes: Emergence and the psyche's deep structure. In *Analytical psychology: Contemporary perspectives in Jungian analysis*, ed. Joseph Cambray and Linda Carter, 32–55. New York: Brunner-Routledge.

Jacobs, Theodore J. 2002. Response to the *JAP*'s Questionnaire. *Journal of Analytical Psychology* 47, 1: 17–34.

Jung, C.G. 1911/1973. On the doctrine of complexes. In CW 2.

———. 1931/1966. Problems of modern psychotherapy. In CW 16.

———. 1934/1969. A review of the complex theory. In CW 8.

———. 1946/1966. Psychology of the transference. In CW 16.

———. 1966. *The practice of psychotherapy*. CW 16.

Knox, Jean. 2004. Developmental aspects of analytical psychology: New perspectives from cognitive neuroscience and attachment theory. In *Analytical psychology: Contemporary perspectives in Jungian Analysis*, ed. Joseph Cambray and Linda Carter, 56–82. New York: Brunner-Routledge.

Mitchell, Stephen A. 1998. Letting the paradox teach us. In *Trauma, repetition, and affect regulation: The work of Paul Russell*, ed. Judith Guss Teicholz and Daniel Kriegman, 49–58. New York: The Other Press.

———. 2002. Response to *JAP*'s Questionnaire. *Journal of Analytical Psychology* 47, 1: 83–89.

Perry, John W. 1970. Emotions and object relations. *Journal of Analytical Psychology* 15, 1: 1–12.

Russell, Paul L. 1998. The role of paradox in the repetition compulsion. In *Trauma, repetition, and affect regulation: The Work of Paul Russell*, ed. Judith Guss Teicholz and Daniel Kriegman, 1–22. New York: The Other Press.

Sandner, Donald F., and John Beebe. 1982. Psychopathology and analysis. In *Jungian analysis*, ed. Murray Stein, 294–334. Chicago: Open Court.

———. 1995. Psychopathology and analysis. In *Jungian analysis*, ed. Murray Stein, 297–348. Chicago: Open Court.

Saunders, Peter, and Patricia Skar. 2001. Archetypes, complexes and self-organization. *Journal of Analytical Psychology* 46, 2: 305–23.

PATRICIA VESEY-MCGREW, NCPsyA, is a supervising and training analyst at the C.G. Jung Institute, Boston where she is past president of that Institute. A member of the Board of Trustees of the National Association for the Advancement of Psychoanalysis and a book review editor for the *Journal of Analytical Psychology*, she has a private practice in Cambridge and Rockport, MA.

3

CULTURAL COMPLEXES IN ANALYSIS

Thomas Singer with Catherine Kaplinsky

On December 3, 1947, Dr. Joseph Henderson wrote to C.G. Jung:

> I am working on an essay, which is possibly going to become a book, called "Protestant Man," in which I am gathering the fundamental attributes of historical development of Protestantism and trying to put them together with the modern *cultural complex* appearing in our Protestant patients on the psychological plane. (Henderson 1947)

Some sixty years later, in 2007, Joe Henderson, the revered elder of the C.G. Jung Institute of San Francisco, died. He never completed the book, *Protestant Man*, or further elaborated on the notion of the "cultural complex," but he did help lay the essential groundwork for building a theory of cultural complexes by describing and differentiating out from Jung's notion of the "collective unconscious" the more specific area of unconscious activity and influence that he labelled "the cultural unconscious." One can conceptualize this as closer to the surface of ego-consciousness than the collective unconscious, from which we understand the archetypal patterns to originate.

The notion of cultural complexes was long implicit and even occasionally mentioned in the literature of analytical psychology, but it was not until the twenty-first century, when Sam Kimbles and Tom Singer put the essential building blocks of Jung's original complex theory and Henderson's work on the cultural unconscious together, that the potential impact of this theoretical extension of analytical psychology could begin to be appreciated and more widely applied (Singer and Kimbles 2004).

There are at least two possible reasons that the concept of the cultural complex remained more implicit than explicit in the Jungian tradition until the last few years. Jung's ill-timed foray into discussions about national character and especially the German psyche in the 1930s (Jung 1936/1970) effectively stopped further detailed consideration of differences among groups of people on the basis of race, ethnicity, and tribal/national identities by Jungians, who were deeply wounded and limited by the charges of anti-Semitism against Jung and his followers. After World War II and the Holocaust, few wanted to take up the subject of "national character" or cultural complexes for fear of being tainted by allegations of discrimination or, far worse, of contributing to justification of genocide. From this, Jungians learned very well that stepping on the landmines of cultural complexes can be very painful and destructive. Furthermore, the introverted bias of most Jungian psychoanalysts contributed to an ingrained distaste for addressing group psychology because group life itself was viewed as the shallow "collective" out of which individuation needed to occur.

Perhaps the willingness of a younger generation of Jungians over the last decade and a half to address more openly the highly charged issues surrounding Jung's attitude to Jews has freed up a considerable store of bound-up energy from a Jungian cultural complex. Now we can once again, more openly, explore the implication of Jung's psychology in relation to the group or collective psyche. As a result of the collapse of the Soviet system and the end of a psychological world view dominated primarily by two colliding super powers, all sorts of new tribal, ethnic, and racial issues have begun to surface in the startlingly rapid process of globalization. This has made it imperative for the Jungian tradition to begin analyzing the collective psyche with a more flexible and open attitude. This means resisting the typical Jungian temptation to reduce every group conflict to an archetypal motif but instead giving more careful consideration to the uniqueness of different cultures, including their separate cultural complexes. The tools to begin this work lay within the Jungian tradition itself, made available by joining Jung's early theory of complexes with Henderson's notion of the cultural unconscious.

Most simply, our theory now holds that large scale social complexes form in the layer of the cultural unconscious of groups and become cultural complexes, as Henderson suggested in his 1947 letter to Jung. This new addition to the body of Jungian theory has the two following very important applications, which this chapter will spell out using separate examples:

1. It offers a unique perspective for understanding a particular layer of the psyche of individuals who find themselves in conflict around their personal and group identity, which inevitably creates internal and external distress.

2. It also provides a unique perspective for understanding the structure and content of the group psyche and especially for elucidating the nature of conflicts and attitudes among groups towards one another. This perspective focuses on the level of the collective psyche where we can consider the mind and behaviour of the group as a body.

THE BUILDING BLOCKS

There are two primary building blocks for a theory of cultural complexes: (1) Jung's original complex theory and its relationship to individuation and the life of groups; (2) Joseph Henderson's theory of the cultural unconscious.

Jung's papers on the Word Association Experiment were published between 1904 and 1909 (Jung 1973, Part 1). Out of those early experiments based on timed responses to lists of words was born Jung's theory of complexes. For many Jungian psychoanalysts today, the theory of complexes remains a cornerstone of their clinical day-to-day work. Like the Freudian theory of defenses, Jung's notion of complexes provides a handle for understanding the nature of intrapsychic and interpersonal conflict.

After a hundred years of clinical experience, the field has come to know well and accept that complexes are a powerful force in the lives of individuals. The complex is defined as an autonomous, largely unconscious, emotionally charged group of memories, ideas and images that cluster around an archetypal core. Jung wrote:

> The complex has a sort of body, a certain amount of it own physiology. It can upset the stomach. It upsets the breathing, it disturbs the heart—in short, it behaves like a partial personality. For instance, when you want to say or do something and unfortunately a complex interferes with this intention, then you say or do something different from what you intended. You are simply interrupted, and your best intention gets upset by the complex, exactly as if you had been interfered with by a human being or by circumstances from outside. (Jung 1936/1976, para. 149)

In Jungian psychoanalysis, an important goal is to make personal complexes more conscious. In this way, the energy that is contained within them is freed up and made more available for psychological development. Elizabeth Osterman, a senior Jungian psychoanalyst of an earlier generation, liked to say that she had learned her complexes would never completely disappear, but a lifetime of struggling with them had resulted in their debilitating effects, including foul moods, lasting only five minutes at a time rather than decades.

Today, we could say that some of the cultural complexes that we are currently exploring have caused uninterrupted foul moods in cultures for centuries, if not millennia. The cultural complex can possess the psyche and soma of an individual or a group, causing them to think and feel in ways that might be quite different from what they rationally think they should feel or think. As Jung put it: "when you want to say or do something and unfortunately a complex interferes with this intention, then you say or do something different from what you intended" (Jung 1936/1976, par. 149). In other words, cultural complexes are not always "politically correct," although being "politically correct" might itself be a cultural complex.

The basic premise of our theory, then, is that another level of complexes exists within the psyche of the group and within the individual at the group level of their psyche. We call these group complexes "cultural complexes," and they, too, can be defined as autonomous, largely unconscious, emotionally charged aggregates of memories, ideas and images that tend to cluster around an archetypal core and are shared by individuals within an identified collective. When it comes to understanding the psychopathology and emotional entanglements of groups, tribes, and nations, we maintain that until now Jungians have not taken full advantage of

Jung's original theory of complexes, and this has left a major gap in analytical psychology.

Just as a theory of cultural complex was more implicit than explicit in Jung's psychology, so too the level of a cultural unconscious was more implicit than explicit in Jung's model of the psyche until Joseph Henderson pointed to its distinct sphere of influence. In his paper, "The Cultural Unconscious," Henderson defined the cultural unconscious as:

> an area of historical memory that lies between the collective unconscious and the manifest pattern of the culture. It may include both these modalities, conscious and unconscious, but it has some kind of identity arising from the archetypes of the collective unconscious, which assists in the formation of myth and ritual and also promotes the process of development in individuals. (Henderson 1990, 102–13)

Over a period of several decades, Joseph Henderson in his teaching and writing expounded on a "cultural level" of the psyche that he called "the cultural unconscious." He posited this realm as existing between the personal and collective unconscious. For many Jungians, Henderson's work opened the theoretical door on that vast realm of human experience which inhabits the psychic space between our most personal and our most archetypal levels of being in the world. Henderson's elaboration of the cultural level of the psyche has made greater space for the outer world of group life to find a home in the inner world of the individual, and this also has allowed those immersed in the inner world to recognize more fully the deep value the psyche actually accords to the outer world of collective cultural experience. However, the potential role of Jung's complex theory remained undeveloped in Henderson's discussions of the cultural unconscious. Extending Jung's theory of complexes into the territory of the "cultural level of the psyche," as first described by Joseph Henderson, is the work that we are now addressing. We feel that it is clinically useful to specify how the cultural unconscious influences the psyche of individuals and groups through the development, transmission and manifestation of cultural complexes.

THE THEORY OF CULTURAL COMPLEXES

It is time now to assemble the building blocks—Jung's theory of complexes and Henderson's theory of the cultural unconscious—and make the "cultural complex" an integrated part of the theoretical framework of analytical psychology. The following is an attempt to do that.

While it must be pointed out that personal complexes and cultural complexes are not the same, they do get mixed together and affect one another. We suggest that personal and cultural complexes *share* the following characteristics:

1. They express themselves in powerful moods and repetitive behaviors. Highly charged emotional or affective reactivity is their calling card.

2. They resist our most heroic efforts to make them conscious and remain, for the most part, unconscious.

3. They accumulate experiences that validate their point of view and create a storehouse of self-affirming ancestral memories.

4. Personal and cultural complexes function in an involuntary, autonomous fashion and tend to affirm a simplistic point of view that replaces every-day ambiguity and uncertainty with fixed, often self-righteous, attitudes to the world.

5. In addition, personal and cultural complexes both have archetypal cores; that is, they express typically human attitudes and are rooted in primordial ideas about what is meaningful, making them very hard to resist, reflect upon, and take apart.

Attending to the personal, cultural, and archetypal levels of complexes requires respect for each of these realms without condensing or telescoping one into the other, as if one realm were more real, true, or fundamental than another. Cultural complexes are based on frequently repeated historical experiences that have taken root in the collective psyche of a group and in the psyches of the indi-vidual members of a group, and they express archetypal values for the group. As such, cultural complexes can be thought of as the fundamental building blocks of an inner sociology. But this inner sociology is not objective or scientific in its description of different groups and classes of people. Rather, it is a description of groups and classes as filtered through the psyches of generations of ancestors. It contains an abundance of information and misinformation about the structures of societies—a truly inner sociology—and its essential components are cultural complexes.

An Example of a Cultural Complex in the Psyche of an Individual (by Catherine Kaplinsky)

The following is an example of how a cultural complex took shape in the psyche of an individual. This was creatively worked through in relation to his personal complexes, and his story illustrates how these were freed up and energy for indi-viduation was released through a transformative experience.

The individual, now deceased, was a White South African man living abroad, a professor in a European university. The shape of the cultural complex expressed itself in a recurrent dream that he communicated in a letter to me, his friend, around the time of South Africa's democratic transition out of the institutionalised racism of Apartheid in 1994:

From the ages of 35 to 40 or so I had a recurrent dream. The dream experience was always pleasant. It was very simple:

A small black boy, who I somehow knew to be Xhosa, sat on a beach. The beach was very long and very beautiful, with heavy surf. If you looked at the surf from the beach it seemed high, with big waves banked up on one another. Above the surf, the air was filled with a light haze. The boy was about 4 years old. He played with a whole lot of cowrie shells, which were "cattle." He was putting these cattle into a kraal (African enclosure) made of sand. He was happy. I was not present in the dream. I could not talk to him, only observe him. . . .

The little boy was a puzzle, and I took a long time to home in on him. Then at one point I had a strong set of feelings about my identity, which was somehow mixed up with *being* Xhosa. I realised that the little boy was—in a curiously inadmissible way—myself. This I think was why I was not present in the dream except as an observer, unable to talk to the little boy.

Why was I the little boy? . . . What I found was the following: In early childhood I was with my mother and little sister in the Ciskei where my cousins and uncles were farmers. My father was "up north" in the army. In that time my "relationship" with my mother was terrible. You can say that she was jealous of my childhood because she wanted to be looked after herself and resented having to be a responsible parent. She was, to all intents and purposes, a competitive child . . . only a grown up one, with great power over me. I have no recollection of meaningful love from her.

On the other hand, I was loved and properly mothered by Rosie Ngwekazi who was a servant-cum-nursemaid in my aunt's house. . . . I depended on her far more than most South African children might depend on their black nursemaids, because of my mother's opting out of her role—and because my mother actually hurt and humiliated me. Rosie on the other hand loved me and was the only source of unconditional loving. . . .

When I discovered this some years ago, I experienced a sort of unbounded joy and freedom. The discovery that I had been loved like that was also my first adult recognition that, like everyone else, I was "lovable" and that it was also OK to love myself.

I came to understand that I had been denied this recognition for so many years (it only came to me at about 40), because after my father's return we went to Cape Town where I was subject at home and at school to extremely strong racist conditioning. I simply could not own a Xhosa woman as my mother. . . . All the black part of me which had come into being in the Ciskei became inadmissible. I could not allow myself to own the experience with Rosie. And although by the age 25–30, I had disentangled a large amount of the racist shit that was pushed into me in the post-Ciskei years, this critical bit remained. After all, it raised very fundamental questions. At the same time, since Rosie's love was so central to my emotional survival, I held on to it in a subconscious way in the dream-sequence.

I saw Rosie at the Feni location when I visited the Ciskei region two weeks ago. It was a wonderful meeting. I was able to thank her for the love she gave me then. She knew perfectly well how important it had been and, very discreetly, made it clear that she knew a great deal about my mother's inabilities. She said that it was important that I had come back because I was Xhosa and because my "navel is buried" in the Ciskei. I know what she means.

So there's your dream. Make whatever use you can of it. I share all the usual reasons for hating Apartheid, but I have my own additional one . . . it prevented me from owning the most important experience of childhood by making it inadmissible. I could not own the central Black part of myself. I don't have the dream any more. It must be because I can own the reality. (Kaplinsky 2008)

It is clear from the dream and the dreamer's "working through" how the interface between cultural and individuation processes has created conflict and stress for him. The dreamer needed both to "own" his experiences with Rosie in order to be "true" to himself, and he needed to "disown" them in order to be "true" to his family and the white racist culture into which he was born. However, he then came to resent the positive experiences he had had to "disown" with Rosie. This propelled him on his personal journey.

A kind of layering of complexes, splits, and shadow formation developed. Firstly he described his mother as having been "terrible." His infant self therefore had to set up a defensive structure, a second skin function, to survive (terrible mother complex). But he also sought appropriate responses elsewhere—bodily and emotional—and he found them in Rosie (positive mother complex). Later, since he "belonged" to, and interacted with white reference groups, he learned to "disown" Rosie, giving rise to a sense of betrayal and guilt that resided in the cultural complex. We can see, therefore, how complexes developed out of an intricate network of affect, absorbed via mother, Rosie, and intimate others who in turn participated and were embedded in this culture.

Themes of power and dependency run through both the personal and the cultural complexes. The dreamer describes the "great power" his mother had over him, thus necessitating his defensive structure. From the cultural point of view, there was an interesting twist. While the Whites dominated and controlled the Blacks economically, they also depended on them not only for their labour but also very often for emotional care—as was the case with the dreamer. To keep the status quo, a rigid political structure was required, which fed the cultural complex. Apartheid means "separateness," thus signifying a rigidification of the "us versus them" dynamics in terms set by skin color. As we know, all manner of negative projections were aimed by the ruling white population at those with non-white skin. Skin color triggered emotional reaction and was the key to the cultural complex.

The cattle game in the dream was the dreamer's attempt to disentangle himself from what he called the "racist shit that had been pushed into [him]" and that made up part of the cultural complex in which he lived. This, in turn, affected his personal complexes.

The cowrie shells were pretend cows. The transition from cowrie to cows is particularly inventive. The hard defensive structure of the shells with a feminine underside became softer creatures that interacted with one another, providing milk and nourishment. They also easily evacuated waste, and they had looser skins. So within the cattle game it was as if the cowrie/cow/complexes were being loosened and shifted about, in and out of the kraal/container, allowing for experimentation and exchange. The dreamer was finding a way to reach into his hidden, vulnerable underside.

The coloring of the cowries is particularly significant when addressing the cultural complex of the Apartheid era. Cowrie shells vary in color, but where the dreamer played on the beach they were generally a mixture of white with blotchy brown, black, or caramel markings. Cows have similar coloring, commonly more defined—possibly addressing a firming up of the dreamer's color consciousness as well as his struggle to loosen his complexes in relation to skin color. He had written: "all the black part of me . . . became inadmissible." His infant self had assumed that he was black and Xhosa, the same as Rosie. Thus we see the transcendent function at work, producing symbols where the multicoloring in a single skin—of both cowrie shells and cows—helped disentangle and loosen both personal and cultural complexes.

COMMENTARY ON CATHERINE KAPLINSKY'S EXAMPLE
(BY THOMAS SINGER)

There are many ways to consider this extraordinary material. Below I have set up a schematic diagram to illustrate how the cultural complex operates in this case with regard to the various levels of the unconscious.

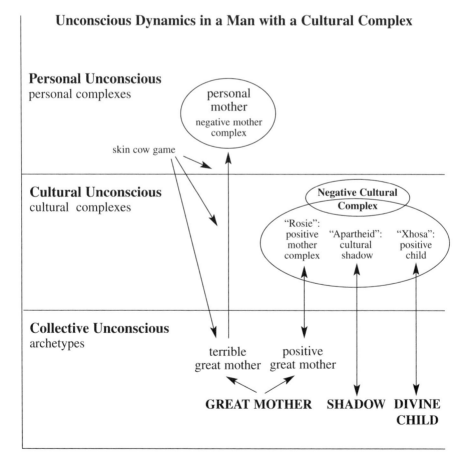

Unconscious Dynamics in a Man with a Cultural Complex

Personal Unconscious
personal complexes

personal mother
negative mother complex

skin cow game

Cultural Unconscious
cultural complexes

Negative Cultural Complex

"Rosie": positive mother complex   "Apartheid": cultural shadow   "Xhosa": positive child

Collective Unconscious
archetypes

terrible great mother   positive great mother

GREAT MOTHER   SHADOW   DIVINE CHILD

Complexes (personal and cultural) and archetypes (shadow, great mother and divine child) interact in the exiled professor's recurrent dream and in his subsequent "working through." The diagram is intended to help understand how a cultural complex takes shape in the psyche and how the energy trapped within it is released, thus bringing a profound sense of renewal for this individual. This occurred in this case through processes of spontaneous active imagination.

Within the collective unconscious, the archetypal patterns act as preconditions for how a psyche may be shaped and develop. Seeds for polar oppositions orginate here, including idealizing and denigrating (splitting) tendencies, as well as shadow energies and the potential for morality. The potentials for extremes–the Great and Terrible Mother, the Divine Child, and so on—are resident here.

Within the personal unconscious of this man, we find the opposites at work when he describes his mother as "terrible" and Rosie as his "only source of unconditional loving." The "all terrible," "all powerful" mother in his family resulted in building up a defensive second skin structure, like the cowrie shell. Later, in Rosie he found the "great and positive mother" and she became an essential part of his individuation process—with powerful cultural implications.

The cultural unconscious came into play when the positive experience with Rosie had to be denied. The love of and from Rosie was obscured by the negative cultural complex that was coupled in an unholy marriage with the shadow projections of the Apartheid era.

The cow game—or cowrie game—is the play that facilitated and symbolized the movement of psychic energies from one level of the unconscious to another, eventually leading to a profound transformation in the psyche. The unconscious memory/energy of the "Positive Great Mother" had been obscured for decades by the unholy union with the "Shadow" of Apartheid and was thus housed within the negative cultural complex at the level of the cultural unconscious. This fusion of positive mother and cultural shadow in the cultural complex was finally dissolved, and the energies contained within the negative cultural complex were released and became available to consciousness for other purposes. The repressed experience of Rosie's love, which could have taken shape as a positive mother complex, now became available to consciousness through the dream figure of Xhosa boy, and the grip of the personal negative mother complex on the ego was then also further relaxed. Thus a new experience of the ego and its identity became possible, and what is sometimes referred to as the ego-self axis could be restored.

FURTHER CLINICAL OBSERVATIONS ABOUT CULTURAL COMPLEXES

Although the previous example of a cultural complex in an individual did not unfold in the context of a formal psychotherapeutic framework, it was chosen because the dream and the narrative provided by the dreamer offer a concise and powerful example of the structure, content, and evolution of a cultural complex in an individual. In *The Cultural Complex* (Singer and Kimbles 2004), Kimbles, Morgan, and Beebe have each offered poignant vignettes of the clinical appearance of cultural complexes in the psychotherapeutic container, and the reader is encouraged to go to those studies for a more detailed description of the clinical manifestations of cultural complexes. Here I will briefly outline some of the more important features of working with cultural complexes when they crop up in analysis.

Cultural complexes are made conscious in analysis in the same way that most other unconscious conflicts become known, that is, through paying close attention to personal, family, and cultural history, through analyzing dream and fantasy material that emerges from the unconscious, through transference/counter transference reactions, through unconscious slips, and through potent moods and/or the breakthrough of powerful affect. Of this, John Beebe writes:

> In Jungian analytic work, which is always about the exploration of complexes, one does not necessarily recognize that the knot one is trying to untie may be a cultural complex. Like any other complex, the cultural complex creates internal conflict; occasions anxiety, anger, and depression; governs the outer situations that are brought to the therapy for counsel; shapes the transference in the therapeutic interaction; and structures the imagery of the patient's dreams. Since these complexities affect the individual, and any person who comes into the emotional field that surrounds the individual, we often assume that they belong solely to the subjective nature of that individual person. Yet, they can represent culture operating at the level of the individual. By following a careful clinical method, a therapist can unmask the intrusion of a cultural complex into the unconscious life of the patient." (Beebe 2004, 223)

With surgical precision, Beebe dissects the appearance of a cultural complex in the dream of a man who was later to die of HIV-AIDs. In the dream, a lesion on the dreamer's thigh in the shape of a bottle cap from a Coke of the 1950s led dreamer and analyst to uncover a cultural complex that literally marked his body and psyche with a terrible homophobic fear of not being strong enough, of not being masculine enough, of not being heroic enough. The homophobia of the 1950s branded the boy with a crippling cultural complex that left him a scapegoat and an outsider. The cultural complex proclaimed itself in the dream, and through careful analysis it became more conscious in both the analysand and the analyst. While neither was able to heroically overcome the HIV virus, they were able to diminish the virulence of the cultural complex.

Another way in which cultural complexes announce themselves in the consulting room is through transference-countertransference reactions of analysand and analyst. Helen Morgan describes her discovery of a racial cultural complex in herself, a white woman, and a patient, a black woman, which made itself known through the emergence of a negative emotional reaction to the patient in the analyst and an unconscious slip of the tongue in the patient. The analyst experienced her patient as a "cuckoo in the nest." "The cuckoo does not build its own nest but lays its eggs singly in the nests of other bird species. The eggs are then incubated and reared unwittingly by the foster parents" (Morgan 2004, 214). Morgan had the intrusive, negative, unbidden thought that she did not want her patient in the room, that the patient was a "cuckoo in the nest." In turn, the patient soon began to express her fears that Morgan wanted to "brainwash" her, but in a slip of the tongue "brainwash" became "whitewash." As patient and analyst began to explore the complex attitudes that emerged through the "cuckoo in the nest" who feared being "whitewashed," the self-loathing and loathing of other at the heart of this cultural complex became conscious—a disparagement of the patient's blackness and later a disparagement of the analyst's whiteness. Morgan writes:

> This complex attitude to her self and to me clearly related to her personal story, but this also illustrates something of the dilemma of the black person in the white society. If what is declared to be good is white, then the fairer one can become, the more one may gain acceptance. The stain, the misdemeanour is in the blackness and so must be whitewashed, but by becoming whitened the individual is lost as is the value of black-ness. There is a wiping out, an annihilation of the diverse when a blanket layer of white is layered all over. In this game, the black is beaten so decisively by the whitener that "he or she fails to score at all." (Morgan 2004, 218)

Samuel Kimbles has documented another form in which this cultural complex can appear. He describes a white patient who revealed fantasies and fantasy fig-ures dating back to her childhood that were subsequently projected onto him, a Black analyst. These fantasy figures functioned in her psyche as an alternately "dreaded and desired Other" in a stereotypical way. Kimbles writes:

> In her fantasies, starting as early as her preadolescent years, the patient has been uti-lizing stereotypes to represent anxieties and conflicts that were active in her early developmental history. That my patient had no actual relationships to the cultural fig-ures of her fantasies and dreams shows the relative autonomy of cultural stereotypes at the level of the cultural unconscious. Her creative use of these stereotypes reveals, however, that a cultural complex may function unconsciously in the individual, just as in the culture, to organize and bind anxiety related to differences. (Kimbles 2004, 210)

As with personal complexes, the making conscious and getting some objec-tivity about cultural complexes in a psychotherapeutic setting is a long, arduous process of disidentification from contents that emerge from the cultural uncon-scious as well as the more familiar personal and collective unconscious.

AN EXAMPLE OF A CULTURAL COMPLEX IN THE COLLECTIVE PSYCHE

Even if cultural complexes are not the direct focus of psychotherapy, the clinician would be wise not to underestimate the power and influence of this part of the collective psyche on individuals in the consulting room. Cultural complexes in the unconscious of the group contribute mightily to the barometric pressure of everyday life and can be thought of as part of the psychic environment of all patients. The following is a brief example of how intersecting cultural complexes have infected the collective psyche of citizens throughout the Western and Islamic world.

In his 1936 essay about Nazi Germany, "Wotan," Jung wrote:

> Archetypes are like riverbeds which dry up when the water deserts them, but which it can find again at any time. An archetype is like an old watercourse along which the water of life has flowed for centuries, digging a deep channel for itself. The longer it has flowed in this channel the more likely it is that sooner or later the water will return to its old bed. The life of the individual as a member of society and particularly as part of the State may be regulated like a canal, but the life of nations is a great rushing river which is utterly beyond human control... Thus the life of nations rolls on unchecked, without guidance, unconscious of where it is going, like a rock crashing down the side of a hill, until it is stopped by an obstacle stronger than itself. Political events move from one impasse to the next, like a torrent caught in gullies, creeks and marshes. All human control comes to an end when the individual is caught up in a mass movement. Then the archetypes begin to function, as happens also in the lives of individuals when they are confronted with situations that cannot be dealt with in any of the familiar ways. (Jung 1936/1964, para. 395)

What Jung wrote in 1936 resonates all too clearly with our current crisis between Islam and the West. The ancient archetypal riverbed of conflict—among Christians, Jews, and Muslims—is once again overflowing with a rushing torrent that threatens to flood the world. Can we say something about this situation from the perspective of the "cultural complex"?

Cultural complexes can have long memories and very powerful emotions embedded within them. They acquire a strong sense of history with the passage of time from one generation to the next and over multiple generations. They enshrine and encrust themselves in the consciousness and unconscious of groups of people and the individual psyches of members of groups. Simultaneously, they intertwine themselves with the cultural complexes of other groups of peoples. Indeed, these intertwining and affect laden energies of conflicting unconscious cultural complexes can form the preconditions for human events to unfold with a fury that can be likened to the natural forces portrayed in a movie of a few years ago called *The Perfect Storm,* when all of the climatic conditions off the eastern seaboard of the United States were uniquely positioned to come together and cause a storm of gigantic proportions.

It is no stretch of the geopolitical, psychological, and spiritual imagination to say that we are living in a time when a rare configuration of swirling cultural complexes have been aligning in just the right combination to unleash massive destructive forces. The best way to know that one is touching a cultural complex—in either a group or an individual—is by the emotional reactivity that certain topics automatically trigger. This is how Jung first came to identify personal complexes—the emotional reactivity of a trigger word caused disturbance in responses. The same can be said about a cultural complex. A hallmark of a cultural complex is the emotional reactivity of trigger words, such as "George Bush" or "Osama bin Laden" or "war on terror" or "holy jihad" or "colonial empire."

I do not want to be understood as equating the origin of cultural complexes with the geographical expansion and contraction of civilizations, but one can see the late fifteenth century—especially 1492—as a critical date for the beginning of the rise of the West and the decline of Islam. To say that the rise of the West is at the core of one cultural complex and that the decline of Islam is at the core of another is, of course, a gross oversimplification. Currently, for instance, multiple local and regional complexes have become caught up in the clashing mega-cultural complexes of Islam and the West. In the West, for instance, former French, German, English, and American rivalries and hatreds have been stirred up, just as in the Islamic world Sunni, Shiite, Kurdish, and other tribal feuds have been activated. All of these cultural complexes, Western and Islamic, have been thrown together to form the conditions for a global "perfect storm" of colliding cultural complexes. But if we take 1492 as a turning point in defining the history of Islam and the history of the West and in giving rise to two very different kinds of cultural complexes, we can begin to sketch some of the characteristics of these cultural complexes:

a. On the one hand, 1492 marks the beginning of the ascendancy of the New World with its "discovery" of the Americas. In addition to the New World providing just the right climate for the creation of a set of remarkable values such as democracy, freedom, and the sanctity of the individual, it has also given rise to a particular type of cultural complex characterized—especially in the United States and its relative newness and youthfulness on the world stage—by:

1. addiction to heroic achievement,
2. addiction to height,
3. addiction to speed,
4. addiction to youth, newness and progress,
5. addiction to innocence,
6. most importantly, a profound belief in the resilience of the Western— and especially, the American—group spirit which can easily translate itself into arrogance and grandiosity.

b. On the other hand, 1492 also marks the beginning of the retreat of Islam from the West and a long steady decline over the past 500 years of Islam's ability to take creative initiative in intellectual, economic, and social realms. This decline in Islamic power and influence has led to a cultural complex in the Islamic world and especially in its groups of radical fundamentalists that can be characterized by:

1. adherence to purity,
2. adherence to absolutism,

3. adherence to tradition,
4. adherence to incorruptibility.

These first four characteristics of the cultural complex of Islamic fundamentalism are almost perfectly mirrored in the cultural complex of Christian fundamentalism in the United States. The next two features I want to highlight are more unique to the cultural complex of Islamic fundamentalism:

5. renunciation of materialism (as so awesomely symbolized and concretized by turning America's addiction to speed, height, and material success against itself in the attack on the World Trade Center);
6. and, most importantly, a profound wound at the center of its group spirit that has given rise to despair and suicidal self-destructiveness. Repeated humiliation is at the heart of much of the Arab world's experience of itself, and the fear of and rage at humiliation constitutes a most dangerous core symptom of the Islamic cultural complex.

I am aware that the description of Islam's 500-year history of decline, resulting in a battered sense of a group self at the collective center of identity, is a gross oversimplification. Cultural complexes, however, collect around and thrive on such oversimplifications that have some truth at the core. Bernard Lewis gives an excellent description of the impact of the West on Islam and the rage of traditional Muslims in the face of the encounter with the West (Lewis 1993, 3–42). Mix together all of these ingredients of the Western and Islamic cultural complexes and one will have a truly horrific recipe for a witches' brew that has mobilized huge energies in the life of nations and at the group level of the psyche in the individual. These activated cultural complexes, transmitted through the cultural unconscious, set us up for the kinds of archetypal possessions and overflowing of ancient riverbeds that Jung described in his "Wotan" essay.

CONCLUSION

About personal complexes, Jung wrote: "Our destinies are as a rule the outcome of our psychological tendencies" (Jung 1913/1967, para. 309). The same can be said of cultural complexes. Our personal and cultural complexes are the hand that fate has dealt us. Jung said rather bluntly in another context: "We all have complexes; it is a highly banal and uninteresting fact. . . . It is only interesting to know what people do with their complexes; that is the practical question which matters" (Jung 1936/1976, para. 175). How we play the hand that fate has dealt us and what we do with our personal and cultural complexes determines who we become as individuals, groups, and societies.

REFERENCES

Beebe, John. 2004. A Clinical Encounter with a Cultural Complex. In *The cultural complex: Contemporary Jungian perspectives on psyche and society*, ed. Thomas Singer and Samuel Kimbles, 223–36. London and New York: Brunner-Routledge.

Henderson, Joseph. 1947. Unpublished letter, December 3, 1947, addressed to C.G. Jung. By permission of the author.

———. 1962/1964. The archetype of culture. In *Der Archetyp. Proceedings of the 2nd International Congress for Analytical Psychology*, ed. Adolf Guggenbühl-Craig, 3–15. Basel and New York: S. Karger.

———. 1984. *Cultural attitudes in psychological perspective.* Toronto: Inner City Books.

———. 1990. The cultural unconscious. In *Shadow and self*, 102–13. Wilmette, IL: Chiron Publications.

Jung, C.G. 1913/1967. The theory of psychoanalysis. In CW 4.

———. 1936/1964. Wotan. In CW 10.

———. 1936/1976. The Tavistock lectures. In CW 18.

———. 1973. *Experimental researches.* In CW 2.

Kaplinsky, Catherine. 2008. Shifting shadows: Shaping dynamics in the cultural unconscious. *Journal of Analytical Psychology* 53, 2.

Kimbles, Samuel. 2000. The cultural complex and the myth of invisibility. In *The vision thing*, ed. Thomas Singer, 157–69. London: Routledge.

———. 2004. A cultural complex operating in the overlap of clinical and cultural space. In *The Cultural Complex: Contemporary Jungian perspectives on psyche and society*, eds. Thomas Singer and Samuel Kimbles, 199–211. London and New York: Brunner-Routledge

Lewis, Bernard. 1993. *Islam and the West.* New York and London: Oxford University Press.

McGuire, William. 1989. *Bollingen: An adventure in collecting the past.* Princeton: Princeton University Press

McNeill, William. 1963. *The rise of the West: A history of the human community.* Chicago and London: University of Chicago Press.

Morgan, Helen. 2004. Exploring racism: A clinical example of a cultural complex. In *The cultural complex: Contemporary Jungian perspectives on psyche and society*, ed. Thomas Singer and Samuel Kimbles, 212–22. London and New York: Brunner-Routledge.

Singer, Thomas, ed. 2000. *The vision thing: Myth, politics and psyche in the world.* London and New York: Routledge.

———. 2002. The cultural complex and archetypal defences of the collective spirit: Baby Zeus, Elian Gonzales, Constantine's sword, and other Holy Wars. *The San Francisco Library Journal* 20, 4: 4–28.

———. 2007. A personal meditation on politics and the American soul. *Spring Journal* 78.

Singer, Thomas and Samuel Kimbles, eds. 2004. *The cultural complex: Contemporary Jungian perspectives on psyche and society.* London and New York: Brunner-Routledge.

THOMAS SINGER, M.D. is a psychiatrist and Jungian psychoanalyst and a training analyst at the C.G. Jung Institute of San Francisco. His long term interest in the intersections between mythology, psychology and society are reflected in books he has edited, contributed to, and written, among which are *The Vision Thing*, *The Cultural Complex*, *A Fan's Guide to Baseball Fever*, and *Initiation: The Living Reality of an Archetype*.

CATHY KAPLINSKY was born in India and brought up in South Africa. She is now a Professional Member of the Society of Analytical Psychology, London and a Training Analyst for the BAP (Jungian Section) and The Association of Child Psychotherapists. She is in private practice.

4

INITIATING A PSYCHOLOGICAL EDUCATION

Josephine Evetts-Secker

. . . we are not really at home in the interpreted world.

—RILKE

We don't need no education
We don't need no thought control.

—PINK FLOYD

"Thought control" has been a standard charge against the whole psychoanalytical enterprise and it remains a possible abuse. We wrestle with the problem of authority in the transferential field, fully cognizant of the power analysts can and do exercise. Our approach to the educational function inherent in analytical praxis has to be reimagined in and for our time.

Jung's early formulation of the structure of the analytical process, evolving through stages of confession, elucidation, education, and transformation, is alien to current practice. Insofar as we might accept these as genuine components of analysis, we do not see them as necessarily sequential or progressive, but rather as variably ordered and more typically concurrent (Lambert 1973, 24). Education is happening all the time. Despite his innate scientific desire to systematize, Jung's actual experience of psyche convinced him that "[i]f the collective unconscious did not exist, everything could be achieved by education" (Jung 1931/1977, para. 720). But the unconscious does exist. He insisted on the necessary work of understanding unconscious forces, but he stressed the danger that understanding might lead to the deadness of Rilke's "interpreted world" (*der gedeutete Welt*).

Nevertheless, as a rigorous academic of his time, Jung valued education as means of formation and direction and he might once have shared Adler's endorsement of the medical scientist, Rudolph Virchow: "Physicians will eventually become the educators of humanity" (Adler 1923, 317). Such was the confidence in education and faith in the process of correction. Something of that Utopian trust survives, but throughout the Western world expectations of education are now humbler, even cynical, *vide* Pink Floyd.

Jung grew suspicious of education, but a cynical Jung is hard to imagine. His wariness came from a different source. It was an early expression of genuine hermeneutic suspicion. In contrast to Virchow, Jung hoped that the "method of medical treatment" would become a "method of self-education" (Jung 1931a/1977, para. 174). He reflected on the danger of "doing violence to the other person or succumbing to his influence," fully aware of the risk of "therapy by suggestion." "I had given up hypnotic treatment . . . because I did not want to impose my will on others. I wanted the healing process to grow out of the patient's own personality and not out of suggestion of mine that would have only a passing effect" (Jung 1961/1976, para. 492). The desired transformation of the personality would "bring with it an enrichment of mind." Such expansion was consequence, not aim, of analysis. But the archetype of the teacher was constellated ineluctably and we might well wonder how consistently Jung practiced what he preached!

There are two verbs in Latin commonly invoked in discussions of education, *ducere* and *ductare*. *Ducere* means to lead, guide, draw. *Ductare* carries similar meanings but also suggests taking-home. *E-ducare* implies leading out, but originally evoked the nurturing process; rearing, fostering, even hatching. In English, both etymologies are significant, though they would not have been available in German. What Jung insistently condemned was in*doc*trination (*docere*, teach). His separation from Freud reflected his rejection of psychoanalytic 'doctrine', his mentor's words weighing heavily: "I beg of you . . . do not deviate too far from me" (McGuire 1974, 18). This contrasted with Jung's evolving conviction that "Every psychotherapist not only has his own method . . . he himself is that method" (Jung 1945/1966, para. 198). The quality of the analyst's *being* in analysis is inherently educative.

In order to grasp Jung's approach to education in analysis, all these senses and other derivatives in the semantic field are needed: *induce, deduce,* even *seduce.* All these inform the experience of genuine education. Jung encouraged diversionary, sabotaging, generative energies as potential agents of the unconscious. He spoke of the need for "a certain re-education and regeneration of the personality," but he came to see that re-education was enacted rather than taught, for "a person is a psychic system which . . . enters into reciprocal reaction with another psychic system" (Jung 1935/1966, para. 1). This 'reaction', occurring spontaneously in the present moment of interaction between partners in the analytical dyad, convinced him that the less the analyst knows in advance the better (Jung 1945/1966, para. 197). Education is not direction or transfer of knowledge, leaving the analysand an "intelligent but still incapable child" (Jung 1931a/1966, para.150). It is, rather, a readjustment of psychological attitude, for "we seldom get rid of evil [*or our complexes*] merely by understanding its causes. . . . the patient must be drawn out of himself into new paths . . . only achieved by an educative will" (ibid., para. 152). Rehabilitation of the analysand's will required freedom from

Jung's own "medical authority as soon as possible" (Jung 1935/1966, para. 43), so that the analysand may "*learn* to go his own way," and "*learn* to stand on his own feet" (ibid., para. 26, italics mine).

It became clear to Jung as he worked with living psyche that teaching in analysis is the wrong modality. Although material arising from the unconscious and manifest in typical behaviors is best related to, and integrated by means of, comparative mythological parallels, and while the well-informed analyst might supply "some kind of context so as to make them more intelligible" (Jung 1944/1968, para. 38; see article below on "amplification"), the model for this is not instruction. Rather, analysts need to model living in dialectical relationship to the archetypal world of the unconscious, enacted in the inner working of the therapeutic dyad. One task of the analyst is to find/forge a necessary language for the work, which will be different for each analysand. Jung remarked with mischievous seriousness that a new theory was needed for each person: each requires an individual idiolect for psyche to speak—idiosyncratic lexis, syntax, accent, and intonation.

Most people discover that what has been most vital in analysis is not learned content, but fresh understandings, imaginative awakenings that release new, more authentic ways of being. This is a far cry from Freud's didactic goal of interpreting patients' meanings that are hidden in the unconscious. This cannot be the achievement of an educating mentor, except through the fostering of the analysand's "experiment with his own nature" (Jung 1929/1966, para. 99). In the course of a lastingly enriching analysis, the individual will become less reliant on material provided by the analyst. Given that "the psyche has a share in all the sciences" (Jung 1945/1966, para. 209), analytical training emphasizes the need to know as much as possible, but such knowledge must be held in transitional space rather than used directly or explicitly.

If there is teaching to be done, it is done by and within the dream, which teaches "like a parable" (Jung 1928/1977, para. 471). This is why we do and must give priority to this communication with unconscious psyche. But here too there be dragons. In training I valued most the urging, "always stay one step behind the unconscious of the analysand" (C. T. Frey). Good advice for analysts with a propensity to teach. I well remember a dream seminar that impressed on me the danger of stealing the dream through mythological knowledge. An innocent dream-cat was amplified comprehensively—Egypt via Athens, and all mythological stations between—until someone risked the naive question, "Does the dreamer have a cat?" Well, yes, she did; a beloved creature run over just before the dream. I was reminded of a poem by Nowlan that still strikes when knowledge makes me a thief. The poet offers a gift to a child-adult, who whispers,

'Nobody will ever get this away from me,'
in the voice, more hopeless than defiant,
of one accustomed to finding that his hiding places
have been discovered, used to having objects snatched
out of his hands. (Nowlan 2004, 138)

How do we avoid such easy robbery by the teacher who might know what analysands do not yet know? More is required than the humility inherent in genuine dialogue.

We need not fear to invoke the love conceived by Socrates as education's agent. Hillman reminds us: "it is as if love had in its nature a mission to ignite, educate and convert, spreading its mercurial fire in the soul, transferring itself from person to person ...[by] its devious indirection" (Hillman 1972, 78). This energy is intrinsic to the lexical play above: fleeting senses, rather than established meanings, that inhabit *ducere* and *ductare* as they pro*duce* multiple associations. Self is source. As Socrates urged that love educates, so Hippocrates insisted that love heals. We know love to be inevitably transgressive, so we expect all our categorical thinking to be sabotaged or penetrated by this daimon. Disturbingly, our educational praxis will prove most efficacious when it in*duces* and se*duces* fearlessly, absurdly, often offending well-tempered, e*duc*ated ego. Psychoanalysis began with noble purpose to explicate psyche's latent purposes and explain neurotic functioning, as means to healing. But psyche's guide is Hermes, who enjoys Eros' "devious indirection". We must orientate our educative intentions accordingly, echoing Adam Phillips's interrogation of our task: psychoanalysis has "become the science of the sensible passions, as though the aim . . . was to make people more intelligible to themselves, rather than to realize how strange they are. When psycho-analysis makes too much sense, or makes sense of too much, it turns into exactly the symptom it is trying to cure: a defensive knowingness" (Phillips 1995, 87). Jung also hoped that analysis would "make us more conscious of our perplexity" (Jung 1939/1976, para. 688). He would approve Wordsworth's call to "Come forth into the light of things, / Let nature be your teacher" (Wordsworth 1959, 377). Neither imagination nor individuation can be taught. Experience of psyche itself educates, with analysts nurturing innate ways of relating to unconscious perplexity.

We have new ways of knowing this to be true, validated by current discoveries in neuroscience. Working metaphorically/mythically creates new neural pathways more effectively than working cognitively. There is not space here to pursue this appreciation of left brain as the tool of interpretation and influence—what Margaret Wilkinson describes as "the creative capacity to make conceptual and affective links across the different realms of knowing" (Wilkinson 2006, 146), but these must be integrated into our perception, initiation and fulfillment of psychological education. This will also make us responsive to that crucial "interpretive moment" when meanings can be let in (ibid., 110). Understanding the educative aspect of analysis initially overemphasized the analyst as source. We may now be capable of a broader, truer perspective, knowing as we do, for example, how the experience of metaphor itself lights up the brain and can be a source for transforming left-hemispheric functioning.

How then might we nourish in our praxis the "experiment with one's own nature"; the facilitation of "letting nature be teacher"; the "enrichment of mind" that comes in the wake of the transformation of personality. In his exploration of

Jung's epistemology, Renos Papadopoulos makes significant contributions regarding the co-creation of meanings, the co-construction of knowledge, and learning how to learn within analysis (Papadopoulos 2006). With this in mind, I conclude with several typical moments from actual praxis that might be recognizably educative.

First, I acknowledge educational reciprocity. Analysts are in the transformative vessel too, and so they are informed, even formed, by analysands. I once gave a seminar series entitled "Tinker, tailor, soldier, sailor" that grew out of the realization of all I had learned from my vocationally varied analysands and how psyche had made imaginative use of each professional discipline. We explored ways in which the work-life of nurse, actor, composer, hairdresser, and lawyer provided raw matter for symbolization through dreaming. This proved to be no mere "day residue," but part of ceaseless psychic processing, facilitating transformation and ego-education. In cutting, styling, dyeing, curling, straightening, coloring, hair-salon translates alchemist's laboratory. Legal praxis, with its pretrial discoveries, plea-bargaining, out-of-court settlements—how precisely, vividly the unconscious imagination lays hold of such data for symbolic recycling! Modulations of key and rhythm speak of mood, feeling, suppressed longing, 'major' delight urgent to transcend 'minor' desolations. Medical procedures, organic functions, surgical interventions in hospital theatres, all provide material for psyche to metabolize. In another theatre, we considered obvious but subtle interplay of characters in conflict and collusion as actors experiment with psyche's "infinite variety" of selves. At the time I also worked with surveyor, rancher, painter, IT-specialist, blacksmith . . . the professional possibilities were endless. How much analysts learn from analysands about the tasks of life and the inventiveness of psyche! If both partners are willing to be affected, education is reciprocal and transformative.

Many come to analysis with no psychological knowledge whatsoever, perhaps even defended against it. A man, scientist by profession, came to my Canadian practice claiming never to have read anything other than a textbook. This, he suddenly realized, he wanted to remedy, though he could not explain why. It was clear from the outset that he suffered from a destructive mother complex and had no intention of going anywhere near this problem in our interactions. Soon after beginning, he went on holiday and asked me to propose some holiday fiction. He came from D. H. Lawrence country, so with apparent innocence I suggested *Sons and Lovers,* quite unprepared for the actual impact this would have. He was ripe to begin deep inner work, but he was afraid. Feeling safely contained in the novel's distant but familiar landscape, two readings gave him all the insight he needed to start unpacking his problems *vis à vis* Mother. It also seduced ego into receiving vivid dreams, providing all he needed to endure the depression out of which new life could spring. Education happened; he learned all he needed to know about how complexes possess and bewitch.

A dance therapist with little conscious knowledge of ancient mythologies did a painting during a body-workshop, which provoked a dream in which the flat figure depicted arose from the paper on the floor, with robe and shield. Athene seemed constellated, of whom the dreamer "knew nothing." The name was all she needed from me. From reading and imagining, an amazing process of self-discovery followed that shaped outer life in unpredictable ways. So began a shocking experiment with her own nature.

What is needed, then, is to find ways of *initiating* psychological education, which then propels itself. We follow psyche's lead for each individual. Transformation and enrichment follow. We are induced and seduced, if we allow Hermes into the work. But in the end, far more important than the resources of education and amplificatory knowledge are the resources of mind and soul, of what Jung calls "amplitude."

> Richness of mind consists in mental receptivity, not in the accumulation of possessions. What comes to us from outside, and, for that matter, everything that rises up from within, can only be made our own if we are capable of inner amplitude equal to that of the incoming content. Real increase of personality means consciousness of an enlargement that flows from inner sources. Without psychic depth we can never be adequately related to the magnitude of our object. It has therefore been said quite truly that a man grows with the greatness of his task. But he must have within himself the capacity to grow. (Jung 1950/1968, para.215)

REFERENCES

Adler, Alfred. 1923. *The practice and theory of individual psychology*. London: Routledge & Kegan Paul.

Hillman, James. 1972. *The myth of analysis: Three essays on Archetypal Psychology*. New York, London: Harper Colophon.

Jung, C.G. 1928/1977. General aspects of dream psychology. In CW 8.

———. 1929/1966. Aims of psychotherapy. In CW16.

———. 1931a/1966. Problems of modern psychotherapy. In CW16.

———. 1931b/1977. Analytical Psychology and 'Weltanschaung'. In CW 8.

———. 1935/1966. Principles of practical psychotherapy. In CW16.

———. 1939/1976. The symbolic life. In CW 18.

———. 1944/1968. Introduction to the religious and psychological problems of alchemy. In CW12.

———. 1945/1966. Medicine and psychotherapy. In CW16.

———. 1950/1968. Concerning rebirth. In CW 9i.

———. 1961/1976. Symbols and the interpretation of dreams. In CW18.

Lambert, Kenneth. 1974. The personality of the analyst in interpretation and therapy. In *Technique in Jungian Analysis*, ed. Michael Fordham, Rosemary Gordon, Judith Hubback, and Kenneth Lambert, 18–44. London: Heinemann.

McGuire, William, ed. 1974. *The Freud/Jung letters*. London: Hogarth Press and Routledge.

Nowlan, Alden. 2004. He sits down on the floor of a school for the retarded. In *Between tears and laughter: Selected poems*. Northumberland: Bloodaxe Books.

Phillips, Adam. 1995. *Terrors and experts*. London: Faber & Faber.

Pink Floyd. 1979. Another brick in the wall. Album: *The Wall*.

Rilke, R. M. 1993. *Duino elegies*. Einsiedeln: Daimon Verlag.

Stein, Murray. 1996. *Practicing wholeness*. New York: Continuum.

Papadopoulos, Renos. 2006. Jung's epistemology and methodology. In *The handbook of Jungian psychology: Theory, practice and applications*, 7–53. London and New York: Routledge.

Wilkinson, Margaret. 2006. *Coming into mind. The mind-brain relationship: A Jungian clinical perspective*. London and New York: Routledge.

Wordsworth, William. 1959. *Poetical works*. London: Oxford University Press.

JOSEPHINE EVETTS-SECKER, M.Phil., taught for many years in the English Department of the University of Calgary, then trained at the Jung Institute in Zurich, and now lives in England where she is a senior member and training analysts in IGAP (London). She has published articles on literature and the interface between literature, psychology, and theology.

5

INSTIGATING TRANSFORMATION

Dianne Cousineau Brutsche

A Transformation Process

". . . the psyche is indistinguishable from its manifestations," says Jung (1937/1958, para. 87), and "psychology is concerned with the act of seeing" (1944/1953, para. 15) and describing empirical facts. In this spirit, I have chosen to base this chapter on a concrete case of a transformation process witnessed within the analytical container.

Christina came to our first session with the following dream: *"I am remarrying my husband. The ceremony is about to begin when I realize that I have not yet taken care of getting an appropriate gown for this very special occasion. Our guests are arriving. I feel panicky. My husband tells me that I could wear a certain dress that I already have and that we both like. But even if that dress would be suited to attend a wedding ceremony, it is certainly not suited for the bride herself. I wake up feeling vulnerable, anxious and disorientated."*

Christina is 64 years old when she starts analysis with me. She is a career woman, divorced for many years, happily living with her present partner and about to retire from her work. Asked about her relationship with her ex-husband, she says it is amiable and mainly revolves around their common daughter and granddaughter. It is obvious for her that the dream is to be understood on the subjective level, especially since her dream-husband is someone totally unknown to her in waking life.

The decision to start analysis is usually triggered by a crisis in one's life. At the time of her divorce, Christina had undertaken therapy to try and sort out her emotional upheaval and its hindering consequences in several aspects of her life. At a certain point of that earlier therapy, it seemed that the objective parts of her presenting problem had progressively fallen into place and that she was retrieving her inner balance. She nevertheless decided to pursue her inner work further in order to investigate deeper dimensions of her psychic life. At the time when she started her work with me, no obvious maladjustment seemed to require any specific attention. Yet she talked about experiencing feelings of inner stagnation, a strange sense of vulnerability as well as vague but persistent anxiety feelings for which she could not find any specific ground. Her initial dream, dreamed one week before our first meeting, made her aware of an inner urgency. The unconscious had taken the lead, and her ego, already well attuned to her unconscious thanks to her previous therapeutic work, followed the impulse.

TRANSFORMATION

In his article "Problems of Modern Psychotherapy" (1931/1966), Jung identifies four successive stages of psychotherapy, each one of them being characterized by specific inner processes, namely "confession," "elucidation," "education," and "transformation." The first three stages belong to any depth psychotherapeutic work. Jung qualifies them as objective, rational approaches, with each of these processes being necessary to come to terms with one's specific symptoms. The fourth stage, which he names "transformation," is the one that most characterizes analytical psychology (i.e., Jungian psychoanalysis). About this fourth stage Jung says that it concerns primarily people who, like Christina, are intellectually and emotionally well functioning, satisfactorily integrated in their social, familial, and work environment: in other words, well adapted but longing for something beyond normality and adaptation. The goal is to achieve psychological wholeness, and transformation is the means towards this goal. The instigating factor is not anymore a dysfunctional attitude in need of being overcome but an unconscious reaction to what is perceived by the individual as an unbearable inner standstill or an inner pressure without grounds in objective, daily functioning. It arises from a subjective need and finds its resolution through a subjective process, in which a nonrational dimension plays an essential part. Even if it sometimes is a path followed by young individuals, the need is most of the time felt by people in the second half of life.

IMAGES OF TRANSFORMATION

The preoccupation of human beings with psychological transformation is universal, and a wealth of images symbolizing it are found in every culture. Jung's predilection for alchemical imagery as evocative of such a process is well known. Another powerful image of psychological transformation is the phenomenon of metamorphosis of the caterpillar into a butterfly. Even if such a phenomenon is a concrete process found in nature, it has been universally apprehended in its symbolic evocative quality (see Stein 2005 and Woodman 1985).

Such images, apprehended symbolically, not only reveal the essential phases of the transformative process but its aim as well. Whether it be the transmutation of base metal into gold or the metamorphosis of the caterpillar into a butterfly, both point towards the manifestation and achievement of what could be called the ultimate identity of a given structure or entity.

The path towards psychological wholeness goes through a succession of transformations resembling the shedding of the snake's skin, another natural process whose symbolic meaning has been acknowledged by all cultures. Following the commands of its own growth repeatedly throughout its life time, the snake develops a new skin and sheds the outgrown one. In so doing it frees itself from the confinement of a previous developmental phase, making room for an expansion of its being. It is therefore not surprising that it has become a powerful image of psychological growth, renewal, and healing.

Christina's dream clearly referred to an impending phase of initiation with the symbol of a renewed wedding: psychologically speaking, her dream was announcing the need for a new "*conjunctio,*" a new relationship to her unconscious, to the Self. The reference to the wedding gown that demanded to be acquired reminds one of the new snake skin that has to grow inwardly so that the old skin can be shed.

THRESHOLDS

In the pre-shed-skin period, when the old skin begins to detach from the underlying new skin, the snake's vision becomes blurred during a certain time, giving rise to an increase in nervous behavior, the blurred vision depriving the animal of its normal orientation in its environment. The snake is experienced by those observing it as being restless, obviously stressed and anxious due to its vulnerability.

Whatever may be the symbolic image one would relate to a phase of psychological transformation, each such period is akin to the crossing of a threshold. Thresholds bring one into a space "betwixt and between," a liminal space (from the Latin *limen*), a "neither-nor place" where one's well-known and reassuring reference points shade off. Deprived of one's usual coping mechanisms or protective garments, one finds oneself in a state of sometimes profound disorientation and objective vulnerability. Naked, unprotected, the psyche is exposed, like a soft-shell crab, to countless predators, whether violently attacked by destructive impulses or attracted by the seductive path of regressive restoration. Such psychic processes of course generate legitimate and unavoidable feelings of anxiety, as expressed by Christina.

Innumerable rituals, present in practically every culture, have been developed to ward off the dangers inherent in the crossing of a threshold, affirming thereby its deeply problematic, risky potential. In fairy tales, monsters and demons often guard the gate to the threshold, either warning against the inherent danger or obstructing the passage, preventing the heroine from accomplishing her task. The ritual that is still most commonly known is the one that surrounds the crossing of the threshold by the bride into her new home. In many ancient cultures, it was believed that the bride's family demons were surrounding her, preventing her from entering her new home, preventing the accomplishment of the transformation. She therefore had to be carried across the threshold without her touching it in order to outwit the demons, a custom that is still often practiced in several of our developed western countries.

While discussing Christina's dream, we both were aware of her being in a deep (albeit still mysterious) phase of transition in which prudence, that is, awareness of a potential danger, was demanded. We also realized that her dream-husband, who was trying to convince her that her already familiar dress (her "old skin") would be good enough, was symbolically playing the role of the bride's "family demons" keeping her from crossing the threshold.

As the dream had made a powerful impact on her, Christina brought it back or referred to it during several sessions, in the course of which its meaning gradually unfolded. One day, as we were once more juggling with its images, she said: "There is obviously a mysterious deadline for which I am unprepared." After a moment of silence, she repeated several times punctuating the words: "A deadline." She suddenly gazed open-eyed: "A death-line," she said. "Is this what this wedding is about?" No particular illness seemed to threaten her life. On the contrary, she was physically remarkably fit. Yet, her sudden insight felt totally congruent with a vague but growing awareness that had been haunting her for a while: the awareness of her life span shrinking slowly, but surely. "Even if I could possibly still have a good 20 years ahead of me, it feels very short," said Christina. "Twenty years ago I met my present partner. It seems like yesterday." The psychological meaning of her having reached the age of her professional retirement suddenly hit her.

TRANSFORMATION IN THE "EVENING OF LIFE"

Commenting about the typical psychological needs that correspond respectively to the first and second half of life, Jung talks about a "psychology of the morning and of the afternoon of life" (1931/1966, para. 75).

In my work with some of my analysands and conversations with friends about to enter or already well into the seventh decade of life, therefore well over what is usually considered as mid-life, I began to discover another kind of shift in the inner life: enlightening similitudes manifested between their processes, echoing my own experience. I came to identify these specific aspects as belonging to what I would like to call a "psychology of the evening of life." In this short chapter, I wish to bear witness to some significant aspects of this psychology of the evening and the transformation process that it demands.

The passage from the afternoon into the evening of life is usually not as dramatically distinct as the one between the morning and afternoon. The shift from one to the other is most of the time so subtle that it may well pass unnoticed, being experienced more in terms of continuity than as a shift. Yet the biological clock is being heard also in the realm of the soul and in some individuals (probably more aware of the impact of time), significant differences may be perceived, giving the process a very specific quality, a special coloration.

Christina's story offers a moving illustration of such a transition phase, as one progressively enters into the evening of life.

THE "DEATH-LINE"

Unless a serious, life threatening illness suddenly strikes, most of us manage to keep the reality of death well encapsulated and stored in a dark, remote corner of the unconscious. Its repression is a healthy reflex in a good part of life. Without it one would never really incarnate into life. As the individual grows older, however, the awareness also grows that time is running and that the years left ahead are rapidly decreasing. From its hiding place, the reality of death gets activated in the unconscious, trying to awaken the ego to its further duties, acting on the psyche in the way a complex does. The quality of the ensuing process depends on whether the ego can relate to it, or on the contrary suppresses it like an unacceptable shadow from which one has to protect oneself.

The readiness to accept this confrontation or on the contrary the struggle to escape it probably has a lot to do with whether or not a person sees death as the termination of life or is able to perceive it as its goal, as Jung affirms in his article "The Soul and Death" (1934/1969, paras. 796–815). The shift from one perception to the other requires by itself a profound inner transformation. Indeed, even if death is perceived as the goal (finality) of life instead of an end, both nonetheless talk about finiteness. Healthy people do not enjoy brooding on their own inescapable destruction. Resistances automatically arise, as expressed in Christina's dream: her dream made her aware of an inner conflict between two opposite impulses symbolized by the dream-ego who perceives the upcoming "dead-line" and the urgency to get the "appropriate dress" for this further initiation, while another, more rational part of her, symbolized by her dream-husband, would be satisfied with going on as before, ignoring the duties required by the need for renewal, oblivious of the fact that, as Christina soon realized, the dead-line of her dream was referring to a "death-line."

Following her awareness of the death-line, Christina went through a painful and unsettling period, her mood oscillating between panic ("This dream is announcing my impending death") and denial ("I am in perfect health. I don't need to worry"). A conflict between two opposite impulses is the most common source of anxiety. When she finally accepted and succeeded in keeping both these opposite voices together, progressively a new perspective started to emerge. Little by little the dream started to loose its doomsday quality (as announcing the impending end of her life) and began to be felt as an invitation to respond to the demands of the evening of her life, that is, the necessary transformations towards the goal, a new contract with life corresponding to this new phase. In fairy tales, the naming of Evil (the Devil or the Witch) can result in its being disempowered. Finiteness having been named and accepted, Christina's symptoms of anxiety from that point on started to melt away progressively.

The concept of wholeness being rooted in the infinite potential of the Self, its full realization goes beyond the limitations of any individual life. Because of its archetypal quality, it is very likely to reveal its ambivalent nature: it can be experienced as an invitation to connect deeper with oneself, but it can also give rise to wishes to set goals that have an inflationary flavor. Christina is what one could call a spiritually ambitious person, that is, one who takes seriously the dictates of her soul, is ready to confront her resistances, and is actively committed to her inner growth and setting for herself highly valuable spiritual goals. However, even if such goals are inner ones, they remain goals that are set by the ego, and because of this even they must be progressively let go of in the evening of life in order to make room for all that one is, as one is and not as one would wish to be. More than ever, in the evening of life the notion of wholeness reveals itself as a path, the path being, like the Tao, its own goal.

Grieving is part of any transformation process: something has to be let go of in order for something new to arise. Christina's process went through a period of grieving for what she called her "unlived lives"; not only for those that belonged to her past, but for those also that would belong to her future. Not only can the past not be redone, but given the limitations of an individual's life span, many of one's genuine potentials will never be actualized. Many wished for transformations will never take place. Paradoxically, however, a profound transformation can come through accepting aspects of oneself that one cannot transform. As Jung points out, healing sometimes is not curing a neurosis but accepting it as meaningful and helpful (1931/1966, para. 11). Grieving in the evening of life is what leads to reconciliation with oneself, to psychological oneness, to integrity, a term that is practically synonymous with wholeness but with a more modest flavor, and thus more attuned to the dictates of the evening of life. Psychological integrity implies an unconditional acceptance and integration of all aspects of one's being, the cessation of an inner split that is sometimes heavily reinforced by our very best spiritual aspirations for the afternoon of life. Many thick skins have to be shed before the split can be mended between what is spiritually seen as valuable and what on the contrary bears witness to one's misgivings and laziness. Many more skins have to be shed for this unconditional acceptance of oneself to be a dynamic movement of surrender to one's full truth and not a simple defeatist resignation. Only through such a dynamic surrender can one genuinely "continue to grow old and ... not merely sink into the aging process," as Helen Luke writes (Luke, 55).

The Mutual Transformative Power of Ego and Unconscious

One day, Christina brought to our session an acrylic painting she had made during the week. It was in the shape of a mandorla resting on and protruding from a dark background. The inside of the mandorla was a sort of stained glass window and looked like a rose-window showing different shapes in vivid colors, each one related to a specific aspect of herself. Some pieces of the stained glass had odd shapes, looking like unpolished stones with uneven outlines. While she was commenting on the mandorla, she pointed to these unexpected shapes: "These are stones," she said. "Parts of me that cannot transform: too heavy, too dense to be penetrated. My hopeless parts." She started naming them: "This is my unmothered unmothering mother," "This is my depressed inner teenager. The passive, lifeless one, sleeping through her depression," "This is the one who will always remain afraid of exposing herself in public and will go on hiding and betraying part of her truth," and so on. She went on naming each one of her stones. As for myself, I could feel the heaviness of these odd shapes, but I was struck by their vivid colors and by the fact that they showed higher relief than the other elements, as if Christina had used several layers of acrylic on them. I said: "They look like gems." She said: "At the beginning I had painted them in dark grey. But at one point I became sad for them and I decided to give each of them a proper wedding gown." She said this with a smile. "I thought that they deserved it. So they ended up turning into gems."

Shortly after that session, Christina had a dream in which she saw herself following a woman walking along a narrow corridor at dusk. Her guide had an angelic quality and a mysterious glow emanated from her. On each side of the corridor all sorts of people were waiting: some healthy and smiling, others wounded and sad. Among them were a young woman dancing, a dog running around happily, also a stillborn baby, a pregnant twelve-year-old girl about to give birth, a dead old man, and even broken parts of a human body—a foot, a liver, and so on. As the angelic woman was passing, all these beings came towards her (even the foot and the liver were moving toward her). The group was forming a procession and growing bigger with each addition. The procession slowly progressed toward an empty room at the very end of the corridor, from which a mysterious soft light was coming. From the point that they had reached to the mysterious room, the distance was impossible to evaluate. The only thing that was clear was that along the further part of the corridor many more familiar or strange, reassuring or frightening beings were waiting to be integrated into the procession.

Psychological transformation is usually perceived as being instigated by an impulse coming from the unconscious and accomplished when the ego submits to its demands. One of Jung's most hopeful and ground-breaking thoughts, however, is the acknowledgement of the power of the ego to bring about a transformation of the Self, an insight that he has particularly elaborated in his "Answer to Job" (Jung 1952/1958, paras. 553–758). When a deep bond has been established between the ego and the unconscious, they become active partners in a process of mutual transformation.

As Christina was telling me her dream, we were deeply touched by what we both felt to be the response of her unconscious to the initiative she had consciously taken when she painted her mandorla. Her compassion towards all parts of her psyche, her conscious decision to provide a "wedding gown" for her most hopeless inner aspects, had instigated an alchemical transmutation and triggered a movement within the unconscious, which immediately reacted. The ensuing dream provided her with the image of a spiritual entity, a Psychopomp, leading her along the path of integration, revealing the creative potential of previously hopeless aspects of herself (the pregnant teenager), but bringing also into the procession the seemingly useless elements, the dead, the stillborn, the dismembered elements of the psyche. An Isis-Sophia figure was leading Christina to the meaning of the process in this phase of her life, performing a task of "re-memberment," the specific task of the evening of life. Without such a reassuring presence, Christina confesses that she would probably have been terrified and tempted to shrink away from the task. Responding to her ego's initiative, the unconscious had provided her with a symbol that would make the impossible possible.

"Habentibus Symbolum facile est transitus" ("To those who have a symbol the transition is easy").

REFERENCES

Jung, C. G.. 1931/1966. Problems of modern psychotherapy. In CW 16.
———. 1934/1969. The soul and death. In CW 8.
———. 1937/1958. Psychology and religion. In CW 11.
———. 1952/1958. Answer to Job. In CW 11.
———. 1944/1953. *Psychology and alchemy.* CW 12.
Luke, Helen. 2001. *Old age: Journey into simplicity.* New York: Parabola.
Schwartz-Salant, Nathan. 2007. *The black nightgown: The fusional complex and the unlived life.* Wilmette: Chiron.
Stein, Murray. 2005. *Transformation—Emergence of the self.* College Station, TX: Texas A&M University Press.
Woodman, Marion. 1985. *The pregnant virgin: A process of psychological transformation.* Toronto: Inner City.

DIANE COUSINEAU BRUTSCHE, Ph.D., was born in Montreal, Canada and earned a Doctorat in French literature from the University of Paris and a Diploma in Analytical Psychology from the C.G. Jung Institute of Zurich. She works as an analyst in private practice in Zurich and is a training analyst, supervisor, and lecturer at the International School of Analytical Psychology in Zurich.

6

EMERGENCE AND THE SELF

Joseph Cambray

At a pivotal moment in the midst of a multiyear analysis, a professional man who was struggling with a change of career had the following short dream:

> *I have come for my session. I'm about to ring your bell and enter when I look up. The light is changing. It is twilight and the stars are coming out. I'm surprised to see a constellation that I've never seen before. It is new and it is nearly overhead.*

While the dreamer was aware that the deeper background, the archetypal configuration upon which he was basing his life, that is his point of orientation, was shifting, the straightforward clarity of the dream imagery impressed and amused him. The dream held compensations both for the abstract, complex nature of his conscious formulations and for his idealizing transference.

At the first layer of metaphor, the locus of the dream action seemed to me especially significant on the last point. The "looking up [to]" is not happening directly in the analyst's office, nor is it removed from his vicinity. The analyst is an absence, anticipated as about to be engaged. The action takes place on the threshold, as if a transit from what appears outside in the world of nature to an interior space, actually a deepening internalization, is about to be made. Through the dream, we are taken to a moment at the edge between worlds, a pause at the interface of conscious and unconscious, as well as between the human and the cosmological. The liminality of the scene is further reflected in the twilight hour. It is in this open state that the new and unexpected vision is serendipitously glimpsed. The affect of "surprise," one of the six or seven inborn emotions—identified in the work of Silvan Tomkins, introduced into the Jungian literature by Louis Stewart (1987)—is noteworthy for its impact on the analysand; this stops him, reorients him, and sets off a process of reflection.

Given this dream, as well as the responses, associations, and reflections engendered by it and future psychological development of this person, a traditional Jungian approach would readily identify aspects of both the personal and transpersonal self engaged in a moment of transformative realignment, with the potential for integration of new attitudes pointing towards greater wholeness of the personality. Rather than directly detailing such a view, which clearly holds much value, I will instead step back and start with a look at a tradition of holism in science as a way of exploring the "new constellation" that is appearing here. This will be brought into contemporary discourse through the notion of emergence and applied to the idea of the self in analytic practice, with an eye to how this might enhance our understanding of this sort of dream encounter.

HOLISM

The peoples of the "prescientific" world had numerous visions of the universe, usually as alive and profoundly interconnected in mysterious, magical ways, and frequently portrayed in their mythologies. With the advent of empirical, observational methods aimed at quantification of nature, chroniclers of the work of the pioneers emphasized the distancing from the prior perspectives, which they often derided as superstitions. The history of mainstream science contains a number of important observers and theoreticians prior to the seventeenth century, most notably figures such as Copernicus, Galileo, Tycho Brahe, and Kepler, who would have counted among such thinkers. However, the rigorous mathematization of basic, universal laws of physics is generally given the place of honor in the story of the origins of the Western scientific view of the cosmos. While inaugurated by Kepler, this quantification of nature is most often traced back to the philosopher-scientist-mathematicians of the seventeenth century beginning with René Descartes with his analytical geometry and the source of our Cartesian coordinates. In philosophy, Descartes championed the total separation of mind from matter/body, initiating centuries of debate on the origins and nature of consciousness, a problem that is (re)gaining attention in the twenty-first century as technological probing of the brain/mind interplay is becoming accessible to scientific exploration.

The greatest exponent of the mathematical approach was of course Sir Isaac Newton who formulated the laws of motion. The success of the Newtonian view resulted in a mechanistic world view, but this achievement was troubled over time on two major points. First, there was the problem of action at a distance. While Newton's laws provided an accurate description of gravitational force and the movement of bodies, especially planets and moons, the means by which this force was transmitted remained uncomfortably mysterious. Secondly, the model Newton proposed held implicitly that space is empty and absolute, that is, a three-dimensional Cartesian framework through which bodies moved. Time was likewise seen in absolute terms, a one-way flow from past through the present to the future, which could be systematically but arbitrarily subdivided into units using mechanical devices such as clocks.

As recent biographers of the scientists of the sixteenth and seventeenth centuries have taught us, the lives of these figures were more complex than can be derived from their scientific accomplishments. Newton, for instance, is now known to have written far more on alchemy than on mathematical physics. Leibniz, the co-discoverer of calculus alongside Newton, likewise was deeply concerned about symbolic thought. For him, mathematics was part of a search for a universal language, and he has been firmly placed within the hermetic tradition by Francis Yates (1966). Most of the scientists and mathematicians of the period had strong philosophical interests that went beyond the bounds of what could be quantified, but these views were edited out of the subsequent eighteenth-century rationalistic, reductionistic ("Enlightenment") reading of nature.

While there have been many challenges to the reductive views, their explanatory power has been very persuasive, and they have persisted into the contemporary world, though increasingly recognized as valid only for select situations and specific conditions. Some of the most serious criticism initially came from philosophers, starting in the seventeenth century itself. Leibniz, who fixed his attention on the continuum (a sort of pleromatic background to the universe, a holistic fundament), opposed the atomistic view of Newtonian particulate bodies. He also presented perspectives linking time and space as relational—this later caused Einstein to declare himself a "Leibnizian" (Agassi 1969). In other words, he rejected Newton's absolutes of time and space. For Leibniz, matter consisted of intensifications of forces, or energy, as dimensionless points in the continuum. While Leibniz's theory of monads is beyond the scope of this essay, it included the notion of a preestablished harmony among monads, which served as one of the key precursors to Jung's idea of synchronicity. Similarly, Spinoza, in rejecting Descartes's dualism, developed a dual-aspect monism (mind and matter as two different aspects of an underlying unity, a radically holistic stance). Strikingly, this last theory has recently enjoyed resurgence among some neuroscientists examining the brain/mind interface (Damasio 2003).

By the end of the eighteenth century, reactions to "Enlightenment science" had set in, especially in German culture. Guided by Kant's Critiques, German romanticism and classicism revived interest in Spinoza through various figures, including Goethe and Schelling with his *Naturphilosophie*. Alternative process-oriented ways of approaching science were suggested. Although at the time this approach had few successes and quickly became marginalized, there was one area of importance that remained—the discovery of the link between electricity and magnetism in 1820 by Hans Christian Oersted, who had studied with Fichte. The observation was made serendipitously in a classroom demonstration when Oersted noticed a compass needle responding to a current passing through a nearby wire. Though his theory about this was not well developed, this observation served as spur to the great British experimentalist, Michael Faraday.

Coming from a modest socio-economic background, Faraday lacked a mathematical education, but he was brilliant in the laboratory and with metaphysical speculations. In his study of electromagnetism, he identified lines of forces and discovered magnetic strain permeating the space around magnetic phenomena. From his work on the effects of magnetism on polarized light, Faraday developed the idea of the field, which he understood as "a space filled with lines of electric or magnetic force" (Cantor, et al. 1991, 77). He first publicly articulated this in June 1845 at a meeting of the British Association for the Advancement of Science (ibid.). From there he went on to develop field theory more generally. Rejecting Newtonian views of space as empty and absolute, Faraday instead envisioned the space around electric and magnetic phenomena as permeated with, even composed of, lines of electromagnetic force, and in a great intuitive leap he suggested that these lines of force could carry the "ray vibrations of light" (Williams, 1980, 116). He also saw that analogous lines of force could account for gravitation. Thus in one stoke he provided a theory for the propagation of light and gravity, questioning the notion of absolute space and dismissing action at a distance. This was the greatest intellectual breakthrough in understanding the physical world since Newton. From a Jungian perspective, we would identify this as the reemergence of an archetypal idea leading to a vision of a wholly interconnected universe, an image that Jung himself would draw upon heavily.

Within the limits of classical physics, Faraday's insights were brought to their fullest expression by James Clerk Maxwell from 1862 to1865. Among his numerous brilliant achievements, Maxwell worked out a completely rigorous mathematical expression for the electromagnetic field, not only unifying electric and magnetic phenomena but also demonstrating that light was a form of electromagnetic radiation with a spectral range extending far beyond visible light in both directions. (The ultraviolet and infrared ends of the visible spectrum of course supplied Jung with his apt metaphor for archetypal processes having both spiritual and instinctual dimensions.) Newtonian notions of absolute space and time as well as action at a distance were now wholly overturned. The parallels between the study of electromagnetism in nineteenth-century science and the fascination with hypnotic phenomena, often referred to as a form of "magnetism," can only be noted in passing here, but they do directly link to the study of mediums as in Jung's medical dissertation.

In a surprisingly brief time Maxwell's own work was used as a springboard for a much more radical revision of physics through field theory. In 1905, Einstein produced four major papers including his article, "On the Electrodynamics of Moving Bodies," which proposed his special theory of relativity (the relativity of all inertial frames of reference). By 1915/16, Einstein had articulated his general theory of relativity, unifying special relativity, Newton's universal gravitation, and a geometric view of space-time. Gravitational acceleration arises from the curvature of space-time by the mass-energy and momentum content of matter. This in turn had a profound impact on psychological theorizing. Jung had Einstein to his house as a dinner guest on several occasions during the period "when Einstein was developing his first theory of relavity. . . . It was Einstein who first started me off thinking about a possible relativity of time as well as space, and their psychic conditionality" (Jung 1975, 109).

Although Jung does not explicitly refer to his model of the psyche as a form of field theory, it clearly owes much to this formulation, which was defining the Zeitgeist especially in the physical sciences and which had been imported into psychology by figures such as William James with his "field of consciousness." Consider for example Jung's view of the archetypes of the collective unconscious, which in effect form a highly interconnected network: "It is a well-nigh hopeless undertaking to tear a single archetype out of the living tissue of the psyche; but despite their interwoveness they do form units of meaning that can be apprehended intuitively" (Jung 1940, para. 302; quoted and discussed in Cambray and Carter 2004, 119). A field description can be understood as a network model with polycentric holism. In terms of psychodynamics, Jung's "Psychology of the Transference" presents an interactive field model emerging from a background archetypal field. The scientific investigations of field theory in physics in relation to holistic perspectives has continued mostly notably in the work of David Bohm and his students on what they term the "implicate order" (for an example see, Nichol 2003).

That such field descriptions themselves derive from archetypal images can be seem through amplification. The *unus mundus* of alchemy is one example; another from Indian and Chinese Buddhist philosophy is "Indra's net." This latter image is one of the primary metaphors of the Hua-yen or flower garland school:

> In the heaven of the great god Indra is said to be a vast and shimmering net, finer than a spider's web, stretching to the outermost reaches of space. Strung at each intersection of its diaphanous threads is a reflecting jewel. Since the net is infinite in extent, the jewels are infinite in number. In the glistening surface of each jewel is reflected all the other jewels, even those in the furthest corner of the heavens. In each reflection, again are reflected all the infinitely many other jewels, so that by this process, reflections of reflections continue without end. (Mumford, Series and Wright 2002, ii)

A holistic, radically interconnected, reflective universe has been recurrent in humanity's imagination, and Jung's theories of the Self and the collective unconscious offer a contemporary psychological reading of this archetypal pattern.

EMERGENCE

Another related strand of holistic thinking in science and philosophy derives from developments in dynamic systems theory, especially from recent studies in "complexity." Systems with multiple components capable of interacting with one another to produce behaviors or properties in aggregate that are of a higher order than the components and not predictable in terms of their known behaviors are thought of as "complex." These systems tend to be open to the environment, dissipating energy and producing greater internal order, and so they are referred to as self-organizing systems. As such, they operate far from equilibrium states and therefore cannot be analyzed using the classical laws of thermodynamics. The high order phenomena associated with the self-organizing features of such systems are termed emergent and tend to appear at the edge of order and chaos (for clinical applications see Cambray 2002). In terms of field theory, emergent phenomena would be expected to occur in just those regions of the field that are undergoing self-organization. Emergent phenomena have been identified throughout nature and the human world—from the organization within clusters of subatomic particle to the clustering of galaxies; in biological systems, such as the behavior of social insects, the immune systems of animals, the organization of and interactions with the brain from which mind emerges, the networks of human interactions producing economic and cultural behaviors. I postulate Jung's notion of the Self is an emergent property of the psyche as will be discussed below.

One additional subset of complex adaptive systems worth noting is those that form dynamic networks through their interactions. These networks have hubs that are highly connected as well as nodes that are less richly linked. Imagine maps of airlines connections showing major cities' airports as hubs with many links along with smaller city and town airports as nodes. The most striking feature of such networks is their "scale-free" properties, that is, they have fractal qualities appearing similar at various levels of scale. For example, consider the shape of a tree, then the shape of its major branches and so on down to the structure of individual leaves. Significantly, scale-free networks are known to have self-organizing properties.

As I have detailed elsewhere (Cambray and Carter, 2004), Jung's model of the collective unconscious, together with his method of amplification, can be seen as manifesting a scale-free network structure, even if his presentation often tends to be a bit too rigid. This formulation could also be used to integrate psychoanalytic models into a Jungian view: the personal complexes residual from childhood could be seen as organized around the major archetypes active during early development, which form the "hubs" in analytic theory. The interactive patterns of object relations, which inform the transference/countertransference field, reveal the interconnections between hubs.

As individuation proceeds out of childhood, through the socially adaptive period of adult life (Jung's "first half of life") towards the psychological challenges of maturity (whether of the whole personality or particular developing aspects of it), the archetypal patterns active also shift away from the more commonly trodden pathways between hubs to explorations of nodal patterns and their linkages that lie at the margins. These patterns at the margins may have hitherto been left unexplored because of various defensive maneuvers of the ego or the self, placing them in the "shadow" region of the dynamic unconscious. Further experiences in life may bring us to the marginal and uncharted aspects of our being, often revealed only after previous unconscious encumbrances have been worked through. The new constellation in the twilight sky of the dreamer in the opening vignette suggests just such a moment of discovery.

THE SELF AS EMERGENT

The literatures of attachment theory, complexity theory, cognitive and neuro-sciences have by now been widely applied to various perspectives on emotions and developmental processes. At the center of this is the experience of self, which is now increasingly understood in its initial stages as an emergent aspect of the mind-brain in an interactive field between infant and caretaker(s). Daniel Stern pioneered this area for psychoanalysis starting in 1985; more recently, Jungian reflections and research have begun to appear, most notably in the work of Jean Knox (Knox 2003).

Moments of emergence of the self in infancy manifest at a multitude of lev-els, from micro-shifts that have been observed in videotapes of mother/infant dyadic interactions (Beebe and Lachman, 2005), to larger phase transitions like the sudden onset of the smile response or stranger anxiety that were noted in clas-sical studies on early development. The latter seem to involve an element of rapid reorganization of neuronal patterns in a self-organizing manner. As this is a large and growing literature, I encourage interested readers to start by exploring the ref-erences cited here. For purposes of the present chapter, I would like to turn now to Jung's ideas on the self as an archetypal, transpersonal, trans-historical reality, especially as articulated in the last chapter of *Aion*, "The Structure and Dynamics of the Self."

Previously, in defining the self Jung had made it clear that this is a transcen-dental concept not wholly graspable by the intellect but one that provides the archetypal basis of personality including the capacity to conceptualize. His ear-lier descriptions had already focused on wholeness: "As an empirical concept, the self designates the whole range of psychic phenomena in man. It expresses the unity of the personality as a whole" (1971, para. 789). As the unity of psychic totality, this wholeness of course includes conscious and unconscious compo-nents of the personality. The imagery associated with the self, as in dreams, tends to reflect or to imply this totality—the appearance of circles, squares, crosses, quarter circles, and so forth; or the depiction of unions of opposites (*yin* and *yang*; royal marriages or (al)chemical combinations; hero and traveling companion or hostile brothers); or imaged in the figure of the "supraordinate personality" (ibid., para. 788). There is frequently a strong affective charge associated with the expe-rience of such images. They feel numinous. Manifestations of the self thus over-lap to the point of identity with the *imago Dei*, the god image from various cultures around the world throughout history, and bring a sense of order or order-ing to situations in which they appear. Edinger notes that Jung borrowed the term "Self" from the sacred texts of the Upanishads through his readings of Schopenhauer and Nietzsche (1996, 163).

A subset of self images that Jung wrote about at length was those from man-dala symbolism (e.g., in CW 8). In brief, he notes:

> Experience shows that individual mandalas are symbols of *order*, and that they occur in patients principally during times of psychic disorientation or re-orientation. As magic

circles they bind and subdue the lawless powers belonging to the world of darkness and depict or create an order that transforms the chaos into a cosmos. (Jung 1959, para. 60)

The transformative quality of these images, especially when spontaneously emerging at the very edge of madness, closely resembles the kind of ordering that arises in self-organizing systems, which are indeed envisioned as coming into being at the edge of chaos. These processes are at the heart of the emergence of the cosmos as a physical and psychological reality.

Late in *Aion* as Jung works his way through "Gnostic Symbols of the Self," he is at pains to represent the multidimensional quality of the self through a set of geometric diagrams. Using a set of four octahedrons—double pyramids (one of the Platonic solids)—each of which he has explicated as an elaborations of a quaternity at differing levels of being from inorganic matter (the Lapis Quaternio) up through images of the transcendental self, the "higher Adam" (the Moses Quaternio—figure 1), he ultimately envisions a set of nonlinear, circular processes (figures 2 and 3). Read in terms of emergence, we can see a close parallel here to contemporary views at the conjunction of complexity and network/information theories. Self-organization reflects the information of complex systems and is an inherent feature in the universe from the micro- to macro-physical aspect of 'inorganic' nature. It extends through the properties of

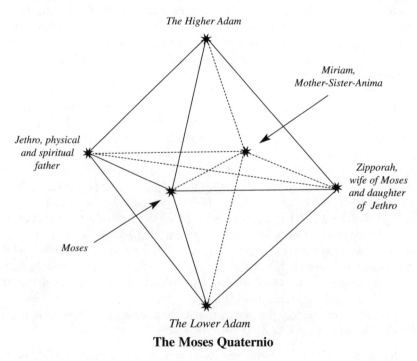

The Moses Quaternio

Figure 1

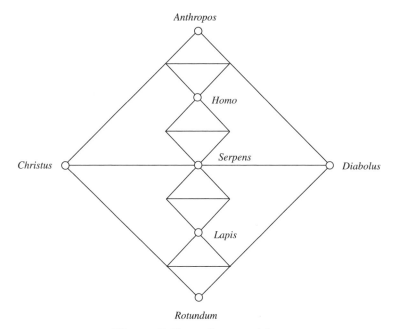

Figure 2 Four Quaternities

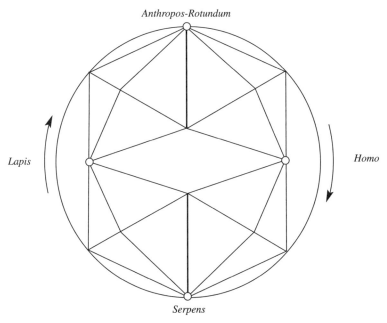

Figure 3 Uroboros Quaternities

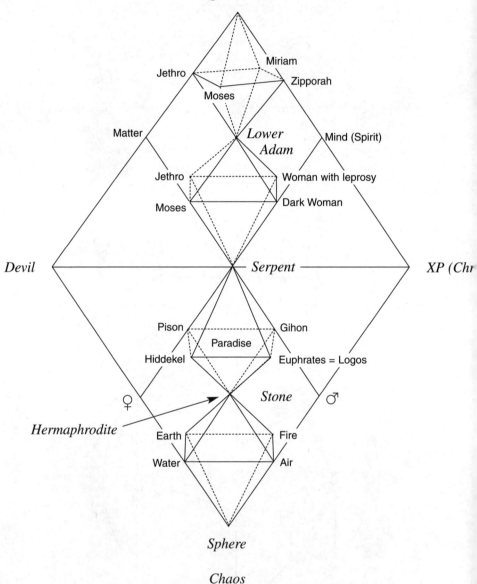

Figure 4 Quaternities in Jung's letter

biological systems to the manifestations of mind, including both individual and collective behaviors, as well as the evolution of cultures, and includes all of the highest aspirations of humans. Jung's stack of four "Quaternios" offers a poetic expression of this knowledge in a densely compacted form. (For more detailed discussion of these levels from a classical Jungian perspective, see Edinger 1996, and for Jung's unpublished detailed drawing that was reduced in *Aion* to what is presented here in figure 2, see Ann Lammers [2007] and the letter of May 21st, 1948 from Jung to Victor White (Lammers and Cunningham [2007]; this will be referred to below as figure 4.)

In these figures, it is evident that Jung was seeking a sufficiently complex way to present his evolving understanding of 2000 years of symbolism. His multidimensional geometric imaginings are closely linked with his attempt to break out of the Trinitarian principles of religion and science as he understood it (space, time, causality) and to express a Quaternitarian view that includes "correspondences," that is, his ideas about synchronicity (Jung 1951/1959, para. 409). In the language of this article, these diagrams represent Jung's struggle to communicate a view of an archetypal self in a manner that places it at the heart of emergent processes. As such, it symbolizes the potential for emergence throughout the hierarchy of levels of being, from the mineral to the spirit.

One striking feature in comparing these diagrams is the breaking of, or reduction in, symmetry in Jung's fullest representation, figure 4. In their general form, figures 1–3 all show highly regular, symmetric features. Even the most complex of them demonstrates rotational as well mirror symmetry. However, unlike all of the diagrams published in *Aion*, Jung's sketch to White (figure 4) shows the top octahedron rotated 90° relative to those below it. This rotation together with the diagonal lines in the larger diamond that link the lower frontal face of the second octahedron with the upper dorsal face of the third octahedron reduces the symmetry of the whole figure to a single mirror plane. Additionally, as noted by Lammers (2007), these diagonal lines from matter to the ♂ symbol and mind (spirit) to the ♀ symbol are omitted from the drawing in *Aion*, again simplifying and symmetrizing the published figure relative to the one in the letter to White. This reduction of symmetry suggests to me that this fullest expression of Jung's idea contains an impulse (I do not know if it was conscious or not) to break out of the excessive ordering that at times accompanied his discussions of the self (as with his own history of producing mandalas). The unacknowledged value in this diminishing of symmetry may be found in the increased complexity that results.

From careful examination of symmetry in relation to complexity, scientists have ascertained that complexity is characterized by the breaking of symmetry. For simple/linear systems where the whole is equal to the sum of its parts, symmetric features are common and introduce redundancy into the pattern, so that one only needs a portion of the information in a simple system to construct the whole. The repetition of a pattern producing order tends to engender an aesthetic experience of beauty, which can of course have a calming effect on the mind and induce a feeling of tranquility in resonance with the harmony of the symmetric form. The building up of symmetric forms is also crucial to early development, hence the value of imitative learning. However, for complex systems the reduction in symmetry is integral to emergence. No aspect of a complex system has adequate information to represent the whole, nor can any single part statistically predict the dynamic behavior of the system, especially when it self-organizes. Symmetry is broken in what are called phase transitions, that is, rapid reorganizations in a dynamic system that radically restructure the system, allowing new forms to emerge (for an discussion of phase transitions in manifestations of the self, see Hogenson 2005; for more a general scientific discussion, see Mainzer 2005). Psychologically, bearing such transitions and reorganizations can be highly stressful for an individual even if ultimately positive in transformative effect.

My suggestion is that Jung wrestled with both sides of the problem in articulating the self. He needed the symmetrical ordering properties associated with historical, aesthetic and religious traditions on the one hand, while also remaining open to the precarious, symmetry-breaking, emergent possibilities of the self on the other. Perhaps his need to remain open to the power of the numinous, which cannot always be reduced to symmetrical containment, informed his diagram to White, just as he spoke of his respect for various religious traditions as the closest approach he could come to faith (Lammers and Cunningham 2007). It seems he needed a more complex view of the divine than he could find in traditional religion.

By centering his discussion of the self on the Christian eon, Jung also points towards historical transformations of the collective expression of the archetype of the self. His discussion is set against the Platonic year with its zodiacal "months." (Due to the precession of the equinox caused by the wobble of the earth, a "year" is one full transit of equinox through the circle of the zodiac, that is, 25,765 earth years. Each month therefore consists of roughly 2200 years). The transition to the next eon, to the by now excessively touted "age of Aquarius," is clearly in Jung's sights. This is where he locates the dilemmas associated with the resolution of opposites (1959, para. 142). From the perspective of the objective psyche, such a shift in basic expression of the form of the self would indicate a large phase transition at the socio-cultural, even global, level accompanying the emergence of a new form. There has of course been much speculation about this, especially with the rise of globalization and the enormous impact of the internet, but it is premature to seek clear identifications.

More reflections about the previous shift, in addition to *Aion*, are becoming available and provide a reconsideration of the transition in terms of emergence. The work of Karen Armstrong on the beginnings of the world's great religious traditions in the "Axial Age" is just such a contribution (2006). In the Jungian community Murray Stein (1998) has explored transformative aspects of emergence in adult life and Hester Solomon in the final chapter of her latest book, *The Self in Transformation*, brings a combination of Jungian and emergentist's readings of this material into a fascinating conjunction (2007). Similarly, the study of cultural complexes (e.g., Singer and Kimbles 2004) will I believe also be advanced by careful study and application of complexity theory to the unconscious dimensions of socio-cultural and historical phenomena. Elsewhere I will explore macro-synchronicities, those that occur at the level of societal and cultural interfaces and have left their mark on history (Cambray 2009).

CONCLUSION

Returning to the dream with which I began this chapter, we may now consider the new constellation that appears overhead. There is insufficient information to know where the dreamer's psyche places this vision with respect to the zodiac. We only know that a new pattern has emerged and is near its zenith on the threshold of analysis, which makes the link between the personal and collective aspects of this material focal and uncertain. What it does suggest is a breaking of the symmetry, perhaps a step out of or breaking "heimarmene" (the compulsion of the stars as bound to the zodiac). Certainly fate is not so simply transcended, but a breaking that leads to increased complexity does make individuation more pressing. The liminality of the dream also contains the impulse for greater differentiation, which it is hoped will intensify the need to articulate the relationship between individual and collective elements of the self, so that what emerges partakes of both but in a way that cannot be predicted. In this the affect of surprise is crucial. As I have previously written, it is the affect most directly linked with the psychological experience of emergence (Cambray 2006).

We end with a return to the unknown, though enhanced, I hope, by ideas from contemporary science that are forming a new paradigm. Jung's concepts, especially of the self, cannot be put through such reflections without some modification, but in this I believe they are strengthened. Jung's entire opus has an emergentist feeling to it. His amazing intuition honed in on many features that could be associated with such a perspective, though he did so without the benefit of scientific explorations, which were not yet available during his lifetime. At times his view seemed too constrained by the longing for order, which caused him to oversymmetrize his models, not unlike Einstein in his search for a unified field theory. Our world faces different anxieties, and if we relax Jung's model of the self towards the totality of a more open polycentric network its vibrancy and vitality will offer much to life in the twenty-first century.

REFERENCES

Agassi, Joseph. 1969. Leibniz's place in the history of physics. *Journal of the History of Ideas* 30: 331–44.

Armstrong, Karen. 2006. *The great transformation*. New York and Toronto: Alfred A. Knopf.

Beebe, Beatrice and Frank Lachman. 2005. *Infant research and adult treatment: Co-constructing interactions*. New Jersey: The Analytic Press.

Cambray, Joseph. 2002. Synchronicity and emergence. *American Imago* 59, 4: 409–34.
———. 2006. Towards the feeling of emergence. *Journal of Analytical Psychology* 51, 1: 1–20.
———. 2009. *Synchronicity: Nature and psyche in an interconnected universe.* College Station: Texas A & M University Press.
Cambray, Joseph, and Linda Carter, ed. 2004. *Analytical psychology: Contemporary perspectives in Jungian analysis.* Hove and New York: Brunner-Routledge.
Cantor, Geoffrey, David Gooding, and Frank A.J.L. James. 1991/1996. *Michael Faraday.* New Jersey: Humanities Press.
Damasio, Antonio. 2003. *Looking for Spinoza: Joy, sorrow, and the feeling brain.* New York: Harcourt, Inc.
Edinger, Edward. 1996. *The Aion lectures.* Toronto: Inner City Books.
Hogenson, George. 2005. The Self, the symbolic and synchronicity: Virtual realities and the emergence of the psyche. *Journal of Analytical Psychology* 50, 3: 271–84.
Jung, C.G. 1951/1959. *Aion: Researches into the phenomenology of the self.* In CW 9ii.
———. 1971. *Psychological types.* CW 6.
———. 1975. *Letters,* 2: 1951–1961. Ed. Gerhard Adler and Aniela Jaffe. Princeton, NJ: Princeton University Press.
Knox, Jean. 2003. *Archetype, attachment, analysis: Jungian psychology and the emergent mind.* Hove and NY: Brunner-Routledge.
Lammers, Ann Conrad. 2007. Jung and White and the God of terrible double aspect. *Journal of Analytical Psychology* 52, 3: 253–74.
Lammers, Ann Conrad, and Adrian Cunningham, eds. 2007. *The Jung-White letters.* London and New York: Routledge.
Mainzer, Klaus. 2005. *Symmetry and complexity.* New Jersey: World Scientific.
Mumford, David, Caroline Series, and David Wright. 2002. *Indra's pearls: The vision of Felix Klein.* Cambridge: Cambridge University Press.
Nichol, Lee, ed. 2003. *The essential David Bohm.* London and New York: Routledge.
Singer, Thomas, and Samuel L. Kimbles, eds. 2004. *The cultural complex: Contemporary Jungian perspectives on psyche and society.* Hove and New York: Brunner-Routledge.
Solomon, Hester MacFarland. 2007. *The self in transformation.* London: Karnac.
Stein, Murray. 1998. *Transformation: Emergence of the self.* College Station: Texas A & M University Press.
Stewart, Louis H. 1987. A brief report: Affect and archetype. *Journal of Analytical Psychology* 32, 1: 35–46.
Williams, L. Pearce. 1980. *The origins of field theory.* Maryland: University Press of America, Inc.
Yates, Francis A. 1966. *The art of memory.* Chicago: University of Chicago Press.

JOSEPH CAMBRAY, Ph.D., is President-Elect of the IAAP and a member of the New England Society of Jungian Analysts and the Jungian Psychoanalytic Association with private practices in Boston, MA and Providence, RI. He is a faculty member of the Center for Psychoanalytic Studies at Harvard Medical School.

PART TWO

METHODS

INTRODUCTION TO METHODS
Murray Stein

Jung was famous for disdaining the notion of "technique" in analysis. It was anathema for him because he feared an emphasis "on how to do it" would create mechanical imitators who would miss the individuality of the person coming for treatment. He was convinced that the most important thing an analyst has to offer is an open and receptive mind, and if technique gets in the way of this it is far better to set it aside and sit with a person without knowing what to do or how to do it. In a sense, the articles in this section contradict Jung's outspoken criticism of method and technique in analysis, but it is only a seeming contradiction and not a real one. As the articles all make clear, no one is in favor of technique over personal presence. The methods, tools, and techniques spoken of in this section are of value if handled properly, which means not "mechanically" and inflexibly but with respect for the uniqueness of each individual soul who comes into analysis.

John Beebe, arguably the world's leading contemporary Jungian spokesperson and theoretician of psychological type, discusses the great value of assessing type as one works with analysands. Type theory is a tool that actually guarantees more individual treatment than might otherwise be possible, precisely because it presupposes that people are different and that one size shoe does not fit all feet. Jan Wiener, equally an authority on transference in the Jungian world today, discusses Jung's expressed ambivalence about the use of transference as a tool in analysis and shows how an understanding of transference, in Jung's own terms, can be critically important for promoting growth of consciousness and individuation in analysis.

Jung's own preferred method for working in analysis was dream interpretation. Warren Colman, in his chapter "Dream Interpretation the Creation of Symbolic Meaning," shows how Jung's approach differed from Freud's and how the modern Jungian psychoanalyst employs dream interpretation centrally and importantly today. The traditional as well contemporary form of dream interpretation in Jungian work is collaborative. Meanings are not imposed or handed down by an authoritative analyst. They are the product of dialogue and exchange within the creative matrix of the analytic setting. John Hill, in "Amplification,

Unveiling Emergent Patterns of Meaning," discusses the analyst's important contribution to this dialogue. The method of amplification was specifically designed by Jung to expand the meaning of dreams and other material from the unconscious to include collective in addition to personal references.

In addition to working with dreams, active imagination was a preferred method employed by Jung for coming into contact with the unconscious. Sherry Salman, in her chapter "Peregrinations of Active Imagination," connects this traditional Jungian method with contemporary discussions on Jungian psychoanalysis and postmodern perspectives and reviews traditional and contemporary forms of using this technique in analysis. A somewhat neglected instrument among Jungian psychoanalysts in recent decades, active imagination is again being highlighted by a new generation as an indispensable technique for working analytically in depth. Mary Dougherty ("On Making and Making Use of Images in Analysis"), Eva Patis ("Sand Play"), and Cedrus Monte ("The Body and Movement in Analysis") extend the discussion of active imagination by introducing specific further techniques that have been developed by themselves and other Jungian psychoanalysts to elaborate the potential of active imagination in various modes.

With all of these methods, instruments, and techniques, the intent is to create a dialectical process between consciousness and the unconscious that will release creative energies and build up a stable psychic structure that is maximally representative of the whole personality. In the wrong hands, of course, they can become straitjackets and be more poisonous than healing. The skilled Jungian psychoanalyst will presumably know when and how to use them, and when to put them aside.

7

THE RECOGNITION OF PSYCHOLOGICAL TYPE

John Beebe

The late Jo Wheelwright, the analyst who in the years between 1940 and 1980 did so much to keep Jung's theory of psychological types alive as a clinically relevant modality of interpretation, liked to say that the ability to recognize psychological type is a "knack." Jo was, as he explained in his inimitable way (Wheelwright 1982), an "extraverted intuitive feeling type," which in his case meant an uncanny ability to enter into the minds of others and to know how they were feeling. Some of his expressions of intuitive compassion, at a time when the term "emotional intelligence" had not yet come into common usage, were legendary. A woman colleague battling alcoholism received a bouquet of flowers from him every week during her first year of recovery. Jo once greeted a younger male colleague with, "It must feel great being in a fresh new suit!" to the amazement of the colleague, who had recently purchased the suit and wondered how Jo, who didn't see him every day, could know that.

To arrive at his type, Jo assumed (1) that he was an extravert (no one who knew him doubted this), (2) that his leading consciousness—what Jung would have called his "superior function of consciousness"—was "intuition," and (3) that his auxiliary function (Jung's term for the "second" function of consciousness that pairs with the first to produce the individual's "type") was feeling. Jo concluded he was pairing "extraverted intuition" with "extraverted feeling" to achieve the extraordinary feats of empathy for which he was noted. But it seemed to me, and to those who had studied type using the Myers-Briggs Type Indicator (MBTI), that Jo was pairing "introverted feeling" (which remembered how certain categories of experience tended to feel deep inside) with "extraverted intuition" (which latched onto the new thing in a person's life on which the individual with whom Jo was empathizing was staking her or his future). Jo himself always insisted that his feeling was extraverted, however, claiming that there was not a shred of evidence that he had introverted feeling. There is a recording of a seminar we shared with Jo's wife, Jane, in which I patiently explain the basis of my competing conclusion while Jo thunders back, until Jane finally shouts to me, "Will you stop it?!"

This argument about Jo Wheelwright's type reflects the confusion Jungian clinicians often experience when trying to use type theory, despite the extensive groundwork laid out by Jung (1921) in *Psychological Types* and by Katherine Briggs Myers (1980) in *Gifts Differing* and the later clarifications in both Jungian and MBTI circles that I have summarized in a recent review article (Beebe 2006). To use the theory with precision, one has to be able not only to (1) recognize and accurately name the main "functions" that a person is using to express his or her consciousness (Jung gives only four choices for this: thinking, feeling, intuition, and sensation), but also to (2) figure out which of the two functions that are likely being most often used is primary and which secondary—and beyond that to (3) make clear the "attitude" with which each function is being deployed. (The choices Jung and Myers give us here are only two, extraverted and introverted, and it is Myers's view, and my own, that if the primary function is extraverted then the auxiliary will be introverted, and vice versa. This natural alternation of extraversion and introversion in our functions of consciousness is, by my observation, very adaptive: it keeps us from becoming too one-sided.)

Even those who recognized both Jo Wheelwright's intuition and his feeling (and there were many who could only see one or the other of these functions) did not always know what to call them (some thought Jo's extraverted intuition was simply intrusiveness, or narcissism), and few could figure out which of these functions was primary and which secondary (most people assumed that he had "extraverted feeling" as his main modus operandi, not realizing, I believe, that they were conflating the extraversion of his superior function (intuition) with the introversion of his auxiliary function (feeling).

Nor should my need to define type so sharply be promoted as a value without my admitting that my thinking function has a need to define type precisely, but also to pull away from the person to do so into an ideal model in my own mind of how a person's type can be parsed. This is so evident in me that it would be easy for the reader to conclude that I have introverted thinking as my leading function. But, no, I would argue, extraverted intuition is my leading function, and introverted thinking my auxiliary. Notice the strange inner confidence in my own thinking that led me to believe I had a right to type Jo Wheelwright at all. Also notice, though, the way this article begins, jumping right into the middle of the type muddle. That is extraverted intuition, and it has a certain verve and immediacy. The article starts to bog down, however, as soon as I try to specify Jo's type or my own too precisely in my thinking way, because then I am writing as if consulting a model of the mind that is particular to me, one not easily accessible to the reader who doesn't already know this model. Now the reader has to work to follow my argument. If the reader consults his or her own experience of reading this chapter so far, the evidence for making a type assessment of its author is already at hand.

To check the assessment that this author is using extraverted intuition and introverted thinking, the reader may consider that neither the feeling nor the sensate aspect of the chapter is its strong point. Have I considered how Jo

Wheelwright felt about the conclusion he had reached about his type—that, as he would have put it, "his thinkings" might "be hurt" by an analysis that contradicted his own? Am I giving the reader much secure fact to base any kind of analysis on? Isn't the overall feel of the chapter so far, despite the personal example, abstract rather than concrete? And isn't it hard to tell what I as author feel about the algorithm of type choices I seem to be trying to convey?

It is not hard to see, if you simply consult your experience while reading this chapter, that its author does not particularly emphasize feeling, and that he exhibits even less sensation. And, if you are already fairly familiar with Jungian type theory, you may find the pattern of my consciousness that is emerging to be consistent with the view that when thinking is the second of the two leading functions, feeling (its opposite on the same axis of "rational" functions) will be tertiary, and that when intuition leads, sensation (intuition's opposite on the axis of "irrational" functions) is going to be the inferior function. Knowing this enables us to map out the type of the author of this chapter—that is, my type—as Jung might have, by starting with a vertical line, which we can label at its top intuition and at its bottom sensation and next by crossing it with a horizontal line to define an axis at right angles to this spine. We will then label this horizontal axis's leftmost extent "thinking" and its rightmost "feeling." The stick diagram that has resulted can then be labeled "John Beebe's type profile." It is meant to convey this author, for the purpose of typing him, visualized as if facing the reader, arms spread apart with his right hand to the viewer's left and his left hand to the viewer's right, and his head, trunk and legs all lined up to suggest an upright spine.

Why would anyone want to turn himself into a diagram? If such model-making is introverted thinking (a function which we might define as the need to make experience conform to a thinking model held and checked within for "internal" consistency), possibly the answer to this question is found by saying: "This is what introverted thinking likes to do!" James Hillman has pointed out that the very word "function" comes from a Sanskrit root *bhunj*, which means "to enjoy," and from which his own introverted thinking draws the conclusion that "The exercise and performance of a function is something to enjoy, as a pleasant or healthy activity, as the operation of one's powers in any sphere of action" (Hillman 1971, 75). In my case, it is true that I enjoy typing consciousness and fitting it into a thinking model.

But I am not performing this exercise in a vacuum, autistically, just for myself. It is my way of teaching, of conveying, even of trying to *take care of* the reader, who I imagine is reading this chapter in hopes of understanding how to use type in an analytic practice. My auxiliary function, introverted thinking, is actually trying to take care of you as you read, by getting you to draw the stick figure of me so that you can visualize both the type theory and the man who is explaining it to you in the typological terms I have found most helpful. Whether you *feel* taken care of, and whether your unclarity about type is actually lessened by this instruction, is of course a result of how you receive me, which depends in part on your own typology. But I can count on your having at least some experience of me while reading this chapter, and it's on that that I want you to build your own sense of my type, just as you would watching and listening a patient presenting himself to you.

Elsewhere (Beebe 2004), I have argued that, regardless of an individual's psychological type, there is a presiding genius associated with each of the ranked "positions" of our typology—superior, auxiliary, tertiary, and inferior—in Jung's original four-function model of consciousness. For each position, an archetype flavors the expression of the function in that place. (Although it is beyond the scope of this short article, I have also identified archetypes associated with the four functions that are in shadow.) It was my discovery that the auxiliary function is used parentally—as a way of taking care of others. (Again, I am focusing on the individual's intent when using a particular type of consciousness.) It follows that when making a type assessment, we need to take into account the archetypal stance that accompanies the deployment of a particular function. If you can experience me as at least trying to take care of you using an intricate, even private, logic, based on my love of my own particular version of type theory, then you can begin to see how my introverted thinking is auxiliary, because that's what an auxiliary function aims at, *taking care of another.*

Following a professional meeting, Jo Wheelwright was once in a hotel bar leading some other colleagues in an informal sing-along when the woman playing the piano suddenly realized her period had come. She stopped playing, got up gracefully and walked to the bathroom, at which point the pool of blood that had been hidden by her skirt was evident on the piano bench. The moment was naturally uncomfortable for all present: no one knew what to say or do. Wordlessly, Jo went over to the bar, picked up some paper napkins and used them to wipe off the bench. Then he sat down and began playing the piano so the sing-along could continue. When the woman reappeared ten minutes later, she was able to resume playing. I believe Jo used his introverted feeling to know how humiliating such an experience might be for the woman and how helpless everyone else might feel about what to do, and he simply concentrated on removing the thing that was producing the embarrassment: the blood on the bench. He himself would likely have read his action as an extraverted feeling one. I think it is clear that it was just as much a parental gesture, one that involved using his authority as a senior analyst to make the caretaking move of cleaning up a junior colleague's mess in his exquisitely calibrated feeling way. I cannot imagine approaching the typology of that story, whether as an example of extraverted or introverted feeling, without also looking at the fatherly way that whichever kind of feeling it may have been was being deployed. And I doubt that few present could have experienced the gesture, though involving the sensation function (wiping up the blood), as motivated by anything other than feeling.

By contrast, the superior function is less involved in the care of others and more in the assertion of self. In describing the night-sea journey of the hero in *Wandlungen und Symbole der Libido*, Jung gives a beautiful depiction of the way a heroic introverted intuition approaches the problem of relating to the unconscious. In asserting this vision of a consciously irrational ego (i.e., an intuitive type), he sacrificed his caretaking role with regard to Freudian psychology, which was the very basis on which Freud had anointed him his "Crown Prince." He was ever after accused by Freud of abandoning the scientific study of the unconscious, which for Freud could only be accomplished rationally through a dialectic of thinking and feeling.

In an essay completed shortly before his death, Jung described how the need to assert his own more intuition-and-sensation-based (and thus in his own language for these functions, "irrational") standpoint developed out of the unconscious itself. He recounts a dream that he shared with Freud when the two men were on their way to America to a conference at Clark University at which many leading psychologists, including William James, would be present. Freud expected Jung to help him "sell" the theory of psychoanalysis to the American psychologists. In the dream, Jung encountered for the first time his own house, which mirrored through its furnishings and contents not only his intellectual history and interests but also a multilayered model of the psyche. Discussing the dream with Freud, he tells us, he had the "sudden and most unexpected insight that my dream meant myself, my life and my world, my whole reality as against a theoretical structure erected by another. . . . It was not Freud's dream, it was mine; and suddenly I understood in a flash what my dream meant" (Jung 1961/1980, 215).

One could say that in response to this dream Jung's identity emerged, and that his identity was expressed through a rather characteristic burst of introverted intuition. In contrast to the type diagnosis of introverted thinking given Jung by many Jungians, including occasionally Jung himself, I tend to read Jung as an introverted intuitive type, with thinking (and I would argue that it is extraverted thinking) his auxiliary function. What is important here is to note that in the way he approaches the dream he tried to share with Freud, Jung asserts his intuition at the moment he sees it as presenting his "own" standpoint. There is narcissism in this as well as a certain heroic combativeness. He is emphatically *not* taking care of Freud, as he does in the more "rational" writings he was publishing at the time of the dream where he uses extraverted thinking to argue for the validity of psychoanalysis. Jung's dream, and the way he interprets it, is compensatory to letting himself be used in this way. The dream fosters the emergence of an extreme self-assertion carried by the intuitive function, which (at that moment of insight at least) became the superior function for Jung (and his preferred guide for thinking ever after).

With a patient in the therapeutic situation, we often have to distinguish between the way the patient asserts self and the way the patient takes care of an other. This is not so hard to do because in the analytic situation the 'other' will usually be the analyst. There is something heroic about self-assertion (it should be noted that many patients have a considerable difficulty asserting themselves with anything like the definiteness Jung describes in taking ownership of his own dream), and there is something parental about taking care of the other. The analyst may want to note the ways the patient is parental in the transference, and not just the ways the patient is infantile. (Developing Winnicott's [1987] notion of the analyst's way of "holding" the patient throughout an analysis, contemporary relational psychoanalysts have implied that the patient holds the analyst during treatment quite as much the analyst holds the patient [Samuels 2008] and of course there are wide variations both in patients' capacities to do this and in the ways they do this, into which both the strength and the typology of the patient's auxiliary function figures.) This distinction helps us to differentiate the patient's (heroic) superior function from his or her (parental, caretaking) auxiliary function, and that can be an enormous help in establishing a reliable type diagnosis. Because of the way Jung's introverted intuition is so involved in his self-assertion at the moment of realizing the possibility of his own theory of mind (and so uninterested in any longer supporting Freud's model), I am led to diagnose Jung's superior function as introverted intuition and to read him as being (when he is being most characteristically himself) an introverted intuitive thinking type.

Although "position" is critical in the assessment of type, it is of little help if one does not also know how to recognize and distinguish the different types of consciousness (eight in all) that can appear in particular positions such as "superior" and "auxiliary." (These two do not exhaust the positions in which a type of consciousness may appear, but I am concentrating on them because they are the most frequent to manifest relatively early in treatment in most people.) One has, in other words, to be able to recognize, and tell the difference, between introverted thinking, introverted feeling, introverted sensation, introverted intuition, and extraverted thinking, extraverted feeling, extraverted sensation, and extraverted intuition. Learning to do this requires conscious practice. It is not unlike the way one learns how to read music. Unfortunately, we don't have a mnemonic song like "Do-Re-Mi," which Mary Martin, and later Julie Andrews, sang in *The Sound of Music*, to learn type recognition the way we learn to recognize the basic tones of the Western musical scale. There is, however, a European story, "A Dinner Party with the Types," which is included as an appendix in Daryl Sharp's book, *Personality Types: Jung's Model of Typology* (113–19), that does a very good job of describing the eight different types of consciousness personified as guests at a dinner party. The hostess, appropriate to her role, embodies extraverted feeling. Her husband, a quiet, slender professor of art history, doubtless excels at noticing the minute differences between similar works of art. He represents introverted sensation. An extraverted thinking lawyer is the first guest to arrive. An industrialist, well dressed but loud, and a greedy though appreciative eater, comes later. He stands for extraverted sensation. His wife, a quiet, extremely ladylike woman with mysterious eyes, the type in whom "still waters run deep," is with him. She exerts a strangely magnetic effect on the other guests with her introverted feeling. An introverted thinking professor of medicine is next. He comes without his wife, and is apparently preoccupied with the disease he has been studying. He is followed by an extraverted intuitive engineer who rhapsodizes about his ambitious plans, which one suspects will come to fruition only if someone else carries them out. While speaking, he gobbles his food without noticing what he is eating. The last intended guest, a poor young poet, forgets to come to the party but, when he realizes his mistake, plans by way of apology to send his hostess the poem he was working on while the party was taking place. (Sharp's own descriptions of these eight types of consciousness follow Jung and are presented at more length in the main section of his book.)

The functions are not as easily recognized in therapy. A real life person, unlike a stereotyped character identified with a single function, has access to all eight functions of consciousness, even if some are in shadow, and will deploy one or another depending on the context and the type of consciousness called for by that context. Also, the patient in analysis is often in the grip of complexes, which notoriously produce what Jung, quoting Janet, called an *abaissment du niveau mentale*, a reduction of the mental level, such that the energy that normally attaches itself to the superior and auxiliary function, allowing them to surface, is absent. When these functions are not active, the tertiary and inferior functions emerge. "Tertiary" and "inferior" are terms that imply that there is a gradient of differentiation in the four types of consciousness that normally describe someone's "ego," at least as that sometimes inexactly defined term is understood by analytical psychology. As the least differentiated of the functions consciously available to the patient, the tertiary and inferior functions tend to be less adapted to reality and more influenced by unconscious complexes, which are in fact usually dominating the psyche when the third and fourth functions emerge in recognizable form. Their presentation is thus often floridly neurotic, easily characterized as obsessive, cyclothymic, hysterical, or paranoid, creating an obvious link to psychopathology. When it is easy to diagnose neurotic traits or character pathology in an analytic patient, it is a tip-off that one is looking not at the patient's natural (superior and auxiliary function) typology but at "a falsification of the original personality" (Jung 1959, para. 214). Naturally, a person can also falsify his or her original personality in a more adaptive way by conforming to the expectations of a family, school, occupation, or culture.

We should be cautious, therefore, in making a type diagnosis. It is best not to try to type someone who has not yet made a connection to the self that would be natural to him or her because all you may be doing is noting the "negative personality" (Jung 1959, *idem*) that has swallowed up the patient's true self (Beebe 1988). Sometimes, however, knowing that the inferior and tertiary functions reflect what someone "is least good at" can be a clue to the actual type. The person who constantly obsesses about small feeling matters, finding other people's feelings an endless burden, may be not an extraverted feeling type for whom other people's feelings matter but who finds it easy to deal with them, but someone with inferior extraverted feeling, that is, an introverted thinking type. Marie-Louise von Franz (1971) has written the definitive text on the inferior function, and in many ways her monograph is also the best book on type for clinicians because it portrays the way many kinds of patients present themselves in the office when in the grip of the inferior function. It should be required reading in all Jungian training programs. A companion essay by James Hillman on the feeling function shows the number of other psychological entities that can confuse the identification of a function of consciousness and the need for clinicians to differentiate all of these. To cite just one example:

> Extraverted feeling ought not to be confused with the persona. Although in Jung both refer to the process of adaptation, extraverted feeling is a function of personality. It is a manner of performing and can be an expression of an individual style. By means of it a person gives values and adapts to values in ways which can be highly differentiated, uncollective and original. The persona, on the other hand, is a fundamental archetype of the psyche referring to the manner in which consciousness reflects with society. The persona in Jung's stricter usage of the term would mean a developed reflection of the collective consensus. If one is a prisoner, or an addict, or a hermit, or a general, one can have a developed persona by behaving in the styles and forms collectively belonging to these patterns of existence. They are archetypal patterns. Feeling may have little or nothing to do with this adaptation, for one can be connected very well to the collective through thinking, intuition and sensation. In a nutshell: classically the persona is a collective way of playing a role in the world; the feeling function is an individual instrument of self-affirmation. (Hillman 1971, 102)

To discover a patient's typology, it is better to wait until the patient shows an original gift for accurately construing or managing some aspect of what comes up in therapy, rather than attempt to "type" the person when he or she is manifesting a collective persona that could belong to anybody in the patient's situation, or when the patient is so evidently suffering from psychopathology that a syndrome has all but replaced the person.

The typology of the true self (defined as the personal, little "s" self in touch with the transpersonal big "S" Self [Gordon 1985; Beebe 1998]) is rarely so stereotyped; rather it opens up the use of the most differentiated parts of the personality in an individual way that is a revelation and a pleasure to experience. It's when the patient is exhibiting his or her strengths as an authentic person that we can begin to appreciate the skill with which feeling, thinking, sensation and intuition are being used. At such moments, we can also see what effective extraversion and introversion are like when they are used as conscious attitudes.

When the patient is using a well-differentiated extraverted function, the function will seek to merge with some aspect of the analyst in a way that the analyst does not find particularly uncomfortable. When *extraverted feeling* is differentiated, the analyst feels appreciated and respected, and there is a sense of one's good will being seen and met. When *extraverted thinking* is highly differentiated, the analyst will find that it is safe to let the patient set the agenda, like a general directing the campaign of the therapy. When the patient's *extraverted sensation* is well-developed, the analyst has the experience of a ready participation in what is happening in the moment and an accompanying impatience with abstractions, as if what is already there is sufficient without much interpretation. *Extraverted intuition* can feel intrusive, but it is also entertaining and astonishing in the way it can pick up on fresh possibilities for developing the objectives of the therapy in the world.

Introversion, when used consciously, is not as easy to discriminate, and indeed the functions of introverted feeling, introverted sensation, and introverted intuition are easily confused with each other. *Introverted thinking* can usually be distinguished by the fact that it tends not to know when to stop, and needs to define everything freshly, to the point that it becomes exhausting and hard to follow. It, like the other introverted functions, seeks to match its experience of an object with an a priori, archetypal understanding of that category of object *already present in the unconscious.* The introverted move away from the outer object is therefore the first step in a process that takes the introverted function's libido deep into the unconscious of the introverted subject, to see if the object really matches up. (That it often doesn't live up to the archetype helps to explain the frequent disappointment that introverted functions register in analysis, a disappointment that must not be confused with a condition to be treated, even if it is dysphoric to the subject. People with superior introverted functions must register this disappointment when the object simply doesn't match up. It's their normal way of reacting.) *Introverted intuition* seeks to match up the experience with an image of an archetype, something like a visual metaphor. *Introverted sensation* likes to establish whether the experience of the object checks out with an inner sense of what has already been established through long human experience as "real." And *introverted feeling* wants to know if the object as experienced is conducting itself in accord with what is fitting for such an object, that is, if a bride is acting like a bride, if a home feels like a home, if the boss is behaving as she should in her role.

The clinician should grow accustomed to the way introverted functions are constantly sizing up what happens in the therapy, to see if it checks out with the rich inner world of already-known, archetypal experience, against which an introverted function measures everything. Recognizing the introverted types in their normal functioning is one way to realize Jung's enormous contribution to opening up the introverted world as a part of healthy functioning. Simply not pathologizing introversion is perhaps the most healing thing a therapist can do in our pathologically extraverted, world-despoiling times. And it is a sign that the therapist is well along in the knack of type recognition.

REFERENCES

Beebe, John. 1988. Primary ambivalence toward the Self: Its nature and treatment. In *The borderline personality in analysis,* ed. Nathan Schwartz-Salant and Murray Stein, 97–127. Wilmette, IL: Chiron Publications.

————. 2004. Understanding consciousness through the theory of psychological types. In *Analytical psychology: Contemporary perspectives in Jungian analysis*, ed. Joseph Cambray and Linda Carter, 83–115. Hove and New York: Brunner-Routledge.

_____. 2006. Psychological types. In *The handbook of Jungian psychology: Theory, practice, and applications*, ed. Renos Papadopoulos, 130–52. London and New York: Routledge.

Dalp, Sammlung. 1952. *Handschriften-deutung.* Bern: Franke Verlag.

Gordon, Rosemary. 1985. Big Self and little self: Some reflections. *Journal of Analytical Psychology* 30: 261–71.

Hillman, James. 1971. The feeling function. In *Lectures on Jung's typology*, 73–150. Zurich: Spring Publications.

Jung, C.G. 1950/1959. Concerning rebirth. In CW 9, i.

_____. 1961/1980. Symbols and the interpretation of dreams. In CW 18.

Myers, Isabel (with Myers, P. B.). 1980. *Gifts differing.* Palo Alto, CA: Davies-Black Publishing.

Samuels, Andrew. 2008. Personal Communication.

Sharp, Daryl. 1987. *Personality types: Jung's model of typology.* Toronto: Inner City Books. First published in German as *Das Diner der psychologischen Typen* ("The Dinner Party of the Psychological Types"), Sammlung Dalp, 1952.

Von Franz, M.-L. 1971. The inferior function. In *Lectures on Jung's typology*, 1–72. Zurich: Spring Publications.

Wheelwright, Joseph. 1982. Psychological types. In *Saint George and the dandelion: 40 years of practice as a Jungian analyst*, 53–77. San Francisco: C.G. Jung Institute of San Francisco.

Winnicott, Donald. 1987. *Holding and interpretation: Fragment of an analysis.* New York: Grove Press.

JOHN BEEBE, M.D., is a Distinguished Fellow of the American Psychiatric Association and an analyst member in the C.G. Jung Institute of San Francisco, of which he is a past president. Over the past twenty-five years, he has lectured and written on psychological types. He is the author of *Integrity in Depth* and co-author of *The Presence of the Feminine in Film*.

8

WORKING IN AND WITH
TRANSFERENCE

Jan Wiener

*Emotions are contagious because they are deeply rooted in the sympathetic system . . .
any process of an emotional kind immediately arouses a similar process in others. . . .
Even if the doctor is entirely detached from the emotional contents of the patient, the
very fact that the patient has emotions has an effect on him. And it is a great mistake
if the doctor thinks he can lift himself out of it. He cannot do more than become conscious of the fact that he is affected.*

—JUNG

This remarkable quote from Jung in Lecture 5 of the Tavistock Lectures brings
home with clarity that Jung's sharp intuitive capacities were alive from the earliest days of his writing and in his clinical practice. Jung knew about transference
in his bones and though rarely acknowledged, he was certainly the first depth psychologist to point both to the inevitability and the usefulness for analysts of their
countertransference affects. Jung's profound beliefs in the archetypal nature of
unconscious processes alive between patient and analyst, in the emotional impact
of analysis and its potential for making meaning, finds generous support at the
beginning of the twenty-first century from contemporary research in the fields of
neuroscience and attachment theory (Schore 1994, 2001; Lyons-Ruth et al. 1998;
Kaplan-Solms and Solms 2000; Pally 2000; Beebe and Lachmann 2002). The
development of a mind and the capacity to make meaning emerges through relationship. Nonverbal and unconscious interactive processes go on continuously in
infancy and adulthood and therefore, by implication, in the transference and
countertransference relationship. Implicit processing that is beyond awareness
can be as important as that which is explicit, conscious or verbal. Jung's quote at
the beginning of this chapter stands up pretty well to the research tests of time,
and this perspective certainly gives us food for thought as to how best to train
potential analysts to fine-tune their affective states in relation to their patients.

    Given Jung's obvious talent in this area, a question to be asked is why the role
of transference in the Jungian world is at best controversial, and at worst a hot
spot for profound disagreements. There are probably at least three central convic-

81

tions that bring us together as analytical psychologists. The first is our strong belief in the power of the unconscious as much greater than the capacity of the ego to understand it; the second relates to the value of the self as an organizing and unifying center of the psyche, seeking to bring together and mediate the tension between opposites; the third is that a symbolic capacity and the development of a transcendent function facilitates the process of individuation. However, when it comes to theories about transference and how to work with transference projections, the Jungian world divides radically. Beliefs about the role and value of patients' transferences to their analysts are predicated not only on views about the nature of the psyche and the development of mental functioning, but also on the aims of analysis and within this, the role of the analytic relationship. We would probably all agree that transference exists as an archetypal process, so why then have Jungians turned to a variety of different methods of making sense with their patients of their transference experiences? What can be made of the observation that the value Jungian analysts across the world place on the significance of the transference within as a "site of therapeutic action" (Colman 2003, 352) varies so enormously? It is these issues that this chapter will address.

JUNG'S AMBIVALENCE ABOUT TRANSFERENCE

One has only to survey Jung's writing on transference to realize his ambivalence about this topic, expressed in his contradictory statements sometimes even in the same paper. Inevitably, this has attracted the interest of a number of authors, each keen to understand why this was the case. Steinberg (1988) and Fordham (1974), for example, carefully surveyed Jung's writings on transference. Steinberg thought that Jung's ambivalence could be attributed to his hurt and anger with Freud and also because he encountered personal transference difficulties with patients that led him to play down the significance of the personal transference. Henderson (1975, 117), recalling his personal relationship with Jung, remembers that Jung tended to refer those patients with too strong a transference to him on to Toni Wolff! Fordham (1974) was generous to Jung, considering that it is possible to find some sense of continuity in his writings on transference if they are viewed within the social and cultural preoccupations of the time. More recently, other authors have been drawn once more to examine a Jungian approach to transference through analytic eyes embedded in a culture of a different time (Kirsch 1995; Perry 1997; Samuels 2006; Wiener 2004; Wiener in 2009).

Jung's inconsistent views about transference are indeed confusing. Looking at the fascinating exchange of letters between Jung and Freud during the spring and summer of 1909 (McGuire 1974), it seems that Jung's vulnerability to the erotic transference experienced at that time most powerfully with Sabina Spielrein, his first analytic patient, may indeed have made him wary of too close a personal involvement with his patients. Even so, the letters convey Jung's strong motivation for understanding and working through this difficult experience. Whereas Freud and post-Freudians were drawn increasingly towards an interest in the nuances of transference dynamics in the analytic relationship, Jung, after the collapse of his friendship with Freud, was much happier working with his beloved dreams and the archetypal images and symbols that emerged from the unconscious.

Faced with the discomfort of Jung's ambivalence, Jungian psychoanalysts have taken different transference directions in their working methods, influenced as well of course by the trends and personalities prevalent in local cultures. Some, including myself, turned to a developmental approach, interested in how complexes are formed from the earliest stages of life, and also specifically to Fordham's ideas about how the self develops in infancy. Psychoanalytic perspectives were essential to advance an understanding of the subtleties of the analytic relationship, including the technical aspects of how to work with transference in the consulting room. Others chose to follow more closely the central ideas of Jung himself, settled in their beliefs that Jung offered future analysts a good enough method with which to work with patients. This has led unfortunately to two transference camps—the developmental and the classical—and a division that endures today. For those interested in a developmental approach, relating and its processes have taken precedence, whereas for those drawn more to the classical approach, gaining access to the contents and creative energy of the collective unconscious has taken on greater significance.

THE NATURE OF TRANSFERENCE

Transference as we understand it today is a natural, archetypal process, multi-beamed and multidirectional in character. It brings different beams of transference including the erotic, the psychotic, the negative, the idealizing, and the addictive. Sometimes it seems to be absent altogether. What is "transferred" is always unconscious: a complex stirred in the present with roots in the patient's past; a mood of the moment, not yet conscious to the patient; an internal object projected into the analyst; an infantile anxiety or fantasy; and then, suddenly, something new and archetypal, activated for the first time within the analytic relationship, like Stern's "moments of meeting" (Stern 1998). Each of these transference projections has the potential to activate the analyst's countertransference affects in different ways and, if carefully processed and returned to the patient in a manageable form, can lead to new insights.

We are helped in our thinking about transference by making a central distinction between working "in" the transference and working "with" the transference. Like it or not, we are always working "in" the transference. The evidence from neuroscience and infant research shows clearly that subjectivity always involves an interactive process. We affect each other from cradle to grave, and the quality of our earliest relationships is likely to influence the biochemistry and the structure of the brain, creating neural pathways connected with emotions that lay down essential patterns for adult relationships. Those of our patients who have experienced a mother capable of mediating and regulating the emotions of her baby are more likely to develop internal capacities to soothe and manage themselves when in distress. Other patients who lack the experience of a mother who could tune in to their emotions remain easily upset and volatile, developing the "hot" responses typical of borderline or psychotic states of mind, or the "colder" schizoid reactions of those who have shut off from relationships, leaving them isolated but protected from frightening intrusions.

Working "with" the transference involves analysts in decisions as to whether, when and how to interpret the transference projections of their patients. Analysts listen with an open mind and use their bodily sensations, thoughts, and imaginative capacities to interpret the transference when it comes to mind to do so. However, this phrase "when it comes to mind to do so," actually involves quite a complicated process. The analyst needs to create a space, a place in the mind, where something can happen. Britton (Britton 1998, 121) refers to this as the "other room." Countertransference takes place in the other room of the mind, a place in the mind that creates itself from right hemisphere to right hemisphere unconscious nonverbal relating; an internal space that is experienced even if what will enter it is not yet known. This is the receptive space with which we meet without prejudice our patients' unconscious communications including transference projections. It involves a letting go, a receptive state of being much like meditation or reverie. But imagining involves a mental function as well as a mental space, and it is this more ego-oriented function that we need in order to appraise and understand the meaning of what it is that we are experiencing with a patient. The difficult task of course is to distinguish which of these news headlines belongs to the analyst and which come rather from patients' transference projections.

CONCEPTUAL CONTROVERSIES

I do not think that Jung's disenchantment with Freud and his challenging experiences with Sabina Spielrein provide sufficient explanation of the controversy that surrounds the topic of transference in the Jungian world today. For this, we have to turn to some conceptual issues that have muddied the transference waters.

Jung used the German word *Übertragung*, meaning to carry something over from one place to another, to define the term "transference" (Jung 1935/1976, paras. 311–12). His emphasis was a broad one and could encompass both the personal and the archetypal transference. His approach to transference was largely theoretical and he did not give us many detailed accounts of his clinical work to show us how he worked with transference material. On the whole, Jung used the term transference vaguely. He did not want to confine the meaning of transference just to the projections of parental imagos, keeping a place at all times for the archetypal; but too broad a definition risks a concept losing its meaning altogether.

In Jung's usage the term transference often became a description of the analytic relationship as a whole. His interest in alchemy and the symbolism of the *Rosarium Philosophorum* (Jung 1946/1966) was intended as a metaphor for the stages of development in the analytic relationship, what he calls the transference, but this has left us with a confusing conflation of process and outcome. Jung contrasted the initial experience in analysis of *participation mystique* (process), what we would today call projective identification, where personal transference projections in the analysis may lead to a state of unconscious identity between patient and analyst with the *coniunctio* (outcome) a higher order psychological mechanism that is "always the product of a process or the goal of endeavour" (Jung 1946/1966, para. 462). In other words, this is the hoped for outcome of analysis when the patient becomes more conscious. But transference emerges in different ways with different patients during analysis. It is an unconscious process, an inevitable part of all analyses, stronger sometimes, quieter at others, sometimes directed onto the analyst; at other times onto other people in patients' lives. I am not sure that it evolves in clear stages as Jung suggests, and we risk muddling process and outcome if we consider the term as a description of the analytic relationship as a whole.

During my training, I studied with interest and enthusiasm the detailed accounts used by psychoanalysts interested in the technical aspects of working with the transference. I realized only later that Freud's and Jung's conceptions of the meaning of transference were quite different. Jung's teleological emphasis on transference as the projection of what is not yet known contrasts with the Freudian emphasis on transference as the return of the repressed, what he called "new editions of old conflicts" (Freud 1916, 454). Jung's conception of the psyche and the unconscious as normally dissociated—a vertical division—and his interest in the not yet known, the unrepressed, and the collective unconscious with its natural symbol-making capacity, contrasts with Freud's horizontal division where he viewed repression as an unconscious defensive maneuver and a more pathological form of functioning. From Jung's perspective, we unconsciously project what is not yet known into the analyst so we can find out more about ourselves. These different models of psychic functioning suggest different attitudes to transference with implications not only for theory-building, but also for clinical practice.

Jung made a clear distinction between the personal and the archetypal transference. He considered that images emerging in the transference from patients' personal experience were qualitatively different from those images emanating from the impersonal structures of the psyche. Jung was much more interested in the archetypal, transpersonal transferences and gave the impression that he wanted the personal quickly out of the way. His distinction seems to me to have become quite problematic. Separating the personal and the archetypal can lead either to the potential for dangerous idealizations of the archetypal and its contents or to a neglect of the personal. We do well to heed Mary Williams's (1963) wise words that the personal and collective unconscious in image-making and pattern-making activities are always interdependent:

> Nothing in the personal experience needs to be repressed unless the ego feels threatened by its archetypal power. The archetypal activity which forms the individual's myth is

dependent on material supplied by the personal unconscious . . . the conceptual split, though necessary for the purposes of exposition is considered to be undesirable in practice. (Williams 1963, 45)

Most Jungian analysts are interested less in the sources of unconscious material than in their meaning. Jung preferred a more educative and synthetic approach to symbols when they emerge in sessions or in dreams, grounded in his largely intrapsychic model of the psyche. Some analysts look for unconscious symbols emerging from their patients' psyches to be elucidated together in the analysis. Others, and I include myself in this category, are more oriented towards the interpersonal, taking the view that unconscious material including the symbolic emerges more naturally in relationship.

CLINICAL CONTROVERSIES

As well as conceptual difficulties, we find two central clinical debates in the field of analytical psychology, one emanating from psychoanalysis and the other from Jung's specific legacy. These highlight significant differences in clinical practice.

There continues to be debate as to whether transference should be given only a limited place in the analytic process, in contrast to the view that the main task is to analyse everything as an aspect of the transference. Transference as the total situation (Joseph 1985) has been a popular approach in the UK. It was developed by Kleinian analysts who considered that the only way to gain access to primitive states of mind and the unconscious was in the here-and-now of the transference relationship. Everything in analysis takes its meaning from the patient's transference to their analyst, and gives clues about their earliest unconscious fantasies. While acknowledging a central role for transference in my own practice, I question whether everything that emerges from the psyche comes only from these earliest states of mind. I also view with some alarm the effects on our patients of relentless transference interpretations. First of all, this means that the analyst is likely to listen only "for" transference material, rather than listening "to" the patient with an open mind. To listen for transference alone means that this preoccupation will increase the tendency for analysts to miss the bigger picture of unconscious communications, accessible through the free of flow of patients' associations during sessions. There is also the danger that patients learn their analysts' language and subsequent interactions become artificial rather than authentic. David Bell (2008), a psychoanalyst, remarked how easily transference can become a fetishized object for trainees, who think that they will be in trouble if they fail to report regular transference interpretations in supervision. This is a far cry from the hope that analysts will be able to use their transcendent function in a flexible and sensitive way with each of their patients, involving "now and then" (Bollas 2007, 95) rather than "here and now" transference interpretations. Bell's comment is not just about trainees, as it is surely their teachers who set the transference tone.

Jung advocated a central role for the analyst's personality in the analytic relationship. What he meant by this is a question that seems to me to become more complicated the more we delve into it. Of course the personality of the analyst influences the progress of an analysis, but we need to use our personality differently with different patients. What is required is the necessary training and skills to recognize the different needs of our patients and how these may change over time. It is easy to confuse authenticity, where analysts make themselves emotionally fully available to their patients, with a too "real" relationship that compromises the analytic and ethical attitude, making it difficult to maintain a nonjudgmental, safe psychic container in which patients may discover more about themselves. Jung's emphasis on personality was in part his reaction against the by now much-caricatured Freudian emphasis on neutrality, abstinence and anonymity, which were in part vestiges of the old medical model. Yet we do well to keep them in mind today. As analysts, we reveal minimum information about ourselves, leaving space for transference projections (anonymity); we try to limit enactments and acting-out (abstinence) and to maintain a nonjudgmental attitude (neutrality). It is actually our self-knowledge that our patients need, which is a carefully considered way of using ourselves in the service of the analytic process. This self-knowledge cannot be separated from personality, but it also involves a number of learned competencies (Wiener 2007). There are good reasons why analysts need a thorough training.

Jung's Attitude towards Method

Jung realized through his own experience that the significance of the transference is as the precursor of something that is about to become conscious. In my view, however, he lacked a coherent method and technique for working with the transference. Jung was more interested in the prospective function of symbol formation and less interested in how it worked, or indeed how it develops or fails to develop in infancy. For many of our less gifted patients and those we know to have experienced early traumatic parental deficits, violent families, child abuse, chronic somatic complaints, or who have a fragile or weak ego, the symbolic capacity is often at best rudimentary and at worst completely absent. For them, states of disintegration are more likely than states where the not-yet-known can be integrated. I can think of many examples in my practice where I have struggled to find in myself ways of working with patients who are seriously depressed, or who have chronic somatic symptoms, or who fall into delusional transferences. They cannot play and often they cannot imagine. Transference analysis can play a key role in helping such patients emerge from these psychic retreats.

Jung was highly mercurial in his attitudes to method and technique, despite his interest in the self and the patient's individuality. In *Memories, Dreams, Reflections*, he upholds an approach that would suit each patient individually: "Psychotherapy and analysis are as varied as are human individuals. I treat every patient as individually as possible, because the solution to the problem is always

an individual one. Universal rules can be postulated only with a grain of salt"
(Jung 1963/1995, 153). Jung then goes on to put forward the idea that holding to
a single method for all patients is not to be recommended: "In general one must
guard against theoretical assumptions. Today they may be valid, tomorrow it may
be the turn of other assumptions. *In my analyses I am unsystematic very much by
intention. . . . We need a different language for every patient*" (Jung 1963/1995,
153; my italics). Of course we need a different language to acknowledge the
unique attributes of every patient, but we still need theory and method to help us
maintain a professional and ethical attitude. Analysis needs some constraints that
define it as a method and while technique can seem to spoil the human aspects of
analysis, I do not think we can manage without it.

Transference and the Development of a Symbolic Capacity

Kast is clear about her priorities when it comes to working with transference:
"Facilitating the development of symbols is more important than the process of
transference-countertransference itself. Symbols are not only the vehicles for the
individuation process, but also refer to life history and future development. . . .
They shape the emotions that are connected with complexes, archetypes and the
real relationship" (Kast 2003, 107). I wonder how she works with those patients
who cannot symbolize, who do not bring dreams? It is here that work with the
transference can be essential to facilitate the development of a symbolic capacity
and a transcendent function.

I am mindful of the views expressed by two Jungian authors writing almost
forty years apart. The first is Plaut who, writing in 1966, says: "a reliance on
images alone leads into a kind of desert unless associated with analysis of personal relationships" (Plaut 1966, 113). Later in the same paper he holds that "the
capacity to form images and to use these constructively by re-combination into
new patterns is dependent on the individual's capacity to trust. . . . Failure in this
area impoverishes life and requires careful transference analysis in order to further the ego's function to trust both in relationships and in one's imagination"
(Plaut 1966, 130). Bovensiepen, writing in 2002, puts it a little differently but the
general thrust of his argument is the same: "if the symbolic attitude is primarily
understood as a relational process instead of an intellectual amplification of symbolic contents, this understanding would expand our treatment options for
patients who are, above all, plagued by difficulties with symbolization"
(Bovensiepen 2002, 253). Bovensiepen also emphasizes that "Jung's prospective
function of the living symbol, which he stressed repeatedly, corresponds to the
need for a living object" (ibid.). From these two eminent Jungian analysts we
learn that it is the analytic relationship, the person of the analyst and transference
analysis, that together help to promote a symbolic capacity. It is hoped that the
analyst's personality is well enough developed to help patients acquire an imaginative capacity for play that will lead them to think about what they lack or what

they have lost. Bion commented that "people exist who are so intolerant of pain or frustration or in whom pain or frustration is so intolerable that they feel the pain but will not suffer it and so cannot be said to discover it" (Bion 1993, 9). Most patients feel pain and this is indeed why they come into analysis, but for some of them the task of learning to suffer their pain in the presence of another is a mammoth task, sometimes lasting many years. For those with early disturbance, difficulties *have* to be worked out first in the transference.

These views of Plaut and Bovensiepen are essential to my argument. I suggest first that we consider the symbolic attitude as a relational process where living symbols herald new meanings that emerge in living relationships and include an important role for the transference. Secondly, although Jung held that the symbol-making capacity of the psyche is a natural, archetypal process, many of our patients cannot use their imaginative capacities. They become blocked, and it is only within an authentic relationship where trust can evolve that takes account of transference and countertransference dynamics, that the self begins to emerge and with it, the potential to trust in new relationships and in an internal capacity to make meaning.

THE TRANSFERENCE MATRIX

It may be that I have exaggerated the significance of the different attitudes to transference observable in the Jungian world and indeed that there is now a greater overlap of approach both to theory and clinical practice than there was before. I hope so. I would like to suggest a contemporary metaphor for transference that honors Jung's commitment to the significance of the symbolic and the effect that patient and analyst have on each other, but that also takes account of recent writing in the fields of infant research and neuroscience and the more detailed clinical research investigating different kinds of transference. Today, I believe that we need an approach to the symbolic that respects not only the psyche's capacity for image-making but also acknowledges that a symbolic capacity inevitably emerges in relationship.

Consider the following dream of a patient of one of my supervisees:

I am visiting a house where there is some kind of party and someone is cooking beef burgers that are still raw in the middle. You [the analyst] are present in the dream. Other people are given books as presents, and I am given a book on architecture. I am disappointed. The book does not reflect my interests sufficiently well. It is black and white and too rigid. I try to change the book for something else. In another scene of the dream, I arrive at your [the analyst's] house and ring the bell. You do not answer immediately, but come to the door when I ring for the second time.

I imagine that readers will agree that this dream involves transference. My initial associations to the dream would be that it is a transference dream bringing to consciousness for Bob, the dreamer, and his analyst live issues about the analytic relationship. Something is cooking, but it is still raw in the middle. The analysis may still be raw, or Bob feels raw. We may wonder why Bob has dreamed this dream at this time and what it could be telling his analyst. Perhaps the analyst is being too rigid, that is, black and white, about something, giving Bob a gift that misses the mark? Bob has to ring the bell twice suggesting that the analyst may not be hearing what he has been trying to convey. Obviously, Bob's personal associations to his dream are crucial in trying to tease out the meaning of his dream, but at first glance it seems that the dream suggests something about Bob's unconscious feelings about his analyst at that moment. The analyst may well be getting it wrong and needs a wake-up call. I wonder how other analysts would associate to this dream. It may be that the alchemical imagery of 'cooking' comes to mind, or questioning whether the reference to the book on architecture suggests that Bob needs to develop something other than his thinking function, perhaps something to do with aesthetics or daily living.

Jung's major text on transference, "The Psychology of the Transference," in which he uses the *Rosarium Philosophorum*, is a visual amplification of the transference, individuation and the unconscious processes between patient and analyst that draws on alchemy as a metaphor. Difficult to understand and thought by some to be of limited clinical usefulness because of its symbolic complexity and its failure to map out in sufficient detail the complexities of the analytic relationship, it is best known for Jung's diagram of the 'counter-crossing transference relationship' (Jung 1946, para. 425) or the *marriage quaternio* in alchemy. This illustrates a conscious and unconscious relationship between patient and analyst.

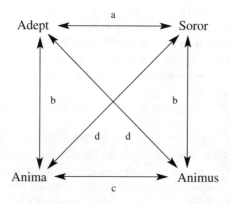

Figure 1

Jung (1944/1952, para. 219) uses the term *vas bene clausum* (well-sealed vessel) to describe the containment of both patient and analyst in the analysis. The *vas* is an alchemical vessel intended to hold disparate elements which when mixed together could ultimately make gold—the emergence of the self.

I would like to suggest that we adopt the term *the transference matrix* as a contemporary Jungian metaphor referring to a co-constructed place and framework for thinking about transference that allows for learning through experience within a relationship. The term matrix comes from the Latin word for womb, a place of origin where babies are carried, protected, and nourished until ready to emerge into the world. The Oxford English Dictionary defines the word matrix as: "*a place or point of origin and growth; a mould in which something is cast or shaped; a mass of fine-ground rock in which gems or crystals, or fossils are embedded.*" From these definitions, the transference matrix may be seen as an environment with potential for personal transferences to emerge, including the infantile as well as precious, archetypal pearls that come from the self.

Winnicott (1965, 33) referred to ego-relatedness as the "matrix of transference" and saw the mother as the infant's psychological matrix. My use of the term *transference matrix* begins as a twosome, a place of potential relationship from the beginning in which the analyst maintains a free-floating awareness of the different levels of patients' experience, including the developmental and the archetypal with space for the not yet known. The matrix contains the analytic pair and allows the analyst to interpret "when it comes to mind to do so." As the above dream suggests, what comes to mind is likely to vary, depending on the relationship and the analyst's belief systems.

CONCLUSIONS

In this chapter I have illustrated how in spite of Jung's remarkable intuitions about the significance of transference in the analytic relationship, his ambivalence on the subject to be found in his writing has left us with some difficult theoretical and clinical differences to manage. Contemporary research findings from our own discipline and related disciplines have provided strong evidence about the profound unconscious emotional effect we have on each other. Each analytic environment is unique, as Jung emphasized, and we are invited to fulfill different and changing transference roles and object representations for our patients. The transference has to be lived before it can be understood. We ignore it at our peril, but paradoxically its overuse fosters a prejudiced listening ear.

For some patients, working in and with the transference is essential as a precursor of a capacity to symbolize; for others it remains always a central place of psychic experience; and for some it is to be treated cautiously. André Green has remarked wryly: "There is no point in the analyst running like a hare if the patient moves like a tortoise. A meeting point in depth is more probable as the thread that links the two travellers also serves to keep them sufficiently apart" (Green 1974, 421).

As a Jungian analyst living and working in London, I prefer a multibeamed approach to transference, keeping in mind as its epicentre the probability that transference projections are happening all the time, each with an unconscious aim that I hope to comprehend. How to choose may be beside the point as sometimes we are "chosen" to enact something in the transference, in the self-to-self relationship between patient and analyst. These are actions of the self rather than actions of the ego, or as one of my supervisees put it recently, "listening to the stillness of the voice within from which she could find her own direction." The transference matrix is not only an image of containment, but it contains within in its walls the matter from which both the fossils and the precious gems of our patient's psyches may be jointly discovered.

REFERENCES

Beebe, Beatrice, and Frank Lachmann. 2002. *Infant research and adult treatment. Co-constructing interactions.* Hillsdale, NJ and London: Analytic Press.

Bell, David. 2010. Bion: The phenomenologist of loss. In *Bion today* (New Library of Psychoanalysis) edited by Chris Mawson. London and New York: Routledge.

Bion, Wilfred. 1993. *Attention and interpretation.* London: Karnac Books.

Bollas, Christopher. 2007. *The Freudian moment.* London: Karnac Books.

Bovensiepen, Gustav. 2002. Symbolic attitude and reverie: Problems of symbolisation in children and adolescents. *Journal of Analytical Psychology* 47, 2: 241–57.

Britton, Ronald. 1998. *Belief and imagination: Explorations in psychoanalysis.* London and New York: Routledge.

Colman, Warren. 2003. Interpretation and relationship: Ends or means? In *Controversies in analytical psychology*, ed. Robert Withers, 352–62. Hove and New York: Brunner-Routledge.

Fordham, Michael. 1957/1974. Notes on the transference. In *New developments in analytical psychology.* London: Heinemann.

———. 1974. Jung's conception of the transference. *Journal of Analytical Psychology* 19, 1:1–22.

Freud, Sigmund. 1916. *Analytic Therapy.* In Standard Edition 16. London: The Hogarth Press.

Green, André. 1974. Surface analysis, deep analysis. *International Review of Psychoanalysis* 1:415–23.

Henderson, Joseph L. 1975. C.G. Jung: A reminiscent picture of his methods. *Journal of Analytical Psychology* 20, 2: 114–21.

Joseph, Betty. 1985. Transference: The total situation. *International Journal of Psychoanalysis* 66, 4:447–55.

Jung, C.G. 1935/1976. The Tavistock lectures. In CW 18.

———. 1944/1952. *Psychology and alchemy.* CW 12.

———. 1946/1966. The psychology of the transference. In CW 16.

———. 1963/1995. *Memories, dreams, reflections.* London: Harper Collins.

Kaplan-Solms, Karen, and Mark Solms. 2000. *Clinical studies in neuro-psychoanalysis.* London: Karnac Books.

Kast, Verena. 2003. Transcending the transference. In *Controversies in Analytical Psychology*, ed. Robert. Withers, 85–95. Hove and New York: Brunner-Routledge.

Kirsch, Jean. 1995. Transference. In *Jungian analysis*, ed. Murray Stein, 170–209. Chicago and La Salle, IL: Open Court.

Lyons-Ruth, Karlon. 1998. Implicit relational knowing: Its role in development and psychoanalytic treatment. *Infant Mental Health Journal* 19, 3:282–91.

McGuire, William, ed. 1974. *The Freud/Jung letters.* London: The Hogarth Press and Routledge & Kegan Paul.

Pally, Regina. 2000. *The mind-brain relationship.* London: Karnac Books.

Perry, Christopher. 1997. Transference and countertransference. In *The Cambridge companion to Jung*, ed. Polly Young-Eisendrath and Terence Dawson, 141–64. Cambridge: Cambridge University Press.

Plaut, Alfred B. 1966. Reflections about not being able to imagine. *Journal of Analytical Psychology* 11, 2:113–33.

Samuels, Andrew. 2006. Transference/countertransference. In *The handbook of Jungian psychology*, ed. Renos Papadopoulos, 177–95. London and New York: Routledge.

Schore, Alan N. 1994. *Affect regulation and the origin of the self: The neurology of emotional development.* Hillsdale, NJ and Hove, UK: Lawrence Erlbaum Associates.

———. 2001. Minds in the making: Attachment, the self-organising brain, and developmentally-oriented psychoanalytic psychotherapy. *British Journal of Psychotherapy* 17, 3: 299–329.

Steinberg, Warren. 1988. The evolution of Jung's ideas on the transference. *Journal of Analytical Psychology* 33, 1: 21–39.

Stern, Daniel N., et al. 1998. Non-interpretive mechanisms in psychoanalytic therapy. *International Journal of Psycho-analysis* 79, 5: 903–23.

Wiener, Jan. 2004. Transference and countertransference. In *Analytical psychology: Contemporary perspectives in Jungian analysis*, ed. J. Cambray and L. Carter, 149–75. Hove and New York: Brunner Routledge.

———. 2007. Evaluating progress in training: Character or competence? *Journal of Analytical Psychology* 52, 2:171–85.

———. 2009. *The therapeutic relationship: Transference, countertransference and the making of meaning.* College Station, TX: Texas A and M University Press.

Williams, Mary. 1963. The indivisibility of the personal and collective unconscious. *Journal of Analytical Psychology* 8, 1:45–51.

Winnicott, Donald W. 1965. *The maturational processes and the facilitating environment.* London: The Hogarth Press and The Institute of Psycho-Analysis.

Jan Wiener is a Training Analyst and Supervisor for the Society of Analytical Psychology and the British Association of Psychotherapists. She is a past Director of Training of the SAP and works in the UK National Health Service and in private practice. She is on the Executive Committee of the IAAP.

9

DREAM INTERPRETATION AND THE CREATION OF SYMBOLIC MEANING

Warren Colman

Despite their differences, all schools of psychoanalysis share an approach to dreams that is definitive of psychoanalytic therapy in general, namely, a *symbolic attitude*. Analysts are trained to cultivate in themselves and their patients a way of thinking in which the whole of the patient's psychic life can be understood in the same way as dreams—that is, as forms of symbolic expression. This is especially true of the way the analyst seeks to understand the surface content of the patient's material and the way they behave toward the analysts as unconscious expressions of the patient's inner world and to communicate these implicit meanings to the patient via interpretation. All such interpretations make use of a kind of symbolic imagination in which apparently ordinary events and statements take on additional layers of metaphorical meaning and, in so doing, utilize the same way of thinking out of which dreams are constructed, where one thing is used to stand for another (displacement) and many things may be indicative of the same underlying issue (condensation). The interpretation of dreams is therefore paradigmatic of the art of psychoanalytic interpretation in general. Similarly, the state of mind that both analyst and patient need to develop to attend to dreams is paradigmatic of the state of mind that is required for attending to psychic life.

SCIENTIFIC THEORIES OF DREAMING

In my view, this way of thinking is inherently nonscientific insofar as science requires forms of measurement, evidence, and proof that are antithetic to symbolic understanding and interpretation. In particular, symbolic meanings are inherently multiple and indeterminate, whereas scientific explanations require precise specification. More broadly, though, science is the expression of a rationalistic mode of thought that is normally associated with waking consciousness, especially in post-Enlightenment Western culture. This is precisely the form of cognition that shuts down when we are asleep. So, by definition, dreams do not conform to the ideation (or ideology) of rational consciousness. The understanding of dreams therefore requires a process much more akin to the appreciation of the arts than the discovery of scientific laws. This process is concerned not with the explication of causes but the elaboration of meaning (Rycroft 1966).

It is probably not surprising, then, that scientific efforts to establish the causes of dreams are more often than not associated with the popular attitude towards dreams, which either denies that they have meaning altogether or regards what meaning they do have as accidental or trivial. Since the late 1970s, the dominant neuroscientific theory of dreaming has been the "activation/synthesis" model put forward by Hobson and McCarley (1977). According to this theory, dreaming is the result of physiological activation of the brain-stem in REM sleep producing randomly generated bits of nonsense which the cognitive efforts of the forebrain attempt to synthesize into a sensible narrative. (For a critique and an alternative view, see Solms and Turnbull 2002). Yet when we take into account the high level of symbolic coherence of many reported dreams, it seems highly unlikely that this is the outcome of an after-the-fact synthesis of meaning out of random nonsense. On the contrary, the detailed exploration of dreams repeatedly discovers a uniquely apt specificity in the images chosen, the associative links between them and their connection with the context of the dreamer's waking concerns and pre-occupations. It is therefore hard to believe that randomly chosen images and memories might eventually produce a dream such as Jung's "Pool of Life" dream in which he dreamed of a magnolia tree in the center of a mandala-shaped city (Liver-pool) and of which he said: "The dream brought with it a sense of finality . . . [it] depicted the climax of the whole process of development of conscious-ness. It satisfied me completely, for it gave a total picture of my situation" (Jung 1963, 224).

There are other famous dreams such as Coleridge's dream of Kubla Khan and Kekule's archetypal dream of a snake seizing its own tail, which revealed to him the structure of benzene, a chemical compound made up of a ring of car-bon atoms. All these dreams suggest a strong link between dreaming and cre-ativity. Similarly, many creative artists describe their inspiration in terms of a dream-like state of intuition and receptivity. Stravinsky, for example, said of "The Rite of Spring" that he was "the vessel through which *Le Sacre* passed." These experiences are indicative of a highly purposive intelligence at work beyond the conscious mind that is capable of generating both dreams and cre-ative works of art.

Of course, it is true such dreams are relatively rare and that most dreams are considerably more humdrum and incoherent. Yet, if dreaming is regarded as an alternative way of thinking carried on while asleep, it is immediately obvious that the same can be said about the way we think while awake. Most waking thought is fleeting and insubstantial, most scientific hunches turn out to be untrue, and most artistic works are failures that end up in the rubbish bin. So the fact that most dreams may either lack meaning or express it in a form that remains inscrutable and therefore unusable as a means of symbolic expression does not mean that dreaming itself is any more random and meaningless an activity than waking thought.

FREUD'S THEORY OF DREAMS

Both Freud and Jung regarded themselves as empirical scientists and were keen
to demonstrate the scientific credibility of their work. Yet both of them developed
a discipline which, at the least, requires a radical reinterpretation of the nature of
science. This was explicit in Jung who became strongly critical of the reductive,
materialist approach to the psyche, which he associated with Freud. However,
while Freud remained committed to a positivist scientific outlook in theory, in
practice his work expresses a quite different orientation that is concerned with the
creation of symbolic meaning and is therefore much more like Jung's.

These two quite different trends of thought can be clearly seen in Freud's
great work, *The Interpretation of Dreams* (Freud 1900/1976). It is almost as if
there are two Freuds writing the book: one is the neurological scientist, determined to construct a scientific theory of the mind; the other is a much more imaginative, intuitive, and poetic sensibility, delighting in the fertile profusion of
metaphorical and symbolic meanings thrown up by dreams and the method of
free association that he uses to interpret them.

Freud's great insight, the "insight that falls to one's lot but once in a lifetime,"
(Freud 1931/1976, 56) turned out not to be, as he thought, his *theory*—that
dreams were the disguised wish fulfillment of instinctual desires—but the *method*
he devised to reach this conclusion. It was only through being able to devise a
method for interpreting the strange language of dreams, so remote from that of
waking rational consciousness, that he was able to demonstrate his theory.
However, as it has turned out, it is possible to reach quite different conclusions
using the same method. This demonstrates the power and flexibility of the method
and shows that it is independent of the theoretical conclusions. In one sense, this
does make psychoanalysis scientific since, while its conclusions may not be
empirically testable or provable, they are subject to critical appraisal and can be
altered, not through scientific experiment but in the light of psychoanalytic experience. So it is not the case, as is sometimes asserted, that psychoanalytic theories
are merely self-validating propositions (Gellner 1985).

Freud's theoretical model is derived from the previously abandoned "Project
for a Scientific Psychology," which attempted to express mental phenomena in
entirely neurological terms. He has his own version of the activation/synthesis
model that could be described as an activation/repression model. According to
Freud, an instinctual wish is activated from "below" through becoming associated
with the events of the previous day ("day residues"). This then meets the opposition of a mental "censor" who acts as a "guardian of sleep" by preventing unacceptable repressed wishes from disturbing the peace of the sleeping ego. Out of
this clash, the "dream-work" creates an innocuous disguise for the "dream-
thought" by utilizing the unconscious mode of thought that Freud called the primary process in which, through chains of association, one idea can be represented
by another (displacement), or many ideas can be compressed into one idea/image
(condensation).

Freud argued that because of the process of disguise, the images and narratives that appear in the manifest dream are merely a distorted form of the real, latent dream, which can only be arrived at through the detailed work of interpretation. Only through decoding each separate image by following the chains of association that lead towards and away from it can the original, undisguised dream-thought be arrived at. Thus, in Freud's view the dream is a kind of husk that can be discarded once the sleuthing analyst has found a way into the hidden kernel.

Freud believed that rational thought, which he termed the "secondary process," developed out of this more "primitive" way of thinking as the infantile ego develops the capacity to delay its wish for immediate gratification and engage with the constraints of external reality (the "reality principle"). In dreams, though, the mind *regresses* to the more primitive level of the pleasure principle. Thus all dreams can be shown to consist of disguised forms of *wish fulfillment*.

Although Freud seemed to believe that the primary process was an inferior mode of thought that needed to be superseded by the rationality of the secondary process, his own interpretations convey a quite different attitude. The dreams themselves, often Freud's own, are rich and fascinating imaginative productions, while the interpretations often show an astonishingly rich and elaborate network of chains of associations, revealing layers of meaning and possibility that go far beyond the simple reductive "solutions" that Freud himself provides. It is in these chains of associations, metaphors, puns, and metonymies that Freud reveals the extraordinary creative abundance of the unconscious, which he simultaneously values and devalues. On the one hand, he shows how dreams are truly psychic phenomena, embedded in a context of meaning that goes far beyond their surface appearance, yet on the other he seems to think that the dream is "nothing but" a disguise which can be *replaced* by the "dream-thoughts" of the latent dream. He does not so much *place* the primary process dream in the chain of mental phenomena as *re*-place it with a secondary process dream thought. Thus, although dreams are supposed to emerge from a layer of the mind that is quite foreign to rational categories of space, time, contradiction, excluded middle, and so on, somehow the supposedly originating dream-thought can be expressed in just such a rational, linear form.

JUNG'S CRITIQUE: THE SIGNIFICANCE OF SYMBOLS

It is here that Jung took issue with Freud. Rather than seeing the dream as a disguised appearance of something else, Jung argued that dreams *are* what they seem: The dream "shows the inner truth and reality of the patient as it really is: not as I conjecture it to be, and not as he would like it to be, but *as it is*" (Jung 1934/1966, para. 304). The dream does not need to be decoded in the sense of being translated into something else; instead, it needs to be *elaborated*. Interpretation, rather than *replacing* the dream, *enhances* it in the way that artistic criticism enhances the meaning of a work of art.

The reason why the dream appears obscure, however, is because it is a way of representing something that, in Jung's term, "compensates" for the conscious attitude—that is, it shows a different view of something that is actually emerging from this "other" realm of thought where meaning is created through metaphor and symbol rather than linear thought. Jung therefore developed an interpretive approach of *amplifying* the dream by showing its connection with the archetypal themes of mythology. In this way, he sought to create a larger network of meaning through which the symbolic themes of the dream might be elucidated. He also encouraged patients to "dream the dream onwards" through active imagination (see chapter 11, below). Since he regarded the dream as an effort at symbolic expression rather than a disguise, he sought to assist the patient to develop that expression by whatever means possible, in contrast to Freud's view that such elaborations were merely "secondary revisions" of the manifest dream that further obscured the latent dream thoughts.

Freud's negative view of the unconscious work of symbolic representation left him struggling to account for artistic creativity, which he tended to see as some form of substitute for instinctual gratification. Here Jung's view of dreaming segues much more easily into the process of artistic creativity, with the caveat that for the creation of art a more directed sensibility is required to mould and shape the spontaneous unconscious images into a more universally recognizable and relevant form. In relation to dreams and active imagination, conscious sensibility is directed towards enabling the emergence of new symbolic forms that reveal the inner, personal meaning towards which the unconscious process is striving. In both cases, though, the process involves the mutual interpenetration of conscious and unconscious modes of thought leading to the creation of a "third" that Jung termed the transcendent function.

It was in their approach to symbols that the differences between Freud's and Jung's view of dreams became most apparent. Freud took a very limited view of symbols in dreams, treating them as figurative representations of repressed elements, especially (and notoriously) parts of the body such as the male and female genitals. Jung argued that this made them *signs* rather than symbols since they could be replaced by a one-to-one correspondence with the objects they signified. By contrast, he suggested that symbols represent not the already known, but the *not yet known*—they are the best possible representation of an unknown psychic fact. So the purpose of a symbol is to represent something that is in the process of becoming known and can only be represented in this complex way. In this view, the symbol contains and transcends *all* the possible associations to it, rather than being reducible to a single "dream-thought."

Jung gives a revealing illustration of this different approach in his interpretation of a dream in which a woman patient dreamed that someone gave her a wonderful, richly ornamented, antique sword dug up out of a tumulus (Jung 1916/1969, paras. 149ff.) Since she associated the sword with a dagger that belonged to her father, Jung suggests that a Freudian reductive interpretation would see the dream in purely sexual terms as a wish for her father's "weapon"—

a phallic fantasy. Jung, though, picks up the association with her father's energetic, powerful temperament and the fact that the sword in the dream is specifically a *Celtic* sword, which the patient associated with her own ancestry, ancient tradition, and the heritage of mankind. He goes on to suggest an interpretation in which the sword represents what the patient *needs*—it is a "compensation" for her own passive and dependent attitude by representing a symbolic image of passion, energy, and will, something that connects her to her heritage and is being "excavated" by the analysis. Thus the sword is a powerful symbolic image that *gathers together* all the associations to it through its capacity to represent and synthesize them in a single image.

Unfortunately, the way Jung's juxtaposes the two kinds of interpretation seems to suggest that they are in mutual opposition. This has tended to produce a regrettable and quite unnecessary polarization in the Jungian world. However, the real strength of synthetic interpretation lies in its inclusiveness. For it is clear that one aspect of the father's power certainly *is* his phallic aspect and this could equally well be expressed, in Freudian terms, as "a wish for the father's penis." This aspect of the symbol *increases* its meaning by adding to it the powerful charge of sexuality and desire—it gives it thrust and lust. The symbol is *all* these things and no doubt more besides. What is more, the symbolic image represents the many powerful *affects* in these associations—the longing, the energy, the drive for power, as well as the sexual desire and perhaps the patient's violent aggressive energies too. In this sense, symbols could be described as *the clothing of affect in image* and since, as Jung says, they are the best possible means of doing so, they have the potential to become *tools to think with*. Innumerable, unspecifiable and complex affects can be represented and thought about through the contemplation of the images by which the dream represents them.

THE DREAM OF THE BOTANICAL MONOGRAPH

I now want to show how these processes of symbolic representation work in one of Freud's own dreams, resulting in a quite different interpretation from the one that Freud himself gives but one that I believe is entirely consistent with it. This dream is mentioned several times in *The Interpretation of Dreams,* firstly in the chapter on the sources of dreams (Freud 1900/1976, 254–62; 279–80), again in the chapter on the dream work (386–90) and finally in relation to affects in dreams (603). The dream itself is a simple one:

> *I had written a monograph on a certain plant. The book lay before me and I was at the moment turning over a folded coloured plate. Bound up in each copy there was a dried specimen of the plant, as though it had been taken from a herbarium.* (Freud 1900/1976, 254)

Freud outlines a prodigious series of associations to this dream (1900/1976, 254–58) that I shall attempt to briefly summarize: he had seen a monograph on cyclamens in a shop window the previous day; cyclamens are his wife's favorite flowers; guilt about not bringing flowers to his wife; the monograph he wrote on cocaine that he hoped would make his name but where his own contribution was eclipsed by a colleague; a conversation with two colleagues the previous night, one of whom was called Dr. Gardener in which "blooming looks" and a patient called "Flora" were mentioned; his headmaster's low opinion of him, associated with an incident involving bookworms in the school herbarium; his failure to identify a plant; his inadequacy at drawing plants; artichokes, which are *his* favorite flowers that his wife brings him; his friend, Fleiss, who had written to him saying he had imagined seeing Freud's book on dreams "lying before me and turning over its pages"; a book of colored plates that his father gave him as a child to pull apart (like an artichoke); and, finally, that collecting books is his favorite hobby, associated with the book worms, debt, and the theme of the conversation with the two colleagues which was that he was "too much absorbed in my favourite hobbies" (258) and "my intimate relations with books" (388).

From this tour de force of "copious and intertwined associative links" (279) Freud concludes that the dream was a self-justification, "a plea on behalf of my own rights" that "I'm allowed to do this." Although Freud is discreet enough not to say so, we can imagine from the associations and his own theory that his "favorite hobby" may well have had something to do with sex, possibly mastur-bation, possibly associated with his guilt that he doesn't bring his wife her favorite flowers. He hints, too, at the significance of the infantile memory of pulling the book of colored plates apart that perhaps might have something to do with a fantasy about mother's body. All this remains speculative, of course.

However, Freud provides plenty of evidence for another key theme of the dream—his burning ambition for professional success, his competitive envy and rivalry with professional colleagues, and his need to justify himself. This features in several other dreams, including the dream that immediately follows his second reference to the botanical monograph dream (280). The "yellow beard" dream refers to two Jewish colleagues who have not been appointed to professorships. Freud interprets the dream in terms of his wish that he *will* be appointed, despite being Jewish. But the dream is also about beards *going grey*, as his own is in the process of doing, thus indicating his fear that he will grow old before achieving his lifetime's ambition of professional success and recognition. And it is this which is represented in the botanical monograph through the key association with Fleiss imagining Freud's dream book "lying before me." Now we begin to see that the botanical monograph *is The Interpretation of Dreams* itself. It is, as Hamlet says, "a consummation devoutly to be wished," the longed for fulfillment of Freud's greatest ambition. *That* is Freud's "favorite hobby," the book into which he has sunk all his hopes, fears and ambitions and which must at some level have occupied his every waking and sleeping moment during this period of his life. The association with the headmaster, his failure to identify the correct plant, and his inadequate drawings link up with the failure of the cocaine monograph and the fears of going grey. Behind the dream, there is a raging battle going on between Freud's overweening ambition and the fear, doubt, and guilt he has to overcome if he is to push onwards with his "favorite flower," ignoring the remonstrations of his professional colleagues (perhaps about him neglecting his obligations to his wife and family?), and bring to fruition the full flowering of his nascent inspiration: the secret of the interpretation of dreams.

Further evidence for this interpretation is provided by Freud's own apparently unconscious flow of associations from the botanical monograph (279) to the yellow beard dream (280) and on to his frustration and rage at the barriers put in the way of Jews in the Austro-Hungarian Empire (280–82). There is an association between pulling apart artichokes and "the dismemberment of the Chinese empire" (279) (another consummation devoutly to be wished?) and also his comment that "behind artichokes lay my thoughts about Italy" (388). Freud's thoughts about Italy are discussed in the passage following the interpretation of the yellow beard dream in which he speaks of his unfulfilled longing to go to Rome (occurring in many dreams) and his identification with Hannibal who crossed the Alps yet, like Freud, was denied entry to the promised land of Rome (282–85). Here Freud writes:

> To my youthful mind Hannibal and Rome symbolized the conflict between the tenacity of Jewry and the organisation of the Catholic Church. . . . Thus the wish to go to Rome had become in my dream-life a cloak and symbol for a number of other passionate wishes. Their realization was to be pursued with all the perseverance and single-mindedness of the Carthaginian, though their fulfilment at the moment seemed just as little favoured by destiny as was Hannibal's lifelong wish to enter Rome. (1900/1976, 285)

And then Freud goes on to describe the incident when his father had told him about an anti-Semitic attack in which his cap was knocked off into the gutter. Freud was deeply shamed to hear that his father had quietly gone into the road and picked it up again and he relates this to his (compensatory) identification with Hannibal and, through him, with Napoleon—that is, his longing for triumphant vengeance against the cruelties and outrages of anti-Semitic prejudice.

There is one more mention of the botanical monograph that cements this interpretation of it as a symbolic representation of Freud's hoped-for triumph over his enemies. Much later in *The Interpretation of Dreams,* where Freud is discussing the apparent suppression of affects in dreams (through displacement), he contrasts the colourless absence of intense affect in the manifest dream with the dream thoughts in which he finds "the most intense psychical impulses . . . striving to make themselves felt and struggling as a rule against others that are sharply opposed to them." In the case of the botanical monograph, he says:

> The thoughts corresponding to it consisted of passionately agitated pleas on behalf of my liberty to act as I chose to act and to govern my life as seemed right to me and to me alone. The dream that arose from them has an indifferent ring about it . . . This reminds one of *the peace that has descended upon a battlefield strewn with corpses; no trace is left of the struggle which raged over it.* (1900/1976, 603, italics added)

So *that* is the wish that is to be fulfilled in the dream of the botanical monograph. This is far from an absence of affect: if we take Freud's image as a further association to the dream (an amplification of it), we can see the sheer violence of the ambition expressed in his identification with military heroes such as Hannibal and Napoleon. Yet we can also see his fear and insecurity, for both Hannibal and Napoleon were eventually defeated. Was this perhaps why Freud later felt so threatened by Jung? The imagery of the dream refers to both these aspects, with the monograph in the dream representing the longed for dream-book that will vindicate him, banish past failures, and vanquish his enemies. And, because of its multifarious associations, the dream-image does this in a far more complex way than an image of his actual book could ever have done. Of course, this is what makes the dream *symbolic.*

In short, this dream is a perfect illustration of Jung's idea of *the transcendent function,* the symbolic image that arises from, reconciles, and transcends the conflict of warring opposites ("the struggle raging over the battlefield"). And even Freud's own discussion, especially with regard to the significance of Rome, makes it plain that at this time he saw symbols as far more than simple substitutes for sexual body parts. Freud's own associations provide copious evidence of complex, coherent, and purposively directed unconscious thought directly related to the dreamer's deepest fears and desires. Freud clearly shows how these unconscious thought processes, breaking the surface as a dream, draw upon an astonishingly wide range of connections, gathering together the dreamer's whole life into a single image of turning over the folded colored plates of a botanical monograph.

THE FUNCTION OF DREAMING

It would be quite possible to interpret this dream as a sort of "message" from the unconscious, along the lines of unconscious encouragement for Freud to pursue his goals and not give in to his doubts (as projected into his colleagues and so on). Some Jungians might even want to call this a message from "the Guiding Self," the wisdom of the unconscious, or some such. Yet it is equally possible and just as true to see in it the expression of Freud's Oedipal wishes—the little Hannibal who seeks to vanquish the father and enjoy mother's artichoke, with its juicy fleshy lips, and so on. The dream is both of these, more than these, and none of these. For the dream is, as Jung says, simply itself and only becomes meaningful through contemplation of it in waking consciousness. Or, as Rycroft puts it, "the imagery in dreaming lacks as yet the meaning that will turn it into a metaphor" (Rycroft 1979, 71). Only then is the symbolic potential of the dream revealed as a web of infinite possibilities. This view of dreaming, while recognizing its immense creative potential, does not require us to privilege dreaming as a special kind of oracular pronouncement from "the Self."

It may well be that as a result of his unusually intense desire Freud's dreams really *were* wish fulfillments, and undoubtedly many dreams would fit this description. Not only children but grown men sometimes have undisguised "hero fantasy" dreams—one patient of mine described them as his "shoot-em-up, Indiana Jones–type" dreams. Freud's interpretations of his own dreams clearly express the powerful constellation of the hero archetype in him, elaborated into something much more purposeful than a wishful escapist fantasy. However, few analysts nowadays would claim that *all* dreams are of this kind. In psychoanalysis, the development of object relations theory has led to a view, similar to Jung's, that regards many dreams as a depiction of the patient's psychic situation, in which the various characters and situations represent the object relations pertaining in the patient's internal world which are also frequently enacted in the transference. As Jung put it, "the dream is *a spontaneous self-portrayal, in symbolic form of the actual situation in the unconscious*" (Jung 1948/1969, para. 505 ital. in original).

For example, the following dream occurred early in the therapy of an ambitious and driven young career woman struggling with a series of psychosomatic illnesses:

> *There is a kind of commando working for the resistance who has been on a mission and is struggling to get back to base camp through cold wind and torrential rain. When he finally gets there, cold, hungry and exhausted, his commanding officer tells him he must rest and recuperate before the next mission, but the commando refuses to rest and insists on going off on the mission right away.*
>
> *In the second part of the dream, there's a young girl in an educational establishment, walking through the corridors and, every now and again, surreptitiously kicking someone in the shins.*

The therapist recognized that the dream exactly depicted the problem that the patient was bringing to therapy—she is unconsciously identified with "the commando" as well as the rebellious girl and is likely not only to resist the remonstrations of the therapist (commanding officer) but give her a kick in the shins for her trouble. Over the course of the therapy, the dream and particularly the figure of "the commando" became a leitmotif of the patient's compulsive drive to keep going on her "mission," regardless of the cost to her physical health. The therapeutic task thus became concerned firstly with elaborating the meaning of this internal figure, especially with regard to her identification with a masculine animus as a "resistance movement" against her unsupportive mother, and secondly with how this internal figure could become more integrated and less destructive to the patient, while recognizing its positive aspects of heroism, self-sacrifice, will and determination. Initially, it was only the therapist who grasped the symbolic significance of the commando but, latterly, the patient became able to use the image to deepen her own self-understanding and to gain some conscious choice over how she wanted to live her life. By being able to imagine the commando, the patient gradually became able to develop a "third position" towards this ferocious internal driver (super-ego).

Dreams like this suggest the presence of an unconscious ally that is silently working alongside the analyst to create meaningful constructions of the patient's difficulties. And while particular dreams may fulfill a wide range of functions (including wish fulfillment), I believe that *all* dreams express, as this one does, the unconscious concerns and preoccupations of the dreamer at the time—hence the significance of "day-residues." And this is for the even more simple reason that *dreaming is the form that thinking takes while asleep*. Just as, in our quiet waking moments we may find ourselves reflecting on our current concerns and preoccupations, especially those with which we are strongly emotionally engaged, so we turn over these matters in our mind whilst asleep. These concerns may range from the simplest of physical wishes to the solutions of the most complex philosophical problems. So dreams may well be concerned with any or all of the various kinds of thinking that engage us while we are awake, although it may well be that while we are asleep and there are no other distractions we find out what is *really* important to us and, if we are lucky, we may also find out why. Emerson expresses this beautifully: "The dream presents an answer in hieroglyphs to the question we would pose" (quoted in Whitmont and Perera 1989, 8). However, since it is plainly apparent that the way we think while asleep is very different from the way we think while awake, the trick is to work out from the dream what it was that we were thinking about!

Yet it is just because our thinking takes such a different form that dreams can provide us with novel and useful ways of thinking about our situation. Looked at from the point of view of cognitive reason, dreaming is an *inferior* form of thinking, since it is just those aspects of mental functioning that are shut down (inhibited) during sleep. But, from another point of view, the inhibition of cognitive reason allows for a much freer, more associative kind of thinking that is able to draw on a far wider range of associations and to draw together in novel and unexpected ways material from disparate areas of the mind, fusing together what waking consciousness keeps separated into categories of time, space and logic. While we may see some things more clearly during the day, we need to dim the sunlight of conscious attention to see the starry heavens revealed to us in our infinite dreamscape.

For these reasons, the psychoanalyst Charles Rycroft proposed replacing Freud's value-laden differentiation between the primary process and the secondary process with the philosopher Susanne Langer's distinction between discursive and nondiscursive symbolism (Rycroft 1979; Langer 1942). Discursive symbolism refers to the sense in which words can be considered as symbols—that is, words are units of representation with definite, fixed meanings that are more or less permanently assigned. In discursive symbolism, meaning is enhanced by precision and specificity. In nondiscursive symbolism, the opposite is true. Nondiscursive symbols have multiple meanings that are indeterminate and gain their meaning and significance through the integration of many meanings into one simultaneous presentation. Rycroft suggests that in this respect dreams resemble works of literature: "Unlike factual statements like 'The Battle of Waterloo took place on June 18th, 1815' or 'Arsenic is a poison' which have only one meaning, dreams, poems and novels either have no meaning or several meanings" (Rycroft 1979, 162). So rather than seeing the associative, figurative thinking of dreams as *regressive* and therefore inferior to the logical, directed rationality of the secondary process, Rycroft suggests that they are merely *different* since they have different purposes and functions. Like Jung (1912/1952/1956), who similarly makes a distinction between directed thinking and nondirected thinking, Rycroft recognizes that the value of symbolic thinking is precisely this multiple indeterminacy of meaning.

As Freud's interpretation of the botanical monograph dream shows so vividly, dream symbols are the expression in condensed form of highly complex networks of association. For me, this is the clearest way of drawing the distinction between the discursive and nondiscursive modes of thought. Rational thought and language uses *linear thinking,* so that clarity is achieved by following a defined sequence. Nondiscursive thought, on the other hand, involves *network thinking,* where all elements of the network are potentially present at once. Therefore the apprehension of the network requires thinking tools that act as network hubs, in which many links in the network converge—in short, *symbols.* The more complex the network, that is the greater the number of associative hubs that are linked together in the overall structure, the greater the potential range of meanings—hence the idea of the dream, or the work of art, as a web of infinite possibilities.

Similarly, then, dream interpretation requires an attitude that is open and allusive, making links and raising possibilities rather than attempting to find a "solution," a "correct" interpretation that closes down the potential of the dream by reducing it to only one thing. Hence Jung's objection to Freud's sexual interpretation of dreams and his preference for amplification. Unlike scientific facts and theories, whose validity decreases to the extent that they are ambiguous or susceptible to multiple interpretations, the value of symbols and their interpretation *increases* according to how multiple and indeterminate are the interpretations of which they are capable. Consider for example, the ambiguity and inherent uncertainty of great works of art such as *Hamlet* or the Mona Lisa. This is the rationale for the "negative capability" recommended by Keats for poets and adopted by Bion as a recommendation for psychoanalysts. Negative capability, the capacity for "being in uncertainties, mysteries, doubts without any irritable reaching after fact and reason" (Keats 1817/1958 I, 193; quoted in Bion 1970) is the requisite state of mind for both the production of symbolic images (the dreamer, the poet) and their interpretation (the psychoanalyst).

The dreaming mind produces metaphors, images and symbols "naturally," spontaneously, in the same negative way indicated by Keats: it is because of what the mind is *not* doing (reaching after fact and reason) that it is able to produce the multiple meanings of the dream. The poet and the analyst cultivate this mental faculty in order to, as it were, learn to speak—and interpret—the "natural" unconscious language of the dream. In both cases, it requires the development of a state of mind that partakes of both waking and sleeping forms of thinking, suppressing cognitive functions sufficiently to allow a dream-like state to develop while maintaining them enough to be able to attribute metaphorical and symbolic meaning to the "dream-thoughts" that emerge. Bion called this the analyst's "reverie"; Jung called it the transcendent function.

If dreaming is a form of nondiscursive symbolism, this would suggest that dreaming, or perhaps more broadly unconscious imagining, is the raw material not only for art but for any creative activity that utilises symbolic imagination as a way of reflecting on the emotional and spiritual aspects of our psychic life— that is, our *subjective* experience. Art, religion and psychoanalysis all provide imaginative arenas that foster the conscious development of imaginal capacity through the elaboration of symbolic imagery. In this way, they might be seen as a consciously cultivated form of dreaming.

THE CONCENTRATION CAMP DREAM: SIGNIFYING THE UNSIGNIFIABLE

I would like to conclude with a dream of my own that came to me in the midst of my analysis over twenty years ago. It is an example of the way the process of analysis can promote the patient's own symbolic function so that it eventually becomes possible to dream an inner situation that had previously been unsignifiable. While such dreams may be horrifying, as this one was, they can also bring immense relief, akin to removing a painful splinter, a feeling of "ah, so now I see what it is!"

This dream occurred after a particularly distressing session with a patient who had discovered his wife in bed with his friend on their first wedding anniversary. I had been deeply disturbed by the violence of the patient's agony and his dark and quite realistic threats to have the pair of them murdered. Identifying with his pain yet repelled by his violent lust for revenge, I was left depressed and preoccupied by this session as if full of something that I might now call "unprocessed." At one o'clock in the morning I awoke from the following dream:

> We are in the concentration camps where I am an unwilling accomplice to an attempted rape. Despite my disgust and horror, the rules of camp life require that I must stay silent and never protest or complain.
>
> Later, we are liberated from the camps, yet in our selves we have not been liberated. By the same rule of silence, this remains unseen and unknown by others. It is a mood of bleak despair too terrible to tell which hangs over us without hope of relief.
>
> Later again, I am retching violently, as if retching up the death, decay and corruption still inside me. But even this is not allowed, and I am surrounded by a gang who intend to punish me for my transgression. I manage to cry out, and through this cry it is at last realised that we have not been liberated at all but are in this far worse state of not even having hope of liberation since no one knows that we are still mentally confined. The dream ends with a food-drop from the air and I awake, sobbing violently with the relief of liberation from this nightmare.

This dream represents its own significance in the image of crying out: the dream *is* the cry that brought to my conscious awareness a lifelong feeling that is symbolically represented as being in a concentration camp. It depicts a situation of knowing something that, at the same time, cannot be known because there are no words to say it—it is unsignifiable. Through this representation of a literally unspeakable inner situation, I became liberated from a previously unrealized sense of oppression. As in the session with my patient, I recoil in horror and disgust from a violent and despicable act, but now I am forced to acknowledge my own complicity and guilt. The "day residue" of the disturbing session and the unprocessed, unsignifiable affects it had touched off in me had now found issue in a symbolic narrative that represented some of the deepest concerns of my inner world. Behind this dream lay feelings of betrayal, hurt and despair associated with an early childhood separation of which I had never been able to speak or know—this was the significance of the theme of not being able to complain. In fact, one of the first interpretations my analyst had made to me was that I needed to complain bitterly—something I had not really understood at the time. Now I knew what she meant. So the dream also expresses an unconscious *coniunctio* between my analyst's understanding and my own struggle to symbolise and thus communicate my inner situation to her.

In the dream I retch up the terrible complex of feelings that had been evoked in me by projective identification with my patient. While some of these feelings may have belonged to him, they had also touched off a complex in me that was now, as it were, vomited up as this agonising dream. And so, despite the threat of punishment, I had been able to overcome the barriers of repression, awakening from a lifelong nightmare in which I, like my patient, had felt imprisoned without hope. In this way, the nightmare itself became a symbol of the oppressive object from which I had been liberated by being able to dream it. It was, as Bion would say, the transformation of beta elements into alpha elements by the unconscious work of alpha function.

This dream has remained in my mind not only because of its content and personal significance, but as a realization of what dreams can do and why they are so immensely valuable to the analytic process. It is because of experiences like these that I, like most analysts, await my patients' dreams with hopeful anticipation of fresh insight and understanding. For this was also the last nightmare I ever had—since then I have welcomed my dreams, no matter how frightening and disturbing, as sources of new understanding and vehicles of transformation.

REFERENCES

Bion, Wilfred. 1970. *Attention and interpretation.* London: Tavistock.

Freud, Sigmund. 1900/1976. *The interpretation of dreams.* In Penguin Freud Library, vol. 4. (Reprinted from Standard Edition, vol. 4–5, 1953.)

———. 1931/1976. Preface to the third (revised) English edition of *The interpretation of dreams.* Penguin Freud Library, vol. 4.

Gellner, Ernest. 1985. *The psychoanalytic movement.* London: Paladin.

Hobson, Allan, and Robert McCarley. 1977. The brain as a dream state generator: An activation-synthesis hypothesis of the dream process. *American Journal of Psychiatry* 134:1335–48.

Jung, C.G. 1912/1952/1956. Two kinds of thinking. In CW *5.*

———. 1916/1969. The transcendent function. In CW 8.

———. 1934/1966. The practical use of dream analysis. In CW16.

———. 1948/1969. General aspects of dream psychology. In CW 8.

———. 1963/1977. *Memories, dreams, reflections.* Glasgow: Fountain Books.

Keats, John. 1817/1958. *The letters of John Keats 1814–1821.* Ed. Hyder Edward Rollins. Cambridge, MA.: Harvard University Press.

Langer, Susanne K. 1942. *Philosophy in a new key: A study in the symbolism of reason, rite, and art.* Cambridge, MA: Harvard University Press.

Rycroft, Charles. 1966. Causes and meanings. In *Psychoanalysis observed.* London: Constable.

———. 1979. *The innocence of dreams.* London: Hogarth.

Solms, Mark & Oliver Turnbull. 2002. *The brain and the inner world: An introduction to the neuroscience of subjective experience.* London and New York: Karnac.

Whitmont, Edward, and Sylvia Perera. 1989. *Dreams: A portal to the source.* London and New York: Routledge.

WARREN COLMAN is a training analyst of the Society of Analytical Psychology and the Editor-in-Chief of the *Journal of Analytical Psychology.* He has published many papers on diverse topics including couples, sexuality, the self, and symbolic imagination. He lives and works in full-time private practice in St. Albans, U.K.

10

AMPLIFICATION: UNVEILING EMERGENT PATTERNS OF MEANING

John Hill

HIT OR MISS

Humans have never stopped telling tales about life's wonders and contradictions. Dreams do the same. Amplification has been acclaimed as Jung's unique contribution to methods of dream interpretation. Differing from personal associations, amplification consists of making available to dreams and dream fragments narratives found in fairy tale, myth, ritual, and "all the branches of the human sciences" (Mattoon, 69). Amplification with motifs from films, literature, history, and contemporary events can also be significant. Personal associations elaborate on dream themes in order to connect them with actual experiences that have been repressed or forgotten. With amplification the analyst usually provides an elucidation of certain dream motifs and symbols with the intention of linking them with universal themes found in the narrative heritage of humankind, of which the dreamer might have no previous knowledge. Amplification might be understood as an attempt to anchor identity within that heritage.

Jungian psychoanalysts are trained to have at their disposal sufficient knowledge of ritual and myth from diverse cultural practices in order to elucidate dream material. It can be most surprising when one such motif provides entry into a dream, which otherwise would remain opaque to consciousness. Amplification however runs the risk of being a hit or miss approach to dream interpretation. Nevertheless the analyst and dreamer may never forget those moments when a universal motif strikes a deep core in the dreamer, sheds light on hidden parts of his or her behavior, opens up new perspectives for the future, or links the dreamer's mind with humanity's cultural heritage. For example, the presenting dream of one young woman began with: "I was a swan." In a flash I remembered the tale of the children of Lir, in which King Lir's daughters were changed into swans by an evil stepmother only to be redeemed many years later. I responded by a dramatic appeal to the dreamer: "I think you need to come down to earth." Twenty-seven years after the analysis had terminated, this same person informed me that this moment changed her whole life.

The above is an example of an impressive hit. What of the misses? On several occasions, when amplifying dreams with motifs from myth and alchemy, my remarks have not hit home and a disconnect in consciousness between dreamer, dream, and analyst occurred. Amplification might be meaningful for the analyst, but resonates in no way with the patient's dreaming mind. Fordham was aware of this danger. Mythic and alchemical motifs may become abstract ideas divorced from the patient's contemporary life, especially if he/she has little knowledge of the historical context in which they were created (Fordham 1978, 145). Nevertheless he did admit that amplification might have a transformative effect for both analyst and patient within the context of transference (1974, 149).

DISCONTINUITY BETWEEN WAKING AND DREAMING

Dream interpretation is primarily concerned with bridging two very different states of consciousness. The human mind is active in both waking and sleeping states of consciousness, although there is a formal difference between the two. In dreaming, cognition and short-term memory are reduced, whereas affect, image, and long-term memory are enhanced (Hobson, 14). Dreams allow us an alternative existence, which we only dismiss as unreal if we assume that consciousness is exclusively limited to waking states of mind. While in a state of dreaming we feel ourselves to be conscious. Once awake we tend to limit subjectivity to daytime consciousness. Analysts may slip too readily into verbal interpretations and risk losing the dream's emotional content. This assumption severely limits our understanding of dreams. We no longer cross the bridge that links the two modes of subjectivity. We lose awareness of the subject who creates those enigmatical landscapes night after night and fail to appreciate the creative powers of the dreaming mind. All attempts at interpretation must reckon with the radical otherness of a mind that creates dreams without daytime awareness.

It is quite easy to create a bridge between the waking and sleeping states of consciousness through the dreamer's personal associations. Biographical material from day residues and the activation of earlier memories often provide the dreamer with sufficient material to link both states of consciousness. The analyst's interventions, support, or comments are attuned to relational components of the client's history that might have become reactivated in transference. Dreams, however, also activate universal patterns of meaning that may initiate another kind of bonding between analyst and client. Here the analytic interventions involve a complex cultural exchange. In approaching the dream, the analyst might not only narrate a mythic motif, but presumably makes some evaluation of it; not just the myth but its meaning is applied to a particular dream. That meaning hopefully is not simply an intellectual, disembodied, impersonal evaluation of the myth, but reflects deeper levels of the analyst's own understanding of myth that might or might not have affinities with the client's quest for meaning. If amplification is to reach into the dreamer's night-time consciousness, the analytic encounter itself must take priority over an explanatory or pedagogical approach to the archetypal.

DISCERNING THE POWERS OF FATE

Amplification is an adventure, a way of engaging in a process that attempts to bring to consciousness emergent patterns of meaning as they appear embodied in the particular and the relational. In amplifying, one risks loosing the threads of an individual life by continually taking the dream back to the archetypal. Yet in assessing biographies and dreams, a Jungian psychoanalyst cannot afford to miss those archetypal aspects of "mother" or "father" emerging in and through personal relationships. We might hear stories about broken boundaries eventually taking on demonic qualities, or the idealization of a parent feeding expectations impossible to fulfill in later relationships. Their developmental process having been severely impaired, victims may find they are unable to remember what went wrong, unable to distinguish the various parts of the puzzle, unable to recognize what belongs to parents, to culture, or to God. At some time, a process of sorting out begins. In analysis, the gathering of personal associations and right timing in the use of amplification becomes crucial to the healing process.

Already in 1909 Jung discovered the archetypal in the powers of fate whose influence over a family could be compared with that of a good or evil spirit (Jung 1909/1961, para. 727). Tracing the origins of fate can be the work of amplification. First we are likely to discover its transpersonal power embedded in identification with a parent figure. It then may be linked with a cultural pattern that has had a life-enhancing or a life-destroying effect on family members over generations. Such patterns, often embodied in primary caretakers, have a massive influence on attitudes to life that fail to respect the individual, such as ideologies controlling people through fear, cultures degrading women, and societies judging people by skin color, religious affiliation, or some extraneous factor.

BRIDGING THE GAP

From a Jungian point of view, the unconscious does not simply store past events in memory but, as creative agency, allows fantasy to spread its wings. Jungian psychoanalysts have not failed to notice resemblances between dream narrative and earlier cultural practices, especially initiation passages concerned with the stages of life, survival, and the furthering of life's potential (Jacobi, 76–78). Exploring the foundations of fantasy, Jung claimed that fantasy, in particular mythological fantasy, is symbolic and considered it an expression of psyche's potential to anticipate meaning. It is not just a turning away from reality, but it has phylogenic roots that were "once open to the light of day" (Jung, 1912/1970, para. 27). What some may interpret as a distortion of reality was once a conscious custom, law, or a general belief that molded the spiritual life of civilizations. In linking individual fantasy with mythological material of earlier cultures, Jung was convinced that the fundamental laws of the mind remain the same and thus have a common explanation (ibid., para. 27–29). The common explanation lies in the mind's ability to create symbols and thereby anticipate meaning.

In dream narratives, cultural symbols might not appear in explicit form. Rooted in a cultural heritage and expressed in a person's embodied existence, dreams also have a biological basis, which has led some neuro-psychologists to interpret the bizarre nature of dream narratives as an expression of random cortical activity. Other neurobiological research, however, suggests that symbol and metaphor tend "to light up more centers in the brain than any other form of human communication" (Wilkinson, 147). Considering Mallarmé's principle, "To name is to destroy, to suggest is to create" (Hederman, 118), and Jung's understanding of the symbol as expressing "something that is only divined and not yet clearly conscious" (Jung 1923/1971, para. 475), the night-time creation of symbols can be considered as an act of an open-ended consciousness that anticipates meaning. Dreams may reflect "the curiosity-interest-expectancy-circuits" of the brain as advocated by Panksepp and Solms (Solms, 171–74), but given the symbol's predisposition towards meaning the curiosity drive would include a meaning-seeking component specific to humans.

In view of the link between the curiosity drive and dream symbolism, amplification can be understood as an attempt to connect the anticipatory, symbolic consciousness of dreams with earlier cultural endeavors created by a society to contain life's transitions in meaningful form and ritual. This is not a question of proving the link through enumeration of parallel material; rather, it is one of comparing, defining, evaluating, and translating affective dispositions concerning mythic or ritualistic images into meaningful discourse between dreamer and analyst. Amplification can bridge the gap between non-discursive and discursive symbolism, between the immediacy of the mythic image and the extension of its meaning in language by means of comparison, reflection, and the use of concept. Its purpose is not to replace image by concept, rather to stimulate the imagination and ground it within an historical matrix. In accord with the work of Susan Langer, it attempts to anchor the human mind within its genetic, social, and historic inheritance: "But the most disastrous hindrance is disorientation, the failure or destruction of life-symbols and loss or repression of votive acts. A life that does not incorporate some degree of ritual, of gesture and attitude, has no mental anchorage. It is prosaic to the point of total indifference, purely casual, devoid of that structure of intellect and feeling, which we call personality" (Langer 1996, 290). The work of amplification is to link embryonic forms of meaning as expressed in affect and dream symbolism to a specific life context, rendering it intelligible within a framework of historical rootedness beyond the personal unconscious. Once the bridging process is underway, the meaning of the symbol translates into the language of daytime consciousness, becoming a vehicle of communication, creating new affinities of meaning not only within the context of the analytic relationship, but also in the social and cultural life of a community.

FOUR VIGNETTES

The following vignettes demonstrate the presence of archetypal material in four dreams, constellated at a time when the dreamer's life processes were blocked. The vignettes illustrate four different approaches in the use of amplification.

a. Intimations of the Archetypal

A young man dreamt that he saw a swamp filled with snake-like dead people. Whenever he touched them, they came alive and the dreamer awoke in fear. At the time of the dream the young man was beginning to gain confidence in his sexuality and relationship with women. The candidate-in-training became a supportive father for his client. With dreams he would gather personal associations; his interpretations remained on a personal level. Aware that the dreamer was frightened of such dreams, he assumed the dreamer primarily needed reassurance. The analyst thought that the dream referred to masturbation and assured the dreamer that it was normal to masturbate to get to know his own body. This approach was helpful for a young man afraid of sexual relationships, but it failed to see the mythic structure contained in the dream. If the analyst had thought of the motif of death and rebirth, he could have asked important questions, without necessarily amplifying a particular narrative, as for example: What has died within you? Do you feel anything is coming alive? Asking such questions, the analyst found the young man began to turn his attention away from him and focus more on his own feelings, his own sexuality, and his own creativity, which had been swamped by a possessive mother. Through this and other dreams, the young man realized that repressed parts of his personality were now in the process of becoming alive again. The motif of death and rebirth established a turning point in the analysis. The dreamer needed less from a "supporting father" and more from a "partner" or "friend" who would help him get on with his own life.

b. Undoing the Knots of Fate

A dream of a young medical student, shortly before an important exam: *I come into the examination hall. The professor sits on a large chair. Those who are allowed to do the exam are sent to the right, and those who are not permitted to do so are sent to the left, to the gas chambers. I am sent to the left and awake in terror.*

When this woman brought her dream to me, she was convinced that fate was against her and she was going to fail the exam. I recognized a disparity between the Christian motifs of the Last Judgment, located in a Nazi setting, and the actual exam situation, understood as a modern initiation about professional identity. In several dramatic sessions, work focused on separating her actual fear of exams from the deeper anxiety of eternal damnation. I confirmed that her preparation for the exam was sufficiently thorough and that her chances to succeed were excellent. The dream was pointing to another fear, a fear of an all-powerful and inhuman God, who had already pronounced judgment over her and the world. For several sessions we kept focus on the two forms of anxiety. Finally in one session she unexpectedly remembered the family governess in charge of the children's education. Every night this person gave the children a lecture on good behavior and warned them if they did anything bad, the devil would come in the night, take them away, never to return home again. Every night of this woman's childhood was a night of terror. No matter what she did during the day, the all-powerful demon of the night would find fault with her. Her fate was sealed; she had no way of defending herself. Amplifying the dream was crucial to our work. We discovered the root of a fatal bonding with a human who had assumed the power of a God, imprisoning this woman's soul in a religion of guilt and fear. Her life had been determined by a cruel fate over which she felt helpless. With the help of amplification she could separate the inhuman from the human. This involved several discussions on sorting out "Christ's Last Judgment," "Hitler," "the governess," and "the professor." In this process she could internalize "the judge" and gain more confidence in her own capacity of self-evaluation. Eventually she decided to disengage herself from the religion of her family that had blurred the boundaries between God, the devil, and the governess. She succeeded in the exam and later in her profession.

c. Psyche's Perennial Creativity

A dream of a thirty-year-old woman suffering from depression:

> *I lay on the ground of a cave where it was pitch dark. I felt tired and empty. I wondered whether I should pray to God to let me come to his kingdom. I was prepared to take all my sleeping tablets and die quietly. The time would be right, my mother wouldn't miss me, and my analyst had been away for so long that he would hardly notice my absence on his return. I suddenly felt the presence of an angel behind me. Although my eyes were closed, I could see his huge radiating wings. He spoke: "There are many other worlds beside this one but they are no better. You may choose to go wherever you like, but God's kingdom is only open to those he calls, and he has not called you yet. There is still a task for you to fulfill on this earth." I asked for a definite order, which I promised to obey. He replied: "The great masses of people need orders, you are told to act freely. Your task cannot be revealed to you until you are ready to live out of your own free will." I felt defeated and afraid when I heard these words. There was a long silence. Then the angel whispered into my ear: "Be careful, time is pressing and your nature works slowly. Therefore you must use the people who are sent to help you more than ever before. I shall watch over you and will be there for help. But remember, I am the angel of strength and I cannot relate to your weakness." I made no reply but felt a growing calmness inside me. The radiance of the wings faded but the angel stayed with me until I fell asleep.*

This dream highlights an aspect of amplification different from the other dreams. Here the analyst is confronted with a level of the psyche that challenges his usual ability to apply amplification. In view of the dream's extraordinary numinosity, one is faced with a dilemma whether to amplify or just remain in respectful silence. I chose neither of the alternatives, considering the work of interpretation is first to make contact with the consciousness of the dreamer. The dream begins with a state of sheer abandonment, a reenactment of her actual childhood. Through the dream the client was appealing to the analyst to empathize with this part of her life; he was far away and was in fact at that time away on his summer holidays. Only after admitting the limitations of my help, and recognizing that my holiday had initiated a re-traumatization of my client's childhood, could we proceed to the deeper levels of the dream. It became clear to us both that the angel had taken over where I had failed. Amplification became a mutual process, and we talked about familiar stories concerning those strange, unexpected and often inexplicable interventions that happen in spite of human failure, found especially in legend and fairytale. We might understand such interventions as a message from God, the voice of the self or the autonomy of the human psyche. Whatever our belief system, the dreamer's night-time consciousness registered this archetypal theme as an angel. The angel's celebration of freedom defeats the injunctions of authoritarian institutions that rule over the human heart with fear. The presence of the angel sensitized the analyst's heart to the extraordinary depth of the dreamer's psyche and lent meaning and direction to future work.

d. A Narrative for All

A fifty-year-old woman had the following dream.

> I am tugging and pulling at a rubber inflatable dingy all grey in color. I am trying to fold it up. I am making great efforts, but nothing is happening. All of a sudden the dingy becomes a small silver vessel and a voice says: "This is the vessel of the spirit; treat it gently." I am holding the vessel in my two hands and feel a great sense of peace.

The dreamer, in hospital and dying of cancer, told the dream to her therapist, who, with her permission, conveyed it to a dream discussion group where I was present. We heard about the patient's suffering body, grey in color and ravaged by the last stages of cancer. She made every effort to die, all to no avail. After the dream she knew her struggle was over, could enter deep relaxation and welcome another kind of life. Those present in the group were deeply moved by the account. It became obvious that the dream had meaning not only for the dying patient, but for us all. Some responded with great sympathy for the patient, several talked about the coming to terms with the inevitable end of life and others were aroused by the deep spiritual intent of the dream. Many tales were told during that session. One person mentioned the solar barque of Pharonic Egypt that brought the souls of the dead to the Otherworld to await new life, another followed with Irish tales of night sea journeys to Islands of the Blest. On that day the dream became a source of inspiration and provided an opportunity to share experiences on a theme relevant to all present.

CONCLUSION

I have outlined four models in applying amplification, corresponding to four different ways an archetypal motif might appear in dreams. The motif common to all four dreams is death and renewal: Rebirth in the first dream, hell in the second, the angel of strength of the third, and the ship of life in the fourth. The context of each dream in the analytic relationship differs and requires another approach to amplification. First are those dreams where the archetypal is only implicit, acting as a kind of background, nevertheless lending structure to the dream. The young man's dream of snake-like beings coming alive does not require explicit amplification. Following Masud's theory of interpretation, Samuels reminds us that analysts do not have to articulate their amplificatory knowledge of myth but use it indirectly to guide their interventions and help them see where things are leading (Samuels, 198). Second are those dreams where powerful mythological themes are so enmeshed in a personal biography that the human and archetypal are scarcely distinguishable. Explicit amplification of the Nazi-Christ was crucial so that the dreamer could gain distance from the governess's puritanical authority, separate that oppressive influence from the actual circumstances of the exam, and internalize a capacity for self-evaluation. Third are dreams that contain archetypal content, seemingly uncontaminated by influential figures of the past. These revelatory dreams represent an autonomous aspect of the psyche that bare unexpected messages deeply significant for the entire life of the dreamer. Nevertheless the purpose of amplification is not to elaborate on the dream's numinosity in an exclusive way, but to include the context of transference. Fourth are dreams in which the archetypal may only be loosely connected with personal biography. They probably spring from the same source that originally inspired humans to create myth and ritual in order to come to terms with life's inevitable changes. These are known as big dreams, bearing significance beyond the individual. Amplification can become an enriching and enlightening experience in a larger social context.

With the veneration of temples of consumption and a purely pragmatic approach to life, so obvious in contemporary culture, older mythic and religious beliefs have either lost much of their meaning or become flagships of collective, often divisive, ideological movements. Night after night we create narratives about perennial themes, especially motifs concerning death and rebirth. Psyche seems to challenge, protect, and contain us as we pass through life's transitions. Perhaps this beneficent holding in a web of emergent meaning secures survival, allows transformation, and furthers a communal consciousness in which psyche's values are upheld. Amplification within the analytical encounter can be understood as a way of containing, anticipating, and differentiating the soul's archetypal intent. It facilitates the discovery of affinities of meaning in a relational way. Should we no longer amplify our dreams, shared human values, such as compassion, solidarity, friendship, and a sense of community in the face of a common human destiny would lose much of their significance. With careful resort to amplification, the analyst can bring to daytime consciousness new perspectives on narratives and rituals that once enabled a society to hold a world together and give it meaning. The analyst, amplifying parallel tales implicitly or explicitly, can help clients reconnect with images of rebirth, hell, angels, or vessels of spirit, inviting each person to rediscover psyche's phylogenic inclinations within the context of their actual life situation.

REFERENCES

Fordham, Michael. 1974. *Technique in Jungian analysis*. London: Karnac.

———. 1978. *Jungian psychotherapy*. London: Karnac.

Hederman, M. 2007. *Symbolism*. Dublin: Veritas.

Hobson, Alan. 2002. *Dreaming: A very short introduction*. Oxford: Oxford University Press.

Jacobi, Jolande. 1967. *The way of individuation*. London: Hodder & Stroughton.

Langer, Suzanne. 1951. *Philosophy in a new key*. Cambridge: Harvard University Press, 1996.

Mattoon, Maryann. 1984. *Understanding dreams*. Dallas: Spring Publications.

Jung, C.G. 1912/1970. *Symbols of transformation*. CW 5. Princeton: Princeton University Press.

———. 1923/1971. *Psychological types*. CW 6. Princeton: Princeton University Press.

———. 1909/1961. *Freud and psychoanalysis*. CW 4. Princeton: Princeton University Press.

Samuels, Andrew. 1985. *Jung and the post-Jungians*. London: Routledge.

Solms, Mark. 1997. *The neuropsychology of dreams*. New Jersey: Lawrence Erlbaum Association.

Wilkinson, Margaret. 2006. *Coming into mind*. London: Routledge.

JOHN HILL, MA, is a Training and Supervising Analyst of the International School of Analytical Psychology in Zurich. He received degrees in philosophy at the University of Dublin and the Catholic University of America. He is the author of articles on The Association Experiment, Celtic myth, James Joyce, home, dreams, and Christian mysticism.

11

PEREGRINATIONS OF ACTIVE IMAGINATION

The Elusive Quintessence in the Postmodern Labyrinth

Sherry Salman

"Active imagination" is the deliberate use of the creative imagination aiming toward quintessential truths and possibilities. As a method, it structures and enhances the natural, spontaneous expression of archetypes and the living stream of constructive and deconstructive psychological process. "Dreaming with eyes wide open," active imagination is at once a process provided for by psyche's natural tendency toward mythopoetic expression, a formal method that has to be cultivated, and at its best an attitude of psyche towards itself and the world. At the same time that we are confronted with "nothing at the center" of the postmodern labyrinth, the active use of imagination can create a virtual viewpoint offering an optic on psychological process that turns the psyche towards radical interactivity with the ever-present other.

In many ways, active imagination is akin to working the various alchemical procedures, but in a postmodern vessel that holds the subject, the images, the act of imagining, and even the intimation of an invisible goal, which is a state-of-being and reality to be found and created. This goal is what the alchemists called the "quintessence," the "celestial balm," and the Philosopher's Stone. The fruitful Stone of active imagination is of course not the rock of literality, nor is it the unconscious, and neither is it imagination's images themselves. It is rather, as quintessence, process qua process, kin to both personal individuation and the larger, cultural Great Work—the Western esoteric project described most succinctly and poetically by Goethe in *Faust*: "Formation, transformation, Eternal Mind's eternal Re-creation" (Act I, 69). For the postmodern psyche, the quintessence of imaginal process is not the objectivity of revealed wisdom, nor the subjectivity of the exalted individual creator, nor the sovereignty of images themselves, but a reimagined relationship between self and what is other(s), wherein meaning emerges in interdependence—as an endless and reflective series of responses.

The story of this elusive quintessence reflects the story of Jungian thought and its possible future in postmodern psychology. As the subjectivity of the artifex has fully entered the vessel of imagination with the images, as the vessel is itself understood as existing in no place and no space—as virtual—as the old gods are gone and what surrounds (if not contains) us, information, corporate globalization, virtuality, and cyberspace is of another order of reality altogether—as even imagination itself is being deconstructed by the undoings taking place in the collective, it may be that what is in the vessel now to be worked is imagination itself and the decentering of images.

This chapter is not primarily a postmodern lament about the crisis, disappearance, or death of imagination. It attempts instead to further the motion and possible futures of a postmodern imagination. It goes without saying that imagination has been colonized: the hijacking of the mythopoetic sensibility by fundamentalisms, the literalized spinning of images by the image industry, and the endless flow of information in virtual space are simultaneously by-products of the breakdown of imagination and the movements of psyche where it currently resides. At the same time that imagination in collective culture appears lost or hidden, it is also being revealed as truly subversive—as becoming itself at the edges of artifice and coercion, in the emptiness of place and cyberspace—listening transparently and reflectively to the happenings of today's psyche and society: further, almost unimaginably, released from both fixity and subjectivity.

ORIGINS

Jungians have historically privileged the imagination in both theory and practice. The preoccupation with the constructive and synthetic, even prophetic, tendencies of psychological process and imagination runs throughout the literature. It would not overstate things to say that the creative imagination is "the way," a mandala-in-motion, an essential regulator and creator of psychological process. The origin of Jung's particular method of using the imagination was his early confrontation with his own psychological crisis, and chronicled and illustrated in the newly published *Red Book* (2009), and elaborated in *Memories, Dreams, Reflections* (MDR). He engaged with the torrent of images that overtook him, and in the midst of it, in 1916, wrote a seminal paper, "The Transcendent Function," his first written statement on active imagination, though not published until some forty years later. It presents a synthetic view of psychological process and a method with which to come-to-terms with intense affect, fear, and imagery such as he had been experiencing. Jung concluded that, left to its own devices, unconscious material impacts us in a potentially adaptive and compensatory way, balancing and shifting psychic energy, even if by means of troubling and bizarre symptoms or intense flooding with emotions and images. The key is to make this process as conscious as possible, to interact with it, and to modify and deepen it. The method aimed at a better, more durable and flexible means of meeting and processing the inevitable difficulties and growth-spurts integral to living. Jung felt that the most important problems of life were by nature insoluble. They could, however, be out-grown, that is, replaced by a more compendious scope of awareness. Active imag-ination was meant to facilitate that outgrowing by stimulating "the transcendent function," a psychological capacity that brings together what were thought of as conscious and unconscious factors into a new relationship.

THE ORIGINAL METHOD OF ACTIVE IMAGINATION IN FOUR STAGES

(1) Concentrate on an emotion or image with the lowered awareness of a trance state (Cwik, 1997). This shifts the psyche into mythopoetic process, into the language of images, story, symbols, and affective fields. Imaginal figures, sto-ries, and feelings will emerge. Give these form in whatever way allows for their spontaneous expression, either verbally, by writing, drawing, dancing, or any-thing that enriches the emotion or image and lets it speak. Stay close to the integrity of the specific image without wandering away into emotional or intel-lectual free associations. At this stage, noninterference is key: just let things hap-pen. Jung said of this first phase:

> Take the unconscious in one of its handiest forms, say a spontaneous fantasy, a dream, an irrational mood, an affect, or something of the kind, and operate with it. Give it your special attention, concentrate on it, and observe its alterations objectively. Spare no effort to devote yourself to this task, follow the subsequent transformations of the spontaneous fantasy attentively and carefully. Above all, don't let anything from out-side get into it, for the fantasy-image has 'everything it needs'. In this way one is cer-tain of not interfering by conscious caprice and of giving the unconscious a free hand. (Jung 1955-56/1970, para. 749)

(2) Then work in a directed way with what emerged, either by trying to understand it on the dimension of meaning, or by elaborating it in accord with conscious artistic sensibility, or both.

(3) The back-and-forth dialogue between undirected and directed psychological processes creates a field in which more compendious symbols, feelings, or positions develop.

(4) The process is completed with a "coming to terms. Conclusions are realized and sacrifices are made as the fruits of the process are implemented in life. This was imagined as essentially an ethical process, an issue of conscience, not just consciousness. This is quite difficult because, as Jung described:

> It is exactly as if a dialogue were taking place between two human beings with equal rights, each of whom gives the other credit for a valid argument and considers it worth while to modify the conflicting standpoints by means of thorough comparison and discussion or else to distinguish them clearly from one another. Since the way to agreement seldom stands open, in most cases a long conflict will have to be borne, demanding sacrifices from both sides. (Jung 1916/1969, para. 186)

At the same time that he was working out this method and for many years afterwards (1912–1930), Jung was laboring devotedly on the wild imaginary characters and dramatic encounters that had come to him at night during his "confrontation with the unconscious," and setting those down in the *Red Book*. Jung showed the text and paintings in the *Red Book* to a few trusted friends and colleagues, but after he discovered alchemy he stopped working on it. After his death it was hidden away in a Swiss bank vault, and was finally published in 2009. As the missing piece of Jung's opus—the monumental work of his own active imaginations—the *Red Book* illustrates exactly what Jung meant by active use of the imagination, and how much he valued the integrity and the unknown but knowable life of the imagination. As Jung said at the end of his life, "My entire life consisted in elaborating what had burst forth from the unconscious and flooded me like an enigmatic stream . . . everything later was merely the outer classification . . ." (2009, vii).

Before exploring the method in more detail and its relevance for a postmodern psyche, it is worth taking a turn even farther back in time. Going back to premodern archaic and mythic times, one sees that the agency of deep change in psychological process was experienced as the mysterious action of spirits, gods, and oracles. These presented nonego images in "objective" form, albeit quite differently. Humanity's presumed projections then became psychological projects as the gods became conscious—or better said, became—the unconscious. Jung would come to differentiate and amplify this "wisdom of the unconscious" in specific images: for example, as the intuitive knowledge of the bush-soul. It became highly differentiated dynamically and practically in the method of active imagination, in which the other appeared now entirely from within, a move which mirrored the collective psyche's ever-increasing turn towards the subject.

Interestingly enough, there is still an aura of both the sacred and taboo surrounding active imagination in Jungian circles, a cult status which both elevates and marginalizes it. This status resonates in part with the method's connection to older mytho-ritualistic approaches to imaginal process, such as the Egyptian ritual of the "Washing and Opening of the Mouth." Performed to reanimate the living soul of the deceased after washing and purifying various images of the gods, the mummified statues of kings and even favored animals had their mouths ceremonially opened by the touch of a blade. This allowed them to see, hear, breathe, and eat—in short, to enjoy the offerings of food and drink made to them, thereby sustaining their living *ka* (spirit). Once this rejuvenation was accomplished, the images could reciprocate and help the living (Rundle-Clark 1959).

The original method of active imagination as practiced by the first generation of Jungians was conceived in this model of dialogue with gods and devils, with the "divine body" in each of us (Dallett 1982, 175). While this dialogic model did the great service of objectifying the autonomy of psychological process in a particular way, allowing an appreciation of an order of reality beyond ego-consciousness, contemporary Jungian psychoanalysts no longer even symbolically open the mouths of gods or kings nor romanticize or reify the image's power to feed us. Moreover, we recognize the hubris in the notion that the ego can somehow assimilate, that is, "eat," the archetypal dynamisms represented by the god-images for it's own "growth." Understanding this also in their own way, our psychoanalytic forbears experimented with automatic writing, hypnosis, spirits and séances, free association, and word association, in an effort to get beyond the margins of the ego's identifications. Jung and the generation he trained were entirely devoted to the techniques of amplification and active imagination, which were validated, they felt, by the historical cross-cultural record of mythologies and the methods of the hermetic traditions, foremost alchemy. They followed the mythopoetic trails of imagination found in dreams and visions in their efforts to get beyond the ego's margins, and they believed firmly in the notion that all culture, including the culture of the individual psyche, originated from incursions of imagination. These incursions, "altered states" of imaginal process, were the portals through which the founders passed as they defined the craft of analysis at its beginnings. What so fascinated the early psychoanalysts were the mythopoetic movements of imagination—and their constructive, healing function. Jungians have since formalized their work with images and imagination in the two classic methods of amplification and active imagination, both of which are used in analysis.

Amplification as a method of interpretation grounds images in mythologems, which are different from scientific explanations or historical referents (see preceding chapter on amplification). It calls on the past, on what is "known" as it has been expressed symbolically in collective and cultural mythology, folklore, traditional symbols, and customs. It amplifies the field of an image from the obscurely personal into the cultural and archetypal. As an experience, amplification can be numinous as it reveals the wonder of connection between one's images and their resonance with the universal. Active imagination, sometimes referred to as natural or unconscious amplification, is an individual evocation and relationship with emerging psychological material, expressed in mythopoetic language and images. As a method, it calls on the present "unknown." It is unlike prayer, art, or meditation, all of which appeal to other aspects of psychological process. Using both

WORKING WITH IMAGES

Amplification   systematized collective imagination
                  draws from extant mythologies (known)
                  extracts essential and relevant mythologems

            Not conventional or scientific explanation.
            Links past collective symbolism to the present.
            Interpretive
            Conservative

Active   natural or unconscious individual amplification
imagination   draws from mythopoetic imagination (unknown)
                  image unfolds it's own meaning
                  may deconstruct collective mythology

            Not traditional prayer, meditation, or art
            Links emerging present to the future
            Experiential
            Subversive

amplification and active imagination, images and unconscious material get linked to the past, the present, and to possible future developments. Both methods assume that an image reveals crucial bits of information and experience, which act to empower the image itself, the imaginer, and what is "other" through mutual fields of resonance (what used to be called "sympathetic magic"). In both methods, images are circumambulated, walked around and through, as well as experienced and analyzed in an on-going circulation between the personal and archetypal fields of psyche and life.

POISON OR PANACEA?

Jung was initially worried about "handling" such unconscious material:

> The essential thing is to differentiate oneself from these unconscious contents by personifying them, and at the same time to bring them into relationship with consciousness. That is the technique for stripping them of their power. It is not too difficult to personify them, as they always possess a certain degree of autonomy, a separate identity of their own. Their autonomy is a most uncomfortable thing to reconcile oneself to, and yet the very fact that the unconscious presents itself in that way gives us the best means of handling it. (Jung 1961/1989, 187)

And he continued to believe that there was a demon in the *prima materia* of unconscious process that could drive people, and whole cultures, crazy.

Whether active imagination is "poison or panacea" has been an ongoing question for clinicians. Although very much in favor of it, Hillman (1983) pointed out that psychopathology is a description in functional and dynamic terms of the same phenomena personified by medieval demonology, and in this sense practicing active imagination opens the door to the devil and all the inhabitants of hell! Is the method poison for a person who is already overwhelmed by emotion and strange images and ideas? Should it be reserved for those with strong ego boundaries? Clinical experience often proves not, especially as we understand psychological processes from a more fluid, multivaliant perspective and less as an ego versus unconscious polarity. Many clinicians have found that, as I wrote in an earlier paper:

> The mythopoetic structure of active imagination and its origin in non-rational process can create an empathic resonance which reaches deeply into early levels of disturbance and process. This becomes particularly pertinent during those altered states of psychological process where alchemical dramas are being enacted—*solutio, mortificatio, separatio*—here we participate most fully in the destruction and creation of old paths and new possibilities. Running counter to the notion that active imagination is not therapeutically effective at early levels of process and may be invasive, it may be that the process can provide empathetic links which are not possible through intersubjective analysis, ego strengthening, or traditional analysis of the transference, as these require cognitive and affective abilities which postdate early levels of experience. (Salman 2006, 186)

At these levels of psychological process in character disorders and at certain points and pockets of more mature process, analytic work with transference can also be a kind of active imagination, if transference is understood as one aspect of, or even as a stand-in for, the transcendent function. This understanding has also led to an altered understanding of analytic neutrality as grounded in images and their unfolding through the transference, not in a stance of either detachment or mirroring. Entering the autonomy of the image through active imagination or amplification yields objectivity in its deepest sense. Seeing through the lens of imagination may achieve a truly functional neutrality, based as it is in a matrix of archetypal dynamics.

Even so, there are cautions regarding the method, similar to those associated with "cooking," "drowning," or "drying" the material in the alchemical vessel. As with all methods and techniques, one needs to respect issues of timing and healthy resistance.

THE POISONS

(A) In the evocation of images and fantasies
    (1) The defensive production of pseudo-symbols which are only reproductions of collective images, a form of fool's gold
    (2) Eruption of, possession by, and identification with the material

(B) In the subsequent understanding and elaboration of images and fantasies
   (1) Defensive degeneration into free association
   (2) Defensive or dissociated aesthetic interest
   (3) Tendencies toward over- or undervaluing the material and related issues of judgments according to both subjective or collective standards
   (4) The pull toward archetypal reductionism, a premature concretizing of psychological process into reified mythologems and categories rather than seeing the process through to its end, which is often a surprise

(C) Regarding the use of the entire method
   (1) The practice of black magic in which other people and events are manipulated
   (2) The practice of ego-psychology in which unconscious contents are seemingly assimilated, or "eaten," by the ego in service to its growth, rather than its relativization
   (3) The twin poles of idolatry: the worship of images as magical messages from the self and iconoclasm, the destruction of images by allegorizing, conceptualizing, and psychologizing them
   (4) A conflation between the ethics of human behavior and the ethics of the image

The alchemists were fooled again and again by thinking that their goal (i.e., gold) had been reached, when what appeared as panacea was actually poison. The same is true in psychoanalysis when we identify with and reify any aspect of theory or practice. That being said, there are nuggets of gold, "non-vulgi" elements of psychological process, which have precipitated out as "panaceas," although not all are incontrovertible.

THE PANACEAS

(1) The psyche is "peopled" not by pieces of "me" but by "others" who make a claim for emotional, relational participation. This view highlights the "reality of the psyche" as nonderivative. One of the figures Jung encountered in his *Red Book* active imaginations was "Philemon," a lame-footed "pagan" who instructed:

> Philemon and other figures of my fantasies brought home to me the crucial insight that there are things in the psyche which I do not produce, but which produce themselves and have their own life. Philemon represented a force which was not myself. In my fantasies I held conversations with him, and he said things which I had not consciously thought. For I observed clearly that it was he who spoke, not I. He said I treat thoughts as if I generated them myself, but in his view thoughts were like animals in the forest, or people in a room, or birds in the air, and added, 'If you should see people in a room, you would not think that you had made those people, or that you were responsible for

them.' It was he who taught me psychic objectivity, the reality of the psyche. (Jung 1961/1989, 183)

(2) Psychic energy is released from unconscious identifications when brought into awareness and engaged. Similarly, energy is released from conscious fixation when enriched by unconscious contents. A psychic complex or archetypal factor exists in both image and affective forms. Images give form to the emotions, and emotions give a living body to images. The releasing of images from the emotions, and vice versa, contributes to breaking up identifications, which is why active imagination also "works" as a therapeutic tool.

(3) There is a difference between active imagination and passive fantasizing, between what the alchemists called "true imagination" (CW12, para.218) and "phantastic imagination," what we experience in psychological process as the unfolding of archetypal factors (true) versus the repetition compulsion of complexes (phantastic).

(4) Active imagination is a way to "know thyself," but not to "know myself" in a personalistic sense. It is not primarily about curing symptoms, abreacting emotions, problem solving, or "working on yourself." It is also not about the practice of ritual magic in a transpersonal sense—not about inviting synchronicities, inducing visions, enhancing prophetic abilities, or "summoning or freeing" the gods. The purpose is rather to heal psyche by increasingly deliteralizing it, which as Hillman points out is "interminable, revelatory, non-linear, and discontinuous. . . . We may fiction connections between the revelatory moments, but these connections are hidden like the spaces between the sparks or the dark seas around the luminous fishes' eyes, images Jung employs to account for images" (Hillman 1983, 80).

In this view of psychological process, what makes the difference, the "solution" or the "solvent," the spaces and the dark seas, is always of a nonrational nature, an energetic process. This view differs from the formulation that conscience and ethics are the "last word" in active imagination.

(5) "Know thyself" opens further into the world with the advent of postmodernism in which the imagination, the images, and the imaginer doing the imagining have all entered the vessel, which has also entered itself. This development shifts active imagination's alchemical sensibility of "co-creation" towards one of simultaneous interactivity. The difference between what is "seen," what is "understood" and what is "done" with it is radically relativized, and the previously conceived linear processes of the method are imagined now to occur simultaneously.

THREE MODELS OF IMAGINAL PROCESS

The various poisons and panaceas can be sorted out into three models, which represent different twists and differentiations on dynamic systems that are applied in analytic work: "polarity," "plurality," and "simultaneity."

DYNAMIC MODELS OF IMAGINAL PROCESS

Polarity
A distinction between 'the ego' and 'the unconscious' exists.
Consciousness and the unconscious function in a dialogic, compensatory relationship.
These opposites cry out for integration, union, or transcendence into a 'third'.
Conscience is the final word.

Rests on an image of unity an and ego-Self axis.

Plurality
There are multiple and separate centers of consciousness.
Ego consciousness is relativized.
Images have their own mandates.
The image-the 'medium'-is its own "message" and meaning.
The final solvent is nonrational.

Rests on images of multiplicity and dissociability.

Simultaneity
Collapse of subject/object, space/time, narrative and linear distinctions.
Meaning of all images and narratives are simultaneous and holographic.
Imaginal process reveals truth greater than images—the medium is not the message.

Rests on image of invisible quintessence—holographic.

SUBVERSION AND THE MOMENT OF TRUTH

Active imagination had been traditionally framed within a "conscious-unconscious" and "ego-other" polarity, pairs of opposites that subsequently cried out for integration or transcendence into a "third." New understandings of psychological process based on images of multiplicity, dissociation, emergence, co-creation, and interactivity have called some of the original formulations into question. We need to ask what of use remains and what needs to be added.

To subvert means "to turn from below," and the active use of imagination sub- verts established mores, authority, and mythology because it comes "from below," from psyche's archaic tendency toward nonrational mythopoetic process and images. Jung commented on the subversive nature of imagination and its deconstruction of collective mythology:

> It is of course ironical that I, a psychiatrist, should at almost every step of my experi- ment have run into the same psychic material which is the stuff of psychosis and is found in the insane. This is the fund of unconscious images which fatally confuse the mental patient. But it is also the matrix of a mythopoetic imagination which has van- ished from our rational age. Though such imagination is present everywhere, it is both tabooed and dreaded, so that it even appears to be a risky experiment or a questionable adventure to entrust oneself to the uncertain path that leads into the depths of the uncon- scious. It is considered the path of error, of equivocation and misunderstanding. I am reminded of Goethe's words: 'Now let me dare to open wide the gate/ Past which men's steps have ever flinching trod' (Faust Part 1). . . . Unpopular, ambiguous, and danger- ous, it is a voyage of discovery to the other pole of the world. (Jung 1961/1989, 189)

There is always a dangerous and "surprise" element in active imagination because psyche's mythopoetic modes of reconstruction do not function just to re-create ancient stories and outmoded realities, but rather to pull those apart, crunch them up, and create new narratives and new variations on archetypal dynamics that point the way toward future possibilities. Always in motion, these variations are often at odds with the prevailing collective mythology, which in turn casts the method, rightly, in a subversive role. Active imagination offers a cri- tique of social norms through the individual psyche's ongoing deconstruction of both personal and collective myths. It also allows us, in subversive fashion, to identify and empathize with what is forgotten, "thrown out," censored, disfigured, or just emerging. Where myth and ritual are often conservative, active imagina- tion can be progressive and democratic, allowing disenfranchised elements of psyche to speak. What's more, the subversive element is not random, simply anar- chic or chaotic, but aims at being psychologically 'true', an unpopular notion in both psychoanalytic and postmodern circles. Amidst the welter of postmodern relativization and artifice, and amongst the multiplicity of the psyche's images and the collective's reproductions, where does the question of meaning and "accuracy" in relation to imaginal process now lie?

Following the alchemists we can reference "true imagination." This was understood as the creation and evocation of images that have a life of their own and develop according to their own logic, an "authentic feat of thought or ideation" (Jung 1936/1976, paras. 396–97) that grasps inner facts and portrays them in images true to their nature. This was in contrast to "fantastic" imagina- tion (fantasy), a "mere conceit" of insubstantial thought, which "just plays with its objects," spinning groundless fantasies on the surface of things, and concerned primarily with "conscious expectations" (ibid, paras. 396–97). The alchemists cautioned (Jung 1944/1968, para. 218) that their work had to be done with "true" imagination, that is with active, purposive creation and not with fantastic imagination. This finds an analogy in analysis, which attempts to differentiate the defensive fantasies generated by complexes that interfere with integration and reconstruction from the trajectory of psyche's true imagination, the coherent synthesis of the real, the imaginal, and the mystery of what might be (Salman 2006).

Under the influence of postmodernism, the splits and the spaces in active imagination between what is seen (the figures and visions), what is understood (the elaborations and amplifications into meaning), and what is done with it all (the ethical issue) are closing. If what is experienced is "true," one becomes, indeed one already is, invested with that truth at the same moment it is "seen." "Who shoots, and what is the mark?" asks a Japanese koan, as subject, object, space, time, and intention collapse into a single moment of meaning, a nodal point of time which the ancient Greeks called *kairos*, the appointed and opportune moment. From this perspective, there is only one single "event," one kairos, one "moment of truth," which is revealed in active imagination. The specific images and temporal sequences observed are by-products of the narrative and imaginal medium, and are not the same as the "message." We can specify the truth of the "message" and also preserve its invisibility, which is its indispensable character in the following way: active imagination expresses essential messages about *the psyche's emerging relationship with itself*, which Giegerich (2001) calls "the soul's logical life," whose domain is the territory of the invisible, the land of what is "not." In the same way that the "stone is not a stone," that the "gold is not gold," images and even imagination have to be seen through and understood as "non vulgi" (not-literal).

The fruits of active imagination are not "true" as one's subjective truth or "the" objective truth. They are true when they "hit the mark" exactly right, when they penetrate into the "heart of the matter." The archetypal symbols of active imagination, with their concurrent ties to subject and object, unfold simultaneously in radical subjective specificity, in all the embodied, objective avenues of experience and expression, in the face of the other, and in their own truth. Even the alchemists always claimed that "The highest Mystery of the whole Work is the physical Dissolution into Mercury, as quicksilver" (Fabricius, 1976). Images themselves must also be "dissolved" into a larger solvent, wherein the truth of psychological life is revealed behind its images—psyche in constant and "liquid" motion in the world. The process of disidentification, even from symbols and images, moves toward becoming more or less complete, at the same time that the apprehension of reality and of others enlarges exponentially. Participation in this process may fulfill a potential inherent in postmodernism.

SYMPATHY FOR THE DEVIL AND EMPATHY FOR THE OTHER— IMAGINATION AT THE ROUND TABLE

If psyche's capacity to imagine does indeed structure both subjectivity and objectivity, the radical thought is that there is little relation to reality without the capacity for imagination. Always interested in scientific developments, Jung would have been delighted to know that studies using brain PET and MRI imaging have demonstrated that when people imagine they are walking down a street, or pressing an experimental button, the same brain areas become active as when they are "really" walking down a street or pressing a button. Moreover, imagining making those movements increases subsequent skill with those actual physical movements. "Practicing" in the imagination is almost as effective as actual training (Frith, 2007).

We are well aware of the contagion and poisonous projections that can reach deeply from one person's imagination into another and into the world. We tend to dwell less upon the more gracious side of this effect, namely the salutary and empathic connections forged by imagination and shared emotions. The fluidity of unconscious process opens the psyche to both the subjectivity and objectivity of other selves and other realities. Active imagination tracks what is "possible," increasing adaptation to the possibilities that both exist already and arise later, and acting to transform those realities. Its symbols are part of engaged experience, mirrored and reflected in various fields of emotional, biological, social, political, and spiritual life, and they claim participation. Active imagination, by taking one deeply into oneself, also brings us into contact with what is more than ourselves. It is a subjective path to objective awareness. Imagination opens the shadow, moving identity beyond its margins into the reality of the psyche and the world, into the heart of darkness of lived experience, into the shock of both internal recognition and of the ever-present other.

Sympathy for our own devils develops hand-in-hand with empathy for the other. Even the specific characteristics of the method support the ideals of democracy and diplomacy: mutuality, pluralism, dialogue, interactivity, negotiation, reciprocity, and the recognition that underneath there is always a "group-psyche" in play. Nothing could be more synchronous with the needs of community and collective life. The dialogue with "the other" is also just that: the forging of an empathic connection to others. Jung commented:

> The present day shows with appalling clarity how little able people are to let the other man's argument count, although this capacity is a fundamental and indispensable condition for any human community. Everyone who proposes to come to terms with himself must reckon with this basic problem. For, to the degree that he does not admit the validity of the other person, he denies the 'other' within himself the right to exist—and vice versa. The capacity for inner dialogue is a touchstone for outer objectivity. (Jung 1916/1969, para. 187)

The original compensatory model of active imagination has long since shifted through our understanding of dissociability and attachment in psychological life. Put another way, it is not that "the unconscious" is somehow "too unconscious," or consciousness "too one-sided," but rather that the lack of libidinal attachment between various psychological contents is what creates disturbance. An emergent field of libidinal attachments amongst psychological factors, idiosyncratic and archetypal, would be a more up-to-date image of the transcendent function. And this libidinal field extends into the interpersonal field, even into the body politic, in which shared images of unconscious dynamics create an intense relational field that can either degenerate into psychic contagion (mobbing) or facilitate empathy and mature bonds.

If active imagination is a medium through which various sectors of psyche can relate to one another, it is empathy and eros that play the definitive role in anchoring these relationships. We know that psychopathy and sociopathy are defined by both lack of empathy and lack of imagination, and furthermore it is clear that the presence or absence of relationships between sectors of psyche is the determining factor in character, "fate," health, and psychological creativity. This also applies equally well to nations and cultures, both internally and internationally. Imagination decentered from subjectivity can open fully to the needs of the other.

One of the last operations in the alchemical process was called "*multiplicatio*," an operation imagined to change the nature of the vessel itself, the Elixir, and the alchemist. In *multiplication*, which the medieval mind pictured as an explosion of stars under the expansive dominion of Jupiter "advancing toward infinity in powers of 10," the Elixir "spills out" of the vessel with "tincturing" power, becoming one with the body politic, active in the world as it moves in all the human soul's activities. The expressions of psyche and the world become simultaneous and inseparable, which Jung intended with the phrase "*mysterium coniunctionis.*" In this way, the refined imagination as an elixir of life is no longer just a "bridge" between subject and object. It becomes what contains, structures, and breathes both at the same time. Imagination, like a "soul," or what Henry Corbin (1969) called the *mundus imaginalis*, becomes wrapped around both psyche and the world.

At our moment in time, as images flood and glut collective life, the notion of a creative imagination seems threatened. This engenders feelings of despair and powerlessness, giving rise to images of a postmodern "wasteland." As Richard Kearny has chronicled in *The Wake of Imagination*:

> Disseminated into the absolute immanence of sign-play, the imagination ceases to function as a creative centre of meaning. It becomes instead a floating signifier without reference or reason—or to borrow Derrida's idiom, a mass-produced postcard addressed 'to whom it may concern' and wandering aimlessly through a communications network, devoid of 'destiny' or 'destination'. (Kearny 1988/1994, 13)

It is important at this moment in history to look both ways—because an aimless "player" also does play—and play is an activity which can be manipulative or communicative, obfuscating or liberating. It appears that the subject, the "medium," the "message," the analyst, the Art, and even all the artifice of postmodern culture have entered the vessel of imagination, which by virtue of it's increasing "virtuality" has also disappeared into itself. This prompts us once again to ask "the Parsifal question" about both postmodernism and active imagination: what does it serve? And this is very much bound up with our understanding of "meaning" in postmodern life.

The "divinely inspired" sensibility of imagination and meaning gave rise in time to the dominance of the creative subject, which has in turn given way to the image of a decentered "player" in a universe of depthless and reproduced signifiers. But there is no way back to 'meaning' in the old mythic-ritualistic sense. Those gods and their images have come and now they have gone. A nostalgic or sentimental clinging to "essentials" in the form of various "fundamentalisms," Jungian or otherwise, is a defense against that loss. Nor are we in thrall to "the Image" as oracle of "the unconscious," or to the Sisyphusian delusion of making the "unconscious conscious," or to the exalted subjectivity of the imagination and its creator. Even the image *qua* image is losing its postmodern luster, as we are invited, in the end, to know psyche abstracted from even its images. Just as there is no longer an "out" in which to throw or even recycle the garbage, or a sacred inner chamber in which to commune with what is "chosen," or a "me" separated from a "you," the active use of imagination in our postmodern times offers the possibility of releasing psychological life from even these images, as "know Thyself" opens to radical interactivity.

REFERENCES

The *illustration*: Mercurius as a winged dragon entering the unsealed Hermetic vessel. Illustration from a seventeenth- or eighteenth-century alchemical manuscript "Sapientia Veterum." The British Museum, London. Courtesy of www.aras.org.

Chodorow, Joan. 1997. *Jung on active imagination*. Princeton, NJ: Princeton University Press.

Corbin, Henry. 1969/1998. *Alone with the alone: Creative imagination in the Sufism of Ibn 'Arabi*. Princeton, NJ: Princeton University Press.

Cwik, August. 1995. Active imagination: Synthesis in analysis. In *Jungian analysis*, 2nd ed., ed. Murray Stein. Chicago: Open Court.

Dallett, Janet. 1982. Active imagination in practice. In *Jungian analysis*, 1st ed., ed. Murray Stein, 173–91. Chicago: Open Court.

Fabricius, Johannes. 1976. *Alchemy: The medieval alchemists and their royal art*. London: Aquarian Press.

Frith, Chris. 2007. *Making up the mind: How the brain creates our mental world*. Oxford: Blackwell Publishing.

Giegerich, Wolfgang. 2001. *The soul's logical life*. Frankfort: Peter Lang.

Goethe, J.W. 1961. *Faust*. Tr. Walter Kaufmann. New York: Anchor Books

Hillman, James. 1983/2005. *Healing fiction*. Putnam, CT: Spring Publications.

Jung, C.G. 1916/1969. The transcendent function. In CW 8.

———. 1936/1976. The Tavistock lectures. In CW 18.

———. 1944/1968. *Psychology and Alchemy*. CW 12.

———. 1955-56/1976. *Mysterium Coniunctionis*. In CW 14.

———. 1961/1989. *Memories, dreams, reflections*. New York: Vintage Books.

———. 2009. *The red book*. Ed. Sonu Shamdasani. New York: W.W. Norton & Co.

Kearney, Richard. 1988/1994. *The wake of imagination*. New York: Routledge.

Rundle-Clark, Robert T. 1959/1978. *Myth and symbol in ancient Egypt*. London: Thames & Hudson.

Salman, Sherry. 2006. True imagination. *Spring* 74: 175–87.

SHERRY SALMAN, Ph.D., has a doctorate in neuropsychology and is a Jungian psychoanalyst practicing in NYC and Rhinebeck, NY. She was a Founding member and first President of The Jungian Psychoanalytic Association. Recent publications include "Blood Payments" in *Terror, Violence, and the Impulse to Destroy* (2003), "True Imagination" in *Spring* (2006), "The Creative Psyche" in *The Cambridge Companion to Jung*, 2nd ed. (2008) and *Dreams of Totality: Where We Are When There's Nothing at the Center* (2011), Routledge.

12

ON MAKING AND MAKING USE
OF IMAGES IN ANALYSIS

Mary Dougherty

Exploring the relationship between image and emotion has long been a central
feature of Jungian psychoanalysis. Jung states in his autobiography: "To the
extent that I managed to translate the emotions into images, that is to say, to find
the images which were concealed in the emotion, I was inwardly calmed and
reassured. Had I left those images hidden in the emotions, I might have been torn
to pieces by them" (Jung 1961, 177). In this chapter, I will attempt to convey my
experience of initiating image making with patients in analysis as a way for them
to find the images concealed in their emotions. I will then discuss ways these
images, once formed, might serve the analytic process.

My use of image making in analysis has been informed by and emerged out
of my practice both as an artist and an art therapist. As a working artist, I had
the strong conviction that as I was forming my work, my work was forming
me. In analysis I realized that the process of making performances and video
pieces out of dream material functioned as transformational psychic events in
my life. This realization in turn influenced my approach to making and teaching art. It also solidified my decision to become an art therapist, and it eventually motivated me to become a Jungian psychoanalyst. In my psychoanalytic
training, however, I found that the normal space, time, and material requirements for the practice of art therapy were at variance with accepted practices
within the analytic frame. To complicate matters a bit further, Jung did not provide a model for how to incorporate imaginal work within analysis, since he
assumed that image making and active imagination would occur outside the
analytic session. In my development as an analyst, I eventually found ways to
incorporate image making within analysis from the perspective that it is possible to move back and forth between synthetic and reductive models of analysis (Cwik 1995, 165 quoting Fordham 1967, 51–65). In other words, imaginal
techniques can be incorporated as a part of analytic practice if that practice is
also grounded in an awareness of the transference dynamics within the analytic
field. In addition, the incorporation of active imagination within the analytic
session can serve as a foundation for the transcendent function as well as for

the development of a symbolic attitude in relationship to unconscious contents (Cwik 1991, 106).

In the process of incorporating image making into verbal analysis, I have modified aspects of my previous art therapy practice in order to ease its integration into the analytic frame. For example, I do not use the word "art" when initiating image making with patients. I present the process as "making marks on paper" rather than "making a drawing" because engaging visual materials can be preceded by doubt and anxiety for many, but especially for nonartists (Edwards 1987, 100). By imagining this process as mark making rather than art making, doubt and anxiety are reduced. Similarly, the product is valued not for its artistic qualities but for its symbolic capacity to generate meaning within the context of analysis. Visual materials are streamlined for easy use within this setting. This emphasis differs from the work of many art therapists who value the art making process as the central component of the therapeutic process with verbal interventions serving mainly to support the psychic integration of the image. Following this point of view, patients use art materials in a space that is set up as an art studio and produce works that serve both aesthetic and therapeutic aims (Case and Dalley, 2006). While I value the work of art therapists who have focused their practice on art therapy as the central modality, I believe there are also some distinct advantages to the inclusion of image making that serves to support verbal analysis.

How This Method Is Practiced

The analyst suggests the use of visual materials within an analytic session in response to a felt sense of something emerging within or between the patient and the analyst. This "something" can feel like a disturbance, sadness, confusion or just a kind of "stuckness." While staying attuned to what seems to be pressing forward for attention, the analyst safeguards the analytic couple from any pressure to engage the imaginal process (Ogden 1997, 161). In making space within an analytic session to engage in an imaginal process, the analyst and the patient enter an imaginal space within which their capacity to be present to emergent phenomena within the analytic field is deepened. Within this space, the analyst provides the necessary holding to allow the patient to access and to experience emerging contents and feelings. Visual materials are introduced into the field of focused concentration on these feeling states. An image materializes as this continued concentration on the internal feelings merges with external media and finds form on the surface of the paper. The image that emerges is a reality that exists within an imaginal play space bridging the opposites of outer and inner, of known and not known. This imaginal space incorporates the process of active imagination into the analytic container and forms the basis for the transcendent function. It is also an intermediate space within which transitional phenomena can emerge (Cwik 1991, 106–7).

As mentioned above, I have streamlined the visual materials used within the context of verbal analysis for easy use within the consulting room. I keep a clipboard (18" x 24") with the same-sized paper attached and a basket of pastels within easy reach. I place the pastels on the couch next to the patient and the clipboard with the paper attached on their lap. The process begins with the analyst inviting the patient to go inward—to close their eyes and to deepen their breath. I do the same. Staying attuned to the patient, I muse aloud about the conflict, sadness, confusion, or stuckness that seems to be pressing forward for attention. I ask them to imagine these feelings in their body—to feel where they are located in their body and to be with these feelings in that place. After some minutes of continuing in this fashion—our eyes closed—I say: "Imagine the color of these feelings." After a short pause: "Open your eyes and pick one or two pastels that align with these feelings in your body." Having selected the color(s), they again close their eyes and continue to observe their breathing, staying connected to these feelings. At some point, I say: "Allow this feeling to move through your body, down your arm, through your hand and pastel and onto the paper—let these feelings make marks on the paper."

This way of giving form to internal feelings is a type of active imagination (see chapter on active imagination, above). It initiates a lowering of waking consciousness, which differentiates active imagination from other forms of imaginative activity such as the free flowing play of children and the creative involvement in painting pictures and creating objects (Cwik 1995, 142, quoting Fordham 1956). Unlike other forms of active imagination in which one's concentration is focused on an internal image, the focus in this imaging process is on accessing and attuning to one's own internal feeling states. The emphasis is to stay imaginally connected to these feeling states as they move down the arm and merge with an external medium to make concrete marks on paper. What I am describing is a mode of being aligned with an instinctual experience of affect as it merges with the chalky substance of the pastel moving against the surface of the paper as it releases the affect onto paper. The image-making process takes place halfway between daydreaming and purposeful or expedient action (Milner 1993, 22). This process exists in an intermediate area of experience in which the patient makes use of a medium as a part of the external world that is pliable and safe enough to treat as a bit of oneself (ibid., 33).

This image-making process can continue with the patient's eyes closed—focusing on the emerging internal feeling states—or the patient can work with eyes open—responding to and expanding on the initial marks laid down. At this stage, the analyst avoids any tendency to anticipate what should happen, but rather remains open to and grounded in her emotional experience with the patient. During the image-making process, the analytic couple is required to endure the liminality of regressive and prospective psychic energies activating infantile residue as well as archetypal potential, all seeking conscious expression through the common channel of the image. Obviously, when a patient makes an image in the presence of an analyst, it can be a meaning saturated experience for both.

The analyst and the patient receive the newly hatched image together, careful in their observation and silent in its presence. The image now exists before them as an external presence, outside the maker of it and, at the same time, temporarily held in a space also inhabited by the maker (Schaverien 1991, 19). The actively imagined *internal* feeling states are now concretized within this *external* image; the image is both a statement about and a depiction of what was formerly an invisible inner state (Edwards 1987, 103). The image is also the ocular evidence emphasized by Jung as necessary to promote a conscious relationship to the unconscious. This ocular evidence counteracts the tendency to self-deception and helps prevent the contents of the unconscious accessed through active imagination from slipping back into the unconscious (Cwik 1991, 103 quoting Jung 1955).

At this point in the process, there is a shift from actively imagining internal feeling states to encountering the newly drawn image. The analyst's first response to the image is not interpretive or directed towards understanding the image for analytic aims. Rather, it is to sit together with the image and with the various ingredients that make up the image: the formal and ideational elements of the image, the affective states now embodied in the image, and the transitional phenomena emerging within and around the analytic couple. This process of responding to the image requires the analyst to tolerate the experience of being adrift, a state that should not be rushed to closure (Ogden 1997, 160–61). The job of the analyst is to create a safe holding environment and allow the patient to discover what is happening in the image. At the same time, the analyst's steady attention to the specificities of the image allows the image to accrue meaning even when a resistant part within the image-maker might wish to avoid particular aspects of the image.

The process of moving toward verbal symbolization of the image can now begin. There are no strict rules governing the interpretation of images in Jungian psychoanalysis (Schaverien 1992, 3). In taking steps towards the verbal symbolization of the image, the analyst begins by gathering a sensory experience of the formal elements composing the image. This is a process of attuning to the physical presence of the medium (pastels) as it exists on the paper and as it resonates in one's body. There are some basic questions to be considered. What is the dynamic quality of line, from its initial point on the paper through its movement along a path that gives shape to the image (Klee 1953, 16–18)? Is the line fast moving or slow, pressured or faint, precise or meandering? Observing the dynamic quality of the lines that form the image can convey qualities of the feeling states they portray. Another question to consider are the colors initially chosen by the maker, their associations to these colors and to the forms made using them. And finally, the size and intensity of the forms, as well as the spatial relationship between the forms made with these lines and colors, need to be considered. Attuning to the sensory experience of these formal elements lays the ground to visualize and to relate to the ideational content portrayed in the image, which often parallels the intensity and energic qualities of the internal feeling states in relationship to the ego's capacity to regulate them. When the analyst and the patient observe the image together in this way, the patient is often struck with an immediate sense of what is happening in the image. Even at this early stage, the newly formed image almost always reveals more than was consciously intended or imagined. At the same time, there can be something in the image or another way of viewing the image that is obvious to the analyst but remains obscure to the patient. In this situation, the analyst provides the necessary holding so that the patient can both witness the iconographic power of image as well as make use of the image at their own pace without being overwhelmed (Edwards 1987, 103; Schaverien 1991, 107).

A CLINICAL EXAMPLE OF THIS PROCESS

Clara could find neither a place nor a situation in her life in which she could experience a sense of competence or enjoy her accomplishments. As a forty-four-year-old professional classical musician, married and a mother, she regularly felt like a "loser" because she was unable to do things perfectly enough. This pressure for perfection had been permanently installed as a competitive structure in her—as well as in her three siblings—by her father's demanding and demeaning presence. As an adolescent, she began to study music in order to become excellent at something no one else in the family could do. At the same time, however, being the best at something also made her feel vulnerable and guilty.

After a year and a half of analysis, Clara told me a story from her childhood in which she remembered being alone in the library of her family home, crying and feeling like a loser. Then, in an attempt to make herself feel better, she pulled herself together to perform gymnastics stunts for her father while he was watching TV. In the process of her telling me this story from the past, the feelings became intense for both of us. It was in response to the intensity of these feelings that I initiated the image-making process.

The initial phase of the imaginal process focused on containing and being present to the feelings brought into our session by this memory and on creating a space within which Clara could reflect on these feelings from a vantage point outside of their destructive power. She selected the black pastel and, without closing her eyes, placed the crying figure on the top right of the sheet. She then encircled the figure with hastily made lines that almost obliterated it. In observing the intensity of these lines, I was struck by the possibility that this was how she treated the part of herself that felt like a loser. Then, shifting focus to the performing part of herself, Clara selected a pink pastel and placed this figure at the top left of the sheet. Still in silence, she then picked up the black pastel and quickly inscribed small black figures under each of the other two, as if she wanted to get the task over with quickly. The haste with which she made these marks coincides with Clara's treatment of herself—giving short shrift to her own self care.

Clara associated the top figures with the two modes of being that dominated her personality. The pink figure on the left was her performing self, and the black figure on the right was the loser. She described these two figures as stamping on the lower ones. The image provided ocular evidence of both sides of the complex:

the unrelenting demand to perform and the self-demeaning conviction of being a loser. The size and placement of the upper figures in relationship to the lower figures portrayed the power that the bipolar complex held over the self-figure beneath them. Another way of viewing the relationships between these figures is that this image could be initiating a process of differentiation between the punishing bipolar complex above and the suffering self-figure indicated below.

This initial image continues to serve as a reference point in the ongoing analysis. It has allowed Clara to identify overwhelming feelings in other contexts as either "pink" or "black." The figures from this initial image also have come to be used as symbolic elements in making additional images. Clara's participation in the imaginal play space of the image-making process has grounded her in an intermediate, mediating process within which she can experience herself and others apart from under the oppression of the complex. In this way, the image-making process functions as a symbolic activity that provides a bridge to the creation of a new attitude in relationship to the external world, based on insights into her inner world (Goodheart 1982, 12).

The price of creating a new reality and of discovering the self is, however, the sacrifice of old comforts (Goodheart 1982, 13). From the beginning, Clara had wanted the analysis to serve as a magic bullet that would free her from the loser part but without having to relinquish the "best part of myself"—the performing part's demand for perfection and greatness. Clara's use of this image and of other images she has made in analysis has gradually allowed her to make small daily adjustments in navigating between the two sides of the complex shown by this seemingly trivial image. This image continues to function within the analysis as a means toward the realization of the transcendent function. It holds our feet to the fire in the process of coming to terms with the opposites it portrays.

REFERENCES

Case, Caroline, and Tessa Dalley. 2006. *The handbook of art therapy*. London and New York: Routledge.

Cwik, August. 1991. Active Imagination as imaginal play-space. In *Liminality and transitional phenomena*, ed. Murray Stein and Nathan Schwartz-Salant, 99–114. Wilmette, Illinois: Chiron Publications.

———. 1995. Active imagination: Synthesis in analysis. In *Jungian analysis*, ed. Murray Stein, 136–69. Chicago and La Salle, Illinois: Open Court.

Edwards, Michael. 1987. Jungian analytic art therapy. In *Approaches to art therapy: Theory and technique*, ed. Judith Rubin, 92–113. New York: Brunner Mazel Pub.

Fordham, M. 1967. Active imagination—deintegration or disintegration? *Journal of Analytical Psychology* 12, 1:51–65.

Goodheart, William. 1981. Book review of Reality and fantasy: Transitional objects and phenomena. *San Francisco Jung Institute Library Journal* 2, 4:1–24.

Jung, C.G. 1961. *Memories, dreams, reflections*. New York: Random House.

———. 1955/1976. *Mysterium conjunctionis*. CW 14. Princeton, NJ: Princeton University Press.

Kalshed, Donald. 1996. *The inner world of trauma: Archetypal defenses of the personal spirit*. London and New York: Routledge.

Milner, Marion. 1993. The role of illusion in symbol formation. In *Transitional objects and potential spaces: Literary uses of D.W. Winnicott*, ed. Peter L. Rudnytsky, 13–39. New York: Columbia University Press.

Ogden, Thomas. 1997. *Reverie and interpretation: Sensing something human*. Northvale, NJ & London: Jason Aronson.

Schaverien, Joy. 1991. *The revealing image: Analytical art psychotherapy in theory and practice*. London and New York: Routledge.

MARY DOUGHERTY, MFA, ATR, NCPsyA, is a Jungian psychoanalyst and art psychotherapist in private practice in Chicago. She is Director of Training of the Jung Institute of Chicago and former President of Chicago Society of Jungian Analysts. As a printmaker and performance artist, she exhibited nationally and internationally and was awarded the "Lifetime Achievement in the Arts" award by the Chicago Women's Caucus for the Arts.

13

SANDPLAY

Eva Pattis Zoja

Presented with a wooden tray (57 x 72 x 7 cm), sand, water, and a large number of miniature objects and figures like plants, animals, humans, and buildings, patients ask: "What should I do with all this?" They are torn between curiosity, inhibition, and the fear of not knowing the rules to this game. Dora Kalff, the founder of Sandplay, usually answered: "Just have a look at all the figures, and maybe you'll notice one or the other that appeals to you." She thereby paved the way to letting the unconscious express itself in a three-dimensional form. During Sandplay the patient ventures into a trance-like atmosphere in which objects are alive. A miniature tree becomes the very essence of "tree-ness." It is also possible not to direct deliberate attention onto the miniatures, but rather to encourage a conscious awareness of inner experience through help of the sand. "Close your eyes if you wish and touch the sand; try to experience consciously how it feels. Can you feel if your hands crave anything?" This is an attempt to reach a psychological state in which unconscious content expresses itself not in the form of images but rather as a sensory experience, as a whole-body state.

On the basis of these two different ways of entering into Sandplay, two theoretical approaches become apparent. In the first, the emphasis is on seeing Sandplay as a nonverbal means of expressing symbolic and archetypal images that can originate from the personal or the collective unconscious. The second approach attempts to gain access to a presymbolic area of the psyche that is similar to the holistic, "psychosomatic" way we experience life in earliest childhood.

Dora Kalff wrote only one small work with a limited but nevertheless impressive selection of case studies. In the past several decades, however, numerous publications have appeared in the USA, Italy, England, Germany, and Japan, with extensive descriptions of the theory and practice of Sandplay. Especially in regard to its range of applications, Sandplay has experienced a significant expansion. Where Sandplay therapists in the 1980s were cautioning against the use of Sandplay to treat psychoses, today it is used in psychiatric hospitals throughout the USA, Italy, Germany, and Japan to treat not only emotional disorders, but also clinical syndromes such as anorexia nervosa, addictive behavior and psychoses.

In 2007 a study on Sandplay with children and adolescents who were offered Sandplay therapy for one year was able to show a highly significant reduction of problematic behavior (Von Gontard 2007). Sandplay can easily be combined with various theoretical approaches. Sometimes it can seem like the three-dimensional, physical embodiment of a psychoanalytical theory. Donald Kalsched writes in his study about trauma and the "archetypal self-care system" how archaic defense mechanisms sometimes seem like giant, primitive sentinels who react blindly to every new emotional experience as if it were a new trauma every time. Many a Sandplay therapist will recall having encountered just such a monstrous figure in Sandplay pictures—an ambivalent huge body guard protecting the ego against new enemies but at the same time keeping it imprisoned—although possibly without understanding its full theoretical significance.

New theoretical insights coming especially from the neurosciences have helped Sandplay fortify its often intuitive practices with a solid theoretical basis and thus enable more effective work on safer ground.

In the following I would like to describe three elements of Sandplay that are not held in common with analysis: first, there is the substance itself—sand; secondly, the triangular nature of the setting; and thirdly, a special form of regression that can occur during Sandplay.

Why exactly is sand the chosen material? It enables a wide scope of design possibilities because one can easily build up or down without any special manual skills being required. By simply drawing a few lines in dry sand, one leaves traces that never look clumsy or unskillful. The precision with which grains of sand react to even the slightest movement or rearrangement creates an atmosphere of attentiveness. The sand behaves like a very sensitive receiving device that can record the slightest influence with infinite accuracy. It is as if a million grains of sand were listening intently and then responding together in perfect synchrony. Little by little patients' gestures grow noticeably attuned to this mood of alertness. They move more consciously, listen to their own voices, their tone and even to their own words in a new way. Furthermore, sand provides both adaptation and resistance in equal measure. It represents matter in its most elementary form, having been ground by wind and water in an infinitely slow process into miniature particles that are barely discernible to the human eye. These miniscule grains of sand are constantly rearranging themselves, and they strive to fill every void as if they were liquid. Sand is solid material, but in fluid form. This unique consistency makes it perfectly suited for visualizing psychological processes.

Sand can embody a whole row of polarities in an uncomplicated way. Depending on how much water is mixed with it, sand can be bright, dry, and light, or else dark, wet, and heavy. Sand can seem clean and pure, symbolizing order, or it can appear muddy and dirty and represent chaos. These few opposing qualities suffice to enable us to see such psychological conditions as depression, mania, or compulsive behavior expressed in the sand. Sand can be compact and suitable for building; or it can be so unmanageable that anything freshly built will immediately start to crumble. Sand can seem persecutory by annoyingly remaining stuck underneath fingernails; or it can have a healing function by gently cooling the palms of hot hands. Sometimes the fine texture of sand brings to mind the feel of skin and arouses a longing to touch and to be touched. On other occasions sand has to endure being roughly compressed, pounded, or even beaten. It can be radically churned about, so that whatever had been at the top ends up at the bottom; and the sweeping, explosive gestures that achieve this can bring about a feeling of release and regeneration. With just a few movements, mountains, valleys, rivers, or deserts are formed. Above all, places are created that are deeply familiar, and yet where no living person has ever been before. Sand formations are easily changed; every destruction almost organically leads to a new creation. Nothing is ever lost. One never has to throw anything away. It is the same sand, ever ready to be reused and ever willing to be transformed again into its own opposite. It becomes clear how similar sand is to what we would call a psychological substance or, in alchemical terms, a substance with mercurial properties.

Often the unconscious becomes so immediately and directly constellated that, after just a few unintentional movements of the hand, a face suddenly appears to be looking out of the dry sand. The patient is taken aback and asks: "Did I make this?" (i.e., he cannot take responsibility for this). Naturally this obvious state of surprise is the very criterion by which the therapist can ascertain whether deeper and more authentic psychological processes are really taking place, or whether the patient's play thus far is still dominated by resistance. Not that there could not be surprises as well even during such a resistive phase, but they would most likely be provoked by the therapist's intervention as when, for example, she were to point out an unexpected aspect of something that has been portrayed in the sand.

A basic rule is that the content of Sandplay itself should never be interpreted or directly commented on by the therapist. One assumes that everything that is formed during Sandplay not only has a reason but also a purpose, the direction of which has yet to reveal itself as time progresses. This process could be severely and irreversibly disturbed by too early an intervention. The therapist's empathetic thinking and feeling can be termed *silent interpretation*, and this is recognized to have an important influence on the outcome of a Sandplay session. Descriptions of the *interactive field* between therapist and patient shed more light on these phenomena (see chapter 19 below on Countertransference and Intersubjectivity). Naturally, this means that the act of playing and its results are rooted in the intersubjective field between the unconscious and consciousness of both parties.

I turn now to a very special dynamic of Sandplay, the triangular constellation of the setting. In the normal analytic setting, two individuals attempt to elaborate a third region of communication, which is the symbolic dimension. Together they create a field of energy that is enriched with unconscious elements, of which they attempt to grasp a few and bring them into consciousness. If they do not succeed, their shared consciousness will tend toward enactments or acting out. Sandplay begins differently. This third and potentially symbolic space is foreseen and present from the start as something concrete and material. It is simply there. This situation often causes a sudden constellation of the patient's other, hidden side. The sandbox is offered as an additional, concrete space, which indeed is more neutral than the analyst can possibly be. The patient has a sense of being more alone, more private. Anything that is painful or is causing emotions such as fear or rage can now make its appearance. The analyst stands far less "in the way" of expressing affects. For the patient, everything bad is now out there in the sand, and not only inside within the subject.

The patient can temporarily create a certain distance from the affect, while nonetheless remaining in touch and expressive of it. For patients whose psyches constellate intense transferences, this means that they have also come into possession of a part of the analyst and can peacefully and quietly take control of it without having to be afraid that the analyst may feel wounded, overwhelmed, or too intensely loved. Everything, even the unimaginable, can first take place in the sand, and only later risk being voiced within the relationship.

Even before anything has been expressed in the sand, this triangular situation can also activate primitive tendencies toward the splitting of the personality. We normally presuppose that unconscious contents allow themselves to be given three-dimensional representation in Sandplay. This holds true for contents which are close to consciousness and which already exist in the form of images. But there are also unconscious elements which have no form at all and no connection with images; they might as yet not even possess psychological substance. In dreams they do not present themselves as images. Instead they can be located in the underlying structure of certain dreams, invisible forces that are highly determinative. Such elements have a tendency to burst out of proportion and become incommensurate. The triangular Sandplay situation makes itself available to precisely such "disruptive" elements. In such an instance, we find scenes like the following. In one session, the patient plays with the sand and is full of initiative. He perceives the sand as pleasant, malleable, protective, and he feels at ease. "If only the analyst weren't here, disturbing things by scribbling away in her notebook," he thinks. "She blocks my creativity. She monitors my every move. If she weren't here, I could make all sorts of things . . ." Next session, the same patient begins by declaring that the sand feels cold and rough. Even its color strikes him as different: it's darker. "What has happened? Nothing at all seems to want to take shape. And the miniatures? They had always been so inviting, but now they just stand around looking so ridiculous—pure kitsch. Luckily the analyst is here; she just sits there so patiently. At least she's someone you can talk to. She'll understand." Once the sand is good and the analyst is bad. Another time the sand is bad and the analyst is good. The patient experiences personally, with all his senses, that the same sand and the same analyst can repeatedly flip sides and reverse their qualities. The patient can become aware of his own unconscious splitting phenomena while they are underway. The analyst allows herself to be used as a neutral object. She might have the corresponding countertransference reactions, at one time feeling poor and useless, at another time important and needed. But she realizes what is taking place and knows that both feelings are really two sides of the same coin.

The third characteristic of Sandplay that distinguishes it from analysis derives from the method itself. Sandplay offers a distinct tendency toward psychological regression, one that is not restricted to the patient's own childhood but, from the point of view of our collective developmental history as a species, a regression of human consciousness itself.

Dora Kalff made concrete use—sometimes even concretistic use—of Jung's ideas. She created conditions in which unconscious contents could be retrieved from matter itself. In terms of the history of consciousness, this amounts to regression. For a concrete object to be charged with psychological substance and to become not simply an image of something else but actually have "power" to work on its own as a "pars pro toto" hearkens back to a distant phase of human development. Jean Gebser, who offers a thorough description of five phases of human consciousness, calls it the "magical" phase (Gebser 1986). It seems that Sandplay gives us the possibility not only to reach far back into individual childhood, as analysis does, but also of regressing to analogous depths in humankind's collective childhoods.

This constitutes an incomparable advantage over other psychotherapeutic practices, but it also bears some dangers. It might explain why Sandplay is rapidly being propagated across the globe on the one hand, and yet is sometimes put off as a mystifying form of therapy on the other hand. Surely one of the main and frequently cited advantages of Sandplay is that it can directly constellate unconscious or semiconscious content that is not expressible verbally. Furthermore, as I have mentioned, it can reach so-called presymbolic regions of the psyche. Depending on the patient's willingness to accept the offer of regression in a "free and protected space," different levels of experiencing take place, regardless of the therapist's instructions. Personal memories may emerge, such as: "This is like when I used to play on the beach as a child"; or symbolic images like: "I want to pile the sand up to form a mountain." Also nonpictorial, formless, whole-body sensations or mental states might occur, such as "something is pulling me down"; "I am feeling cold and cramped"; or "everything is deathly quiet, and nothing is breathing." These are often intense experiences of the senses that cannot be connected to any specific memory. These are realms into which "the talking cure" of analysis can reach only rarely. Traumatic occurrences that were encapsulated, wordless and formless, are frequently made accessible to conscious experience. The term "presymbolic" describes something that lies beyond the boundaries of simple representation. Often the only way of getting hold of these elements is through *projective identification*. This means that the therapist must first come in contact with the patient's traumatic experience in her own body and in her own emotions. If the therapist succeeds in processing this experience by realizing that it is part of the patient's life, while at the same time filtering out the share of her own life history, then the patient can begin to depict the "inexpressible" in the sand and confront it from the outside. The patient's very inner self is reflected back from out of the sand. And though the patient formed it, until now it had been unknown and nameless. No sooner has something been formed in the sand than it is already in the process of changing. This is why anything that is made during Sandplay never just describes the "status quo," but already starts to process it as well.

Sandplay may enable us to constellate a creative process without requiring knowledge of any techniques in advance. This would make it a shortcut to a state where psychological change is possible. The shortcomings of Sandplay have to do with regression, with the possibility of travelling back to a state in which matter and psyche are not yet separated. The possible dangers are "thinking in magical terms," identification with unconscious contents, idealization of the method, and inflation. Precisely because Sandplay can release such highly potent psychological energy from an earlier level of consciousness in our developmental history, it becomes all the more important to stand securely rooted in the coordinate system of psychological and psychoanalytical basic principles. Sandplay is most effective when it is conducted within the context of analysis.

SANDPLAY WITH CHILDREN

Sandplay makes use of an innate behavior, common to all cultures, with which children react naturally and spontaneously to every difficulty, trauma, fear, or insecurity, namely play. Play belongs to a child's healthy behavioral repertoire and is the child's very own innermost way of approaching the world. One can even say children experience the world through play. It is like a filter through which all new impulses and experiences are translated into the child's own language and only thereby can become appropriated. Being a child and playing is one and the same thing. Play lies on the border between reality and imagination, which Winnicott describes as *transitional space*. Within this special area, psychological substance is shapeable, and the psyche is capable—within certain boundaries—of healing itself. Through play, certain changes take place in the psyche that serve psychological growth and differentiation. Bad experiences might, for example, be played through as often as it takes for their emotional load to be weakened. In playing, new behavioral strategies are refined and rehearsed until a better adaptation to the world is achieved. Apart from the pure joy of experimenting and expressing oneself, there is always also a purpose in play. Boring games are never played for long. Play demands risks, new challenges, finding one's own limits and trying new variations on things already familiar. This happens all by itself.

If a child is encouraged enough in its development, then the child's play will freely blossom into infinite, creative variants, and will rejoice in itself like an artwork or a bird's flight. If this process is hindered, however, then play will automatically put itself completely in the service of the child's psychological development. The themes of a play will immediately circle around whatever constitutes the blockage. In ever new and often dramatic variations, the child illustrates what is wrong, what is amiss, and how things would be if it were not for the blockage. Large amounts of psychological energy are mobilized to approach the inner and outer obstruction from all sides. Again and again the conflict is represented in play. If no help is offered from the outside, then these representations become ever more dramatic, chaotic, and cryptic to the observer. If the child's psychological development does not progress, its play will be confined within ever smaller boundaries. The variations will become fewer, until there are only very few elements left, repeating themselves. The child's surrounding situation can sometimes become so threatening that play ceases altogether. In these cases the child's psychological life is seriously and irreversibly threatened. As soon as there is even just a small prospect of change, variants and possibilities of increasing this small spark of hope will be tried out untiringly. And, quite frequently, symbols spontaneously emerge during play, which allows a new developmental level to be reached. In these cases the psyche has healed itself through play.

In Sandplay, the provision of the free and protected space and the presence of the assisting adult intensify the process, and this has saved the lives of many a child in an extremely precarious situation. Through Sandplay, they carefully began reapproaching the healthy behavior they had temporarily lost—even if this amounts to nothing more than kneading some sand for weeks on end. Something incomparably special about Sandplay becomes apparent here. An emotionally shocked and traumatized child will hardly want to use color pencils, or talk, or take part in group activities. But sitting at the sand tray—a separate, enclosed, protected area—and just patting the sand, as if its very existence first had to be tested in order to answer the question if there is indeed anything at all left in the world that will hold—this much seems to be possible. Sand is adaptable, but also solid. It can convey a calming feeling of being something simple—elemental— not frightening, that doesn't expect anything of one, and that just is.

GROUP SANDPLAY FOR CHILDREN—NEW DEVELOPMENTS

In Johannesburg (South Africa) and in Guangzhou (southern China), a simplified form of Sandplay called "Expressive Sandwork" has proven to be helpful in various aid projects for children. The children in Johannesburg came from the poorest quarters, the shack towns, and were badly looked after and emotionally traumatized. These children had never talked to a social worker about their problems, but they described their living circumstances in the sand and weren't shy to explain what each of the figures represented. Here, the Sandplay images should primarily be taken literally. A house is the actual home, and the figures are people out of the children's lives, but at the same time there are always hints of allegorical or symbolic meanings. A six-year-old boy represented in the sand how he lived in a shack with his two brothers. The figure representing the elder brother had a chain around his neck. The boy explained that this brother was mostly drunk, beating the other children, and the chain meant he was imprisoned by drinking. Questioned if there were no adults living with them, the boy answered that the parents had left a long time ago. All this information turned out to be correct and so the boys could be helped by the social workers. Being allowed to work in the sand had helped the boy over his feeling of shame and was more effective than any questioning could have been.

In another case the help came too late. A seven-year-old boy pictured how his stepfather beat his mother and threatened to kill her. There was a house, the mother, the stepfather, and the boy himself who was running to the police station. Three days after the boy's Sandplay session the mother was dead, killed by the stepfather. Fortunately the boy could be taken care of and could also continue the Sandplay sessions. In the following sessions he pictured his mourning in various ways. He pictured the grave and also himself playing with a crocodile. One could think that in this context the crocodile may symbolize his traumatized emotional world, or also the inhumane, cold-blooded aggressiveness the boy is exposed to and that he needs to process, to prevent becoming an offender himself one day. On the other hand, like every symbol the crocodile also has an opposite meaning—in this case motherly protection. In African children's stories the mother crocodile is often described carrying her young in her mouth, where they are in safety behind her sharp teeth.

These two examples, though just a tiny sample, show what immense potential Expressive Sandwork has to offer in situations such as these, where psychotherapeutic help normally does not reach.

In southern China, Expressive Sandwork in small groups is offered at private kindergartens. The success of this project allowed Sandplay to be introduced in three state-run orphanages. Not only psychotherapists work with the children there, but also teachers, psychology students, and social workers. It is not meant to replace psychotherapy but has, in remarkably short time, produced changes of behavior in emotionally disturbed children, provided they are also guaranteed basic needs (food, a minimum of emotional attention, and play). The basic principle of Sandplay remains the same in these situations. The free and protected space is provided by an adult, who has learned not to approach a child pedagogically, but to allow it every freedom of expression, no matter how incomprehensible or chaotic that might be.

I would like to close with an example of a Sandplay process—in this case of a three-year-old boy from a middle-class family in the USA—which shows how even very young children already know what it is that they require. The boy had not yet begun to speak, although his hearing was in order and his cognitive abilities normal for his age. In the first Sandplay session he took two plastic cups and began pouring sand from one to the other. This he repeated over and over again for many sessions, without taking special note of the therapist. The therapist either spoke to the child or watched in silence. Either way, the therapist made it clear that nothing more was expected of the boy than what he was already doing and that his actions were being perceived and reflected upon by another person— sometimes also verbally expressed. After a few sessions, the boy began to look up at the therapist more frequently, and eye contact became longer and longer as the sessions progressed. His play with the sand and the cups, meanwhile, continued as it had been. After three months, the boy began to speak and never had a relapse.

The meaning of his action is easily comprehensible. It is a strikingly simple representation of communication: something needs to be passed from one person to another. Apparently this principle first had to be worked out physically, by hand, as if the boy first needed to gain certainty that this form of back-and-forth can even be possible. Whatever the reasons for the delay in the boy's development had been, one can say that he first learned and practiced to speak on a prelingual level through the help of Sandplay. No symptom-oriented strategy was used in this case, and no attempt was actively made to seek out the underlying psychological reasons for the symptom. All the therapist really did during the Sandplay sessions was to assure the boy this free and protected space, and to put his own personality at the boy's disposal, in the sense of offering him a relationship. In all peace and quiet and at his own pace, the boy could assure himself of the fact that it is indeed possible for things to be transmitted from one to another: first sand from one plastic cup to the other, then eye contact between two human beings, and finally spoken words. Once he had made this experience, he was ready to speak.

Over the past years, Sandplay has established itself as an inherent part of Jungian practice. In some training institutes, experience with Sandplay is part of the curriculum. But Sandplay is also offered as one of numerous means of expression in various other types and disciplines of psychotherapy. It is sometimes also used merely for diagnostic purposes, similar to the *szeno test*. This last use is somewhat problematic, however, because in Sandplay even the first session already sets a process in motion. After children have finished such a diagnostic Sandplay session and have poured their heart and soul into the work, they often rightly feel betrayed because the process, which is often not even fully understood by diagnosticians, does not continue. Sandplay is never just a depiction of a current state but also always the beginning of a process and of change. Using Sandplay merely for the pursuit of short-term aims is like heating one's fireplace with antique furniture. The room will certainly be nice and warm, but a whole different scale of potential is not only completely overlooked, it also risks being lost.

REFERENCES

Gebser, Jean. 1986. *The ever present origin*. Athens, OH: Ohio University Press.

Kalsched, Donald. 1997. *The inner world of trauma: Archetypal defense of the personal spirit*. London: Routledge.

Pattis Zoja, Eva. 2003. Digging in the air: Inflative fantasies in Sandplay therapy. *Journal of Sandplay Therapy* 11, 1: 49–62.

Von Gontard, Alexander. 2007. *Theorie und Praxis der Sandspieltherapie, ein Handbuch aus kinderpsychiatrischer Sicht*. Stuttgart: Kohlhammer Verlag.

EVA PATTIS ZOJA holds diplomas as analyst and child analyst (C.G. Jung Institut Zurich) and is a Sandplay therapist (ISST). In private practice in Milan, Italy, she lectures, teaches, and trains Sandplay therapists in Europe, USA, China, South Africa, and Argentina.

14

THE BODY AND MOVEMENT
IN ANALYSIS

Cedrus Monte

When an individual has been swept up into the world of symbolic mysteries, nothing comes of it; nothing can come of it, unless it has been associated with the earth, unless it has occurred when that individual was in the body. . . . Only if you first return to your body, to your earth, can individuation take place; only then does the thing become true.

—C.G. JUNG *(Visions Seminar,* 1313–14)

During my mid-twenties I entered an impasse. Although I was far from being crippled, I could not stand for more than fifteen or twenty minutes without experiencing debilitating pain. To counteract the exhaustion, I slept for hours during the day. The doctor finally suggested an operation to fuse the vertebra of my lower back. This was clearly not an option for me, so I began researching different modalities of treatment. Eventually, someone told me about a little known approach called Rolfing, a method of physical manipulation developed by Ida Rolf (1990). In those days, there were only about thirty Rolfers in existence, all trained by Ida Rolf herself. Today, Rolfing is practiced worldwide.

After the series of treatments, I was structurally and psychologically different, very different. Among many other changes, I stood straighter, naturally, becoming taller by almost one-half inch; without effort, my head rested differently on my torso; my shoe size changed considerably with my feet widening, allowing greater contact with the ground; and most importantly, I no longer experienced pain, a condition which has remained to this day, decades later.

All the energy used to uphold the structural imbalance and withstand the pain was now released, available to propel me forward into life. I felt the ground beneath me as never before; I could stand more readily on my own two feet. I had the energy and strength to meet the world and was eventually able to develop and promote my own work as an artist. In Jungian terms, one might say that the negative complex around which nearly all my libido had been focused was addressed to the extent that I became less regressively bound, constructively aligned with my own individuation process, no longer at such odds with who I was and with how I could serve in the world.

Soon after I was Rolfed, I entered Reichian therapy, a somatically-oriented psychoanalytic approach developed by Wilhelm Reich. Although Reich was a colleague of both Freud and Jung, his work was largely ignored. During the two-year period of my Reichian therapy, the unconscious was approached using the combination of direct hands-on address of body armoring as well as the psychological insight that is part of Reichian work. I was able to understand the deeper psychological significance of the process that unfolded. Most significantly, I became an active participant in the process. I became increasingly sensitive to what was happening physically in my body, at the same time learning to understand the psychological dimension of my feelings and bodily sensations. What I experienced somatically was the mirror image of what I experienced psychologically. As the armoring in my body gradually released, so did the regressive pull of psychological wounds that kept me armored and self-protective.

In time, my somatic explorations as a patient began to shift into somatic training as I continued to seek out and engage other ways of working, including approaches that do not necessarily require direct, hands-on manipulation. These approaches include exercises that employ the weight and positioning of the body as leverage for releasing body armoring and increasing the flow of energy in the body. They also include ways of embodying, through movement, imaginal material from the unconscious such as dreams, waking images, archetypal energies, and psychosomatic symptoms.

During the same year I was Rolfed, I was introduced to C.G. Jung's writing. As is the experience for so many, I was deeply touched, his words giving shape and life to what had until that time lay unformed in my own mind. It would not be until some fifteen years later, however, that I would enter Jungian training in Zurich where I began to interweave Jungian psychology with my work as a visual artist and the psycho-physical realm of the body. Well into my training, I also encountered the work of other Jungians involved in body-centered analysis, including that of Joan Chodorow (1991) and Marion Woodman (1996).

I have been asked by some, "Do you work with the body in your sessions, or do you work analytically?" From my experience, there is no dichotomy between the two, between working with the body and working analytically with the unconscious. This is not just a theoretical idea. As the reader might understand from the personal story I have shared, it is a deeply felt, experiential knowing of the spirit-matter continuum Jung so carefully traced in alchemical literature and which became pivotal in his work, including his understanding of synchronicity. From my own perspective as an analyst, the "soulwork" that analytical psychology offers can only be fully entered through the experience of the body-mind, psyche-soma unity, a unity that can be understood as the territory itself of the analytical opus. Any separation of body and mind, soma and psyche, in this context is artificial and unnecessarily divisive.

Before describing elements of a somatic, body-centered session, I would like to introduce two points the reader may find useful to understanding how I view the body within analytical psychology. The first discusses the transference; the second, quality of movement.

THE TRANSFERENCE IN BODY-CENTERED ANALYSIS

Traditionally, the transference in analytical psychology is formed between the analyst and analysand at conscious and unconscious, knowable and unknowable, archetypal and personal dimensions of interaction. Additionally, an important aspect of the transference describes the analyst as "holding" the inherent whole-making, or S/self-healing of the analysand, mirroring it back to the analysand until he or she is able to claim and integrate the whole-making process more readily and more independently.

The same is true for a body-centered Jungian approach. There are, however, from my perspective, notable differences, described in part by the following.

Assuming that individuals are open to working somatically, it is possible for them to gain insight and understanding of unconscious material directly through the body. Even at the beginning of the work, this can take place without the intervention of interpretation from the analyst. This is only possible, however, as a result of the analyst's direct experience of bodily-triggered insight through his or her own personal work. Only then can the analyst encourage the analysand to grow in trust and confidence regarding what is offered up somatically.

I understand this somatic offering as the wisdom of the body, otherwise expressed as the Self contained within the flesh, as the flesh itself (Monte), the experience of which becomes a vehicle for rebuilding and strengthening one's experience of wholeness. Working somatically, the Healer archetype—initially transferred or projected onto the analyst—can more readily become embodied in the analysand. Through direct understanding at the instinctual, bodily level, insight is more fully the analysand's, thus engendering a greater sense of autonomy from the outset. An individual can retain the memory of inner experience more readily than outside interpretation. To this end, accessing bodily knowing can become an immediate resource for positive support and psychic sustenance. We discover that we can rely on ourselves more readily. We learn that we are able to access knowing through the ever-present resource of our own body.

We know what we know because we have experienced it in the flesh of our own being, not because someone has told us it is true.

The transference phenomenon in body-centered analysis or other forms of psychotherapeutic bodywork can, therefore, move quite readily from the interaction between analyst and analysand as primary or ultimate, to bodily experience as the medium which can reflect wisdom, self-awareness and the experience of Self. In other words, the transference field can shift from the interaction between analyst and analysand to a more intra-psychic exchange—that is, between the analysand's experience through the body and the ensuing self-reflection. The analysand relies far less on interpretation from the analyst and is, rather, encouraged to give voice to somatic experience and, most importantly, to the meaning of that experience.

Thus, there is a turning from the more hierarchical approach with the analyst as "the one who knows," to an approach that fosters direct, instinctual wisdom—the somatic Sophia.

MOVEMENT AS A VEHICLE TO AND FROM THE UNCONSCIOUS

It is often the case that in dance and dance-like movement one expresses a feeling, an image, or a sensation; for example, sadness, sitting alone by a river, deadness or rigidity. Since the images provided by this kind of expression are quite often recognizable, one is given a comfortable frame of reference. While this approach is by no means to be excluded from the repertoire of a body-centered analytical approach, the broader idea of movement, for me personally, lies in deeper layers than the expressive one.

In deeper layers, movement is no longer employed in the body to express an image; rather, movement arises in the body as a result of being impressed and moved by the image.

To enter this realm one needs to trust enough, one needs to risk the perceived terrors of entering the darkness of what is not known. Put differently, one allows somatic impulses to momentarily take over without trying to devise a way to express or to control what emerges. When we can empty ourselves of preconceived ideas about how we should move, we create space to receive an impression or impulse from the unconscious. We can allow ourselves to be guided into the movement's own meaning.

Further, the movement becomes that which is being moved. It is not a representation of it. It is not a pantomime. We become, in our physical being, the image from the unconscious: You dream of a door opening. . . . How is "a door opening" experienced within you, as you?

When speaking about dream images Jung says, "Image and meaning are identical, and as the first takes shape, so the latter becomes clear" (Jung CW 8, para. 402). The impulse or image in the body, in movement, also carries its own meaning: as the movement unfolds, the meaning becomes clear. For this to happen, however, one needs the willingness to be moved, to surrender one's ego long enough to be pierced by the visitation from the unconscious in impulse and movement.

As I experience it, accessing the wisdom of the body lies in the ability to listen and to let ourselves be moved by something greater than ourselves. We no longer move our ego, but we are moved by that which moves us. Only when we wait, without being attached to outcome, can that which longs to be born from the unconscious be birthed.

To help illuminate these ideas, I offer the following journal entry from personal somatic explorations:

The other day, my friend took me to a new place in the forest. This would be a good place to die, I thought, to just let go and allow my spirit to find release, to let my body dissolve into the earth.

The challenge for me has been to let my rational, conscious awareness be as subsumed as possible by the impulses of the natural world, including my own body. I have come to realize, however, that I scarcely have enough intelligence to do this. I would risk saying that at one point, maybe twenty-five years ago, this intelligence was stronger in me, but over the years the need to be someone has made me dull. I have become so dense, so filled with information and thoughts and expectations, the natural world has a difficult time finding a way in.

When I returned to the forest this morning, I thought I would work on the "movement of dying." I had a plan, in other words. I would do this and this and this, and then this . . . which is, of course, no real dying at all. Fortunately, I found a way out of this folly or, better put, a way out found me.

Standing in the midst of the trees, they found a way in. There was no longer "me" trying to move. For a grace-filled few moments, the trees were moving me, speaking a kinetic, wordless text. By grace again, "my plans" to die deceased. Through the earth and into my feet old roots and long memories filled my limbs. A tempest storm raged. Mute cries of outrage and tortured screams. Whose memories were these? Whose tempest storm? Were these the trees speaking, or were these my own flesh memories unearthed and uprooted?

I believe the only answer to this question is, Yes!

This place of trees was speaking the same speaking in me.

ANALYTICAL BODY-CENTERED WORK IN PRACTICE

Somatic exploration in individual sessions can take many forms. Perhaps a dream has very strong images that beckon. It is also possible to explore certain archetypal, polar-opposite energies particularly germane to the mover: depletion/vitality, creation/destruction. An embodied exploration of polarized energies can often yield a "third" element arising unexpectedly and surprisingly to inspire resolution.

In the sessions and courses I conduct there is no specific method employed. Rather, I listen very carefully to the emerging needs of the moment and then draw from a variety of approaches gathered over a period of almost thirty years.

Within the context of this essay, I can offer only limited examples. Although it is virtually impossible to communicate the actual experiences in words, hopefully the following will illustrate at least some dimension of the ideas here presented.

This is from the journal of a person with whom I worked over a concentrated period of time and is used here by permission from the participant:

I focused on a dream I had . . . about my father. As I dropped more deeply into his gestureless gesture [in the dream], I noticed how strongly my attention was pulled to my/his left arm—the one which was broken and torn off by the oncoming car when I was 4 years old. And sewed back on and held together by metal pins for the rest of his life. As I dreamed into his body, as I sank deeper and deeper, away from my mental body and into micro-sensations, I was aware that my left arm was completely cold! The rest of my body was warm.

Re-emerging from this process, feeling my father in a visceral way, somehow opened the door of compassion [for him]. He was tormented by the death of my brother, his favorite son, and his love/disease of alcohol.

I remember Cedrus' words: "When we drop deeply into our experience, physical, psychic and emotional defenses begin to crumble. . . . Let the image drop from the mind into the body. That which listens, listens from the inside. Let the body become the ear in listening. If you feel like you're falling apart, that's perfect. If we stay intact, we'll never open up enough to be able to listen well."

As mentioned above, I also work with the embodiment of analysands' images that come from other than dreams. In this instance, we worked with a painting the analysand made when starting the analysis.

This particular painting was of a female torso standing on a surging sea of fang-like waves. Streaming out of the pelvic area was a large arc of dark red paint. She said she had no idea what the painting was about, but that she just "had to paint it." She was very concerned about the dark red area in the pelvic region.

I asked if she wanted to explore the painting through her own body, especially since it was an image of the body that she had painted. Although she expressed fear about what would come up, her desire to learn more took precedence. I asked if she would like to lie down on the floor; I put a pillow under her head and covered her with a blanket, letting her know that she could stop at any time. As she explored the image in her pelvic area by deeply connecting with that part of her body, that is, by moving her awareness down, listening, waiting for any impulses or sensations, she began to cry. She cried for a very long time, without saying anything. After she returned from this internal voyage, she said she realized the painting was about the abortion she had had years ago.

As a result of letting herself be guided by the body's impulses and sensations, prompted by the image from the unconscious in the form of her spontaneous painting, she was able to connect with her pain and grief. She was able to mourn the loss of her child and begin to release the oppressive shame and guilt that had engulfed her as a result. She had never told anyone before, holding the experience down, deep in her body for many years. Her long-held fear of never having a successful relationship or a child dissolved in the course of the analysis into a loving marriage and three beautiful children.

EPILOGUE

It is my experience, as both patient and practitioner, that working through the body to access the unconscious is one of the most empowering venues for self-generative healing. Working through the body, we include aspects of life that have become dangerously marginalized. We begin to heal the wounding split that is created by the disenfranchisement of the very thing this approach embraces: the wisdom of the body, the somatic Sophia.

REFERENCES

Chodorow, Joan. 1991. *Dance therapy and depth psychology: The moving imagination.* London: Routledge.

Jung, C.G. 1998.*Visions Seminar 2: Notes of the seminar given in 1930–1934*. London: Routledge.

———. 1954/1960. On the nature of the psyche. In CW 8.

Monte, Cedrus. 2005. Numen of the flesh. *Quadrant* 35, 2: 11–31.

Rolf, Ida P. 1978/1990. *Rolfing and physical reality*. Rochester, Vermont: Healing Arts Press.

Woodman, Marion. 1996. *Dancing in the flames*. Boston: Shambhala.

CEDRUS MONTE, Ph.D., is a graduate of the C.G. Jung Institute in Zurich. Originally from the San Francisco Bay Area, she now lives and practices in Zurich, Switzerland. The organizing principle in all her endeavors has been the vitalizing force of the creative impulse.

PART THREE

THE
ANALYTIC
PROCESS

INTRODUCTION TO
THE ANALYTIC PROCESS
Murray Stein

In his late writings, Jung's preferred metaphor for discussing the analytic process was the alchemical opus, as evidenced in his use of the alchemical text, *Rosarium Philosophorum*, in the major work "On the psychology of the transference" (CW 16). With this trope he meant to communicate a manifold of possibilities for transformation inherent in the enterprise of analysis. In the analytic process, he argued, both reductive and synthetic movements run in tandem, the one deconstructing a fixed and one-sided conscious position and identity, the other building up a new conscious set of attitudes, images, and identities grounded in a union of conscious and emergent unconscious elements. How contemporary Jungian psychoanalysts work to bring about the conditions that will generate these results is the subject of discussion in this section.

The reflection begins with Paul Ashton's evocative and poetic chapter, "Beginnings and Endings." The formal analytic process has a start and a finish, although as Ashton makes explicit the beginning and end are not so clear-cut when one considers the broader context of a lifelong individuation process. Kazuhiko Higuchi picks up on this theme of boundaries in his reflection on analysis in Japanese culture, which is famous for its indirect style of communication.

All contemporary Jungian psychoanalysts subscribe to the importance of establishing a tight and solid analytic "container" in which to practice the analytic opus. In alchemical parlance, this is referred to as a *vas bene clausum* ("a well-sealed vessel"). August Cwik writes insightfully about the nature of this essential structure in the chapter, "From Frame through Holding to Container." The *vas* is a kind of womb, the place of growth where a new type of consciousness can be nourished and out of which it can eventually emerge and become viable and independent.

The process that takes place within the vessel of analysis was indelibly named by a patient of Freud's when she called it a "talking cure," and so it has remained to a large extent in Jungian work, though with some modifications and extensions as the chapters by Dougherty, Pattis, and Monte in the previous section show. A chief difference between the classical Freudian and Jungian forms of the talking cure was that in the former the talking was done almost exclusively by the patient, whereas in the latter talking took the form of an active dialogue between two people, analyst and analysand. The work of transformation in Jungian psychoanalysis is collaborative, akin to what is illustrated so often in alchemical pictures that show the alchemist working with a *soror mystica* in the laboratory or two figures in a bath, and so forth. Claus Braun and Lilian Otscheret in their chapter, "Dialogue," discuss three paradigmatic models of dialogue that characterize various schools and eras and argue that Jung's own stated model is close to the contemporary view of intersubjectivists.

At the heart of the analytic process is, of course, the relationship that develops between analyst and analysand. Jean Knox employs her extensive study of attachment theory in early infancy and childhood to discuss the profound connections that develop between the two protagonists in the analytic drama in the chapter, "The Analytic Relationship." Linda Carter continues this discussion in "Countertransference and Intersubjectivity," and she adds further insights from contemporary science and psychoanalysis to the Jungian perspective on the role that the analyst's psyche plays in the process of change and transformation within the analytic container.

To the views expressed in several of the foregoing chapters Angela Connolly poses some critical questions, which deepen the reflection on how analysts can effectively stimulate change in the psyches of their analysands. Her chapter, "Analyzing Projections, Fantasies, and Defenses," highlights the importance of maintaining a degree of objectivity and analytic distance even within the intimate intersubjective field generated in analysis.

One of the perennial perplexities of the analytical relationship circles around the perceived presence of gender, which is the theme of Joy Schaverien's reflection in "Gender and Sexuality: Imaginal, Erotic Encounters." As Schaverien picks up on the theme of gender and its implications for sexuality within the alchemical field constellated by the analytic dyad, so Birgit Heuer introduces a topic that might be considered its polar opposite in the chapter, "The Experience of the Numinous in the Consulting Room." Between the two chapters one might discern the historic tension that arcs between a traditional psychoanalytic emphasis on instinct on the one hand and a classical Jungian emphasis on spirit on the other. In his late theoretical work, "On the Nature of the Psyche" (CW 8), Jung describes this arc as a rainbow with one end of the spectrum merging with the body and the other disappearing into pure spirit. Both of these authors recognize the profound links between sexuality and spirituality and demonstrate how contemporary Jungian psychoanalysts work in these highly charged energy fields.

Lest we forget that analysis and psychotherapy take place within specific cultural settings, Kazuhiko Higuchi's chapter, "Jungian Psychoanalysis in the Context of Japanese Culture," reminds us that to work with the psyche of individuals deeply implies also encountering and engaging cultural habits and expectations. His fascinating article tells of how a method of analysis originating in a central European cultural context has been taken up and subtly transformed in the very specific and traditional Eastern cultural context of Japan.

15

BEGINNINGS AND ENDINGS

Paul W. Ashton

"Once upon a time . . ." or "In the beginning . . ." is how the stories start that are about the becoming of consciousness. In a strictly symbolic sense, "beginning" carries the suggestion of something positive, open-ended, fresh, possible, opening the door onto a new world, birth and growth.

"In the 'beginning'—in truth before the 'beginning'—myth and religion identify a matrix of protean images, 'pre-creation' symbols we may call them, which hold the potential for all that is to be created. These are the Abyss, the Void, Chaos, Alienation, and Darkness which enshrouds them all; and, of course, a Creator." So writes Louis Stewart (Stewart 1995, 1). I would lump all those images together under the general title of "void" and suggest that even the creative spirit is part of that void (Ashton 2007). And I would say that the dark void of painful unknowing, "in the beginning," may imperceptibly become the white void where it is acceptable to not know. This state, which Bion called "O," to stand for "ultimate, unknowable reality" (Bion 1967, 145), is one in which we can embrace the unknown with awe of it rather than shame for ourselves, and it is this state which can be thought of as the aimed-for end-point of an analysis if not of a life.

There are various levels or aspects of consciousness—mental, symbolic, subsymbolic, sensorimotor, instinctual (Sylvia Perera 2006, Seminar in Cape Town). In the beginning, something in one or more of those domains is missing, and towards the end something is found even though what is found may not be what was sought. According to psychoanalyst Gilda de Simone, the themes of aims and endings are interlinked so that "(t)he level reached at the end cannot be viewed separately from that at the beginning" (de Simone 1997, 1). For her a satisfactory conclusion is tied to the solution of the initial conflicts; certainly we need an initial plan to help us asses whether the conclusion we have arrived at is adequate or not. (This is particularly true in "evidence based" assessments of treatment.)

Jung writes: "Initial dreams are often amazingly lucid and clear-cut" (Jung 1934/1966, para. 313). He then suggests that dreams may lose their clarity as the work progresses and that similarly the analyst may feel that s/he has a good understanding of the patient at the start of an analysis but as time goes on s/he becomes more confused. He writes further that there is "nothing more unbearable to the patient than to be always understood" (ibid.). I understand this to be about knowing and not knowing. These aspects must somehow be held together. The knowing or understanding will always be only of an aspect of a person and the not knowing may be of his or her totality, which can never be completely known. Paradoxically, patients who begin analysis in a confused and alienated state may begin to "feel themselves" more and more even as the analyst's understanding wanes.

I remember one ten-year-old whose mother was finding him difficult to handle. He drew a picture of a boy surfing in front of a huge wave, and in the wave behind the surfer was an enormous shark. When I interpreted his anxiety he retreated behind an impenetrable defense from which the analysis never recovered. For him to be known as the fearless "bruiser" was more important than being known in his completeness.

T. S. Eliot articulates the paradoxical nature of beginnings and endings in *The Four Quartets* where he says: "What we call the beginning is often the end / And to make an end is to make a beginning." (Eliot 1974, 221) Or, more succinctly: "In my beginning is my end" (ibid., 196).

Becoming more conscious results in the island of the ego, of consciousness, becoming larger, and thus its shoreline or the point of contact between ego and self, the ego/self connection, becomes bigger. (Murray Stein seminar in Cape Town, 1997) The unconscious, being infinite, does not diminish while consciousness increases. So we may become more and more conscious of quite how unconscious we are (a painful awareness) and yet as the ego-self axis becomes more accessible we feel a greater and greater connection with "what is."

In the beginning there is a longing for preconscious oneness, the participation mystique. As consciousness increases, so does differentiation and so the sense of oneness diminishes. In *Psychology and Alchemy* (1944) Jung describes how some people leave analysis for one or other reason but others just hang on. This may look like a continued searching for union with another, a sort of dependence, but it may also finally lead to the union of opposites within a person and so toward wholeness or individuation (quoted in Fordham 1974, 101).

One patient past middle age entered analysis because of feelings of depression and depletion and a sense of meaninglessness. The emptiness surrounding him began to be filled with a certain degree of awe, and he began to feel a state of connection with the world. When I was away for about six months he felt fine and thus stopped his analysis, but a month after my return he began it again. My understanding was that he valued the presence of an attentive other without whom he was unable to maintain the engagement with his psyche that he needed in order to feel that life was meaningful.

Soon after his "new beginning," he had a dream that intimated that his analysis was quite meaningless and only consisted in a construction of meaning out of the meaninglessness that was his dream-world. A week after this he was shocked to dream of sleeping with his mother. Although he knew she was dead, she was relating to him. At the same time as sharing her bed, he envisioned her on a raised black marble throne, like a goddess. Later, he was taking a shower in a narrow black bath and was overcome with guilt and shame as he remembered what he had done. (These shameful feelings stayed with him during the next few days.) Later that night he dreamed of helping his youngest son search for a toy saxophone in a pile of junk that had fallen off his bed. A young girl stated: "The sun is shining which will make it easier to find." Sure enough, they discover a full-sized golden trumpet which he, surprisingly, was able to play adequately. It is morning, the sun is shining, and there is dew about.

The shame engendered by dreaming of sleeping with his mother virtually closed down my patient's capacity to reflect or be curious about his dream material. But having been able to cope with that shame through my understanding and acceptance, he was open to the transformative energies from within. Perhaps the stopping of his analysis helped him separate from his analyst so that he was doing his own thing, but doing his own thing brought him to the realization that he needed certain aspects of his analyst to aid him in his work. He could start again, not dependent on his analyst but able to use him.

Some individuals start their analysis before they actually meet their analyst, but others may come for many sessions before they can be said to have really begun their analysis. It has been said that 100 hours of analysis are needed before a deeper process is begun, and this is why seeing a patient who has been in a prior analysis is often rewarding, since they can get straight into it.

Recently I took a six-month sabbatical from my practice, and soon after my return I was telephoned by someone who had had me recommended to him by one of my patients four months previously. This middle-aged man had been powerfully affected by reading a book by James Hollis that had been given him by the person who recommended me. In his mind, it slowly transpired, wise James Hollis and "brilliant local analyst" became conflated, and I could not say anything that was not deeply helpful to him. It was flattering, although also anxiety producing, to have an intelligent patient who was deeply affected by the "wisdom" of my interpretations, but I also realized that he had idealized me long before we met and had probably been having "conversations" with me that were entirely driven by his projections.

I have recently been alerted to the fact that the Internet makes one as an analyst potentially more "knowable" to the patient/analysand than one was before its common usage. If you have published, patients may have read about the author with avidity, and it is surprising what can be discovered by an enterprising surfer. This means that the analyst may be better known to the patient than the patient to the analyst, and the analyst will probably be unaware of the fact that he is far from being a "blank screen" even at the first session.

Freud begins his chapter "On Beginning the Treatment" with a reference about selecting patients and makes the suggestion that in the absence of knowledge about a particular patient it is wise to see him or her "provisionally," for an assessment period of one to two weeks (Freud 1958, 124ff.). This seems to have been particularly to uncover cases of schizophrenia, which would not have been amenable to treatment. He then advises that the patient be told of the length of time necessary and given details of the frame that he or she is expected to keep to. Freud used to "rent" out the hours to a patient and see him or her from three to six times a week. From his point of view, the beginning of analysis was a delicate time during which the (positive) transference should develop as it was this transference that would hold the patient in the analysis in spite of later unavoidable vicissitudes.

Even in an established analysis each separate session has a beginning, and these may be differently problematic. They may constellate dread in either the analyst or the analysand; "Can I be what he or she wants me to be: Clever enough, warm enough, even distant enough, mature enough?" On the other hand, beginnings may be an expression of hope or renewal, and the expectation may be of something positive rather than negative. Each fresh beginning may be an opportunity and a pressure on the therapeutic couple to do it better.

Perhaps because of its intrinsically negative connotations, "ending" (which suggests closing off, shutting down, completing, the loss of possibility, closing the door on the past and the future, death and burial) has received more attention than "beginning" in the psychological literature. De Simone stresses the "continuous and inexhaustible possibility of change." This means that no analysis can ever be complete, and she uses the word "unsaturatedness" to describe that incompleteness. I like her suggestion that we could think of analysis being "interrupted" rather than "concluded" as, after a termination, this gives permission for the patient to reconnect with his or her analyst as necessary. She states: "analysis as a concrete experience is terminable" and yet "it offers interminable possibilities for experience" (de Simone 1997, 60–61).

In a chapter on "The Post-Analytic Phase," she questions whether "the ending of analysis (is) the conclusion of a process or only of a relationship" (ibid., 63). This again is a useful differentiation that permits a separation in one's mind between the internal and the external process. For some it is true that it is only when the analytic relationship (in the external world) has ended that the deepest connection with his or her own self, individuation, can take place.

Relationships end when projections do not fit anymore. That ending makes possible a new beginning. Every end can be a beginning. Beginnings and endings are thus multiple, repetitive and seemingly circular. In fact, they are closer to being spiral in that each round is always in a slightly different place. The initial beginning and the final ending take place in the void.

There are many questions such as when is the ending and who decides and even which part of whom it is that decides. Fordham differentiates between "stopping" and "ending." For him, stopping is a unilateral decision by either analyst or analysand, whereas ending "is separation to which both analyst and patient agree" (Fordham 1974, 100). One reason for stopping is when the sense of connection to "the All," or "Oneness," is seen to have no relevance to, or at least to be independent of, the analyst. Ending may seem appropriate when it feels that nothing more can be attained or learned.

Analysis begins with certain hopes, desires, or purposes, and stopping is sometimes because of a realization that the analyst is unable to meet those expectations. But this disillusionment with the analyst or with the process may lead either to a termination or to the beginning of a deeper analysis.

One sensitive patient arrived for a session on a public holiday when I was not working. Certain that I had not informed her, she came to one more session to tell me how bad I was before disappearing for good. A male analysand became very disillusioned with me when I let him know that I did not read the many dreams that he left in my hands and only addressed the ones that he had spoken about. It was touch and go whether he would stay in the analysis as he was so angry with me and felt so betrayed, but talking about his expectations and sense of betrayal resulted in a new depth to our work together.

Sometimes the disillusionment or sense of failure is felt by the patient within him or herself. S/he feels that s/he disappoints the analyst, cannot meet his/her desires, and then s/he may leave because of that.

It is not often that we achieve or enjoy a perfect ending. I had been seeing a latency child for about two years because of his lingering distress following the loss of his mother through cancer in infancy. This had resulted in his sometimes acting out violently at school and demanding more than his share of attention from his stepmother. We had been going through a period of play in the sand-tray where he was often in opposition to me and deliberately flaunted any "ethical" rules so that he could demolish my "forces." I might interpret these attacks as him letting me know what it felt like to be amorally destroyed as when his mother died, and the attacks slowly abated. Soon thereafter he said that although he enjoyed coming to see me he no longer felt it was necessary and would like to stop in the not too distant future. After consultation with his father and stepmother we set a date four weeks in the future and deliberately "counted down" to that date. He and I and his parents all felt that the ending was entirely appropriate and congruent.

Although I have written above that the analytic process, as a spiral, begins and ends in a void, the void of meaninglessness or of the unknown, I have realized that I find it difficult to allow it to end there. When I am accompanying someone through an Active Imagination, I do not like it to end when there is no "solid ground," and in spite of being a realist pessimist, I generally allow an Active Imagination to end when meaning is present. I encourage keeping on through the dark emptiness until something positive emerges. Contrarily, when there is light and sense and connection I am unlikely to suggest an Active Imagination "to see where it goes" because we are already where we want to be. In other words, although I do not suggest to an analysand what s/he should think, I do weight the process in the direction of meaningfulness. I am unlikely to suggest termination when my patient is in a black hole.

Some would say that ending is never okay because the work is never complete! But perhaps one could say that an ending could happen when s/he can maintain the process by her/himself, or, more appropriately, when the person can maintain the process that s/he wants for her/himself by her/himself. Even after the analyst and analysand stop seeing each other, the analysis continues. What the analyst has learned becomes assimilated and is used for other patients, and what the patient has internalized, in terms of the analyst and the analytical process, continues to affect him or her.

From the perspective of void states, it may be said that a person enters analysis because of a void inside. He stays in analysis because, when he is in the presence of the analyst, the void feels tolerable. He may leave when the void becomes desirable and he needs to be alone in order to experience it. For this to happen the analyst needs to be nonimpinging so that the individual can experience, in a nonthreatening way, being alone in the presence of the analyst (Winnicott 1965, 29–36).

Endings are rarely satisfying for the analyst. They may leave a sense of loss, experienced as a feeling of emptiness or void within the analyst, or they bring relief which may be tinged with guilt ("Did I do enough for him/her?") or shame ("I am an inadequate analyst").

During my years as an analyst there have only been a handful of individuals who I hoped would leave. One was a young professional who had had it made a condition of being permitted to continue her training that she attend psychoanalysis. She did not want to be there, and the material that began to be uncovered was too excruciating for her to assimilate. I began to think that one day she might kill me, and I used to hide sharp objects such as scissors and the letter opener before her session. Her capacity to curl up in her chair and fall asleep I welcomed with relief, but, nevertheless, when she did end the analysis and change her career I felt (along with the release) that I had let her down in some way.

There is no true end to the analytic process, one simply goes deeper or experiences oneself in life more fully. But that process does not have to take place in the presence of the original analyst. A "trial separation" could be to assess whether a patient is able to keep the process going in the absence of the analyst rather than noticing despondently how many complexes he or she falls into. I used to feel that one was either in analysis or out of analysis. If you were "in," that meant seeing your analyst frequently and regularly, and if "out" then you did not see your analyst at all. I am now much more flexible and feel that a person can dip in again for a few sessions, perhaps to refuel, perhaps to reinstate the therapeutic-observer within her/him. This is long-term work, and the analyst should remain available for this "postanalytic phase." But then when is that protracted connection a dependence that is unhealthy for both the analyst and his/her patient and when is it simply a healthy albeit prolonged association? This can be likened to the relationship to parents from whom some individuals never separate, and thus never take on their own lives, whereas others separate completely even though that may mean cutting themselves off from a potential source of something positive. Yet others maintain a lifelong connection that changes over time as the life stages are cycled through. The relationship with one's parents does not end as one leaves home, and neither does the relationship to one's analyst, especially the internal analyst, end when one leaves analysis.

Jung states: "Besides being the prima materia of the lowly beginning as well as the lapis as the highest goal, Mercurius is also the process which lies between, and the means by which it is effected. He is the beginning, middle, and end of the work" (Jung 1943/1967, para. 283). If we accept this description and T. S. Eliot's statement, "In my beginning is my end," then the separation of beginnings from endings becomes impossible.

And yet not only must we try to manage the beginnings and endings of an analysis but also the sessions within an analysis. To do this we should wonder how they are negotiated. It has often been noted that material is brought up at the very end of a session. Is this because session time is too short or because the analysand is ambivalent about becoming fully conscious of whatever it is that s/he raises? Sometimes that which is raised in this way drops into the void never to be seen again, but sometimes it seems to fill the gap between sessions, bridging the emptiness. At times it may seem like a seduction that entices the analyst to grant a little more time or perhaps a Scheherazade figure, by evoking the analyst's curiosity, is ensuring that she is not "terminated." Her analyst will want to know how her story will unfold.

There are some who linger and must be practically forced to leave at the end of a session whereas others tend to watch the clock, seeming to hate being told "it is time." The end of a session, "the mini-death" or "mini-termination," may be a rehearsal of the final ending and can be used by both parties as an indicator of progress or readiness for that termination. One of my patients used to "rent" the first and last sessions of my working week until I went on sabbatical. After my return she changed her times so that we saw each other at the end of my first day of the week and at the beginning of my last day. It seemed to me that the way that she uses the analysis has changed. In the beginning the analysis was a container for her very existence, but now it has simply become part of her working week. Each session-ending is no longer a cataclysmic event, and this suggests her progression toward the possibility of being able to tolerate ending the analysis in the future.

Although I have Bion's injunction to engage with each patient "without memory or desire" ringing in my head, this is not quite as easy as it sounds (Bion 1967, 143ff.). I am aware of many emotions during the course of an analytic hour and aware too that beginnings and endings are tied up with those emotions and may be part of their expression or be used to dull my awareness of them.

But if we can, like Eliot, see that "The end is where we start from" then we can optimistically embrace the world of possibility that our patients are moving into as they move away from us . . . that Brave New World.

REFERENCES

Ashton, Paul. 2007. *From the brink: An exploration of the void from a depth psychological perspective*. London: Karnac.

De Simone, Gilda. 1997. *Ending analysis: Theory and technique*. London: Karnac.

Eliot, T. S. 1974. *Collected poems 1909–1962*. London: Faber and Faber.

Fordham, Michael. 1969. On terminating analysis. In *Technique in Jungian analysis*, ed. Michael Fordham, Rosemary Gordon, Judith Hubback, and Kenneth Lambert, 100–107. London: William Heinemann Medical Books Ltd.

Freud, S. 1958. *Collected works*, vol. 12. London: Hogarth Press.

Jung, C.G. 1934/1966. The practical use of dream-analysis. In CW 16.

———. 1943/1967 The spirit Mercurius. In CW 13.

Stewart, Louis. 1995. The primal symbols of pre-creation. (Copyright the author, used by kind permission of Joan Chodorow.)

Wheelwright, Joseph. 1994. Termination. In *Jungian analysis*, ed. Murray Stein, 111–19. La Salle and London: Open Court.

Winnicott, Donald. 1965. *The maturational processes and the facilitating environment*. London: Hogarth.

PAUL W. ASHTON, M.D., is a psychiatrist and Jungian psychoanalyst and a training analyst with the South African Association of Jungian Analysts. He practices in Cape Town, South Africa. He has published a monograph entitled *From the Brink* and edited a collection of essays, *Evocations of Absence*.

16

FROM FRAME THROUGH HOLDING TO CONTAINER

August J. Cwik

This chapter will discuss three rich metaphors for the structure in which analytic process occurs: the frame, holding, and the container (Siegelman 1990). These tropes have become part of our psychoanalytic lexicon because of their ability to evoke the experience of being in a truly healing analytic space. They are interrelated but form a continuum from the concrete to the "spiritual" or nonmaterial dimensions of the therapeutic situation. These interwoven elements form a psychological membrane that protects and allows the complex system of analysis to occur.

Every Jungian psychoanalysis is informed by Jung's fundamental insight that the relationship of analyst to analysand is dialectical in nature and forms "a third thing" (Jung 1946a). The nature and experience of this unconscious third during analysis directs the process at any given moment and is shaped by underlying archetypal patterns. Both participants are mutually transformed by an analysis that goes to any depth, resulting in deeper felt connections to the unconscious in both participants. This in turn leads to being able to live a more fully symbolic life—a life lived with a sense of aliveness imbued with meaning and purpose. Analytic structure, with its three components of frame, holding, and container, supports and facilitates the functioning of this system and leads to the individuation of both analyst and analysand.

"Frame"—the word itself denotes a sense of rigidity in the structure that surrounds, literally frames, the therapeutic process. The reasons to have a solid and consistent frame in therapy and analysis are legion. Langs (1979) extensively explores the frame in analysis as well as the significance of listening to the symbolic communications of the patient. He lays out the value of the setting of treatment and the general ground rules of therapy: confidentiality, the setting of fees, setting of place and time, proper boundaries and limits, and the basic stance of the therapist (1973). He often goes into great detail about concrete aspects of the

169

office environment, even to the extent of questioning whether a tissue box should be offered by an analyst. He forces us into awareness that anything and everything can be significant in its impact on the patient. Analysts tend to have a one-size-fits-all mentality, and Langs finds verification of his theses in the immediacy of patients' unconscious responses. Using the idea of "derivative communications" based around adaptive contexts or triggers that stimulate the unconscious of the patient, he demonstrates time and again that patients themselves unconsciously monitor the intactness of the frame and quickly respond to any alteration in ground rules. At best, he provides a hard line *ethical* critique for any tendency toward "freewheeling analysis." When it veers from the standard operating procedure, it needs to be questioned. Goodheart goes the furthest to integrate these ideas on the importance of the frame into a Jungian perspective. His work provides a much needed corrective for any laxity around the maintenance of solid boundaries. The secure frame fosters the translation of actions and emotions into words.

The shadow side of this "solidness," which can become unbending and inalterable dedication to frame for its own sake, is addressed by Winnicott who sees the analytic framework as a possible expression of the analyst's *hatred* of the patient. He writes, "the end of the hour, the end of the analysis, the rules and regulations, these all come in as expressions of [the analyst's] hate [of the patient], just as the good interpretations are expressions of love, and symbolical of good food and care" (Winnicott 1945, 147). These words derive a good deal of their persuasive power from the fact that analysts do express their hate in these actions. This is immediately recognizable by any analyst as part of the experience with virtually every patient. Winnicott is recognizing/interpreting the unspoken expression of hate that analysts unconsciously and preconsciously experience (often accompanied by a feeling of relief) in "throwing the patient out" (by ending each meeting on time), and by establishing the limits of what they will provide for patients. Moreover, analysts' fear of the destructiveness of their hatred toward patients can lead to destructive breaches of the frame (Ogden 2001).

Langs finds the unconscious to be not only a receptacle for repressed and unwanted impulses, thoughts and feelings, but also a "deep unconscious wisdom subsystem system" (Langs 1994, 24). Searles posits that even infants "can be viewed as an intended psychotherapist . . . to help the other to fulfill his or her human psychological potentialities" (Searles 1979, 381). This type of reaction from the unconscious is attempting to "heal" an unwitting analyst who breaks a boundary by providing *valid unconscious perceptions*, as opposed to transference projections, to rectify the situation. Patients need analysts who can function analytically and not act out beyond the rules of treatment. Although Langs has been criticized for expressing his assumptions with undue certitude (see Siegelman, 1990 for an excellent critique of Langs), it must be stated that he offers a bracing way to listen to patients who are desperately crying out for a therapist who can be reliably and usefully present.

The structure of analysis is, however, so much more than just the concrete parameters of the frame. As McCurdy states: "Structure is not an *a priori* entity used or provided by an analyst, but rather a complex of several interrelated areas of the analytical process, involving issues that range from the atmosphere of interchange to the technique of the analyst" (McCurdy 1995, 82). While Jung had the genius to see that a "third" was created in the analytic setting, he did not describe how this unconscious construction is experienced and utilized in the clinical encounter. In *The Psychology of the Transference*, he even notes: "The reader will not find an account of the clinical phenomena of transference in this book" (Jung 1946a, para. 165). Nevertheless, Jung was the first to present an interactive model of analysis in which the analyst is fully engaged in an embodied way. This understanding is demonstrated by statements such as the following:

> It is inevitable that the doctor should be influenced to a certain extent and even that his nervous health should suffer. He quite literally "takes over" the sufferings of his patient and shares them with him. (ibid., para. 358)

> The doctor, by voluntarily and consciously taking over the psychic sufferings of the patient, exposes himself to the overpowering contents of the unconscious and hence also to their inductive action. (ibid., para. 364)

> The patient, by bringing an activated unconscious content to bear upon the doctor, constellates the corresponding unconscious material in him, owing the inductive effect which always emanates from projections in greater or lesser degree. (ibid., para. 364)

> Psychological induction inevitably causes the two parties to get involved in the transformation of the third and to be themselves transformed in the process, and all the time the doctor's knowledge, like a flickering lamp, is the one dim light in the darkness. (ibid., para. 399)

In the intersubjective school, Ogden (1997; 1994; 1999) explicates his notion of the "intersubjective analytic third." This refers to a third subject in the analysis, which is co-created by the analyst and analysand. It takes on a life of its own in the interpersonal field between the two. While both individuals participate in the creation of the analytic third, they do so asymmetrically (Jung's "the flickering lamp of the doctor's knowledge" taking a bit of the upper hand). Because it is basically an unconscious creation, the analyst frequently has greater access to it through their "reveries." Ogden uses Bion's notion of reverie as being composed of the natural and mundane contents of mind, such as every day thoughts, feelings, ruminations, preoccupations, daydreams, bodily sensations, and so forth. The mother's reveries while holding her child are thought to create structure in the infant, that is, they perform psychological work for her child and eventually create a matrix of mind. The importance of monitoring the analytic third through the use of reverie is emphasized in Ogden's statement: "in my own clinical work, the use of my reverie experience is the *emotional compass* upon which I most heavily rely (but cannot clearly read) in my efforts to orient myself to what is happening in the analytic relationship in general, and in the workings of the analytic third in particular" (1999, 3, italics added). Ogden notes that he speaks *from* the actual reverie experience: it informs him what might be happening unconsciously between analyst and patient. He infrequently speaks *directly about* the experience itself.

This concept is very similar, if not identical, to Jung's notion of an unconscious third in the interactive field. Jung's sense is more that the third is not as much "co-created" by analyst/analysand, but that the third is a natural function of an interactive field; it is archetypally determined and later "discovered" by the analyst. This was his original intent in using alchemical plates to demonstrate the dynamics of transference. But Ogden gives us the gift of his astute clinical acumen by describing how the third is experienced, and how he uses it to inform his interventions in numerous clinical examples. Ogden understands that the analytic third carries such informative material for the analytic situation due to the mechanism of projective identification (Ogden 1979). The patient places unwanted unconscious aspects of the self into the analyst, and in turn the analyst's unconscious responds to and reworks these contents. In the literature of analytical psychology, this creative capacity of the unconscious third to inform both analyst and analysand has been discussed as the dynamics of the archetype of the wounded healer (Groesbeck 1975; Sedgwick 1994). Here an analyst, relating through his unconscious wounded self, unconsciously communicates with the patient's inner healer. Such a system could easily comprise the "wisdom system" theorized by Langs providing input and correction to an analytical dyad through valid unconscious perceptions provided by the patient. It may be one of the primary ways the Self manifests in the therapeutic encounter to move both participants towards individuation.

Ogden presents reverie as the only way an analyst gains access to the analytic third. But other contents of the analyst's mind and body provide a subtle in-between associational field moving from indirect forms such as reverie into more direct forms of association, that is, archetypal amplifications (Samuels 1985). These contents arising between analyst and patient and shaped by the nonego psyche are all valid material informing the analyst about the nature of the third being formed. Perhaps even better than reverie, the Jungian technique of active imagination would describe the workings of an analyst's mind during the analytic encounter (Cwik 2006, 215–17; Schaverien 2007). The analyst, in a slightly altered-state, allows the free flow of images, thoughts, feelings, and bodily sensations to come into awareness. This mercurial field is engaged by the analyst in an active imaginal manner in order to extract some sense of what is happening in the field. Schaverien gives a number of clinical examples describing forms of active imagination within the transference as well as discussing countertransference as active imagination (Schaverien 2007, 427).

HOLDING

The idea of therapy providing a "holding environment" has been taken into the minds and hearts of therapists and analysts everywhere. Evocative of the good enough mother holding and being able to soothe her child, the concept is both practical and imaginative. Even Langs adopts it when he states, "Do not allow the framework analogy to suggest something wooden, inanimate, non-human or iso-lated. The therapeutic framework is a very human frame filled with fluctuating unconscious communications. It is a way of *holding* the patient, offering him a sense of safety, creating conditions for open communication . . ." (Langs 1979, 108, italics added).

Winnicott (1971) observed the mother/infant dyad and suggested that it is vital for the mother to provide for the baby's needs *just as they are occurring*. There is "a magical understanding of need" in the good enough mother. This immediate meeting of primary needs creates the "illusion" in the infant that mother and child are ultimately and intimately one. It appears that the baby's love, or its need for food and comfort, creates the breast, the need satisfier. This illusion is necessary for healthy maturation and leads to the infant's felt sense of omnipotence, a component of healthy narcissism. The child feels that the environ-ment "magically" will meet its needs. Winnicott sees this as a necessary prereq-uisite for a creative self. This deeply affective experience is what he means by "holding" (Cwik 1991a). The transitional phase begins to occur when the child is capable of creating objects that stand for, yet are not, mother, the beginnings of symbol formation. This demonstrates the child's first capacity for play. For Winnicott, psychotherapy can be summed up as two individuals *playing together*. Where this is not possible, the role of the analyst is to help bring the patient to a place where playing is possible. The holding function of the analyst supplies the affective component for this process and "holding . . . often takes the form of con-veying in words at the appropriate moment something that shows that the analyst knows and understands the deepest anxiety that is being experienced, or that is waiting to be experienced" (Winnicott 1963, 240). Ogden expands on this by stat-ing, "Holding, for Winnicott, is an ontological concept that he uses to explore the specific qualities of the experience of being alive at different developmental stages as well as the changing intrapsychic-interpersonal means by which the sense of continuity of being is sustained over time" (Ogden 2005, 94).

Ogden extends the metaphor of playing into that of dreaming, as theorized by Bion. Again, using a very poetic and evocative image he states that, "Dreaming involves a form of psychological work in which there takes place a generative conversation between preconscious aspects of the mind and disturbing thoughts, feelings and fantasies that are precluded from, yet pressing toward conscious awareness (the dynamic unconscious)" (Ogden 2005, 99–100). Dreaming is a capacity to do unconscious psychological work—to transform raw sense impres-sions into linkable material used for thinking and memory. Using two categories of sleep disturbance—night terrors and nightmares—in a metaphorical manner, Ogden deepens analytic sensibility into two broad areas of psychological func-tioning. In the case of a person suffering from night terrors, the individual cannot sleep, hence cannot dream. He/she cannot use basic sense impressions for thought and feeling. The individual can be thought of as suffering from "undreamt dreams," unmetabolized material. Patients of this kind cannot do psychological work, so the work of the analyst is to "dream the undreamt dreams" for and with the patient. This occurs when the analyst creates conditions whereby the intersubjective analytic third is experienced through reverie and spoken about with the patient. In the case of repeated nightmares, poetically referred to as "interrupted cries," the analyst provides an auxiliary ego in the work of containing overwhelming affect which prevents the patient from continuing to dream.

While Langs seems to imply that all patients require the same kind of "holding," Winnicott's description of the "holding environment" is of a deeply subjective phenomenological experience; only the patient knows if and when he/she is being held by the analyst/mother. Winnicott was known to change aspects of the frame, such as lengthening a session and then keeping to this modified structure. We can think of the "fusional experience," or attunement, created by anticipating the needs of the patient as also being replicated when an analyst is able to speak from the place of the analytic third. Or when, as Ogden lyrically states, we help patients to dream their "undreamt dreams" and contain their "interrupted cries." Only from this place can the necessary "illusion" be created that the patient is with someone who knows, or at least understands, his or her deepest needs. Over time, the patient begins to introject this capacity for holding and containment.

CONTAINER

Jung's view of the container or vessel of analysis, influenced by his alchemical understandings, is a deeply symbolic image. He speaks of it as *temenos*, or sacred precinct, strongly implying a numinous and religious feeling related to it. "The *vas bene clausum* ("well sealed vessel") is a precautionary measure very frequently mentioned in alchemy, and is the equivalent of the magic circle. In both cases the idea is to protect what is within from the intrusion and admixture of what is without, as well as to prevent it from escaping" (Jung 1944/1968, para. 219). The assumption is that the well sealed vessel has everything it requires for the transformation of the materials within. The corollary for analysis is that the analytic third contains all of the information necessary to provide the "emotional compass" for guiding the direction of the analytic endeavor, if only it is understood correctly in the moment. Ogden, amplifying Bion's theories of the container-contained, adds to the standard psychoanalytic understanding of the container: it is not only what is thought but the way in which we think it. The container-contained concept describes how lived experience is processed and what may occur psychically when psychological work cannot be done with some aspects of a person's life experience. "The 'container' is not a thing, but a process. It is the capacity for the unconscious psychological work of dreaming, operating in concert with the capacity for preconscious dream-like thinking (reverie), and the capacity for more fully conscious secondary process thinking" (Ogden 2005, 101). What is being contained, on the other hand, is in actuality thoughts and feelings that are issuing from lived emotional experience.

The vessel itself is paradoxical in nature. Newman writes: "For it is both the container and that which is contained, in that it holds the contents worked upon, while, at the same time, it is also that which is worked on. It contains the process as well as being the process" (Newman 1981, 230). Here uniqueness is emphasized rather than any one-size-fits-all mentality. The shape of the vessel conforms to the process itself. Jung, quoting the alchemists, stresses the utmost importance of finding the just right container: "the 'vision' of the Hermetic vessel is more to be sought than the scripture'" (Jung 1944/1968, para. 350). The singularity of this type of container can easily be sensed in Ogden's statement: "Feeling known in the analytic situation is not so much a feeling of being understood as it is a feeling that the analyst knows who one is. This is communicated in part through the *analyst's speaking to the patient in such a way that what he says and the way he says it could have been spoken by no other analyst to no other patient*" (Ogden 2004, 866–67, italics added). When an analyst uses jargon or speaks through theory, the patient feels isolated and abandoned.

Another experience associated with the container can be seen in the operation of certain kinds of synchronicity. Winnicott held the notion of the analyst saying or providing exactly the right thing at the proper moment, but sometimes it is the world itself that provides what is "magically needed" through synchronistic experiences. The notion of synchronicity, as developed by Jung, is an *acausal* connecting principle or meaningful coincidence (Samuels et al. 1986). In its seemingly serendipitous connecting of an inner event with outer experience, it is the epitome of "magical." Coming at just the right moment, synchronicity often functions to "contain" analyst and/or patient. A clinical example of such containment through synchronicity happened to me during a period of analysis when a patient was uncovering memories of abuse and dreamed of a huge tiger. For her, this image held the promise of greater things to come—it gave her a feeling of hope. As the affect connected to the memories of the abuse began to overwhelm her, the "nightmare" functioning described by Ogden took hold and she became suicidal. I was unsure whether to hospitalize her or not. While traveling home that evening and absorbed by my own anxiety over the situation, I noticed that I was following a truck that had what seemed like a large Rorschach-like design on the back. I dropped back some distance and realized that it was actually the face of a huge tiger—the logo of a delivery service I had never noticed before. The patient's tiger dream came back to me, and there was a palpable shift in my anxiety. The meaning that emerged was a felt sense that we were on the right track. This shift in emotional state is the hallmark of containment and an indication that psychological work is being accomplished. The patient was able to continue in her regression without hospitalization. There were a number of other synchronistic phenomena surrounding the work with this borderline patient. Very often containment is brought about by such occurrences. (See Cambray 2001 for an account of an analytic day focusing on the presence of synchronistic phenomena.)

We may well ask why such synchronistic phenomena occur in certain analyses. Are they best understood as compensations for something lacking in the relationship of the dyad to the analytic third? By definition, however, these occurrences are *acausal*. Rather than linking that occurs through and in the analyst's reverie/active imaginations, synchronicity's linking of the psychic to the material world manifests a different level of the analytic third. The "outermost *vas bene clausum* may well symbolize the *vas rotundum* which the . . . [alchemists] related to the world-soul, or cosmos, that encompasses the physical universe from outside" (Newman 1981, 231). This may be the channel through which the Self works most directly in guiding the participants towards individuation.

Due to its archetypal nature, the energy released during synchronistic experiences can easily inflate the "illusional" element of the relationship to the delusional. Then the fusion becomes infused with a sense of specialness and merger. Here is an example of synchronicity leading to an attempt to break the frame. A woman was seeking hypnotherapy for the amelioration of intractable pain incurred in an accident. (Hypnotherapy can be viewed as operating in and through the conscious creation of illusion [Cwik 1991b].) She was suing for damages, and the trial was imminent. When asked why she desired treatment before the trial, she emphatically stated that she needed relief as soon as possible. During the hypnotic work, she was able to move the location of the pain slightly (a common protocol for working with pain management—if you can move the pain you can eventually control and lessen it.) She left the session in a highly excited, hypomanic state. During her ride home she heard a presentation on the radio about wizards and their power. She contacted me stating that we needed to have our next session in the forest so as to draw on the healing power of nature. By holding the boundaries, we were able to analyze her conflict and guilt about the realization that she was not as damaged as she had previously thought and stated. Her seeking treatment before the court hearing was an indication that she unconsciously knew the truth about her pain. But the realization of this fact coupled with the synchronicity threw the patient into a near delusional state.

The vessel or container image of analysis draws on psychoanalytic understandings as well as alchemical symbolism. So much more than concrete parameters, it enriches our approach to the structure of analysis into a more spiritual or nonmaterial, dynamic sensibility.

CONCLUSION

The three concepts of frame, holding, and container pose differing yet overlapping perspectives on the structure of analysis. Rational and deeply psychoanalytic, yet imaginative and emotionally gripping, these concepts have become fertile seeds enlivening the apprehension of the analytic situation. Like psychic energy itself, which Jung sees as oscillating between the ultraviolet of instinct and the infrared of archetype and spirit (Jung 1946b), the structure of the analytic situation reverberates through the spectrum from concrete, literal frame to sacred temenos container. When an analysis becomes too dangerously inflated with a sense of uniqueness and/or specialness, hard-line frame parameters should be stressed. This end of the spectrum grounds the analysis in professional and ethical reality and provides a space for the "aggression" of analyst toward patient. In a too "tight" frame, the analyst may need to accommodate the specific needs of the patient and strive for a more individualized container. In the end, the primary function of the analyst is the care and handling of the frame/holding/container triune through conscious monitoring of the literal setting and subtle awareness of the unique third created by the analytic dyad that allows patients to play/dream themselves into wholeness.

REFERENCES

Cambray, Joseph. 2001. Enactments and amplification. *Journal of Analytical Psychology* 46: 275–303.

Cwik, August J. 1991a. Active imagination as imaginal play-space. In *Liminality and transitional phenomena*, ed. Nathan Schwartz-Salant and Murray Stein, 99–114. Wilmette, IL: Chiron.

———. 1991b. Jung, hypnosis and active imagination. Thesis, C.G. Jung Institute of Chicago.

———. 2006. The art of the tincture: Analytical supervision. *Journal of Analytical Psychology* 51: 209–25.

Goodheart, William. 1980. Review of Langs and Searles. *San Francisco Jung Institute Library Journal* 1: 2–39.

Groesbeck, C. Jess. 1975. The archetypal image of the wounded healer. *Journal of Analytical Psychology* 20: 122–45.

Jung, C.G. 1944/1968. *Psychology and alchemy*. CW 12.

———. 1946a/1966. The psychology of the transference. In CW 16.

———. 1946b/1969. On the nature of the psyche. In CW 8.

Langs, Robert. 1973. *The technique of psychoanalytic psychotherapy*. New York: Jason Aronson.

———. 1979. *The therapeutic environment*. New York: Jason Aronson.

———. 1994. *Doing supervision and being supervised*. London: Karnac.

McCurdy, Alexander. 1995. Establishing and maintaining the analytical structure. In *Jungian Analysis*, 2nd ed., ed. Murray Stein, 81–104. Chicago: Open Court.

Newman, Kenneth D. 1981. The riddle of the *vas bene clausum*. *Journal of Analytical Psychology*, 26: 229–341.

Ogden, Thomas H. 1979. On projective identification. *International Journal of Psycho-Analysis* 60: 357–73.

———. 1994. The analytic third: Working with intersubjective clinical facts. *International Journal of Psycho-Analysis* 75: 3–19.

———. 1997. Reverie and metaphor: Some thoughts on how I work as a psychoanalyst. *International Journal of Psycho-Analysis* 78: 719–32.

———. 1999. The analytic third: An overview. http://www.fortda.org/Spring_99/analytic3.html.

———. 2001. Reading Winnicott. *Psychoanalytic Quarterly* 70: 299–323.

———. 2004. This art of psychoanalysis: Dreaming the undreamt dreams and interrupted cries. *International Journal of Psycho-Analysis* 85: 857–77.

————. 2005. On holding and containing, being and dreaming. In *This art of psychoanalysis: Dreaming undreamt dreams and interrupted cries*, 93–108. New York: Routledge.

Samuels, Andrew. 1985. Countertransference, the mundus imaginalis and a research project. *Journal of Analytical Psychology* 30: 47–71.

Samuels, Andrew, Bani Shorter, and Fred Plaut. 1986. *A critical dictionary of Jungian analysis*. London: Routledge & Kegan Paul.

Schaverien, Joy. 2007. Countertransference as active imagination: Imaginative experiences of the analyst. *Journal of Analytical Psychology* 52: 413–31.

Searles, Harold. 1979. The patient as therapist to his analyst. In *Countertransference and related subjects: Selected papers*, 380–459. Madison: International Universities Press.

Sedgwick, David. 1994. *The wounded healer: Countertransference from a Jungian perspective*. London: Routledge.

Siegelman, Ellen. 1990. Metaphors of the therapeutic encounter. *Journal of Analytical Psychology* 35: 175–91.

Winnicott, Donald W. 1945/1975. Primitive emotional development. In *Through paediatrics to psycho-analysis*, 145–56. New York: Basic Books.

————. 1963/1965. Psychiatric disorder in terms of infantile maturational processes. In *The maturational processes and the faciltating environment*, 230–41. International Universities Press.

————. 1971. Transitional objects and transitional phenomena. In *Playing and reality*, 1–25. New York: Basic Books.

AUGUST J. CWIK, Psy.D., is a Jungian psychoanalyst in private practice in the Chicago area and a training analyst in the Chicago Society of Jungian Analysts. He is an assistant editor of the *Journal of Analytical Psychology* and has published articles on alchemy, supervision, dreams, and active imagination.

17

DIALOGUE

Claus Braun and Lilian Otscheret

Psychoanalysis represents a leap from the attempt to heal by directly influencing the unconscious through trance/hypnosis to healing by means of consciousness. From the very outset, psychoanalysis was a dialogue, a therapeutic encounter between two people at the level of language, with the aim of identifying and altering neurotic and unconscious attitudes and complexes.

Dialogue, as a philosophical method of recognition, is as old as philosophy itself, its initial pinnacle first reflected in the Socratic dialogues of Plato. First and foremost, we owe the discovery of the relational function in dialogue—the discovery of the significance of the other, of the 'you', the surmounting of the subject-object split—to the philosopher and Hegel scholar, Ludwig Feuerbach (1804–1872). It was he who recognized that self-knowledge is only possible through the other person and in the encounter with the other (Jung 2005, para. 228 ff.). At a later date, Martin Buber (1887–1965) compared the objectifying "I-It" relationship with the "I-You" encounter in dialogue, and in his wake Emmanuel Lévinas (1906–1995) pointed out the fundamental significance of the other for our relationship with the self and the world. Today it is Jürgen Habermas (born in 1929) who presents the notion of a "domination-free dialogue." Central to this mode of thought is the figure of the other and its "otherness," which can only reveal itself from within its very self (Lesmeister 2005, 38 ff.).

The history of psychoanalysis can be described both as the history of the rules and procedures applied in treatment and as the history of the relation or the relationship between the actors involved: the patient and the analyst, each with their own "horizons of expectation." It is to be noted that the history of the psychoanalytical position and psychoanalytical technique of treatment do not in any respect follow "logical consequences derived from research." In fact, the roots of all subsequent developmental directions are to be found at the very beginning. Given certain constellations of persons and history, they gain momentum as they gather their powers of persuasion. For example, as evidence for the currently fashionable intersubjective view as "always existing," reference could be made to the attempts undertaken by Ferenczi to carry out "mutual analysis" and to the works of C.G. Jung on the intersubjective character of the analytical process.

We can start with three paradigmatic models of psychoanalytical interaction (cf. Lesmeister 2005, 29 ff.), corresponding to three forms of psychoanalytical dialogue.

The model of the "classical" standard technique, which is characteristic in drive psychology and ego psychology, understands analytical practice as analogous to a scientific "objective" situation in a laboratory. The unconscious psychodynamics of the patient are observed by the investigator, the psychoanalyst, particularly in transference, and interpreted by attribution to constellations in the patient's history. The type of dialogue taking place is frequently not unlike collecting "criminological evidence," as exemplified by Freud in the Katharina case: "So when she had finished her confession I said to her: 'I know now what it was you thought when you looked into the room. You thought: "Now he's doing with her what he wanted to do with me that night and those other times." That was what you were disgusted at . . .' (because you remembered the feeling when you woke up in the night and felt his body)" (Freud 1893, 192).

Neutrality and abstinence are the pillars of the classical technique of interpretation. The analytical position is founded on the ideal of the analyst's anonymity and on the illusion that the analytical situation could evolve "relationship-free." Psychoanalysts that are guided by an object relations theory with a specific focus on internalized object relationships and their reenactment in the here and now of the transference, as well as the analysts of the classical Kleinian school, are oriented by this same type of technique.

In the "two-person theory" models, on the other hand, the analyst leaves the attempt at impersonality. The notion of the "corrective emotional experience" in the psychoanalytical process places the relationship at the center stage of technique (Ferenzci, Balint, Kohut, Ornstein). The subjectivity of the analyst has been upgraded. The motto of the English school postulating the object relations theory (Fairbairn, Guntrip, Bowlby, Winnicott) reads: "The ego does not seek to satisfy the drive, but the object" (Fairbairn 1952). In France, the new outlook established itself thanks to Bion's further elaboration of the Kleinian model coupled with the rise of the language-oriented theory of Lacan. It could now be ascertained that the analysts themselves create a space for a relationship during the course of therapy, making use of their own relational functions (empathy, holding, containing). As yet, there is no genuine reciprocity. Focus is still on "technique," applied solely by the analyst, however now within a relationship in which the analyst becomes available as an ideal model (or object).

This is also where the self psychology of Kohut is anchored. The mirroring responsiveness of a 'self-object' can be utilized by the patient to build up a continuous, coherent, and positive self. The therapy's principle of healing is the positive experience of a self-object that enables the patient to experience him/herself anew. Although self psychology categorically does not cover intersubjective relatedness and Kohut favors a neutral and objective attitude in the analyst, the school does acknowledge that besides interpretation empathy and relatedness are essential to psychoanalytical healing.

The new patient-analyst relationship, now set up as "two-person psychology," develops in intersubjectivity theory—radically altered notions of the analytical process, the analytical position, and the technical concepts associated with them. The paradigm of intersubjectivity postulates that the analytical process embodies a continuous matrix of reciprocal influences that can only be appropriately seen and adequately understood as the intersubjective-interactive phenomena of the analytical pair. During this process, the analyst is seen not as a new object, such as he was with Ferenczi, Balint, Winnicott, but rather as the medium of a *subjectivity* in which, admittedly, the analyst is not totally available and transparent but whose personal presence is considered to be legitimate and of benefit to the process (Lesmeister 2005, 30 ff.). The analytical encounter now takes on the character of "nonsymmetrical equivalence" (Treurniet 1996, 26), which is characterized by a higher degree of transparency, authenticity, and reciprocity.

With the new paradigm, the patient's isolated psychic apparatus and the conflicting dynamics within its inner structures are no longer the object of attention, but rather the manner in which the self interacts with its environment from the beginning of its development and how intrapsychic processes are coupled with intersubjective processes.

This shift in paradigm is most clearly visualized by viewing the therapeutic relationship from the perspective of transference and countertransference. The traditional term, transference, previously denoted a distortion in perception on the patient's part alone, a product of various dynamics and projections. From this viewpoint, the analyst was not involved in the interaction and remained a mere observer (a mirror or projection screen).

The interactional use of the term transference (Bettighofer 1998), on the other hand, denotes intensive interaction between analyst and patient. Both react subtly to one another and both actively shape the transference and the therapeutic relationship. It is impossible not to involve oneself, even through remaining passive (saying nothing, doing nothing, showing reserve) or by attempting to remain abstinent. Neutrality and abstinence have just as much impact on the patient as tangible actions. In all transferences, the perceptions of the patient always embody a "grain of truth."

In his understanding of the process of transference, C.G. Jung described how intensively two people encounter each other at conscious and unconscious levels and how their projections merge. He characterized the transference as "coniunctio" or as "Hierosgamos" (Jung 1946, para. 358) and compared it to a chemical reaction in which two substances react to each other, both of them being changed by the process. He saw the therapeutic process as an exchange between the conscious and the unconscious aspects of both involved parties, in which unconscious contents are reciprocally projected (transferred/countertransferred). To him, becoming conscious meant that the subject withdraws the projections/transferences. In so doing, Jung endeavoured to differentiate the part of the transference that is derived from the projection of ideas stemming from archetypal patterns from the parts that result from the previous life experience of the individual. Despite concentrating on the archetypal aspects of the transference, Jung was one of the first to recognize the clinical significance of countertransference. To illustrate neurotic countertransference, he referred to the clinical picture of "psychic infection" when the analyst tends to identify with the patient because they are similar in their unconscious motives and dispositions (Jung 1946, para. 365). Jung was convinced that only the ability to hold an "inner dialogue," that is, confront the voice of one's own unconscious, renders any "outer objectivity" possible. This allows the argument of the other to stand and creates the fundamental condition of human togetherness. Whoever is unable to concede to the argument of the other, fails to confer the right of existence to the "other in himself" and vice versa (Jung 1916, para. 187).

Another complication observed by Jung was that ego-consciousness and the supremacy of the will can be endangered by complex constellations that lead to a disorder in the ability to hold a dialogue (Jung 1934, paras. 199 ff.). This is where his early research interest in complexes and their effects on consciousness came into play. The insights from infancy research and attachment theory and theory of mind were not available in his time, which today are compellingly suggestive of an intersubjective view of human development and of analytical processes of change and individuation.

In Germany it was above all the Berlin Group (Dieckmann 1980) and in Switzerland Mario Jacoby (1993) who addressed the intersubjective gap in therapeutic techniques, that is, the issue of transference in terms of relationship rather than only projection. To Jacoby, the analyst's ability to form a genuine I-Thou relationship, as defined by Martin Buber, is determinative, which requires, however, that closeness and distance are so regulated that the analyst is able to have "one foot in the relationship and one foot outside." The "being inside" denotes the empathy for the patient's experience. The "being outside" is necessary as demarcation in order to reflect psychologically on the inner phenomena and the clinical situation.

Jacoby comments on the irreconcilable contradiction between transference and relationship. Transference denotes the I-It relationship but can alter to become a I-Thou relationship if the projections are withdrawn.

According to Buber (1923/1970), existence evolves in the interplay between the "sphere of subjectivity" (I-It) and the "sphere of the in-between" (I-You). The I-Thou relationship can be described by immediacy, reciprocity, and equality; it is the world of true relationship. By contrast, the I-It sphere is characterized by subordination and a focus on the ego, denoting the world of experience of objects. The principle of dialogue in psychoanalysis is open and consciously concedes validity to thesis and antithesis. Mutual responsibility is not eliminated by the need for synthesis. Contradictions are to be defused neither by compromise (synthesis) nor by suppression (extremism).

The social philosopher Goldschmidt (1964) calls the acceptance of contradiction and the restrictions thus entailed the "state of adulthood" in humankind.

It means letting go of the desire for omnipotence and confronting conflicting facts.

The uniqueness of the relationship between patient and analyst can be seen as a special form of encounter, featuring *restricted reciprocity*. Here the relationship remains asymmetric. The analytical relationship has a definite goal: it seeks to further the relationship between the ego and the unconscious of the patient and to render differentiation possible, thus achieving a degree of evolution of consciousness. This is both natural and artificial. This relationship can produce intimacy while at the same time remaining professional. An important factor is that the analyst is able to let him/herself be "used" by the patient.

Considering the theme of intersubjectivity and its therapeutic consequences, one must also turn one's attention to the "barb of asymmetry." An additional complication is generated by the contrast, described in depth by Lesmeister (2005) in particular, between therapeutic technique on the one hand and a relationship that is in permanent danger of being deleted or even perverted into "relational technique." The antagonism between technique and relationship in psychoanalysis remains. It constitutes a dilemma that cannot be solved. We agree with Lesmeister (2005, 55) in his claim that paradoxically it is only an open attitude towards this dilemma that will allow any symmetry to evolve in which the patient feels understood in a way that can heal.

Here lies an important prerequisite for the striking formulation of Orange (2004), namely that "understanding" heals. The relational experience and the emotional availability of the analyst open the door to a second development of relatedness between self and object. This is founded on the willingness and the ability of the analyst to immerse him/herself into the emotional life of the patient: "Psychoanalytical understanding means making sense together" (Orange 2004, 25). Orange views all experience as given and as already interpreted. This compound notion of experience calls for our ability to bear ambivalence and uncertainty. Psychoanalytical understanding also requires memory. "Emotional memory" is the quintessence of our relational past. "Our history rests inside our entire being" (ibid., 156). Insight and emotional understanding can relieve pathological repercussions from established life history and slowly render that history manageable and tolerable.

Jung's writings are in fact strongly intersubjective in tone: "A person is a psychic system, which . . . enters into reciprocal reaction with another psychic system" (Jung 1935/1966, para. 1); "a good half of every treatment . . . deeply consists in the doctor's examining himself, for only what he can put right in himself can he hope to put right in the patient" (Jung 1951/1966, para. 239); "the therapist is no longer the agent of treatment, but a fellow participant in a process of individual development" (Jung 1935/1966, para. 7); "the doctor is as much 'in the analysis' as the patient" (Jung 1929/1966, para. 166); "there is no single theory in the whole field of practical psychology that cannot on occasion prove basically wrong" (Jung 1951/1966, para. 237); "the therapist must abandon all his preconceptions and techniques and confine himself to a purely dialectical procedure, adopting the attitude that shuns all methods" (Jung 1935/1966, para. 6). The dialectical procedure should be free from authority and desire to influence, it should consist of a comparison of mutual findings (Jung ibid., para. 2), Jung states, from which he appears to assume that reciprocal transference and counter-transference are to be put aside, thus ensuring that the "dialectical procedure" takes place in the real relationship and beyond countertransference. The impending danger of the ego being flooded in the dialectical procedure by contents from the collective unconscious is compensated by a process of alignment derived from the unconscious, by the appearance and the impact of a new personality centre, the self (Jung 1941/1966, para. 219).

   This process is the individuation process, described by Jung as an "internal and subjective process of integration" and, at the same time, as a "process of objective relationship" (Jung 1946/1966, para. 448). The decisive factor here is the significance or the role that can be attributed to the "process of objective relationship" in the process of individuation. According to Jung, the unrelated person does not embody "wholeness" combining I and you as parts of a transcendent unit: "Wholeness is a combination of I and You, and these show themselves to be parts of a transcendent unity whose nature can only be grasped symbolically. . . (Jung 1946/1966, para. 454). However, by introducing "wholeness," Jung sees the value of the "you" and of the external relationship in relative terms, which is primarily of interest as a medium of the individual's projections and is seen as auxiliary and an "early stage of individuation." The important factor is the withdrawal of one's own projections, not primarily the ability and possibility of a relationship (Höhfeld 1997, 190). At most, the other engages as an "interacting system" devoid of actual relational reality and is renounced in favour of the notion of a primarily "introverted individuation" (Braun 2004).

   In view of the developmental findings of modern psychological research in infants and the neurophysiological insights into the development of the network structures of the CNS, however, we can no longer avoid directing the greatest of attention to the intersubjective genesis of self. According to Altmeyer (2000), who places emphasis on the intersubjective constitution of self, the self learns to watch itself from the outside and to take on the perspective of the other as it interacts. As a result, it acquires consciousness in the sense of self-reflection. "The self evolves from the mirroring experienced with the other" (Altmeyer 2000, 206). In particular, the ability to "*see oneself with the eyes of the other*" is now considered, even in neurobiology, to be the intersubjective prerequisite in order for any feeling of identity to evolve.

   It is possible to regard intersubjective acknowledgment as the core of the successful development of identity (Benjamin 1995). Paradoxically, the "destruction of the object" (Winnicott 1965) renders the transition possible from a merely intrapsychic relatedness with the other to his actual use, that is, to establishing a relationship with a counterpart that is objectively perceived as existing outside of one's own self, as a being in her/his own right. If the other survives the offensive without taking revenge or withdrawing, then we also know that she/he exists outside our self and is not simply a product of our imagination. This is where Benjamin sees the fundamental tension between denial and confirmation of the other, between fantasies of omnipotence and acknowledgment of reality. By accepting that the mother who leaves her child is not bad but merely independent, the child gains independence of her/his own. From this, a picture of the self evolves that permits intrapsychically different voices, asymmetry and contradiction, that endures ambivalence and refrains from shaping a perfectly uniform consciousness.

Individuation as a process of organizing experience takes place both "internally" (intrasubjectively) as well as "internally" and "externally" between a "subject" and an "object." Further—in our opinion of paramount significance—it takes place "intersubjectively" in a living system that is produced from overlaps and interplay between subjective worlds.

We describe this encounter as an intersubjective and *dialogic process of understanding,* when common efforts are made to "search for conflicts and meaning." The partners of the dialogue incorporate their subjective perspectives so as to better understand cognitively and emotionally more about the other and the other's experience.

One of the major responsibilities of the analyst is to so shape the dialogue with the patient that the *inner working models of relationships and emotional patterns of expectation* (Bovensiepen 2004) are able to develop into mature relational functions in the sense of achieving the "depressive function" (Klein). This is important because the *structural characteristics* of persons have an enormous influence on their definition of self and on the *type of conflicts* which they are able to experience and to overcome.

In case of structural impairments, it is mainly the affective but also the distinguishing and differentiating functions required to regulate the self and its relationships that are only restrictedly available (Rudolph 2005, 48ff.). Structural characteristics are above all anchored psychically in the *implicit relational memory.*

The self is formed as *original primary self* (Fordham) not just in relation to the other, but from the very beginning there is a virtually differentiating, albeit rudimentary, archetypal premonition of the other and hence of one's own self. Realization of this premonition is rendered possible by an *early perceptive ability* and a *primary pleasure in "conversation."* From the outset, we are "dialogic" beings, and the experience acquired from our interactions and conversations set the pace for the further shaping of our "dynamic emotional syntax" (Trevarthen), our "rhythmo-affective semantics" (Molino), or our "psychic texture" (Bollas) as contents of the implicit relational memory. On the one hand, the implicit relational memory has direct repercussions on further cerebral development; on the other, it also affects all future "conversations" and relationships.

These findings give backing to the idea of the significance of "early disorders" for the development of a person's *structural characteristics.* With "early disorders," which are specific impaired conditions of mentalization, the world is largely experienced as shaped by archaic and fearsome interactions in the past.

Because of easily evocable and excessively negative affects, recent social situations will feature, in terms of inner experience, what C.G. Jung described as "introversion of the libido," in terms of object relatedness what Melanie Klein called the "paranoid-schizoid position": it is no longer possible to envisage a "good interaction." Thus seen, "early disorders" are first and foremost long-lasting pathognomic disorders of the interpersonal affective tuning possibilities, that is, of affect attunement (Stern), that are embodied psychically in the implicit relational memory as a result of the complexes formed.

Summarizing therefore, we can say that the dialogic principle introduced in the "dialectical procedure" of C.G. Jung is currently undergoing further development through intersubjectivity theory and the philosophical and developmental requirements to which this is subject. It is thereby taking on a form that accords particular recognition of the "unknown other" in its constitutional significance for the development of the self.

The dialogic principle effects a total change in the psychoanalytical process. It alters the understanding and the handling of transference and countertransference and makes it possible to view abstinence and neutrality in a new light. It brings greater symmetry and reciprocity into the relationship shaped during analytical therapy. Finally, the dialogic principle is open to new territory "beyond interpretation," by placing attention on "moments in the now," or "moments of meeting," which create a new intersubjective environment and an altered domain of "implicit relational knowing" (Stern et al. 1998, 909).

REFERENCES

Altmeyer, Martin. 2000. *Narzißmus und Objekt: Ein intersubjektives Verständnis der Selbstbezogenheit*. Göttingen: Vandenhoeck & Ruprecht.
Benjamin, Jessica. 1995. *Like subjects, love objects: Essays on recognition and sexual difference*. New Haven: Yale University Press.
Bettighofer, Siegfried. 1998. *Übertragung und Gegenübertragung im therapeutischen Prozess*. Stuttgart: Kohlhammer.
Bovensiepen, Gustav. 2004. Bindung—Dissoziation—Netzwerk. *Analytische Psychologie* 35: 31–53.
Braun, Claus. 2004. Der Mythos der introvertierten Individuation. *Analytische Psychologie* 35: 423–47.
Buber, Martin. 1923/1970. *I and Thou*. New York: Scribner.
Dieckmann, Hans, ed. 1980. *Übertragung und Gegenübertragung*. Hildesheim: Gerstenberg.
Fairbairn, W.R.D. 1952. *Psychoanalytic studies of the personality*. London: Tavistock
Freud, Sigmund. 1893. Katharina. In *The Standard Edition of the Complete Psychological Works of Sigmund Freud*, II, 125–34. London: Hogarth Press.
Goldschmidt, H.L. 1964. *Dialogik*. Frankfurt a. M.: Europäische Verlagsanstalt.
Höhfeld, Kurt. 1997. Individuation und Neurose. *Analytische Psychologie* 28: 188–202.
Jacoby, Mario. 1980/1985. *The longing for paradise: Psychological perspectives on an archetype*. Boston: Sigo Press.

————. 1984. *The analytic encounter: Transference and human relationship.* Toronto: Inner City Books.

Jung, C.G. 1916/1969. The transcendent function. In CW 8.

————. 1929/1966. Problems of modern psychotherapy. In CW 16.

————. 1934/1969. A review of the complex theory. In CW 8.

————. 1935/1966. Principles of paractical psychotherapy. In CW 16.

————. 1941/1966. Psychotherapy today. In CW 16.

————. 1946/1966. The psychology of the transference. In CW 16.

————. 1951/1966. Fundamental questions of psychotherapy. In CW 16.

Jung, Christine. 2005. "Der erste Gegenstand des Menschen ist der Mensch": Ludwig Feuerbach entdeckte die Dialogik. In *Im Dialog mit dem Anderen*, ed. Lilian Otscheret and Claus Braun 2005, 216–35. Frankfurt: Brandes and Apsel.

Lesmeister, Roman. 2005. Technik und Beziehung. Erkundung eines Widerstreits. In *Im Dialog mit dem Anderen*, ed. Lilian Otscheret and Claus Braun, 29–56. Frankfurt: Brandes and Apsel.

Otscheret, Lilian, and Claus Braun, eds. 2005. *Im Dialog mit dem Anderen.* Frankfurt: Brandes and Apsel.

Rudolph, Gert. 2005. *Strukturbezogene Psychotherapie.* Stuttgart, NY: Schattauer.

Stern, Daniel. et al. 1998. Non-interpretive mechanisms in psychoanalytic therapy. The "something more" than interpretation. *International Journal of Psycho-Analysis* 79: 903–21.

Treurniet, N. 1996. Über eine Ethik der psychoanalytischen Technik. *Psyche* 50: 1–31.

Winnicott, D.W. 1960. *The maturational processes and the facilitating environment.* London: Hogarth Press.

CLAUS BRAUN, MD, is a medical specialist in psychiatry and neurology and a training analyst in the C.G. Jung-Institutes Berlin/Munich. He is presently a co-editor of the quarterly journal, *Analytische Psychologie*.

LILIAN OTSCHERET, Dr. phil., is a psychologist and Jungian psychoanalyst living and working in Munich, Germany. She is currently President of the C.G. Jung-Institute Munich and a co-editor of the quarterly journal, *Analytische Psychologie*.

18

THE ANALYTIC RELATIONSHIP: INTEGRATING JUNGIAN, ATTACHMENT THEORY AND DEVELOPMENTAL PERSPECTIVES

Jean Knox

Jung placed the relationship between analyst and patient at the heart of the analytic process and, in doing so, offered an entirely different model from the interpretative approach developed by Freud. In place of the modernist (and to our eyes now, rather simplistic) view of analysis, in which a thoroughly analyzed analyst would cure the patient by carefully timed and accurate interpretations of unconscious drives, fantasies, and defenses, Jung described a much murkier process, in which both analyst and patient descend into mutual unconscious entanglements and projections, and out of which individuation and understanding will eventually emerge. Jung's model of analysis requires the analyst to be drawn in at a deep unconscious level and to use his or her emotional responses as a countertransference guide to define the analytic task (Jung 1946/1966, para. 365).

Michael Fordham extended Jung's research in this area and finally came to consider countertransference as an expression of projective identification and as a useful source of information about the patient's state of mind, if the analyst accepts that "an analyst might find himself behaving in ways that were out of line with what he knew of himself, but syntonic with what he knew of his patient" (Fordham 1979/1996, 165). He suggested that "something of the same nature might be contained in countertransference illusions" and concluded that "the whole analytic situation is a mass of illusions, delusions, displacements, projections and introjections" (172). I think what Fordham was outlining here was that an essentially relational process is the necessary basis for understanding and interpretation.

In this chapter, I want to explore this fundamental Jungian approach to the analytic relationship in the light of recent research in attachment theory, neuroscience, and developmental psychology. I suggest that much of this research supports Jung's view of analysis as a process in which the conscious and unconscious relationship with the analyst provides the essential foundation for individuation. These new disciplines are leading many psychoanalysts towards a paradigm shift in terms of the nature of analysis, with an increasing emphasis on facilitating and understanding unconscious relational processes and less emphasis on the accurate identification of specific mental content (BCPSG 2007). I have argued elsewhere that this changing perspective means that psychoanalysis will eventually have to come to terms with Jung's understanding of the analytic relationship, which anticipated many of these insights in contemporary attachment-based psychoanalysis (Knox 2007).

I have also suggested that this increasing body of research helps us to take a truly developmental approach to the analytic process itself and to define more clearly the different ways in which the analytic relationship can be used in the service of individuation. Attachment theory research gives new depth and precision to the concept of individuation, clarifying the self-organizing nature of the psyche and the developmental processes that contribute to psychological and emotional maturity. It supports the view that the analytic relationship needs to be more flexible than either the classical psychoanalytic interpretative or the classical Jungian archetypal models would allow; in place of the uncovering of specific mental content (e.g., repressed oedipal material or the collective unconscious) an attachment-orientated analyst accompanies the patient on a developmental journey, one that will sometimes require interpretation of such material but will also allow for new experiences to emerge in the analytic relationship.

This developmental approach therefore demands that the analyst's use of technique needs to be attuned to the analysand's current unconscious developmental tasks. Joseph Sandler (Sandler 1976, 44) coined the phrase "role responsiveness" to describe the way in which an analyst allows the patient to project a particular role onto him or her, a view that resonates with Fordham's view, outlined above, that projective identification is not a force to be resisted by the analyst, but one that provides a useful source of information via the analyst's countertransference reactions. I would like to extend this idea by suggesting that "developmental attunement" requires the analyst to use his or her countertransference reactions to identify the particular nature of developmental inhibition that the patient brings to the analysis and to use the appropriate analytic techniques in response. This does not mean a total identification with a particular projective identification. It sometimes requires an attuned affective response or sometimes a countertransference feeling from which an interpretation will be made.

So what does attachment-based research tell us about the processes that lead to psychic maturity, for which Jung coined the term individuation? There is already a vast literature, with authors focussing variously on different aspects of neurophysiology, interpersonal relationship and self-development. But all seem essentially to agree that there are three fundamental developmental tasks involved in the achievement of "unit status" (Winnicott 1960, 44). These are the development of affect regulation, of the capacity for mentalization, and of a secure sense of self. But it seems to me that the last of these is rather less precise a concept than the other two. In my view, it is the development of self-agency that more accurately describes this particular developmental task. I suggest, therefore, that the analytic relationship can provide the context for the development of:

- affect regulation
- the capacity for mentalization (the basis for reflective function)
- a sense of self agency.

In practice, these developmental tasks are mutually interdependent in their trajectories, so that progress in one area depends critically on progress in the other two. It is also the case that analytic work in each of these three areas will make different demands on the analytic relationship at different stages of the analysis, sometimes requiring a state of unconscious entanglement between analyst and analysand and sometimes a process of increasing separation and differentiation. Jung's detailed study of alchemy explored these changing aspects of the analytic relationship and offers a framework in which these three aspects of the analytic relationship can be examined.

AFFECT REGULATION

One of the functions of any therapy is to help the patient develop the capacity for affect regulation in the context of an intense relationship. The transference is the main focus for this work. Allan Schore has summarized much interdisciplinary research evidence, which indicates that "therapist-patient transference-countertransference communications, occurring at levels beneath awareness, represent rapid right hemisphere-to-right hemisphere nonverbal affective transactions" and that the therapist's facial expression, spontaneous gestures and emotional tone of voice play a key part in that unconscious emotional interaction. These "affective transactions within the working alliance co-create an intersubjective context that allows for the structural expansion of the patient's orbito-frontal system and its cortical and subcortical connections" (Schore 2003, 264). Such attunement also provides the countertransference experience from which interpretation is drawn. In other words, change in therapy crucially depends on the affect regulation that gradually develops from relational interaction; the emotional regulation offered by the relationship creates the conditions necessary for the neural development in the orbitofrontal cortex and other areas, on which affect regulation depends.

In practice, a great many aspects of the analytic relationship can therefore help to promote the process of affect regulation. When the patient's emotions are out of control, consciousness becomes flooded with inchoate emotions and bodily experiences, and at this moment the analyst's attempts to create a process of self-reflection through interpretation will be unlikely to succeed. Interpretation depends upon words which, by the very fact that we need to use them, convey the separateness of one mind from another and so may be unbearable to someone who cannot yet be sure that he or she can be allowed to have a much more direct emotional impact on the analyst. The patient needs to discover that the analyst is not afraid of the patient's need for close attunement, and that this need will not destroy the analyst and his or her analytic function.

In these situations, the analyst's tone of voice, body language, and facial expression play a crucial part in affect regulation. An attuned response, a Kohutian mirroring, may create a new experience of object relationship and offer containment through the analyst's instinctive downward modulation of affect. This would be largely an intuitive and unconscious response by the analyst, the equivalent in analysis of the parent's attuned response to a baby's cues (Beebe and Lachmann 2002). Attachment theory and neuroscience lend strong support to the argument that this attuned, empathic attitude from the analyst is a necessary precondition for the mourning process which is an integral part of analytic understanding (Schore 2003, 52–57). It was Jung who first recognized that it is the experienced analyst's countertransference which can guide his or her judgement about how much close attunement or interpretation is appropriate at any moment in the analysis (Jung 1931/1966, paras. 163–67). Separation and loss must occur at the pace the infant or adult patient can manage. If they are forced or imposed too early, they lead, not to cycles of deintegration and reintegration, but to disintegration, dissociation, and encapsulated autistic states of mind, which become more and more impenetrable (Fordham 1979/1996, 36).

But affect regulation also develops out of containment created in other ways in the analytic relationship. This includes the clear structure and boundaries of the analytic setting, the analyst's consistency and reliability, and his or her focus on symbolic meaning rather than concrete enactment. When the patient's capacity for affect regulation is highly unstable, the simple act of naming emotions, identifying the cues that trigger them, and helping the analysand to anticipate their impact on him/herself and on others all contribute to the capacity for affect regulation. When affect regulation is already more firmly established, the task of understanding and interpreting the patient's unconscious internal world contributes to the development of reflective function and so to affect regulation. The ability to self-regulate in analysis is inextricably bound up with the interactive regulation offered by a consistent, empathic, but also boundaried and reflective analyst. The focus of the analyst's approach also needs to reflect the level of self-agency at which the patient is functioning (see below).

The analyst must, of course, have developed the capacity to self-regulate, to manage his or her own affective responses to the patient. This includes paying careful attention to his or her countertransference reactions. Jung's own example of his dream about a female patient in a tower on a high hill, whom he had come to find rather irritating and boring, revealed to him the unconscious contempt he had felt for her, and he recognized the compensatory function of the dream, that he should "look up" to her more. This demonstrated his highly developed capacity to reflect on and to use his own emotional reactions to understand the unconscious aspects of the analytic relationship (Jung 1937/1966, para. 549). His exploration of alchemy was the earliest detailed research into the transference-countertransference dynamics and the way these aspects of the analytic relationship contribute to the analytic task of individuation (Jung 1946/1966).

MENTALIZATION AND REFLECTIVE FUNCTION

One of the main tools for developing affect regulation is the analyst's use of his or her reflective function, by which he/she makes sense of the patient's conscious and unconscious experience through interpretation. The simple act of identifying and naming feelings is containing in itself, just as is a parent's naming of the infant's sensations. Analysis provides a framework for the development of the capacity for mentalization and reflective function, the ability to relate to and make sense of ourselves and each other in mental and emotional, not just behavioral, terms (Fonagy 1991). This depends both on transference experience and also on the detailed exploration of personal history and the gradual construction of analytic narratives, which depend on an understanding of one's own and other people's desires, needs, and beliefs. The capacity to link experiences in a meaningful way is a crucial part of human psychological development and is intuitively nurtured by parents in the early development of their children. Stories are crucial vehicles for the development of mentalization. One of the defining features of any bed-time story is that it links events in a meaningful way through the desires and intentions of the people who play the various roles in the story, whether fictional or not. In any narrative, it is minds that are the agents of change, giving rise to decisions, choices and actions that produce effects and link events into a coherent structure. Without mental agency, there would be no story, no meaningful thread tying events together, and those events would appear random and meaningless.

Holmes has coined the term "narrative competence" to describe this ability to make sense of experiences and has linked deficits in the development of narrative capacity to differing patterns of insecure attachment. Holmes also highlights the fact that narrative is a dialogue: "There is always another to whom the Self is telling his or her story, even if in adults this takes the form of an internal dialogue" (Holmes 2001, 85). This dialogue is also itself a constructive process of increasing complexity in which a story is created first by one person and then taken over and retold on a new level by the other.

This process wherein the narrative, initially belonging to the parent then taken over by the child, is also mirrored in the analytic dialogue. Analytic theories are narratives of a sort, which we construct so that we can provide an analytic reverie that allows us to find meaning in our patient's verbal and nonverbal communications, often when the patient herself cannot yet do so. A successful analytic narrative is one that can become meaningful to the patient so that she can take it over, use it for herself and adapt it to establish her own sense of psychic causality, the links between intrapsychic experiences and the external world. Holmes describes the psychotherapist's role in this respect as that of an "assistant autobiographer," whose role is to find stories that correspond to experience. This role starts in the assessment interview, where the therapist will "use her narrative competence to help the patient shape the story into a more coherent pattern" (Holmes 2001, 86). He suggests that the patient then gradually "learns to build up a 'story-telling function', which takes experience from 'below' and, in the light of overall meanings 'from above' (which can be seen as themselves stored or condensed stories) supplied by the therapist, fashions a new narrative about herself and her world" (ibid, 85).

This aspect of the analytic relationship is very familiar to Jungians across the spectrum of our theoretical orientations. The active and creative role of the unconscious, shown through dreams, fantasies, paintings, sandplay and other forms of symbolic expression, has regularly been given careful attention in Jungian clinical practice. A "developmental" Jungian analysis may result in analyst and patient co-constructing a different kind of narrative from that which emerges in a more "classical" Jungian analysis, but in both approaches the patient's unconscious is seen as playing an active and creative role in the emergence of a meaningful analytic story.

A SENSE OF SELF-AGENCY

Analysis is also a context in which the inhibited development of self-agency can be overcome. An increasingly complex and psychic self-agency can emerge, in which the sense of self does not depend on the direct physical or emotional impact one has on another person but on the capacity for self-reflection and awareness of the mental and emotional separateness of self and other.

A sense of self-agency develops in a series of predictable stages, summarized by Fonagy et al. (2002):

1. Physical Agency 0–6 months.
   Awareness that actions produce changes in the physical environment (perfect contingency).

2. Social Agency 3–9 months
   Actions produce behavioural and emotional mirroring (imperfectly contingent) responses in other people-action at a distance.

3. Teleological Agency 9–24 months
   Sense of purpose; actions seen as goal-directed. Capacity to choose action to bring about desired outcome. Intention not yet recognized as separate from action.

4. Intentional Agency 2 years
   Recognition of intentions as distinct from action. Actions are seen as caused by prior intentions and desires. Actions can change mental states.

5. Representational Agency 3–4 years
   Actions seen as caused by intentions that are also recognized as mental processes. Mind is represented to itself, so intentions are not just means to an end but mental states in themselves.

6. Autobiographical Self
   Organization of memories as personally experienced—linked to self-representations and awareness of personal history.

(Fonagy et al. 2002, 204–7)

These stages of self-agency are levels of psychic organization, nonconscious implicit internal working models that structure experiences while themselves remaining outside awareness. The earlier stages in the development of self-agency are not fully replaced or erased by later developmental stages but remain hidden behind them until some psychic breakdown allows them to predominate again if later stages of self-agency—the stages of reflective and autobiographical self—are insecurely established or fail to develop. Jung recognized the importance of this process of "reculer pour mieux sauter" as an essential contribution to the process of individuation (Jung 1935/1966, para. 19).

I suggest that the patient's level of self-agency will profoundly influence the effectiveness of the analyst's approach, requiring the developmental attunement I referred to earlier in this article. The analyst needs to focus intuitively on the analytic technique that is most appropriate to the level of self-agency that unconsciously predominates, and this is a complex and constantly shifting skill developed during many years of analytic practice. If a person's sense of self-agency is functioning at the teleological level, in which they only feel real when they are controlling the actions or feelings of another person, then interpretations which rely on that person's reflective function will be doomed to failure. This is frequently the case with borderline patients. At the intentional level, forbidden desires or wishes may feel dangerously powerful, able to create wishes and desires in the other—for example, in the analyst. In this case, interpretations of incestuous wishes, for example, may be vehemently resisted because the patient's unconscious belief is that if the analyst knows about those wishes he or she may be seduced by them.

I have explored elsewhere (Knox 2005, 2007) some of the life-long consequences when the development of self-agency has been impaired in infancy. There I suggested that the most serious problems arise when a child grows up with the fear that to have any emotional impact on another person is bad and destructive. This is based on the experience of parents who could not bear any awareness of the child's own emotional needs and hence cannot relate to him or her as someone with his or her separate identity. The child comes to fear that to love is to drive the other person away.

It seems that this might be exactly the situation in which the analytic relationship needs to re-create the highly attuned, as near perfectly contingent, mirroring that was lacking in that person's infancy. This is not a simplistic tactic to provide a corrective emotional experience. It is a form of analytic containment necessary to allow regression to a developmental stage that provides the secure sense of self-agency that is the essential foundation for separation and the individuation process. Neuroscience and attachment theory tell us that the sense of self is fundamentally relational, requiring an internalization of the mirroring other for a secure sense of self and self-agency to develop and that this is based on right brain to right brain communication from the earliest moments of infancy. This lends support to the view that a "confirming relationship" must be the basis for any analytic work with an analysand whose early experiences have not provided the foundation for a secure sense of self. In Jung's alchemical model, this kind of close attunement might be thought of as the stage of immersion (Jung 1946/1966, para 453).

Later stages of self-agency require a different approach, in which the emphasis is on separation rather than close attunement. It was Winnicott who recognized the crucial role of destructiveness in the "subject's placing of the object outside the area of the subject's omnipotent control" (Winnicott 1971, 89). Winnicott argued that the object's repeated survival of destruction enables the subject to recognize the object as an independent entity in its own right. Winnicott suggested that for many patients the main analytic task is to help the patient to acquire the capacity to use the analyst: "The analyst, the analytic technique, and the analytic setting all come in as surviving or not surviving the patient's destructive attacks. This destructive activity is the patient's attempt to place the analyst outside the area of omnipotent control, that is, out in the world" (Winnicott 1971, 91). There is an equally important reverse side to this coin. Viewed from the perspective of self-development, the repeated destruction in fantasy of the object and the gradual recognition that the object survives such attacks and goes on being is not only the basis for the sense of object constancy. It is also the means by which the infant becomes increasingly secure in the knowledge that he or she also exists separately and independently of his or her effect on the object. If the object survives the attack, the subject can discover that being is separate from doing and that existence is independent of one's physical actions. The child goes on existing and knowing he or she exists even when having to recognize the continuing and independent physical and psychic survival of the other person whom he or she has just tried to destroy. The object's survival of destructive attacks drives the move from the teleological and intentional level of self-agency, in which one knows one exists only through the physical or emotional impact one has on the other, to the true psychic autonomy of the representational level, at which mind can reflect on its own processes rather than automatically convert them into physical or emotional action. *In this sense, true psychic separateness and autonomy directly depend on the recognition of one's powerlessness to control or coerce others.*

In infancy, narcissistic grandiosity—the sense of omnipotent and magical control over the object world—is essential as a form of psychic protection against the terrifying awareness of helplessness. However, in order to move from the teleological level, its gradual erosion is also essential, even though the painfulness of the accompanying disillusionment contributes to the tantrums and rage of toddlerhood. For many people who come to analysis, it is also necessary to go through a similar experience of rage in adult life, as analysts know especially from work with patients with a history of severe trauma. The analytic relationship needs to be one that allows for the patient's repeated destructive attacks on the analyst, which both analyst and patient can survive.

It is this intensive work with the negative transference that enables the patient gradually to relinquish the coercive control of the analyst, which accompanies the teleological and intentional levels, and to allow the experience of separation and difference, which reflect truly psychological and symbolic self-agency.

THE ANALYTIC RELATIONSHIP AND THE PROCESS
OF INDIVIDUATION

At the heart of all these aspects of analysis is the relational dynamic that Jung called the "transcendent function." Jung's view was that in symbols "the union of conscious and unconscious is consummated" (Jung 1939/1968, para. 524). In attachment theory terms, the transcendent function can be understood as a constant dynamic process of comparison and integration of explicit conscious information and memories with the more generalized knowledge which we accumulate unconsciously in the internal working models of implicit memory, a key part of which constitutes the sense of self. This process of "compare and contrast"—in attachment theory called "appraisal"—is an unconscious process by which experiences are constantly screened and evaluated to determine their meaning and significance. Bowlby wrote: "Sensory inflow goes through many stages of selection, interpretation and appraisal before it can have any influence on behavior, either immediately or later. This processing occurs in a succession of stages, all but the preliminary of which require that the inflow be related to matching information already stored in long-term memory" (Bowlby 1980, 45). New experience is therefore constantly being organized by unconscious internal working models, and unconscious implicit patterns are constantly being identified in conscious language. Jung's theories about self-regulation and compensation thus anticipated the contemporary concept of appraisal, in that he considered self-regulation to be a process in which unconscious compensation is a balancing or supplementing of the conscious orientation. From a relational perspective, James Fosshage has described psychoanalytic therapy as an "implicit-explicit dance," in which there is a constant two-way flow of information between explicit and implicit memory systems (Fosshage 2004). Siegel offers neuroscientific support for the central role of emotion in this process, suggesting that "such an *integrative process* may be at the core of what emotion *does* and indeed what emotion *is*" (1998, 7).

Meaningful experience, therefore, depends on the transcendent function, a process which compares and integrates the following:

- internal objects (the internalized "other") and the self
- a new event and past experience
- explicit and implicit knowledge
- cognition and emotion
- left brain and right brain
- orbito-frontal cortex and subcortical networks

Consciousness or unconsciousness are not fixed attributes of either pole of these dyads but are distributed in varying degrees between the two poles, reflecting the variety of ways in which mental content may be processed and stored.

The essence of the mechanism underlying self-organization, from an attachment perspective, is one of "compare and contrast," the constant evaluation of similarity and difference between new information and existing knowledge. The alchemical metaphor highlights the fact that some patients need to regress to a state of merger, a mutual descent into unconsciousness. This analytic experience is focused on regression to infantile experiences of "perfect contingency," when similarities rather than differences are discovered and explored, and when the illusion of fusion is not challenged but allowed to run its course (Gergely and Watson 1996). Marcus West has drawn on Matte Blanco's model to suggest that an affective appraisal mechanism is predominantly an unconscious preference for sameness, so that too much difference is at first ignored (giving the impression of primary narcissism) but then gradually sought/allowed (West 2007).

Gergely and Watson suggest that this stage is followed by increasing separation, as the infant begins to be more interested in "imperfect contingency," which means that their interest shifts from similarity to difference. Others, such as Tronick and Beebe, differ somewhat from Gergely and Watson, in suggesting that disruption and repair are as essential to the unconscious attachment dynamics of mother and infant as regularity and predictability, even in the earliest weeks of infancy, as part of the process of unconscious categorization which is fundamental to the development of meaning.

In both models, however, these developmental processes eventually lead to the achievement of "unit status," the recognition of the complex and ever shifting similarity and difference between self and other, which forms the basis for the capacity to have deep emotional relationships without fearing a catastrophic loss of self. Similarly, in adult analysis the unconscious exploration of similarity and difference are inseparable from each other and also from affect regulation. For example, emotional stress seems to lead to a position of preferring sameness and resisting change. Exploration, the curiosity about difference, gives way to the retreat to a secure base—that which is safe and familiar—because stress indicates danger.

AN INTEGRATED VIEW OF THE TASKS OF THE ANALYTIC RELATIONSHIP

I suggest that the wealth of information from other disciplines does, for the first time, put us in the position where we can attune the analytic process and the analytic relationship to the developmental task a patient is struggling with at any point in the process. We can construct a table in which the three main analytic goals I described at the start of this chapter:

- activating the attachment system to facilitate the development of secure attachment
- developing the capacity for mentalization and reflective function

- facilitating the development of self-agency

can be correlated with three main therapeutic approaches:

- interpretation, allowing conscious awareness of repressed or dissociated mental contents.
- new relational experiences, in which the analyst is a new object for the patient
- facilitating regression (reculer pour mieux sauter).

This table then allows us to place a variety of specific analytic techniques in the context of the particular task and the particular broad analytic approach that the analyst feels most closely corresponds to the task:

	Interpretation (narrative linking)	**New Experience (analyst as new object)**	**Facilitating Regression**
Developing Secure Attachment	transference interpretation in the here and now	empathic mirroring attunement containment	enabling projection experiencing the past in the present
Developing Reflective Function	transference interpretation linking past and present.	analyst's focus on symbolic rather than concrete	recalling and working through painful past experience
Development of Self-Agency	interpretation of dreams, fantasies, symptoms as intentional/ creative	analyst's survival of destructive attacks	active imagination art, sandplay

With this kind of multivectored model, different analytic theories can be seen to reflect differing emphases among analytic groups on their own particular view of the analytic relationship. This is why a developmental, process-based model becomes essential in order to improve our understanding of the analytic relationship because it can encompass a range of analytic approaches. It also places a responsibility on the analyst to give up the "secure base," the safe territory of his or her own familiar analytic model, and to explore difference and the ideas generated by other analytic approaches and other disciplines, including neuroscience and attachment theory. We need to be able to adapt our analytic approach to each patient and not to impose a "one size fits all" model of the analytic relationship in our clinical practices. Just as infants guide their parents' responses to attune to their developmental needs, so our analytic patients can guide us in the analytic relationship.

REFERENCES

Beebe, Beatrice, and Frank Lachmann. 2002. *Infant research and adult treatment: Co-constructing interactions.* Hillsdale, NJ and London: The Analytic Press.

Bowlby, John. 1980. *Attachment and loss, 3. Loss: Sadness and depression.* London: Hogarth Press.

Boston Change Process Study Group (BCPSG). 2007. The foundational level of psychodynamic meaning: Implicit process in relation to conflict, defence and the dynamic unconscious. *International Journal of Psychoanalysis* 88:843–60.

Fonagy, Peter. 1991. Thinking about thinking: Some clinical and theoretical considerations in the treatment of a borderline patient. *International Journal of Psychoanalysis* 72, 4: 639–56.

Fonagy, Peter, Gyorgy Gergely, Elliot Jurist, and Mary Target. 2002. *Affect regulation, mentalization and the development of the self.* New York: Other Press.

Fordham, Michael. 1957/1996. Notes on the transference. In *Analyst-patient interaction. Collected papers on technique*, ed. Sonu Shamdasani. London and New York: Routledge.

———. 1979/1996. Analytical psychology and countertransference. In *Analyst-patient interaction. Collected papers on technique*, ed. Sonu Shamdasani. London and New York: Routledge.

Fosshage, James. 2004. The explicit and implicit dance in psychoanalytic change. *Journal of Analytical Psychology* 49, 1: 49–66.

Gergely, Gyorgy, and John Watson. 1996. The social biofeedback theory of parental affect-mirroring: The development of emotional self awareness and self-control in infancy. *International Journal of Psycho-analysis* 77: 1181–1212.

Holmes, Jeremy. 2001. *The search for the secure base.* London and New York: Brunner-Routledge.

Jung, C.G. 1931/1966. Problems of modern psychotherapy. In CW 16.

———. 1935/1966. Problems of modern psychotherapy. In CW 16.

———. 1937/1966. Problems of modern psychotherapy. In CW 16.

———. 1939/1968. Conscious, unconscious and individuation. In CW 9i.

———. 1946/1966. The psychology of the transference. CW 16.

Knox, Jean. 2005. Sex, shame and the transcendent function: the function of fantasy in self development. *Journal of Analytical Psychology* 50, 5: 617–40.

———. 2007. The fear of love. *Journal of Analytical Psychology* 52, 5: 543–64.

Sandler, Joseph. 1976. Countertransference and role responsiveness. *International Review of Psychoanalysis* 3:43–47.

Schore, Allan. 2003. *Affect regulation and the repair of the self.* New York and London: W.W. Norton & Co.

Siegel, Daniel. 1998. The developing mind: Towards a neurobiology of interpersonal experience. *The Signal* 6, 3–4: 1–11.

West, Marcus. 2007. *Feeling, being, and the sense of self: A new perspective on identity, affect and narcissistic disorders.* London: Karnac Books Ltd.

Winnicott, Donald. 1965. The theory of the parent-infant relationship. In *The maturational process and the facilitating environment.* Studies in the theory of emotional development. London: Hogarth Press.

————. 1971. The use of an object and relating through identifications. In *Playing and reality.* London: Tavistock Publications.

Dr. Jean Knox is a Senior Member and Training Therapist of the British Association of Psychotherapists, a Training Analyst of the Society of Analytical Psychology, Consultant Editor of the *Journal of Analytical Psychology* and Honorary Senior Lecturer at the University of Kent. She is the author of *Archetype, Attachment, Analysis: Jungian Psychology and the Emergent Mind.* Her current research centers in the issue of self-agency and its expression in language and other communicative acts in the therapeutic relationship.

19

COUNTERTRANSFERENCE AND INTERSUBJECTIVITY

Linda Carter

Although Jung valued Freud's reductive method of psychoanalysis with its emphasis on early history and causality, his own view of the process of individuation was concerned with transformative processes of change and the prospective unfolding of the psyche. With his synthetic or constructive method, he looked to unconscious symbols as they anticipated progressive development toward a new attitude (Jung 1943/1966, para. 159). For Jung, the meaning of the symbol, which holds conscious and unconscious elements in tension, is elaborated through the process of amplification (see chapter on amplification, above) in which the fundamental archetypal pattern inherent in the symbol is matched with an analogical image from myth, fairy tale, or cultural example. Using this amplificatory material, the analyst and analysand engage in a collaborative effort to expand and deepen the meaning of the symbol as it is expressive of and emergent from the analytic dyad, which in turn is embedded in a larger cultural context.

Like Freud, Jung was keenly aware of transference and countertransference, but he saw this as a process of mutual influence, as is evident in the *Psychology of the Transference* (Jung 1946/1966) where he uses alchemical imagery and operations to amplify the multiple levels of analytic transactions, both conscious and unconscious. Out of the conscious/unconscious tension within the individual and out of the tension between the analyst and analysand comes the emergence of the third as new life, in what Jung calls the transcendent function, the synthesis of opposites (Jung 1921/1971, para. 828). These fundamental ideas are stunningly prescient and resonate with contemporary notions of interaction/intersubjectivity, emergence, and Complex Adaptive Systems (CAS). We could almost think of Jung as a proto-systems theorist.

Psychoanalysts and infant researchers interested in intersubjectivity are challenging the conception of transference and countertransference as located within each of the individual constituents of the analytic pair, rather than in a realm between the two that has been mutually co-constructed. The multiplicity of selves of each person, including past history and expectancies, meet in the consulting room, where old patterns emerge along with new interactive possibilities. The analytic dyad is an emergent phenomenon that is contingent on interaction in a given moment and is nested within an archetypal field. Without question, reconstruction of family history and life narrative are important in terms of understanding and insight, but the process of being together with another in relationship in the current moment is highly relevant. The past reveals itself in the present moment so that repetition is involved, while at the same time the present is always unique and moving toward the potentially predictable but unknown future.

Rather than look narrowly at countertransference, I prefer to look at the analyst's use of self (or multiple selves) within the multitiered analytic system (brain, mind, and culture) of two interacting individuals. Phenomenological description, deepened through image, metaphor, and amplification, keeps the understanding of the analytical transaction open to emergent process rather than reducing it to theoretical structures. The term countertransference can be weighed down with historical and theoretical baggage as it harks back to psychoanalytic notions of a one-person psychology. Jung's alchemical account of the transference/countertransference dynamic is fundamentally a two-person psychological system containing intra- and interpsychic aspects. The analyst does not "own" or "have" a countertransference; he is "in" a phenomenological experience co-created with the other. The two people of the analytic dyad are in conjunction, symbolically held by the alchemical vessel constructed through the analytic relationship. Countertransference can never be fully analyzed because it is not one thing or entity in itself; rather it is emergent in a given moment and in a given relationship. Certainly, understanding the narrative content of a patient's history is central for the analyst's practice, but simply making the unconscious conscious is not enough for change and individuation. Understanding how one is "with another" is essential, along with the capacity for reflective function and for play with metaphor and analogy.

Development of a broader understanding of the analyst's use of "self in relation" rather than specifically focusing narrowly on countertransference is furthered through consideration of the multimodal, multifaceted communication process of the dyad, not just the individuals. The use of metaphor, myth, and dream have been central means of communication for Jungians, but we must consider more carefully nonverbal communications (via facial expression, voice, body movement) and nonverbal processes such as rhythm and flow of moment-by-moment interaction in an analytic hour. It would seem that the analyst's simultaneous, internal reflection on thoughts, feelings, perceptions and images in the midst of engagement in the dyad is a complex process requiring a well developed analytic attitude and consciousness.

Ultimately, there can be no analyst without an analysand and no countertransference without transference. The two form an intersubjective matrix as described by Ogden who states: "I do not conceive of transference and countertransference as separable psychological entities that arise independently of, or in response to one another, but as aspects of a single intersubjective totality" (Ogden 1997, 78).

Although Ogden continues to use the traditional language of transference and countertransference, it seems to me that a more general term like intersubjective interaction better characterizes the complex, mutually constructed, ever-changing and amorphous relationship that emerges between the analyst and analysand in a nested, dyadic system. Contemporary psychoanalysts, infant researchers and neuroscientists are struggling to understand and describe the nature and therapeutic value of this interactive exchange that transpires in the liminal realm of the consulting room. There is something that happens "in between" two people, "in between" outer and inner life, "in between" unconscious and conscious, which is co-created and potentially therapeutic and life-giving.

Along these lines, Ogden speaks of the analytic third as the third subject created by the unconscious interplay of the analyst and analysand. He sees this analytic third as something continually in a state of flux, as a process not an entity. It is not experienced identically by each personality system, in other words, it is experienced asymmetrically (Ogden 1997, 30). Connecting some of Ogden's ideas to Jung, Joe Cambray suggests that dreams can be seen as emanating from the analytic third and believes that Jung suggested this kind of intersubjective constellation on several occasions as in the following example:

> [Jung] commented in 1934 to James Kirsch on a series of explicit transference dreams that one of Kirsch's patients was having: "With regard to your patient, it is quite correct that her dreams are occasioned by you. . . . In the deepest sense we all dream not out of ourselves but out of what lies between us and the other." (Cambray 2002, 427)

INTERSUBJECTIVITY AND SYSTEMS THEORIES

Jung's early considerations of the dynamic interaction in analysis seem to be precursors for contemporary intersubjective perspectives and systems theories that substantiate some of these early ideas and offer more refined ways to consider old analytic stand-bys such as the notions of transference and countertransference. Before discussing Jung's alchemical model as a poetic, imagistic rendering of the intersubjective field, I would like to offer some fundamental aspects of intersubjectivist thinking and of Complex Adaptive Systems (CAS) theory.

There is not one clear definition of intersubjectivity, however it can be said that "all theories of intersubjectivity are theories of interaction" (Beebe et al 2005, 4). Simply put, intersubjectivity "refers to what is going on between two minds . . . [it] encompasses the full complexity of how two minds interrelate, align, fail to align, or disrupt and repair alignment" (ibid., 73). According to Beebe and colleagues, psychoanalysis has addressed the concept of intersubjectivity primarily in the verbal/explicit mode while infant research has focused on the concept of intersubjectivity in the nonverbal/implicit mode of action sequences, or procedural knowledge. Further, infant research has studied the presymbolic mind while psychoanalysis has attended to the symbolic mind (ibid., 1–2). It is then argued that "an integration of explicit/linguistic and implicit/nonverbal theories of intersubjectivity is essential to a deeper understanding of therapeutic action in psychoanalysis today" (ibid., 2). These intersubjectivist approaches weave multiple strands together into nets and systems, and they share with Jung constructivist and holistic views. Interaction is the critical element for connecting elements that emerge into ever more complex systems like the neurons of the brain forming webs out of which the mind comes forward and interacts with other minds thus forming social systems. The analytic dyad emerges from a many-layered relational matrix of a Complex Adaptive System whose engine is interaction/intersubjectivity.

Complex Adaptive Systems (CAS) perspectives have been discussed in the Jungian literature by Tresan (1996), Knox (2003, 2004), Hogenson (2004, 2007), Cambray (2002, 2004) and others. I have in particular been following the literature of infant research applications to adult psychoanalysis as found in the work of Beebe and Lachmann (2002), Beebe, et al (2005), Stern (1998, 2004), and Tronick (2007), who look with gratitude to the pioneering work of Louis Sander (1982, 2002). All of these researchers and theorists consider CAS theory to be foundational.

The theory of Complex Adaptive Systems can be enormously helpful in understanding human interaction and specifically the transference/countertransference constellation. Cambray describes CAS as follows:

> These are systems that have what is termed emergent properties, that is, self organiz-
> ing features arising in response to environmental, competitive pressures . . . CAS form
> gestalts in which the whole is truly greater than the sum of its parts. In the words of
> Steven Johnson, in these systems agents residing on one scale produce behavior that
> lies one scale above them. . . . The movement from low-level rules to higher-level
> sophistication is what we call emergence. (Cambray 2002, 45)

We operate within a network of interacting component parts that lead to the emergence of ever greater complex systems beginning with micro, local level connections moving toward larger, macro level patterns of organization. Think here of the interaction of neurons which "fire together and wire together" (Hebb's Law). Neurons form neural nets that in turn form the brain out of which the mind emerges, so that the brain and the mind are necessarily self-organizing and complex systems influencing each other as elements of the human organism that is relating to an environment. This bottom up development is not hierarchical or planned with the explicit conscious awareness or the overview of a grand designer; rather, natural patterns come into being implicitly and can only be comprehended in large numbers or with distance and perspective. Think of looking down on an ant colony or having an aerial view of city neighborhoods.

The understanding of complex systems has been advanced through computer simulations, which allow large scale patterns to emerge. We are influenced by repeating patterns allowing for continuity and by surprising breaks, which lead to change. For example, mother and baby develop expectancies of "being with" each other that are forged through repetition. This offers needed continuity. Then suddenly, one day a new sequence of behaviors emerges in the dyad and the system moves to a new level. Memory of this event, if it is ongoing, becomes incorporated into interactive expectancies. Such interaction moves the mother/baby system toward new levels of complexity and simultaneously changes brain function of the participants (Schore 2003, 97). In discussing Sander's work, Beebe and Lachmann say: "an interactive system is always in process, with a dialectic between predictability and transformation" (2002, 30), a view that would seem quite harmonious with Jung's ideas about a dialectical relationship in analysis.

DYADIC SYSTEMS AND INFANT RESEARCH

In their work, Beebe and Lachmann define dyadic systems models as those approaches that integrate the contribution of the individual and that of the dyad to the organization of behavior and experience. They use terms such as *co-construction* and *co-creation* to convey the mutual contribution of two partners in an ongoing co-ordination of both self and interactive regulation. They state:

> a theory of interaction must specify how each person is affected by his own behavior—
> that is, self-regulation and by the partner's behavior—that is, interactive regulation. . . .
> Each person must both monitor the partner (influence and be influenced) and at the
> same time regulate his own state. Self- and interactive regulation are concurrent and
> reciprocal processes (Gianino and Tronick, 1988). Each affects the success of the
> other. They are optimally in dynamic balance to move back and forth. (Beebe and
> Lachmann 2002, 26)

Tronick furthers these ideas when he talks about dyadic states of consciousness:

> At the moment when the dyadic system is created, both partners experience an expan-
> sion of their own state of consciousness (brain organization). Their states of conscious-
> ness become dyadic and expand to incorporate elements of consciousness of the other
> in a new and more coherent form. At this moment of forming a dyadic state of con-
> sciousness, and for the duration of its existence, there must be something akin to a
> powerful experience of fulfillment as one paradoxically becomes larger than oneself.
> (Tronick 2007, 408)

This fundamentally emergent idea of dyadic expansion seems quite resonant with Ogden's notions of transference and countertransference being "aspects of a single intersubjective totality" (Ogden 1997, 78). To my mind, Jung is attempting to deal with the same relational phenomena in his alchemical studies, where he describes the conjunction of the opposites as a union in a field of mutual influence. Through the alchemical images in the *Psychology of the Transference*, he is trying to work with visible, conscious, verbal engagement as well as with invisible, unconscious (and maybe nonconscious) forces at both the personal and archetypal levels.

EXPLICIT AND IMPLICIT MEMORY

To further an understanding of what happens in the analytic transaction, a discussion of what is meant by implicit and explicit memory is helpful. For this, I will turn to neuroscience and consider how these findings are being integrated into contemporary intersubjectivist perspectives.

Explicit memory, also known as declarative memory (Siegel 1999, 33), tends to be verbal and requires conscious awareness and focal attention for encoding. It includes both semantic (factual) memory and episodic autobiographical memory, which begins to operate at about age two. Implicit or nondeclarative, procedural memory (ibid.) is present at birth and is devoid of a sense of recall. This includes behavioral, emotional, perceptual, and somatosensory memory. These memories have never, for the most part, been "conscious" and therefore cannot be forgotten. (There are exceptions; for example, to learn a new skill such as riding a bicycle, one needs focused, conscious attention. However, once the skill is acquired, procedural memory takes over and riding the bicycle happens automatically.) The implicit is often conveyed through vocal rhythm, intonation, cadence, timing, and through body movement and sensations usually outside of conscious recognition. Coordination and integration of these two domains are influenced through early attachment experiences (Beebe and Lachmann, 2002; Stern, et al. 1998; Tronick, 2007) and profoundly effect self and interactive regulations. How one relates to others and to one's internal world emanates not simply from internalization of the object but from the emergence of the "process of mutual regulation" (Stern, et al. 1998, 907). This is not about internalization of objects; rather, infant researcher/psychoanalysts such as Stern and Beebe have found that through interpersonal connection interactive patterns form as ongoing relational "expectancies." These are rooted in personal history, and they influence and shape what we have previously called transference and countertransference.

Implicit memory is also known as the nonconscious, which resonates with analytic models of dissociation such as were proposed by Jung. The dynamic unconscious model founded by Freud, which is based on repression, does not account for implicit memory. According to Regina Pally, "Neuroscientists use the term 'nonconscious' rather than 'unconscious.' The psychoanalytic term 'unconscious' implies that experience is repressed or split off for defensive purposes" (Pally 2005, 193). These new differentiations of implicit and explicit memory confirm Jung's sense that there is more to the unconscious than the repressed aspects of historical trauma. Traditional psychoanalytic notions of therapeutic process that are based on defenses such as resistance and repression in the dynamic unconscious cannot account for the powerful effects of the nonconscious described here.

Daniel Stern and colleagues (1998) certainly honor the importance of the transference, but they are also interested in the emerging "new" relationship that is co-created within the analytic dyad which comes about through the interplay of explicit and implicit domains. Stern et al. (1998, 908) note that interpretation rearranges the explicit relationship and *moments of meeting* rearrange implicit relational knowing. By *moment of meeting*, Stern et al. mean that it is a moment of intersubjective "fittedness . . . where both partners share an experience and they know it implicitly" (Stern 2004, 168). The therapist's response must be authentic and spontaneous, matching the immediate situation and reaching beyond a neutral, technical response (ibid.). This idea of the new relationship unfolding into the future propelled by interactive moments fits well with Jungian ideas related to the prospective function of analysis. These co-creative moments foster linkages between two people and within oneself. Understanding the influence of the past, played out through historical expectancies of each partner, is critical for analysis, the possibility of the future and a new way of being is equally as important. Despite the fact that the models of Stern and colleagues, Beebe and Lachmann, and Tronick are grounded in multitiered systems theory, they are missing the transpersonal link provided by an archetypal understanding, which links the analytic dyad to universal patterning across cultures and across time.

JUNG AND SYSTEMS MODELS

The famous images of Sol and Luna (Sun and Moon, King and Queen) from the *Rosarium Philosophorum* (1550), the focus of Jung's attention in *The Psychology of the Transference* (Jung 1946/1966), beautifully illustrates a system of interacting complexity and emergence. He examines communication between individuals (represented archetypally as Sol and Luna) along several axes: conscious/conscious, conscious/unconscious, and unconscious/unconscious. The case for Jung as a proto-systems theorist can be made when considering quotes such as the following:

> For two personalities to meet is like mixing two different chemical substances: if there is any combination at all, both are transformed. In any effective psychological treatment the doctor is bound to influence the patient; but this influence can only take place if the patient has a reciprocal influence on the doctor. You can exert no influence if you are not susceptible to influence. (Jung 1946/1966, para. 163)

Jung is describing here a system of bidirectional influence that is consonant with the intersubjective approaches previously noted. Doctor and patient are engaged in a reciprocal (but, as Ogden might say, asymmetrical) dialogue at multiple levels. Infant researchers have been mapping the nonverbal, multi-modal domain of the intersubjective nonconscious that profoundly influences interaction through facial expression, gaze, spatial orientation, touch, posture, and the prosodic and rhythmic dimensions of vocalization (Beebe 2005, 23). Trevarthen (1989) has created a diagram of mother/infant face-to-face exchange with cross-current arrows between mother's eyes, hands, mouth, and ears and the corresponding aspects of the baby that attempts to illustrate the complex transactions of nonverbal, nonconscious relating. This diagrammatic mapping has in common with

Jung's alchemical schema the attempt to explore the interactive *process* of two mutually influencing systems. What is important here is that Jung, through amplification with alchemical imagery and metaphor, was able to capture the *dynamic process* of (intersubjective) interaction in analysis. In the following, he speaks of the reciprocal process of two psychic systems engaged in the dialectic of psychotherapy:

> Psychotherapy is . . . a kind of dialectical process, a dialogue or discussion between two persons. Dialectic was originally the art of conversation among the ancient philosophers, but very early became the term for the process of creating new syntheses. A person is a psychic system which, when it affects another person, enters into reciprocal reaction with another psychic system. (Jung 1946/1966, para. 1)

New syntheses emerge creating ever-more complex systems. In Jungian parlance, we may think of this as the transcendent function, which holds the tension of opposites and presents as a symbol, a synthesis, a third creation. Jung is speaking here of course of adult psychic systems, which unlike mother/infant dyads have a capacity for symbolic thought and language. Adults have two modes of communication, while infants are limited developmentally to nonverbal communication and presymbolic thinking. Understanding the intricate interweaving of these two modes is central to the fullest appreciation of both process and content in analysis and to achieving a holistic view. We have a great deal to learn from the infant researchers who believe that "much of the organization of nonverbal communication remains similar across the lifespan" (Beebe and Lachmann 2002, 26).

What do Jungians have to offer the analytic discourse regarding intersubjectivity and the value of terms such as transference and countertransference? Myth, story, and imagery open possibilities for metaphoric, nonlinear, ambiguous play in the space "in between." Moving from the personal to the collective is a move to another layer of the mutually influencing system. When intersubjective matching is activated in the co-constructed dyad and there is a true sense of affective resonance (this is critical), the vibration reaches to and is felt at the archetypal level. The image that evolves "in between" represents a synthesis of the interaction of two minds, two bodies, two psyches meeting consciously, unconsciously, and nonconsciously in a "dyadic state of consciousness," a "moment of meeting," as the "transcendent function." We struggle to find words to describe the experience. Perhaps that is why the indirectness of metaphor is so valuable. Metaphor presents in pictures, possibilities, undefined images and allows for the mystery of the unknown.

Hovering over these alchemical operations is the figure of Mercurius (Samuels, 1984), the dual natured god of communication who transgresses boundaries as he moves with winged feet and wears the cap of invisibility functioning as a "psychopomp" or guide of souls to the underworld. To me, he is the god of fluidity, flexibility, and possibility, and he occupies the space "in between." Metaphorically, his presence creates an atmosphere of flow, facilitating dialogue, linking, and connection at all levels—body, mind, and soul. Submission to his fluid and flexible nature leads the analytic dyad between the opposites of order and chaos toward transformation. He is the invisible, intangible spirit of relationship and transformative process. Says Jung, "Besides being the prima materia of the lowly beginning as well as the lapis as the highest goal, Mercurius is also the *process which lies between*, and the means by which it is effected. He is the 'beginning, middle, and end of the work.' Therefore he is called the Mediator, Servator, and Salvator" (Jung 1948/67, para. 283; emphasis mine).

Amplification when used well is an art. It is not necessarily employed with *explicit intentionality* but is instead an *emergent phenomenon* that captures the essence of a psychological constellation. It connects the personal and the archetypal and should be presented tentatively as an option—a possibility to be entertained, something to be played with. With careful attention to the analysand's explicit and implicit responses, engagement in metaphorical language and image has the potential to connect body and mind within the containing relationship. Arnold Modell writes of this: "Metaphor is a fundamental and indispensable structure of human understanding" (Modell 1997, 219). And: "Metaphor not only transfers meaning between different domains, but by means of novel recombinations metaphor can *transform* meaning and generate new perceptions. Imagination could not exist without this recombinatory metaphoric process" (Modell 2003, 27).

A CLINICAL MOMENT

A man in his fifties was in the midst of divorce, the presenting reason for beginning treatment. At the outset, he was struggling with pain, sorrow, and humiliation related to the end of his marriage. Relatively quickly, he and I developed an ease in relating with a rhythmic back and forth, good eye contact and a range of affect between us. His educational background was such that he easily quoted poetry and associated often to characters in novels, allowing for playful exchange. Dealing with shame over recent life decisions and events, he seemed to be grieving the diminishment of his integrity, which had brought with it the loss of friends and of his previous good reputation in the community.

He was overwhelmed by what a mess his life had become. During one session, he recounted a recent scene in which he was sitting on the threshold between the house that he had shared with his wife and their three-bay garage. Smoking a cigar and drinking a beer, he looked out over the three bays completely filled with twenty-five years worth of possessions and felt that the task of sorting it would be impossible. Telling this story, he sat slumped in the chair with a terribly sad expression on his face. He seemed weighed down, heavy.

In response, I felt sad and overwhelmed by how much there was to sort. In this specific clinical moment, seeing the patient (in my mind) sitting on the threshold with mountains of things to organize, another image simultaneously emerged unbidden by consciousness. What came to me was the memory of a beautiful and heart-wrenching picture of the mythological figure Psyche, forlorn and abandoned, faced with the challenge of sorting mountains of tiny seeds in order to regain the relationship with her lover, Eros. I had always found this picture to be deeply moving.

I simply said to my patient, "Maybe you feel like Psyche and the seeds." (Without consciously thinking about it, I knew that he had a good grasp of mythology and that he would relate emotionally to the story.) He began to cry. I began to cry. There was a sense that something transcendent had happened. A metaphorical image emerged between us and captured the essence of a profound life experience both at the personal and archetypal levels. The two pictures/stories—my patient on the threshold and Psyche weeping—were a kind of gaze experience where we were co-coordinated in a "matched" state like that of the mother/infant situation.

Tronick's notion of dyadic states of consciousness is relevant here. He and others from the Boston Process of Change group argue that there is "something more" than interpretation that is curative in therapy. He says that "these states of consciousness emerge from the mutual regulation of affect between the patient and the therapist" (Tronick 2007, 410) and are "the creation by the therapist and the patient of new and unique dyadic states" (411).

Psyche's beautiful, metaphorical story of love, loss, and finding oneself and the other in relationship is one of unfolding, creation, and emergence. Psyche as soul and Eros as love convey the suffering and joy of relationship and the potential birth of new life born of their conjunction as the baby Voluptas, or joy. In thinking about this mythological pair, Hillman says, "What transpires *in* our psyche is not *of* our psyche; both love and soul finally and from the beginning belong to the realm of archetypal reality. . . . No matter how personally we feel them as our 'own,' eros and psyche are archetypal powers that find their final and original 'home' when placed where they belong, as transpersonal events which paradoxically form the ground of personality" (Hillman 1972, 104–5).

For me, Jung's analytical psychology with inclusion of the archetypal dimension brings a depth of meaning not found in other psychologies. The cultural and collective layers of the psyche are ever present and influencing intrapsychic and interpersonal interactions. At the personal level, emergent moments in analysis as the one described above could be seen as a "moment of meeting," or a constellation of the "transcendent function." Under such circumstances, Jungian psychology offers words and language for the spiritual, mysterious or numinous experience that comes into being through these moments of interaction that really transcend individual psychologies and dyads reaching farther to webs of connection and communication as a transpersonal collective psyche.

REFERENCES

Beebe, Beatrice and Frank Lachmann. 2002. *Infant research and adult treatment: Co-constructing interactions.* Hillside, NJ and London: The Analytic Press.

Beebe, Beatrice, et al. 2005. *Forms of intersubjectivity in infant research and adult treatment.* New York: Other Press.

Cambray, Joseph. 2002. Synchronicity and emergence. *American Imago* 59, 4: 409–34.
———. 2004. Synchronicity as emergence. In *Analytical Psychology: Contemporary perspectives in Jungian Analysis*, ed. Joseph Cambray and Linda Carter, 223–48. New York: Brunner-Routledge.
Cambray, Joseph, and Linda Carter. 2004. *Analytical Psychology: Contemporary perspectives in Jungian Analysis*. New York: Brunner-Routledge.
Gianino, Andrew, and Tronick, Ed Z. 1988. The mutual regulation model: The infant's self and interactive regulation, coping and defensive capacities. In *Stress and coping*, ed. Tiffany M. Field, Philip McCabe, and Neil Schneiderman, 47–68, Hillsdale, NJ: Erlbaum.
Hillman, James. 1972. *The myth of analysis*. New York: Harper Colophon Books.
Hogenson, George. 2004. Archetypes: Emergence and the psyche's deep structure. In *Analytical Psychology: Contemporary perspectives in Jungian Analysis*, ed. Joseph Cambray and Linda Carter, 32–55. New York: Brunner-Routledge.
———. 2007. From moments of meeting to archetypal consciousness: Emergence and the fractal structure of analytic practice. In *Who owns Jung?* ed. Ann Casement, 293–314. London: Karnac.
Jung, C.G. 1921/1971. Definitions. In CW 6.
———. 1943/1966. On the psychology of the unconscious. In CW 7.
———. 1948/1967. The spirit Mercurius. In CW 13.
———. 1946/1966. The psychology of the transference. In CW 16.
———. 1973. *Letters* 1, ed. Gerhard Adler and Aniela Jaffé. London: Routledge and Kegan Paul.
Knox, Jean. 2003. *Archetype, attachment, analysis: Jungian psychology and the emergent mind*. London: Bruner-Rutledge.
———. 2004. Developmental aspects of analytical psychology: New perspectives from cognitive neuroscience and attachment theory. In *Analytical Psychology: Contemporary perspectives in Jungian Analysis*, ed. Joseph Cambray and Linda Carter, 56–82. New York: Brunner-Routledge.
Loewald, Hans. 1986. Transference-countertransference. *Journal of the American Psychoanalytic Association* 34: 275–87.
Modell, Arnold. 1997. Reflections on metaphor and affects. *Annual of Psychoanalysis* 25.
———. 2003. *Imagination and the meaningful brain*. Cambridge, MA: MIT Press.
Ogden, Thomas. 1994. The analytic third: Working with intersubjective clinical facts. *The International Journal of Psycho-Analysis* 73:517–26.
———. 1994. *Subjects of analysis*. Northvale, NJ: Jason Aronson.
———. 1997. *Reverie and interpretation*. Northvale, NJ: Jason Aronson.
Pally, Regina. 2005. A Neuroscience perspective on forms of intersubjectivity in infant research and adult treatment. In *Forms of intersubjectivity in infant research and adult treatment,* ed. Beatrice Beebe et al., 191–241. New York: Other Press.
Samuels, Andrew. 1985. Symbolic dimensions of eros in transference-countertransference: Some clinical uses of Jung's alchemical metaphor. *International Review of Psychoanalysis* 12: 199–214.
Sander, Louis. 1983. Polarities, paradox, and the organizing process of development. In *Frontiers of infant psychiatry,* ed. Justin D. Call, et al., 333–45, New York: Basic Books.
———. 2002. Thinking differently: Principles of process in living systems and the specificity of being known. *Psychoanalytic Dialogues* 12, 1:11–42.

Schore, Alan. 2003. *Affect dysregulation and disorders of the self.* New York: W.W. Norton & Company, Inc.

Siegel, Daniel. 1999. *The developing mind.* New York: The Guilford Press.

———. 2007. *The mindful brain: Reflection and attunement in the cultivation of well-being.* New York: W. W. Norton & Company.

Stern, Daniel, et al. 1998. Non-interpretive mechanisms in psychoanalytic therapy: the 'something more' than interpretation. *International Journal of Psychoanalysis* 79: 903–21.

———. 2004. *The present moment in psychotherapy and everyday life.* New York: W.W. Norton & Company.

Tresan, David. 1996. Jungian metapsychology and neurobiological theory. *Journal of Analytical Psychology* 41, 3: 399–436.

Trevarthen, Colwyn. 1989. Development of early social interactions and the affective regulation of brain growth. In *Neurobiology of early infant behavior*, ed. Curt von Euler, Hans Forssberg, and Hugo Lagercrantz, 191–216. London: Macmillan.

Tronick, Edward. 2007. *The neurobehavioral and social-emotional development of infants and children.* New York: W. W. Norton & Company.

Wilkinson, Margaret. 2006. *Coming into mind: The mind-brain relationship: a Jungian clinical perspective.* London and New York: Routledge.

LINDA CARTER, MSN, CS, practices in Providence, RI and in Boston and is a training analyst in the Jungian Psychoanalytical Society of New York. For the *Journal of Analytical Society*, Linda is the US Editor, and she is Assistant Editor for *The Jung Journal*.

20

ANALYZING PROJECTIONS, FANTASIES, AND DEFENSES

Angela M. Connolly

If, as Jan Wiener says, "it would be difficult to find a Jungian analyst around the world who would dispute the inevitability of transference projections making themselves felt within the analytical relationship" (Wiener 2004, 149), at the present moment what Jungians risk losing, in a certain sense, is the specificity of the classical Jungian clinical method with its emphasis on the importance of the intrapsychic dimension and of the analyst's imaginal processes. It is perhaps paradoxical that it is the Freudian world that seems to be more aware of the risks of an excessive focus on the interpersonal or relational element in analysis. Increasingly, according to Lombardi, our analysands tend to demonstrate serious deficits in their capacity to integrate sensory experiences at a symbolical level, and in such cases an excessive emphasis on "the interpretation of the transference risks reinforcing primitive fusional/confusional mechanisms or strengthening imitative mechanisms thus creating obstacles to a real individual participation in the analytical experience" (Lombardi 2000, 693). In this discussion of how I analyze projections, fantasies, and defenses, I will be referring to the primitive mental states typical of these kinds of analysands as it is exactly here that the classical Jungian method is relevant.

First, however, I propose to discuss very briefly psychoanalytical models of psychic functioning that show interesting parallels with Jung's ideas and offer us potential theoretical tools for the integration between the classical and the developmental approaches. This is fundamental if we are to create a specifically Jungian account of clinical concepts such as fantasy, projection, and defense. Jung's model of the psyche is essentially a stratified model that presupposes different levels of consciousness. These go from the most lucid, characterized by a predominance of abstract thought, to the most unconscious psychoid levels, where time and space are no longer relevant. This is a model that has much in common with that of Matte Blanco. The model to which I wish to refer, because of its clinical relevance, is that of the Italian psychoanalyst, Armando Ferrari, which stresses that when we analyze we have to take into account not only object relations and transferences but also the relationship between mind and body.

Ferrari has hypothesized that the body is the concrete original object, which "represents each individual person in their original aspects . . . it is not related to the process of introjection and is not formed from external contributions" (Ferrari 2004, 48). Mental functioning commences with the first registration of a perception, so that the operations of perceiving a sensation and registering it take on different meanings, thus creating a passage from the unity of the body to the duality of a body and a mind with its representations and symbolic activities. With the eclipse of the centrality of the body, the area occupied by the sensory world is gradually reduced, giving rise to the constitution of a mental space and the possibility of projective-introjective dynamics. The mother's role is to support this relationship, and any failure in the mother's capacity for mirroring and for reverie will lead to disturbances in this relationship. Thus, there are two different types of basic relationship: a primary vertical one between the mind and the body, and a horizontal one between mother and child. A disharmonic functioning of the mind-body relationship can lead on the one hand to a predominance of sensory phenomena, which can jeopardize the reflective functioning as in psychosis, or to a prevalence of intellectual abstraction in which there is a partial or total rejection of corporality. According to Ferrari, when there has been a failure to establish the vertical axis the task of the analyst becomes one of facilitating representation and dimensionality in the world of primitive sensations and affects rather than on the more generally explored one of the transference.

This emphasis on the importance of the vertical axis in certain analyses is very similar to the ideas of Jungians such as Cambray and Carter (2004) who see psychic development as a self-organizing emergent process in which the psyche develops along a vertical axis, moving from more simple levels to ever more complex levels in response to the pressures of the environment. They too suggest that analysis is an emergent process in which the analyst's affective and imaginal responses play an important role in catalyzing the transition from one phase to another.

This suggests that in any discussion of how we analyse projections, fantasies, and defenses the central issue is to be able to determine the level of these phenomena at any particular moment in the analytical process and to track what we do exactly in order to bring about a transformation from one level to another. One way to do this is to reflect on the different imaginal responses of the analyst, as demonstrated for example in the work of Joy Schaverien (2007) on countertransference. To take this further, I propose to go back to Jung's definitions of fantasy and imagination so as to create correlations between the kind of imaginative activity characteristic of the different levels of unconsciousness, the different forms that projection and defenses can take, and the different responses they may provoke in the analyst. I will then illustrate this by taking a fresh look at two very different analyses conducted by myself in a classical Jungian setting and concluded successfully many years ago, in which something happened that changed the course of the analysis without my being able to fully understand at that time just how these transformations had come about.

FANTASY

Jung uses the term "fantasy" to refer to two different orders of ideas: to the fantasm and to imaginative activity (Jung 1921/1971, paras. 711–22). The fantasm refers to a complex of ideas that has no objective referent in external reality but springs directly from the psyche. Imaginative activity, on the other hand, is considered to be a creative act of the psyche, one of its highest forms, whose function is to create links and to bring together and unite the conscious and unconscious personality, inner and outer worlds (ibid., paras. 77–78). Thus as we see that there are several facets to Jung's ideas about fantasy. On the one hand, there is fantasy as an image-creating function whose aim is, as Carvahlo notes, one of revelation: "to render whatever it is that we call 'mind' as if it were visible to itself in analogical form so that it is available to the subject for symbolic manipulation and scrutiny" (Carvahlo 1991, 331–32). If we think in terms of Ferrari's model, however, we would see that before the mind is presented to itself, it is first necessary to present the body to the mind. Fantasy in the sense of the creation of images is a primary, biologically adaptive activity of the psyche, whose function is to render visible or to represent the unprocessed sensations and emotions. On the other hand, fantasy as imaginative activity works by linking images in order to build up ever more complex representational schemas, and through the creation of symbols it brings together consciousness and unconsciousness, a function Jung later refers to as the transcendent or symbolic function. Important here is Fordham's distinction between imaginative activities such as play, which are in the service of the ego, and active imagination whose function is to strengthen the ego-self axis (Fordham 1956, 207).

There are problems in Jung's conceptualization of fantasy, imagination, and dreams. In as much as he sees fantasy and imagination as innate and spontaneous activities of the psyche, he shows little interest in the quality of images or in pathologies of fantasy. Furthermore, he makes no allowance for the problems of not being able to dream or the nonrepresentation in certain pathological states such as trauma. Instead, he prefers to concentrate his attention on the content of fantasies rather than on the processes themselves or on the apparatuses responsible for producing images and for dreaming. The tools of the classical Jungian method are all instruments aimed at increasing what Hogenson (2004, 161) calls the symbolical density of images, but where there are serious deficits in ego functioning it is the imaginative activity of the analyst, her capacity to provide an image or to give metaphorical depth to impoverished images, that becomes so essential.

PROJECTION

In *Psychological Types*, Jung defines projection as "the expulsion of a subjective content into an object" (Jung 1921/1971, para.783). For Jung, such contents are usually unconscious, and projection results from "the archaic identity of subject and object" or in other words from a state of *participation mystique*. Projection is a universal phenomenon that is both normal and pathological, and it lies at the basis of empathy and transference (Jung 1921/1971, para 486).

Gordon has pointed out that Jung's ideas on projection actually refer to rather different psychic experiences some of which can be more usefully thought of in terms of Melanie Klein's projective identification. For Gordon, terms such as *participation mystique* suggest that Jung is actually thinking of something very similar to projective identification (Gordon 1965, 129), and indeed references to projective identification have become frequent in Jungian literature. There are problems with the idea of projective identification, however, mainly because there is no general agreement as to what this term means. Does it refer to a purely intrapsychic fantasy or to an interpersonal mechanism? Is it a purely pathological defense or a universal if primitive mode of communication? Is it something genetic present from birth or does it is follow a developmental path? Does it exert its effects through induction or is there an actual transfer of unconscious contents, a kind of thought transference? Kernberg, in a sophisticated analysis, traces a developmental path "from projective identification which is based on an ego structure centred on splitting as its essential defence, to projection which is based on an ego structure centred on repression as a basic defence" (Kernberg 1987, 797). Ogden stresses, however, that for projective identification to take place there must already be "some sense of inner space into which one can project an aspect of oneself or into which one can take an aspect of the object" (Ogden 1989, 135). Fordham, too, seems to have some intuition of this difference when he speaks of projections onto and projections into (Fordham 1963, 7), as does Bick who describes a primitive type of narcissistic identification that she terms adhesive identification, in which the idea of getting into is replaced with the idea of getting in contact with, of surfaces stuck together with no space between them. All this suggests that beyond projection and projective identification there are other more primitive ways of transferring a content from the mind of the analysand to the mind of the analyst, and what I wish to do give a description of these kinds of projection, of what is transferred, the defense mechanisms used, and the effects exerted on the mind of the analyst.

ANALYZING PRIMITIVE PROJECTIONS, FANTASIES, AND DEFENSES

While infant observation and cognitive studies challenge the idea of primary fusion or at-oneness and suggest that objectively there is no confusion between self and other at any point of infancy, nevertheless analytical experience stresses that from the subjective point of view it seems very probable that the infant has some experience of oneness or fusion with the caregiver. In infancy, this subjective experience of at-oneness is created through maternal mirroring. If the maternal mirroring, which comes about through the mother's capacity for imitation, emotional atunement and reverie, fails or is inadequate, then I would suggest there is a potential risk of regression to one of two different pathological states of at-oneness: in one, the subject models himself or herself on the other through imitative mechanisms such that the self is reduced to the mirror image of the other; in the other, there is omnipotent control of the other who becomes reduced to the reflection of the self. In the first, which I will call autistic projection, there is no distinction between inner and outer, no boundary between self and other, and thus no inner space and no representational capacity to transform sensations and affects into images. It is here that the analyst may find herself regressing to a state described in a recent paper by Carvahlo in which the confusion between analyst and patient is such that any attempt to trace the transference is futile. In such cases, the task of the analyst is rather that of registering physical sensations and affects in order to "translate them into the currency of mind" (Carvahlo 2007, 234). In autistic projection, the failure of maternal mirroring leads to the failure to internalize a containing skin function, fundamental for the creation of inner space. The lack of inner space for representations means that sensations become a source of chaotic disintegration, and the result is either degeneration into psychotic confusion or a profound dissociation between mind and body, between thoughts and affects and sensations. In such cases, imitation and mimesis become the dominating mechanisms of defense, and the individual equates him- or herself with the surface qualities of the object in order to create a "second skin" or containing surface to prevent feelings of disintegration and to be able to hold onto "attributes of the object in the absence of the experience of having an inner space in which the other person's qualities or parts can in phantasy be stored" (Ogden 1989, 136). In the second, which I will call contiguous projection, the mother has some capacity for mirroring, but the image that she transmits back to the infant is a pure reflection of what the child has transferred to the mother. In other words, it is unmodified by reverie. Here there is a rudimentary experience of inner space, but it is a flat space, capable only of containing two-dimensional representations. The infant has some capacity to mentalize and to represent sensations, but the representations are merely indexical or iconic, that is to say they are concrete images formed on the basis of similarity or contiguity, devoid of any metaphorical power. In contiguous projection, the individual lives in a sensation-dominated world in which bodily sensations are experienced at a purely concrete level, as things to be utilized in filling up the holes in the second skin, as in certain sexual or sado-masochistic rituals. There is a profound dissociation between the representations of sensation and affect, which can only be discharged, never represented. In such cases, the other is experienced as a flat surface capable only of reflecting back what has been projected onto it. The impossibility of tolerating absence because of the failure to establish an affective image of the other in inner space forecloses any capacity to attribute symbolic significance to bodily sensations and affects.

In each of these phenomena, the experience that is transferred is very different and will produce different imaginal responses in the analyst: in the first, the image-producing function has failed and what is transferred is a traumatic, purely bodily experience, a memory trace of the perception of a nonevent, something that should have taken place but did not, rather than a representation, whereas in the second what is transferred is a kind of denuded flat image, lacking in affective depth and metaphorical significance. I will now use two clinical events to illustrate these processes.

MAGGIE

Maggie drifted into analysis on the advice of a friend who told her she was depressed and could benefit from analysis. It rapidly became clear that Maggie existed only as a disembodied mind, and her body was experienced as a useless and inanimate "thing" that she dragged around with her. Her whole life was spent trying to cover up her feelings of nonidentity through a mimetic process of adapting to the wishes and needs of others, and all she expected to get from me was a new and hopefully better image with which to identify. After a few sessions she brought a dream:

> *I am in front of a mirror taking off my make-up with make-up remover and cotton wool but I can't seem to get it all off and the cotton wool is always dirty and I feel panic that the layer of make-up never seems to get any less. Then I think that I must have forgotten to remove my make-up for a very long time and I feel less afraid and I keep on taking off the make-up until the cotton wool is quite clean. At the same time I am talking to someone who I can't identify.*

At the time, I was aware only of the apparently positive transference aspects of the second part of this dream, that is, the presence of another which allowed her to think that it was possible to remove the mask. I failed to take into sufficient consideration her terror that perhaps under the make-up there was nothing. It is this image, in fact, that suggests that her feelings of not being alive were linked to the fact that she had no representation of her own face and her own body.

After a few months the initial positive feelings had given way to her usual feelings of despondency and lifelessness, and it became increasingly clear that what was going on was an imitation of a good analysis and that in reality nothing was happening. It was at this point that something dramatic occurred. Maggie arrived at a session saying to me that she felt hopeless and incapable, but this time unusually she described a physical sensation of a heavy weight on her stomach. When I asked her to imagine this weight, she replied that it made her think of something brown, earth, a mass of earth, but there she stopped. I then suddenly had an olfactory image of almost hallucinatory intensity of the smell of damp earth that then translated into a haptic image of earth pressing on a face and then into a visual image of a freshly dug grave. Instead of holding the image as I would usually do, I found myself saying to her that perhaps this earth was the grave of a bad little girl who had never been able to live. Maggie became extremely agitated and distressed with acute feelings of depersonalization and said that thinking of this image made her feel as though she was split into two, as though she was doubled and she was only gradually able to calm down sufficiently to be able to leave the consulting room. This image of a dead baby remained with her, however and indeed became central in the analysis and in her dreams, in which there was a progression from an infinity of dead babies to one dead baby and finally to images of giving birth to a live baby. This series of dreams enabled her to begin to represent her feeling that her body had never really existed for her, and it permitted us to gradually help her to integrate her body, with its sensations and emotions, into her self image.

SILVIA

The next person I will describe was very different from Maggie, in the sense that Silvia had a representation of her body but the body image was that of a two-dimensional surface rather than three-dimensional container. Her bodily sensations were dissociated from affects and reduced to the level of concrete happenings that she manipulated in masochistic rituals of self-harm in order to shore up her fragile sense of self, while the dissociated affects were evacuated into empty space with no possibility of transformation. Silvia was referred to me because of a depression brought on by a separation from her lover, with whom she had an extremely sado-masochistic relationship, a factor that rapidly made itself felt in the transference-countertransference dynamics. She insisted that I adapt the setting to her specific needs, constantly devalued me and my interpretations, and left me no space for reflection, while at the same time experiencing me as an extremely sadistic figure.

Silvia had many dreams filled with fascinating images, but I gradually became aware that these images were characterized by a peculiar flat quality, rather like the images of a cartoon. Nothing ever really happened in her dreams, nor did she show any emotional reaction to the images either within the dream experience itself or when she narrated the dream. Thus she was unable to use the dreams in any meaningful way to gain insight or to enrich her impoverished psychic reality. As the analysis proceeded, it became clear that we were going nowhere, something clearly expressed in a dream:

> *I am with you in a room but you are sitting behind a desk. I go round to your side of the desk to be close to you but you tell me to go back to the other side of the desk. I try again to come close to you but you send me away, making me understand that I must sit down. There is no chair, however, so I pretend to sit, but it's very uncomfortable and I can't keep my balance. I am upset that you make me do something that is senseless and useless.*

At the time I thought in terms of projective identification and indeed made countless useless efforts to interpret along these lines, with the result that Silvia felt increasingly persecuted and began to talk about leaving analysis. As I look back at the situation now, I can see that Silvia was dehumanizing me to the point that

I was merely a "thing in her dream," to paraphrase Lewis Carroll, but this had nothing to do with having any feelings towards me or being able to use me in any way. It was simply her way of expressing what it felt like to be Silvia. Again, as with Maggie, something happened that changed the course of the analysis. Silvia brought in a dream in which she is at a wedding. Every now and then images of wedding dresses appeared. One particular dress was rather strange, she thought, as the skirt of the dress was really two trouser legs held together by a white zip. I was struck by this image, and in a playful, rather flippant way, which was usually impossible with her, I said: "It's difficult to get married if you don't know if you want to be the bride or the groom." As usual there was no reaction to this interpretation, but that night she called me in a panic, saying that she had been unable to give her mother an injection as her hand was shaking so much. But as soon as she heard my voice, she began to calm down. From this point on the analysis changed dramatically. Silvia began to experience me as a container into which she could project her affects, as we can see from the dream she brought in the next session. There we are sitting cosily together in her bedroom, and I tell Silvia a rather confused story about my parents saying that I feel resentful towards them.

What I was unable to understand at the time was how this apparently banal interpretation worked when so many others had fallen on deaf ears.

DISCUSSION

If we look at what had happened in the session with Maggie, what seemed to have occurred was that in that moment Maggie and I found ourselves in a state in which there was no distinction between inside and outside. Here it is a case of something in the air, an unmentalized sensation that I picked up. This is what I referred to earlier as autistic projection. What is important is that what is transferred is neither an image nor an affect but a perception, and it is the imaginative work of the analyst the linked Maggie's sensation—the weight on her stomach and her partial attempt at visualisation, the earth—to my sensation—the smell of earth—which then became combined with a different sensory modality, the earth on a face, which then gave rise to an image, the dead little girl. It is only with the communication of this image that Maggie's terror of nonexistence, brought about by the fact that she experienced herself only as her mother's double, became thinkable.

My capacity to transform her sensation provided Maggie with an image of her experience of her body, an image that presented her body to her mind in order to bring about the beginnings of a capacity to imagine her body, thus reestablishing the fractured vertical axis. This is what the Botellas refer to as the analyst's work of "figurability," a work that can only come about when the analyst is able to accept a regression to the most unconscious levels of the psyche in which he or she becomes the analysand's "double" (Botella and Botella 2005, 71).

In the case of Silvia, on the other hand, what was transferred was a two-dimensional image with no metaphorical meaning, and it was through the imaginative activity of the analyst, the capacity to play with the image, to imbue it with an as-if quality, that allowed the image to reverberate inside Silvia, thereby releasing the unconscious sadistic rage that she felt towards her mother and father. At the same time, however, the imaginative activity of the analyst also gave Silvia the feeling that the analyst was not merely a surface but a potential container capable of reverie into which she could project her unmetabolized affects (a true projective identification), confident that the analyst would be able to render them thinkable, expressed in the image of the calm analyst who nevertheless has problems with her father.

CONCLUSION

Much of Jung's work was directed principally towards the study of the intrapsychic dimension of the constitution of human subjectivity and his method, insofar as we can talk about a Jungian method, was designed to develop this dimension. In this sense, Fordham's insistence on the importance of the relational dimension of human development and on the necessity of a method that could facilitate the unfolding of the transference-countertransference dynamics was a useful counterbalance. But equally, as I have tried to show in this brief account of the analysis of projections, fantasies, and defenses in primitive states of mind, there are analyses in which the systematic interpretation of the transference is meaningless, if not positively counterproductive. In the cases described, it was the imaginative activity of the analyst that brought about transformation: In the case of Maggie, it was my image-producing function that provided an image for her experience of her body as something dead, without emotions or sensations; in the case of Silvia it was my imaginative activity that was able to give metaphorical depth to her impoverished body image. Imagination is, as Coleridge says, a "synthetic and magical power" (1983, 12) that allows us to enter into and exit from the objects that present themselves to us. Without it there can be no analysis.

REFERENCES

Bick, Esther. 1968. The experience of the skin in early object-relations. *International Journal of Psycho-Analysis* 49:484–86.

Botella, Cesar and Sara Botella. 2005. *The work of psychic figurability.* Hove and New York: Bruner-Routledge.

Cambray, Joseph, and Linda Carter. 2004. Analytical methods revisited. In *Analytical Psychology: Contemporary perspectives in Jungian Analysis*, ed. Joseph Cambray and Linda Carter, 116–48. Hove and New York: Bruner-Routledge.

Carvahlo, Richard. 1991. Mechanism, metaphor. *Journal of Analytical Psychology* 36: 331–41.

———. 2007. Response to Astor's paper. *Journal of Analytical Psychology* 52, 2: 233–37.

Coleridge, Samuel Taylor. 1817/1983. *Biographia literaria*. Vol. 2. Princeton: Princeton University Press.

222   *Angela M. Connolly*

Ferrari, Armando. 2004. *From the eclipse of the body to the dawn of thought*. London: Free Associations.
Fordham, Michael. 1956. Active imagination or imaginative activity. *Journal of Analytical Psychology* 1, 2: 207–8.
———. 1963. Notes on the transference and its management in a schizoid child. *Journal of Child Psychotherapy* 12, 1: 7–15.
Gordon, Rosemary. 1965. The concept of projective identification: an evaluation. *Journal of Analytical Psychology* 10, 2: 127–49.
Hogenson, George. 2004. The self, the symbolic and synchronicity: Virtual realities and the emergence of the psyche. In *Edges of experience: Memory and mergence*, ed. Lyn Cowan, 155–67. Einsiedeln: Daimon Verlag.
Jung, C.G. 1921/1971. *Psychological types*. CW 6.
Kernberg, Otto. 1987. Projection and projective identification: Developmental and clinical aspects. *Journal of the American Psychoanalytical Association* 35: 795–819.
Lombardi, Ricardo. 2000. Corpo Affetti, Pensiero: Riflessioni su alcune ipotesi di Ignzio Matte Blanco e Armando Ferrari. *Rivista di Psicoanalisi* 46, 4: 683–706. (my translation).
Matte Blanco, Ignazio. 1988. *Thinking, feeling, being*. London: Routledge.
Ogden, Thomas. 1989. On the concept of an autistic-contiguous position. *International Journal of Psycho-Analysis* 70: 127–40.
Schaverien, Joy. 2007. Countertransference as active imagination: Imaginative experiences of the analyst. *Journal of Analytical Psychology* 52, 4: 413–33.
Wiener, Jan. 2004. Transference and countertransference. In *Contemporary perspectives in Analytical Psychology*, ed. Joseph Cambray and Linda Carter, 149–75. Hove and New York: Bruner-Routledge.

ANGELA M. CONNOLLY, M.D., a psychiatrist and Jungian psychoanalyst, is a training and supervising analyst at Centro Italiano di Psicologia Analitica (CIPA), Rome. She is currently a member of the Executive Committee of the IAAP. She has published widely in both Italian and English.

21

GENDER AND SEXUALITY: IMAGINAL, EROTIC ENCOUNTERS

Joy Schaverien

The aim in this chapter is to consider gender and sexuality in the consulting room as both real and imaginal experience. There are times when the erotic element in the transference / countertransference dynamic engages both analyst and analysand in a powerful mix. Jung (1946) has graphically shown that the erotic transference is central in analysis, even at times challenging the bounds of the analytic relationship. Following Jung, I have explored this type of analytic engagement in depth (Schaverien 2002, 1995). However, this intensely intimate connection is only one type of analytic encounter that importantly involves the theme of sexuality. There are many times, especially in the early stages of analysis, when the sexual material presented is far from erotic. Often this reveals precisely the problem with which the analysand struggles in life. The difficulty, I will argue, resides in the psychological link between sex, gender, and imagination. Two vignettes from analyses will illustrate this from very different perspectives. In the first example, imagination was frozen because of an unconscious fear of psychosis; in the second, there was much evidence of imagination but a lack of relatedness. In both, there was a profound fear of intimacy, and therefore little symbolic meaning was attributed to sex. For these reasons, the sessions, though filled with discussion about sex, initially lacked the intimacy of an erotic encounter.

When Jung (1946) linked alchemy to transference, he connected material reality to the imaginal. Samuels (1985) drew attention to the fact that this was a metaphor, thus symbolic of the therapeutic relationship. The therapeutic relationship is a symbolic and imaginal, as well as an erotic, enterprise. However, at certain times it is as if there is little imaginative alchemy in the encounter. Imagination is then far from active. Three factors play a part: an absence of eros, a lack or fear of imagination, and an inability to relate in a symbolic manner. For the analysand whose view of gender or sexuality is rigidly fixed, the task of analysis is to transform the psychological attitude from the concrete to the symbolic. This opens the way to a depth approach to relationship through fantasy and imagination.

We start from the very real situation—the meeting—at the start of analysis. A phone call is usually the first approach. In that initial contact there are many clues about who this person is. The first thing the analyst hears, whether conscious of it or not, is their gender. On most occasions, the analyst knows immediately from the voice that this prospective analysand is male or female. This may influence the phone conversation, and occasionally it might even influence whether or not the caller is accepted into an initial session. In most cases, however, gender makes little difference at this early stage but, whether conscious or not, awareness of gender is part of the impression formed at the point of initial contact.

Prior to this call, the prospective analysand might have given gender some thought and perhaps selected the analyst on the basis of gender. They might be actively seeking a man or a woman analyst because of a conscious preference. In women's therapy centers, for instance, the approach is usually based on an assumption that certain aspects of female experience can best be understood by another woman. Williams (2006) discusses how such a choice might be based on unconscious idealization, denigration, or avoidance. Similarly, a gay analysand might seek a gay analyst in the anticipation that their sexuality is more likely to be understood. The point is that this is part of the reality of a situation that is bound to be tinged with anticipation, hopes, and fears, as a person approaches the journey that is analysis.

My use of the terms "sex," "gender," and "sexuality" needs to be defined and elaborated at this point. Here I follow Stoller (1968, 9), who distinguishes between sex and gender. He regards sex as biological, a collection of physical characteristics, and the terms that apply to this reality are male and female. Sex is distinguished from gender, which is psychological and cultural. The terms for this are masculinity and femininity. This distinction is therefore significant in differentiating biological reality from the lived experience associated with it. Masculinity and femininity are not rigidly fixed to male and female: "There are elements of both in many humans, but the male has a preponderance of masculinity and the female has a preponderance of femininity" (Stoller 1968, 9). One can see some parallels with Jung's work on psychological contra-sexuality, the opposites as presented by the masculine and feminine principle in the psyche (Jung 1928/1969, 1946/1966). Stoller argues that lived experience is conditioned by both biological and cultural factors, which lead to formation of "gender identity" and "gender role" (Stoller 1968, 29–30). In the late sixties and seventies, this differentiation became a feminist theme and, following Stoller, the sociologist Oakley argued that "gender has no biological origin . . . the connections between sex and gender are not really 'natural' at all" (Oakley 1972, 188). Her view was that we need to look to the psychological and social construction of these concepts to understand how men and women might experience the world differently.

These arguments against an essentialist, or fixed, view of the association between sex and gender are significant for Jungians because in the past the tendency has been, using Jung's views of the opposites, to argue that men and women are psychologically different because of the biological difference between the sexes. It followed therefore that women were attributed femininity and with it the feminine role in relation to men, and vice versa for men. Thus gender was too closely tied to biology. Awareness of the more contemporary views is vital for the Jungian psychoanalyst in the twenty-first century. Although there is not space here to fully reference the literature, it is important to acknowledge that some of the work in the area of gender and sexuality has been done by Jungians, (Colman 2005; Hopcke 1989; Young-Eisendrath 1987, 1999; Samuels 1995, 2001; Schwartz-Salant and Stein 1992). Sexuality might be understood to be a result of the conjunction of biology and culture; although sex is fixed to biology, gender (masculine and feminine) can be apportioned to sexuality in varying degrees. It is the form that sexual relations, whether physical or psychological, take. Of note in this context are Samuels's (2001, 38–39) proposal that a healthy attitude toward gender and sexuality might be a fluid rather than a fixed one and Hopcke's observation that "an individual's sexuality might change over the course of a lifetime" (Hopcke 1989, 187) .

This viewpoint is well expressed by the feminist psychoanalyst Chodorow, who writes: "To understand femininity and masculinity and the various forms of sexuality requires that we understand how any particular woman or man creates her or his own cultural and personal gender and sexuality" (Chodorow 1994, 92). While biological differences are a factor, there are many ways in which gender might be imaginally fluid leading to fulfilling sexual relationships. However, this is a sophisticated level of relating that requires the symbolic attitude.

TRANSFERENCE AND REPETITION

Analysis inhabits and also engenders the world of memory and imagination. The analysand, troubled in the present, journeys into memory of the recent past. As analysis progresses, memories of the long distant past may emerge. Imagination is brought into play as repetition in the transference evokes earlier connections and associations. This psychological interplay is symbolic, peppered with fantasies and imaginings and shadowed by memories of past close relationships.

This may be observed in the way analysands present themselves in a session. Some will enter the consulting room showing confidence that they will be appreciated—loved even; others enter showing shame and fear of rejection. At the heart of each is the anticipation of repetition of parental delight or denigration; the unconscious body memory of contact with the first carer. Sometimes sex and gender have played a significant part in forming this attitude. The analysand who was welcomed unconditionally into the world feels confident in their embodied state. The one whose sex or gender was an issue in childhood may suffer conflict, anticipating abuse or rejection. These early developmental experiences may be ameliorated or compounded by those of adolescence. Such childhood experience may reverberate emotionally throughout life, affecting the ability to access imagination and so to make loving relationships. Confusion about gender and gender role as well as about sexuality may result in rich potentials of life being unlived. This may be due to the psyche unconsciously holding rigid for fear of a psychotic breakdown.

Clinical Vignette 1

Ms. X's analysis developed with little discernible erotic color, and there was little space for symbolic or imaginal thinking in relation to sexuality. A professional musician in her forties, she was referred to me in a confused state. Ms. X was a small woman with long blond hair tied back in a rather severe style. She had grown up in a family in an Eastern European country where, on the surface, all was apparently very normal and middle class. Her father, an eminent politician, was often absent from home. Mother stayed at home with the children. There were two brothers, one older and one younger than Ms. X. At the time she was referred to me for analysis, Ms. X had concluded that the ideal relationship she and her mother had appeared to have had been a sham. This realization had emerged soon after her move to this country, when, horrified, she started to remember the years of psychological abuse that had filled her childhood. She tried to speak with her father about this, but by this time he was elderly and he appeared oblivious to her distress. It seemed to Ms. X that he did not want to know about the nature of her mother's cruelty and so he was tacitly complicit in it.

Neither of her brothers appeared to have experienced the subtle abuse to which Ms. X was subjected; therefore the abuse seemed to have been gender specific. The mother abused her daughter in a quite bizarre manner. While putting on the appearance of having a close relationship with this child, she would whisper in the girl's ear that she was just like her brothers, also really a boy.

As a consequence, Ms. X grew up with an insecure sense of her sex and this affected her gender identity. She feared that her genitals were not normal. She wondered if she could check this with a doctor but was too worried about it to ask. At the time she came to me, although the opportunity had presented itself several times, she had never dared to have a sexual relationship. Each time it had been possible, she had withdrawn from contact and the relationship had not developed. Parallel to this, although she was a trained musician, she had been unable to develop her professional life to a satisfactory level. In my view, both failures to develop normally were due to an inability to access the world of imagination, symbolization, and metaphor. Because of the terror that dominated her inner world, she was unable to move ahead psychologically. She lived in a rigid, frozen world of concrete fixities.

She presented in my consulting room in a very paranoid state, and it took several months for the above story to be told. The mother's constant psychological abuse had affected the center of her being and created a serious handicap to her psychological welfare and sense of embodied gender identity. She would think that she heard comments in the street, or when she was with people she knew, insinuating that they knew she was really a man. Although to all appearances she was a female, she had little concept of how others saw her. Eventually, after much thought and some consultation with a colleague, I concluded that this very concrete fear could not be resolved by psychological means alone. Symbolic interpretations did not connect with her, so I suggested that she make an appointment to visit a woman consultant specializing in sexual medicine. There she was told that she was exactly as she should be and that she was biologically fully female. The effect of this was immediate relief from this worry, and the problem never surfaced again. Ms. X believed the consultant.

The point here is that Ms. X was biologically female but her *gender identity* had been disrupted by the family environment. There was nothing physically wrong with her, but her ability to imagine herself as a woman had been interrupted. Her need was to be able to mentally conceive of herself as one of the female sex, and so to give birth to herself as a woman. This would enable her to take up the *gender identity* and *gender role* appropriate to her sex. Ms. X had been frozen with unconscious terror. Little symbolic work could take place until the legitimacy of her sex was proved to her. It was only then that she could begin to have a sense of her embodied self as a gendered being.

By denigrating her daughter's female sexuality and by constantly insinuating that she was really a boy, Ms. X's mother had effectively damaged the girl because it ruptured her connection to her own body. Within the therapeutic relationship, it was necessary to work at a rather concrete level with Ms. X because of the possibility that her fragile sense of self would be lost, possibly plunging her into a full psychotic state. Her capacity for imagination was volatile with the possibility that it could become paranoid and get out of control, and she compensated by remaining very concrete in her thinking.

SYMBOLIZATION THROUGH TRANSFERENCE

With Ms. X in mind, I will turn now to consider the facets of the therapeutic relationship that lead to symbolization. Greenson's (1967) rather linear discussion of processes that are far from linear is helpful in considering the difference between the symbolic and real aspects of the therapeutic relationship. Following Freud, Greenson discussed the therapeutic relationship in terms of three elements: the real relationship, the therapeutic alliance, and the transference. The *real relationship* is what is real between the two people who initially meet and agree to work together. The *therapeutic alliance* is based on trust and nonsexual liking and so may demand a psychological split since the analysand is alongside the analyst in observing their own *transference*. When considering sex and gender, this artificial division is helpful. The sex, gender, and sexual orientation of the analyzing pair are parts of the real relationship. However, although we live an existence limited by the body we inhabit, in fantasy we can be fluid. In *the transference*, past and unlived potential patterns of relating emerge in the therapeutic relationship, thereby becoming accessible to consciousness and transformation through the development of the conscious attitude. Transference is characterized by unconsciousness, repetition, and being inappropriate to the present situation. This is revealed in behavior, in and outside of analysis, as well as in dreams. The thera-peutic relationship provides a space set apart where transference is activated through the combination of the real and imaginative interplay between analysand and analyst. This aspect of the analytic encounter is symbolic.

With Ms. X we saw that there are times when the real situation needs atten-tion while working in the therapeutic alliance. In this analysis we had to take seri-ously the material reality of her situation. Ms. X could not permit herself to experience the transference fully because unconsciously she was afraid of the negative and critical mother becoming active again in the present. Because I was aware of this potential transference, we worked in the therapeutic alliance and did not delve too deeply into the realms of imagination and of the negative maternal imago. In this case, the reality of questions about sex played a role in this fear. The strongest form of transference she could allow herself was a sisterly one, where I could accompany her and witness her distress, identifying with it as a woman.

TRANSFERENCE—INCESTUOUS AND EROTIC

Transference, like a dream, can evoke imagination, and it may temporarily seem very real. However, to confuse it with reality leads to unreal expectations and, in some cases, to a powerful impulse to act on the feelings that emerge. This is espe-cially so when there is an incestuous dynamic and the encounter is erotically charged. Jung's view (CW 16 and CW 5) was that incest fantasies experienced in the transference have "a meaning and purpose." They evoke past emotional pat-terns in an attempt to resolve a situation that was not adequately worked through in the family. Thus the transference represents unfinished psychological business with a strong potential for development in the future. While the erotic transfer-ence is the glue that binds the analysand to the task of analysis, it also evokes fear and dread. These emotional patterns engender some of the most personal and inti-mate of human experiences. Jung writes of the incest element in the transference that it "is the hiding place for all the most secret, painful, intense, delicate, shame-faced, timorous, grotesque, unmoral, and at the same time the most sacred feel-ings which go to make up the indescribable and inexplicable wealth of human relationships and give them their compelling power" (Jung 1946/1966, 15).

It is little wonder, then, that analysands avoid consciousness of such power-ful material. Elsewhere I have written that when the erotic transference begins to become active many male analysands, working with female analysts, terminate analysis abruptly (Schaverien 1995, 2006). This is one way of avoiding con-sciousness of the erotic transference. Another is through sexual acting out.

Clinical Vignette 2

Rather than think about the emotional situation, analysands may choose to engage concretely in sexual behavior. We can regard this as a failure of imagination. Mr. Z could have been one of the "men who leave too soon." but instead he remained in analysis and for a time engaged in a good deal of sexual activity around the analytic sessions. For Mr. Z, sex was mixed up in his mind with incestuous desires, and so the emergence of eros in analysis was fearful to him. However, remarkably enough he stayed and confronted it.

Mr. Z, a married man with no children, worked as an executive in a bank. He was tall, with receding fair hair, and in his mid-thirties. He had been referred to me by a colleague who thought that he would benefit from analysis with a woman. The material from a series of closely linked sessions illustrates the move from a concrete attitude toward sexuality to a more symbolic one where he could bear to think. He had a very rich imaginal life, which led to fascinating dreams and creative writing, but he found intimate relationships problematical.

There was an occasion when I had to cancel Mr. Z's appointment. In the following session, he said that although he did not want to finish analysis yet he had been thinking that it might be time to take a break. After allowing this to rest in silence for a while, I wondered aloud if it might be helpful to try to understand why it was now that he was thinking of this. I reminded him that I had been away the previous week. He responded to this with amusement, saying that he had known that I would make that link. The topic seemed to be left there. Then, after a pause, he said that he had thought of attending a massage parlor instead of coming to his session today. This had been a regular feature of the earlier phases of the analysis, but it had been sometime since he had mentioned it. It seemed that he was making it clear that he could compensate adequately for my absence.

As I reflected to myself on this remark, it occurred to me that this was his way of denying my importance to him, which he found very disturbing. It also felt denigrating of the analysis and of me as a woman. Recently, some of the sessions had been sexually charged, and he had been very uncomfortable and aware of being alone with me. He enjoyed it, but he was worried that *I* would enjoy *him* too much; this he would find overwhelming. It was okay for him to have sexual feelings as long as he did not suspect that it was mutual. In response to this, I felt uncomfortably aware of him sexually.

I use the term sexual here rather than erotic deliberately. The sessions with Mr. Z at this time were sexual but not erotic—that is, there was an uncomfortable awareness of sex in the air but little sense of the deeply felt intimacy that characterizes a truly erotic, and therefore creative, connection. It was not surprising that there was a problem in this area for Mr. Z, since there was a history of a rather unboundaried situation with his mother whose delight in her only son had bordered on the incestuous. Mr. Z grew up with the sense that he, rather than his father, was the mother's true partner. Without engaging concretely in acts of incest, this had been a psychological violation where the generational boundaries had not been adequately established and maintained. Reflecting on this history, it became evident that in the transference he was unconsciously replaying his discomfort with the ambiguous signals he had picked up from his mother. Therefore the discomfort I had experienced during these sessions was a countertransference response.

The session described above was the first in a sequence where sex featured, leading to a change from the focus on sex to Eros, from relating in a concrete sexual manner to an imaginative one. Mr. Z arrived smartly dressed for his next appointment, explaining that he was dressed up like this because he had attended a formal business meeting in a nearby town. He had had some time to wait between the meeting and his appointment with me, so he had been to a massage parlour. He described how the attractive woman there had performed very professionally; it had been an enjoyable but professional meeting. After reflecting on this for a while, I concluded that the implied parallel with his analysis needed to be made explicit. I suggested that perhaps he recognized some similarities. This too was a professional meeting, and he paid me to perform professionally with him like he did the woman in the massage parlor. He appeared relieved that I had picked this up, and then emboldened by the implicit permission to speak of it he considered what he paid for her services as compared with what he paid for mine.

My point here is that he was attempting to diminish the intimate, and therefore creatively erotic, connection between us by likening analysis to an anonymous sex act. By denigrating me and what I was offering in this way, he was able to maintain a sense of control of the situation. As discussion of this developed further, it became evident that he was amused and relieved at the metaphorical link. He was open to explore why he was compelled to engage in brief, anonymous sex acts—with men as well as women. He admitted that he found the sex exciting in the moment but finally not very satisfying. As we explored this, I suggested that perhaps he was worried that if he found the analysis satisfying some unspecific demand would be made of him. As long as he could keep it as a merely "professional meeting," for which he paid, he could avoid the thing he most feared, which was intimacy. Thus we began to approach the psychological meaning of his anxious need for anonymous sexual encounters.

The following week he arrived ten minutes late for his session and apologized by saying that he had been delayed because he was having sex with his wife. It was becoming clear that he had to empty himself of his sexual feelings and desires in order to make analysis safe. If he had had sex beforehand, then that would get it out of the way. He may well have felt that he would be less likely to be exploited by me, the incestuous object of desire, if he was not in a sexually aroused state when he saw me. He felt that he was responsible for maintaining the generational boundary. The fact that on this occasion the sex took place with his wife instead of with a prostitute indicated a more relational form of intercourse. Still, since it took place just before his analytic hour with me, it indicated something of his fear of me. My response, as a woman, was to feel not interesting to him sexually. However this was analysis and so clearly this was a countertransference that needed understanding. The transference here evoked an outdated pattern of relating that had defended him in the past from being fully conscious of his sexual interest in his mother. The behavior on this occasion was a defense against the excitement aroused by the analyst, like his mother, a woman.

This raises the question of whether this material would have surfaced in quite the same way had his analyst been a man. It might well have played out through a homosexual transference evoking a reciprocal countertransference, but this would have raised different responses in the analyst. My interest is in the specific differences in the countertransferences evoked by the gender of the analyzing pair (Schaverien 1995, 2006). A female analyst is likely to experience such material rather differently than a male analyst. In this case, her sense of her self as a woman was affected and, even though not directly discussed, her body was part of the material. Thus I think the gender of the pair here was an important factor in the analysis.

Reminding him of the previous session, I commented on his compulsion to have sex before his meetings with me. It seemed he wanted to get sex out of the way before the session. This led to exploration of his fear of me and what I might demand of him. He used the couch, but it made him anxious because he felt sexually open there and vulnerable. He wanted to permit himself to be open with me, but he could not trust me to maintain the appropriate distance. Now he visibly relaxed and, permitting himself to explore his feelings in the room, a powerful, imaginal experience emerged.

He described an image. There was a big breast that was hovering over him, being offered to him, and he wanted it. There was silence for a considerable time as he permitted himself to go with the fantasy. Then he said how small he felt and that it was not a sexual image. I was impressed by how much he seemed like a baby in that moment as he curled himself up towards the imaginary breast. Then he said that he worried he would be too much for it—he wanted to get really angry and kick, but then he became aware that he was a grown man and that made it difficult. Thus it was that after we had discussed his fear of having to perform for me, that is, to have sex, with a mother/ woman analyst, his dependency needs emerged. This was an imaginal, symbolic experience that developed out of the beginning of trust in the therapeutic relationship. It seemed that he could not trust his mother not to sexualize their relationship even when he was very little. While he had found this very exciting, it had left him with an unmet infantile need and that became confused with sex. After this session, I felt easier in his presence and more connected to him in an intimate way. The erotic connection could begin to emerge between us, and it seemed that the sexual contact with his wife prior to the session had facilitated it. A symbolic space emerged in the therapeutic relationship permitting space for imaginal experience.

In the next session, he reported that on his way to his appointment with me he had done a detour. This was because when he had passed a certain street previously, he noticed a massage parlor that advertised that he could have two women at the same time. He liked that idea. He had gone there on his way to see me, and he had been in the place, in a waiting area, when he became aware that he was choosing a brief sexual encounter instead of his analytic session. He left the massage parlor and arrived for his analytic session on time. He was very pleased because it felt like a breakthrough. He had been able to prioritize intimacy over sexual gratification. The two women at the same time might be taken to represent his wife and me, who were both offering him intimate attention but in different ways. Triangulation opens up the space for symbolic thinking and thus for an imaginal connection to be made.

In this phase of analysis, Mr. Z began to separate out and differentiate sex from intimacy in his mind. His genuine desire for an intimate connection to another human being had been compromised by his sexual behavior over the years. In various ways, sexuality can be used as a distraction from problems with intimacy. Mr. Z had feared that he would be aroused by me in the present of the therapeutic hour or, worse yet from his point of view, that I would be aroused by him.

The countertransference is a way of gauging the quality of a connection. The analyst needs to gain full awareness of her or his feeling in order to understand the nature and meaning of sex and eros in any particular analysis. I did not feel desire for Mr. Z, despite the fact that he was an attractive man, but I did feel a sexual tension that was characterized by anxiety. Sometimes I felt sexually denigrated. Later, as he engaged at depth, the relationship changed, and then I could feel a deeply intimate connection to him. As a general rule, when sexuality becomes conscious and can be discussed, it loses some of its power. Once the sexual was brought out in the open, we could both relax in each other's company.

As already stated, this referral was made on the basis of gender by a colleague who sensed that Mr. Z needed to see a woman. Thus gender difference was a factor from the start. In some analytic circles, it is considered that the same material will arise irrespective of the gender of the analytic dyad. In others, gender is considered so significant that an analysand is expected to see both a man and a woman in the course of their analytic experience. Jung, for example, would refer an analysand to a woman colleague either at the same time as he was seeing them, or after terminating with them (Bair 2003, 377). Certainly, the quality of the engagement in this material would have been different had I been a man. It is quite different for a man to discuss visiting a prostitute—man to man—than it is to discuss it with a woman. Moreover, it is possible that had his analyst been a man Mr. Z's maternal complex would not have replayed in the same way. I hope to have shown how sexuality and gender offer a particular element in symbolization and that imagination is central in this process. This is significant if the patient is to stay in analysis rather than leave at the point at which the erotic transference emerges.

REFERENCES

Bair, Deidre. 2003. *Jung, a biography*. Boston, New York, London: Little, Brown and Company.
Chodorow, Nancy. 1994. *Femininities, masculinities, sexualities: Freud and beyond*. Lexington, KY: University of Kentucky Press.

Colman, Warren. 2005. Sexual metaphor and the language of unconscious phantasy. *Journal of Analytical Psychology* 50, 5: 641–60.

Greenson, Ralph. 1967. *Technique and the practice of psychoanalysis*. London: Hogarth Press.

Hopcke, Robert H. 1989. *Jung, Jungians and homosexuality*. Boston and London: Shambhala.

Jung, C.G. 1928/1969. On psychic energy. In CW 8.

———. 1946/1966. The psychology of the transference. In CW 16.

———. 1956/1970. *Symbols of transformation*. CW 5.

Oakley, Ann. 1972. *Sex, gender and society*. London: Maurice Temple Smith Ltd.

Samuels, Andrew. 1985. *The plural psyche: Personality, morality and the father*. London and New York: Routledge

———. 2001. *Politics on the couch*. London: Karnac.

Schaverien, Joy. 1995. *Desire and the female therapist: Engendered gazes in psychotherapy and art therapy*. London and New York: Routledge.

———. 2002. *The dying patient in psychotherapy: Desire, dreams and individuation*. London and New York: Palgrave/Macmillan.

Schaverien, Joy, ed. 2006. *Gender, countertransference and the erotic transference: Perspectives from analytical psychology and psychoanalysis*. London and New York: Routledge.

Schwartz-Salant, Nathan and Murray Stein, eds. 1992. *Gender and soul in psychotherapy*. Wilmette, IL: Chiron Publications.

Stoller, Robert J. 1968. *Sex and gender*. London: Hogarth Press.

Williams, Sherly. 2006. Women in search of women. In *Gender, countertransference, and the erotic transference : Perspectives from analytical psychology and psychoanalysis*, ed. Joy Schaverien, 145–56. Hove, East Sussex, New York: Routledge.

Young-Eisendrath, Polly, and Florence Wiedemann. 1987. *Female authority: Empowering women through psychotherapy*. New York: Guilford Press.

Young-Eisendrath, Polly. 1999. *Women and desire: Beyond wanting to be wanted*. New York: Harmony Books.

JOY SCHAVERIEN, Ph.D., is a Professional Member of the Society of Analytical Psychology in London, a Training Therapist and Supervisor for the British Association of Psychotherapists Jungian Section, and Visiting Professor in Art Psychotherapy at the University of Sheffield.

22

THE EXPERIENCE OF THE NUMINOUS IN THE CONSULTING ROOM

Birgit Heuer

INTRODUCTION

Recently I have found myself pondering the subject of professional maturity. Thus I have wondered whether professional maturity stimulates the capacity to open ourselves up to changes in the core analytical approach we have learned and practiced for many years. This in turn might mean changes to the core clinical paradigm one's work is based on. In time, such changes might facilitate paradigmatic flow in the wider context of the profession. For the individual analyst, it might require giving oneself permission to consider different clinical views and to let them enter one's horizon. Such views might originate in other approaches within the profession or come from outside the profession. The theme of the numinosum in the clinical hour and particularly in the therapeutic relationship, in my view, is a case in point, as Jungian clinical discourse—for a variety of reasons and depending on approach—tends to limit the clinical scope of the numinosum. Thus it might be confined to the symbolic contents of patients' dreams or the archetypal aspects of the transference. In this article, I would like to suggest that the Holy become part of the clinical hour in more fundamental ways, entering the transference/countertransference relationship and the embodied/being experience of both patient and analyst. The Holy as temenos might also include the physical reality of our consulting rooms.

The growing number of books and articles written about spirituality and analysis at present indicate the importance of my theme. When I presented a paper at the IAAP conference in 2001 that mentioned the possibility of praying for patients as part of analytical work (Heuer 2003), I was struck by the intensity of my colleagues' response. There emerged a sense of secrecy and a feeling of needing permission clinically to consider prayer, which I myself had also encountered in writing the paper. From a spiritual point of view, I find it deeply painful that something so central to many of our lives should feel unacceptable in our work, as though it were shameful, or there had to be tight boundaries towards the numinous as a felt reality rather than a symbolic entity. This emphasizes the need for clinical creativity with regard to paradigmatic flow, which requires the capacity to be open to changes to the core of one's clinical approach. As a profession, we might also lead by example: As we foster change to core beliefs and experiences in our patients, we would do well to encourage the possibility of change in our own clinical core beliefs.

In this chapter, I shall attempt to trace my theme in a variety of ways. As one intention is to contribute to paradigmatic flow in clinical discourse, I shall need to provide epistemological context. Thus I need to make intelligible the view of reality that provides the most convincing context for the theme of spirituality in the consulting room. At present, epistemic input comes from contemporary quantum physics, providing paradoxical rather than Aristotelian logic and affecting a shift in what is viewed as real, referred to as quantum reality. This is of import, for the various features of quantum reality overlap conceptually with mystical reality in the broadest sense as the direct, unmitigated experience of the Divine and of Divine grace. In using quantum-mystical reality as paradigmatic context, the theme of the Holy in the clinic is enhanced by being birthed more fully and housed more appropriately.

I shall also attempt to describe the experience of the numinous in my own consulting room. Here I shall consider the Holy with regard to the therapeutic attitude, the transference/countertransference-relationship, the physical aspects of the consulting room, and the boundary and contractual aspects of the work. Overall, I shall approach the Holy in a manner that emphasizes its felt and embodied reality.

In addition, I shall consider the concepts of ego and Self, attempting to reevaluate their clinical status. Ego and Self tend to be differentiated clinically in linear ways, so that, depending on approach, one is usually emphasized over the other, either in a temporal manner, where one is considered clinically to come after the other, or in an evaluative manner, where one is considered lower or higher than the other. My suggestion shall be to consider ego and Self as coinciding from a quantum-reality point of view and explore the clinical implications of this paradigmatic image.

The final section of this chaper will consider what I have termed a psychology of grace, employing a reworked concept of ego and Self, contemporary empirical quantum research and mystical experience to subtly interweave within the ordinary clinical hour. This enables a delicate, yet potentially profound movement in paradigmatic flow, as a central concern in clinical discourse changes shape. A conceptual preoccupation with pathology and its manifestations gently fades as the Holy, or a clinical paradigm of grace, emerges in the reality of our consulting rooms.

METHODOLOGY AND EPISTEMOLOGY

The writing brief for this chapter favored bringing out our own bold vision over scholarliness. Thus I shall not pursue any specific argument, nor shall I attempt to define key concepts such as the Holy and the numinous or trace their origin. It will suit the purpose of this work better to keep key terms fluid, allowing their meaning to evolve through context and the medium of resonance. This chapter then is written more in the spirit of exploration and reflection than argument. At times, meaning will be communicated by resonance, at others, conversely, it will be more reasoned.

My theme needs some epistemic clarification, however, as it is approached—in part—via mysticism. Mystical experience is often regarded as incompatible with the logos of language, and this might be because it comes with a somewhat different view of the world. Mystical experience shares an paradigmatic world view with what has come to be known as quantum-reality (Heuer 2008). A key epistemic feature of this is the capacity to hold paradox, to allow for two logically opposing facts to be true at the same time. Another aspect is the receding of causality—mystical or quantum "facts" co-cause each other—and the emergence of nonlocality whereby "things" move faster than the speed of light, bypassing space. From this follows the idea of a deeper connectedness that is—paradoxically—as symbolic as it is concrete. Similarly, mysticism is steeped in an experience of the Divine that is deeply immanent and personal, while at the same time being utterly transcendent. Thus the capacity for paradox lies at the heart of mysticism. Paradox, though, requires a specific type of reason, with particular features, rather than the suspension of reason, which is why mysticism is an epistemic concern as well as an approach to the numinous.

The conceptual capacity for paradox is also a central feature in much of Jung's thinking. *Mysterium Coniuctionis* and "The Psychology of the Transference" in particular can be argued to employ paradoxical-mystical processes and the use of alchemical metaphor as epistemological context for the purpose of clinical change. For reasons of space, such considerations are beyond the scope of this article and reference to Jung and many others, though richly available, must be kept to a minimum.

THE HOLY IN THE CONSULTING ROOM

For me, psychotherapy requires as its location literally and symbolically a Holy place, Jung's temenos. A Holy place needs to be delineated to keep its identity and integrity. This, then, emphasizes the boundary aspects of psychotherapy and puts them in the context of the Holy, rather than the reified "rules" of therapeutic behavior they sometimes turn into. Therapeutic boundaries become meaningful as enabling and containing the holiness of the work. This includes the contract, the patient's times, confidentiality, the analyst's continuous ethical attitude, and the physical space. Acknowledging the temenos of psychotherapeutic boundaries also means that there is a tight boundary around the spiritual aspects of my approach, so that I never actively bring the spiritual dimension into the content of the work but am, of course, receptive to my patients' doing so. Yet I am aware that my orientation does communicate itself through the quality of my being with the patient.

I view my actual physical consulting room as a temple, of which I am the caretaker. Thus I am aware of the consulting room's energy: On a physical level, I will regularly fill it with fresh air. Some colleagues burn a fire to the same effect. I also energetically prepare the room and myself every day before I start working. I stand in the middle of the room, breathing deeply and becoming still. Then I connect myself to the universal source of all light, and I ask for protection around my being. I ask for my consulting room to become God's healing temple, for it to be consecrated, and for the miracle of healing to unfold within. I also ask for the room to be filled with the substance, essence, and presence of the Divine. At the same time, I sense the energy in the room shifting and my words becoming energetic reality. I then feel/see my consulting room subtly overlaid with a temple of light and myself surrounded by a protective goldish orb. This effect can be faint if I have gone through the ritual rather quickly, or more intense if I have taken time over it. At the end of the working day, I ask for the temple to be cleansed by mentally filling it with light, and for its energy to be freshly repatterned. I also cleanse my own energy, briefly feeling light emerging from within, cleansing the orb. When I return to work the next day, I sense a fresh, clean, sparkling atmosphere in the room. As my patients enter the house, I might silently bless them and, after they leave, I usually spend a moment behind the closed door, praying for Divine light to surround, protect, and heal them. As these rituals flow from a meditative state of mind, they seem effortless, taking no time at all.

The numinous in the clinic also encompasses the therapeutic attitude. As patients enter my consulting room, I am aware of their uniqueness, their beauty, and their transpersonal quality, which is similar yet different in each patient. I see them equally as Divinely beloved, perfect in the eyes of the Divine and thus Holy, and as struggling with whatever they are bringing to the session. This attitude translates into the quality of my being with the patient, into the way I look at them and into the manner and tone of voice I speak to them. A colleague recently described to me how she had "offered" a somewhat challenging interpretation to her patient "as one might present an offering to a goddess" (Dickinson 2007). This attitude describes a clinical stance which combines an awareness of the Holy with clinical vigor. (I prefer this term to the more usual "clinical rigor" for its friendlier connotations.) The numinous in the consulting room thus is not confined to "special occasions," as it were. Rather—like Solomon's (2001) continuous ethical approach—it becomes an integral part of the analytic attitude, extending to all aspects of clinical work. The analyst then is open to the reality of the Holy—within and without—at all times.

THE SELF AND THE EGO

Traditionally, the clinical aspects of the numinosum have been wrapped up conceptually in the Self, which has recently received renewed attention. But how does the Self function in post-Jungian clinical discourse? At present, there tends to be a dualistic clinical view of ego and Self and their respective competencies, where the focus is either on one or the other. Because of this conceptual delineation, there can be an implicit view that clinical vigor and an emphasis on the Holy tend to be mutually exclusive, or that one comes after the other, first psychological integration or individuation and later, the Holy. Moreover, there might be an implicit fear of inflation in giving clinical scope to the Holy, as though it were secretly regarded as a corrupting force. Or the spiritual might be viewed as mainly about exalted states, which are clinically suspect. The Holy as love toward the patient might be feared as potentially seductive. A clinical approach that centers around the transference/countertransference might view the Holy as a contamination of this. Thus a differentiation is made whereby the ego is assigned the task of dealing with ordinary reality (i.e. emotional reality, one's own pathology, the reality of self and other) whereas the Self is assigned all aspects of transpersonal reality. This conceptual split between ego and Self rests on a linear exclusivity, which found its historical expression in splits between societies, or between analytic approaches, such as archetypal versus developmental.

In my view, such exclusivity is not necessary and an integration of these clinical stances is considered helpful. What might clinical practice look like when it is both vigorous and yet suffused with spirit and based in the Holy? Can the relation of ego and Self be reconsidered paradigmatically? For this, importantly, a mystical point of view adds a new perspective. In the broadest sense, a mystical approach has to do with the direct inner and/or outer experience of the Divine and a manner of receiving knowledge that encompasses all four functions at once, so that knowledge and experience coincide. A case in point is Jung's answer: "I do not believe, I know," when asked, whether he believed in God (McGuire and Hull 1977, 414). It is important to distinguish between such mystical knowledge, which is gained epistemologically without an empirical frame, and fundamentalism. Jung's "I know" is descriptive of the method by which the knowledge is arrived at and does not necessarily imply a value judgment or exclude other views.

When the relation of ego and Self is reconsidered from a mystical point of view, then —through the loving eyes of the Divine—ego and Self coincide. This is because mystical experience epistemically requires paradoxical reality, in which logical contradictions are able to co-exist and/or resolve. From a mystical perspective, the extreme power coupled with the extreme yielding softness of the loving Divine, easily and naturally includes transpersonal as well as personal experience. Moreover, the mystical flow of Divine grace brings with it an all-encompassing acceptance and thus continual forgiveness and transformation. Yet the atemporal, loving eye of the Divine sees only perfection, so that all transformation that may need to unfold has already occurred. Even more fundamentally, the Divine holds in mind both our perfect diamond-Selves and our ego-experience, enfolding both in the same Divine love. This love is so powerfully inclusive and so infinitely encompassing that all distinction between ego and Self becomes thinly insubstantial and/or falls away. I am aware that this is a somewhat radical view spiritually as well as clinically, even though Christ's words: "I and the Father are one" express a similar dynamic. Paradoxically, mystical reality allows for differentiation to co-exist with identity, so that two elements—ego and Self—while being essentially one, may also act upon each other from within their identity, as it were, and effect changes that unfold in a temporal manner. From this point of view, no overcoming of the ego is necessary spiritually and no second half-of-life activation of the Self psychologically.

How might such epistemic mysticism translate clinically? It suggests, for example, that when a new patient arrives the work is already done, yet simultaneously unfolding, while, from yet another perspective, we are always at the beginning. It also implies that the patients we are sitting with bring their diamond-selves, their holiness, and their Divinely inspired goodness, while they also struggle. Thus I often picture the patient as the Divinely beloved when she or he is struggling in relation to themselves or me. At such moments I might mentally whisper: "Behold Thy deeply beloved" and sense the Divine ardor flowing towards the patient. I might also picture the shape of a heart around the patient. While a deep part of myself is engaged prayerfully and meditatively, I feel myself, at the same time, to be also available relationally and transferentially. When there is a sense of unbearable pain or rage in the room, I tend to silently repeat: "Christ have mercy" until a shift occurs. This happens in the silences of the ordinary analytic work, so that I am engaged both transpersonally and personally at approximately the same time, which has become my ordinary state in the consulting room. I am aware that I am using Christian language and references, as this is my tradition. This is not meant to express a perceived preference, for, in my view, the Divine is equally fluent in any language and equally responsive, however conceived of or addressed.

A Psychology of Grace

To me, Divine grace lies at the center of the clinical hour in that I always base myself in it and wait for it to unfold. It is as if there is a stillness at the heart of the clinical hour in which I am always waiting upon God. In this place, the good outcome is as certain as it is not known. Grace is like a subtle substance that pervades the physical space, the temporal space, and the therapeutic relationship. To me, it seems like an infinite gentleness or softness, which is equally capable of any necessary firmness. From grace springs the need and the capacity for acceptance. Ordinary analytic work, when going well, strengthens the capacity to face and tolerate reality, while grace is necessary to facilitate the acceptance of that reality, so that deep acceptance then allows for shifts and changes in reality. The mystical flow of Divine love and grace inspires this process in which ego and Self cowork as well as coincide. Everything that is deeply accepted both gains more structure and texture and equally falls away. In this nonhierarchical conceptualization of ego and Self, there are no lower aspects nor is anything post-poned. This is mirrored by the way in which, mystically, reality and eternity act upon each other for transformation, even while they, profoundly paradoxically, coincide.

In a previous paper, I developed the idea of grace as a principle underlying positive clinical change (Heuer 2008). For this purpose, I explored the conflu-ence of the mystical, direct experience of Divine grace and the implications of contemporary quantum research. Quantum research reveals a subtle cosmic dimension that features extremely powerful harmonic principles which inspire a holistic and holographic type of order that is also of a responsive nature. These dynamic principles underlie random processes and seeming chaos. Cosmologically, this might be imagined as a responsive universe which renders everything we create more graceful, whole, and Holy. These are very subtle, nonlinear, acausal processes in that they are objective in Jung's use of the term, yet they cannot be coerced. In mystical imagination they recall the subtle, yet all powerful, constant and responsive flow of Divine grace. As quantum laws were found to operate in living cells (McTaggart 2001)—rather than being confined to subatomic matter—this suggests a coincidence as well as a creative interplay of quantum and ordinary reality strikingly similar to the mystical conceptualization of ego and Self explored above. Of import here is the way in which a world view based on the second law of thermodynamics—epistemically set in a Newtonian paradigm—becomes superimposed by interweaving with inherently more pow-erful quantum laws. Beyond the emphasis on disintegration and destructiveness implied by the second law of thermodynamics, there arises a sense of an all pow-erful, yet all yielding, responsive, yet noncoercive, force. This force is known via the empirical research of contemporary quantum physics, yet its nature suggests description in mystical terms: grace. The mystical apprehension of Divine grace is conceptually perfectly equal to the complexity of a stronger-than-imaginable yet softer-than-imaginable transformational power that is both transcendent and immanent. In clinical terms, this means that the numinosum is not restricted to the inner, archetypal world of the unconscious but also extends to the corporeal and the interpersonal realm. The Holy then subtly interweaves all aspects of the clinical hour as grace. Because of its encompassing conceptual nature, a clinical paradigm of grace works with most clinical approaches whilst gently altering core paradigmatic beliefs in clinical discourse. Engaging with the patient's pathology and suffering softly ceases to be a central clinical concern as the immanent Self recalls the patient's goodness, love, creativity, and perfection. Yet there need be no radical changes to the clinical hour. A minute shift in awareness provides all the opening needed for grace to flow in easily and the Holy to become subtly visible.

At the same time, the holistic and holographic prepatterns of quantum research or the mystical Divine will see to it that anything we struggle with reveals itself, strengthening our capacity for reality. In unburdening itself, the soul needs to be laid all bare. Yet this process can be held by grace. From a mystical point of view, the patient profoundly is the Divinely beloved at all times, regardless whether the clinical focus is colored by the patient's hate or love. Paradoxically, with the passage of time, the Divine ardor only increases, so that the patient, even though Divinely beloved beyond comprehension, becomes yet more so. Conversely, the mystical Divine, unable to stand by any suffering, including hate, must embrace it and co-suffer, while the numinosum as mystical grace attends all suffering faster than the speed of light. Scientifically, the discovery of mirror neurons (Bauer 2001) adds to this dimension, for it emphasizes the neurological basis of the human capacity for deep empathy. The Holy in the clinical hour then includes the analyst's capacity for empathic embrace of everything that to the patient feels entrenchedly untouchable within. When the analyst engages in this spirit, the quality of struggle—both in the patient's dynamics and in the analyst's countertransference—undergoes a small but potentially profound shift. Similarly, in quantum experiments, small movements like the proverbial butterfly's wing, have powerful effects. As clinical thought and practice become suffused with quantum and mystical knowledge, the Holy in its many guises gains a clearly acknowledged place in all aspects of the clinical hour.

CONCLUSION

In this chapter, I have considered the experience of the numinous in the clinical hour using the confluence of contemporary quantum research and the mystical experience of the Divine as paradigmatic background. Thus the experience of the Holy is both evoked and becomes more intelligible. In this context, I have reworked the concept of ego and Self and utilized the mystical concept of Divine grace as a clinical healing principle. In exploring the numinous in my own consulting room, I became mindful of the need to nurture a clinical language of the Holy. Thus the numinous is a profoundly clinical concern for many colleagues, though this may not have registered sufficiently in clinical discourse, owing to the sense of prohibition mentioned earlier and to a lack of clinical terminology. Naturally, my account represents only one of many possible ways of the numinous coming alive in the clinical hour. In ending, I should like to recall the words from the Delphic oracle that Jung had carved over his door "Vocatus atque non vocatus deus aderit": "Called or uncalled, the Divine is ever present."

REFERENCES

Bauer, Joachim. 2001. Integrating psychiatry, psychoanalysis, neuroscience. *Psychotherapie Psychosomatik Medizinische Psychologie* 51: 265–66.
Dickinson, Paddy. 2007. Personal communication to the author, September.
Heuer, Birgit. 2003. Clinical paradigm as analytic third: reflections on a century of analysis and an emergent paradigm for the millennium. In *Contemporary Jungian clinical practice*, ed. Elphis Christopher and Hester McFarland Solomon, 329–39. London: Karnac.

————. 2008. Discourse of illness or discourse of health: Towards a paradigm-shift in post-Jungian clinical theory. In *Dreaming the myth onward*, ed. Lucy Huskinson, 181–90. London: Routledge.

McGuire, William, and R. F. C. Hull. 1977. C.G. *Jung speaking*. London: Thames and Hudson.

McTaggart, Lynne. 2001. *The field*. London: HarperCollins.

Solomon, Hester. 2001. Origins of the ethical attitude. *Journal of Analytical Psychology* 46: 443–54.

BIRGIT HEUER is a Jungian Analyst of the British Association of Psychotherapists, London. Having trained previously in body-oriented psychotherapy, she has practiced privately for thirty years. She was also clinical supervisor at Kingston University Health Centre and has served on the BAP Jungian training committee.

23

JUNGIAN PSYCHOANALYSIS IN THE CONTEXT OF JAPANESE CULTURE

Kazuhiko Higuchi

My subject has emerged from a quiet question that I have held in my mind since beginning analytical work, especially the analysis of dreams. The question concerns basic differences between the processes and goals of analytical work in the East and in the West. From the time of my return to Japan to practice analytical psychology and to teach in our universities, now forty years ago, I've thought that my work must be immature, since I could not fully conceptualize the analytical process with my analysands or clearly grasp just what it is that I am doing. I have felt that this immaturity might be keeping my work from reaching to heart of Jung's deep analytical insights.

Whenever I've listened to a Westerner present a case, I have admired the clarity with which he sees the process and his insight into the analysand's psyche. Many times my head has agreed with his explanations regarding the cases he presents, but I find my heart saying, "Something feels different." I am now eighty years old and, having some experience in our field, I would like to attempt to reflect on the differences that I've felt.

Let me begin by referring our attention to the famous Japanese Noh plays. I came across these by chance. I am not an expert on Noh, or a Noh actor. I have not struggled to understand Noh in a classical sense. Rather, I am simply an interested student, observing Noh from the perspective of my work with dreams in analysis. In looking at Noh, I have been struck by some similarities, both in process and goal, with my work as a Jungian psychoanalyst. I believe these similarities offer an entry into a reflection on the differences between how analysis is practiced in the East, in my case in Japan, in contrast to how it is carried out in the West.

When a Noh play begins, a character appears who, through his spiritual and psychic sensibility, calls forth from the invisible worlds the main character in the drama. This initial character, the *waki*, never wears a mask. In many plays, the *waki* is a traveling monk. He pauses on his pilgrimage at a place where he senses spiritual energy, an elusive something, and begins to pray. He continues to pray, revealing his compassionate heart, for the well-being of everything and everyone he senses present there. Responding to this compassionate interest, the main character, the *shite*, slowly emerges from the invisible realm. The *shite* can be of either gender but is always masked. She or he may change masks several times during the recitation of their story, which often begins with regret or a grudge that they are carrying from their previous existence. Wearing different masks, the shite tells a tale, taking on the faces of the psychic characters from the past that have influenced and inspired the core personality of this protagonist. When the story has been heard and witnessed, the *shite* again fades back into the invisible realm.

This drawing out of a story, which is enacted in the Noh play, is comparable to the creation of a narrative, drawing on conscious and unconscious materials, which is such an important part of the work of analysis. In the coaxing out that occurs, the multiple features (faces, personas) and eventually the true face of the character appear. The *waki's* receptivity, sensibility, and compassion make the apparition possible. The *shite's* story can then be fully and truthfully told.

In Noh, the *waki* is a supporting actor. He never controls the drama. His costume is plain compared to those of the other characters. He symbolizes ordinary life. He is of the real world, or the world of reality. An analyst is also a person of the real world. An analyst charges a fee. This money stands for the reality of the work. If he denies the reality of his work and refuses a fee, perhaps out of spiritual sensibility, it is easy for him to slip from his position in the real world. An analyst must have a standpoint both within and beyond ordinary reality.

So, the *waki* does not have the leading role. Rather, he earnestly puts his heart and soul into his position behind the scenes. When the true main character, the *shite*, is introduced, the *waki* usually just sits down to the side of the stage and silently listens and watches as the drama unfolds. The leading character is the *shite*, but the *waki* has a unique privilege of sitting and watching at the *shite's* side. This is similar for the analyst. We sit, using our abilities, our training, and our compassion to coax the various masked forms of the *shite*, each deeper than the one before it, to appear. Like the *waki*, as we wander about in our work, we sometimes sense that a particular place is where we must stop. In Noh, this place may be where a famous poem was written or a tragic event took place. It is perceived much as an animal might use his sense of smell to find something important. When we arrive at such a place with an analysand, we feel we cannot pass by. There is a certain gravity of soul that keeps us from moving on. This is also the case when we make a choice to work with a particular analysand. We can call it transference or countertransference, or we may simply call it mystery.

Some of the places that have been important in my own life, places where I've felt a strong sense of spiritual gravity, have been Vienna, Zurich, Ascona, and Kyoto. Like the *waki*, we are travelers in the external and the internal worlds, pilgrims of the soul, men and women on the road that has no final destination or end. Like the medieval medical doctor Paracelsus, we wander here and there. Like the *waki*, we are ever on the road, seeking the totality of being human.

THE NOH STAGE

The only setting for a Noh play is a bare stage with a pine tree painted at the back. The floor, made of plain polished wood, heightens sound and the perception of movement to its utmost. This simplicity allows for maximum play of imagination from the actors and audience. Several quiet footsteps symbolize travel of a thousand miles. A slight upward movement of a mask symbolizes pleasure, and a downward movement denotes sadness.

In a modern Noh play composed by the immunologist Dr. Tomio Tada, a traveling monk appears on stage (as usual) and approaches a well. He meets there the ghost of a young fisherman whose heart was removed for transplant after an accident had left him brain dead. A young woman, the recipient of his heart, also appears at the side of the well. The fisherman begins to talk about begrudging this young woman his heart. In this way, Dr. Tomio Tada reveals a problem in modern medicine. Organs are simply considered parts of the body without reference to the transcendent reality of the soul. They are body parts and can be harvested without thought about how this young fisherman might suffer at the loss of his heart. In this play, the young woman is the *shite* and the well is the special place where all may meet.

Sound plays an important role in Noh. It is even more important than words. One sharp note from an ancient Japanese flute, or the sounds of a drum, are more effective at communicating the feelings of the characters or the gravity of a situation than dialogue. Such sounds provoke our spirits to ponder what we are really about with our modern approach to medicine and our way of life.

The simplicity of the Noh stage and narration makes me think of how different it is from the scene in a usual Western-trained analyst's consulting room. The walls are generally covered with paintings, diplomas, and books. Rooms are filled with furniture, carpets, and art objects. There is no negative space. In words, too, simplicity is often best. Rather than endless repetition of the analysand's stories or the analyst's explanations to the client, a short "Oh" might be more effective at moving the heart of analyst and analysand. Such a well placed "Oh" can provoke the spirit of the patient, bringing forth their truer soul.

BEGINNING AND ENDING ANALYSIS

In a modern Western play, the action begins when the curtain goes up and ends when it comes down again. In analysis, too, we often have fairly clear beginnings and endings in our work. We could say that this special therapeutic relationship, with its beginning and end, actually defines analysis. However, in the East, especially in Japan, this relationship will last an entire lifetime, ending only at death. It is a master and disciple relationship. Before death, no end is possible. Yet, there are milestones on the relational journey, just as there are in Noh plays.

In Noh, there is a special offstage room called the Kamaginoma—literally a room for milling about. There is also a bridge, called the Hashigakari, which is between the Kamaginoma, a waiting room, and the stage proper. This is quite a special place, neither on nor off stage. When the actors approach and cross the bridge, the audience anticipates the drama that is to come. When they retreat back across the same bridge, the audience savors the flavor of what has occurred on stage. Usually, during these transitional times the audience remains silent but feels a great wave of emotion.

When we consider this, we might say that analysis begins before the actual first meeting between analyst and analysand. In Japan, the preanalytical period is very important. Our society is a closely related community. It is very easy to gather information about a patient before they ever appear in my consulting room. I learn about them simply from their names, or from a colleague, through a rumor, or from their voice on the telephone. Our relationship begins before we ever meet. For that reason, Eastern analysts must accept that the relationship with the analysand is not solely between the two of them. It includes as well the level of family, social group, locale within the country, and so on. If you receive a person, you also receive his entire family and society. It is very difficult to say no to this extended situation. No is truly difficult in our society. The patient's need can be so demanding, so intensely strong, that we need a kind of bridge, like the Hashigakari of Noh, which is neither beginning nor ending, but a place in between. If this middle place and time, this coming in and going out, is handled skillfully, all will go well. If not, it ends in misery.

In Japan, we sometimes say that the moment when the sun rises is the moment the day begins. We cannot say that the moment we see the moon is the moment the day ends. The moon often appears while there is still light in the sky. It is also partially light before the sun appears. In the East, the beginning and ending of many things take place in twilight rather than in fully sunlit clarity.

THE WANDERING SOUL

In Japan, people often feel that the spirits of those who are dead carry a kind of grudge toward this world and their circumstances during their lives. Often they are angry ghosts. Even modern people still hold secretly to this idea. Perhaps this is the reason that we Japanese are still so deeply influenced by shamanism. Even Buddhism has this idea, joining forces with our native Shinto, and holding that every creature has the spirit of the Buddha. Natural phenomena such as animals, plants, rivers, mountains, and waterfalls are alive with spirit. All things have the ability to be saved, becoming consciously one with their inherent Buddha Nature, when they are aided in this transition through prayers and the chanting of sutras, mantras, and dharanis. If this does not occur, their souls wander aimlessly through this earthly world. This sense of things also found its way into Noh.

In the medieval age, about the same time that Noh first appeared, many monks wandered through Japan chanting for those who had died and for those whose souls were abandoned by their relatives. They also chanted sutras for all natural things. Since all beings had Buddha nature, it was important that they be worshipped as the Buddha.

Otherwise, their souls would wander forever. For this reason, many medieval Noh plays focused on the unhappy circumstances of life such as injury, aging, sickness, and death. The monks in the plays wandered the country and listened to the stories of these pains and grudges. They heard of tension between parents and their children, husbands and wives, star-crossed lovers, and other miserable tales.

Things are not so different today. Analysis deals with these same issues. Stories of unresolved tension, unreasonable demands, and the various pains of the soul are the stuff of the analytical hour. We deal with life's unsolved problems. The monk in Noh walks the country roads praying for the wanderers whose lives are unresolved. He wishes to evoke the deepest figure within that soul so that it may appear and tell its story. Are we Jungian psychoanalysts so different from that monk, the *waki* of the Japanese Noh?

WOMEN IN NOH

I am astonished at the variety of masks worn by women! There is such differentiation and richness of expression. Among them, there is a very strong mask known as Mad Woman. It expresses the negative aspect of woman. The mask portrays a woman who is ferocious in her anger, suffering from unbearable envy, her forked-tongue cracked and dry like a snake's suffering in a raging fire. Another mask shows a beautiful girl who has changed into a huge serpent.

Perhaps women in the medieval age suffered greatly when the Japanese Samurai tradition became dominant. Before that, aristocratic Japanese women were very independent and enjoyed great sovereignty. They created their own literary styles, writing prose and poetry in the Imperial Court. In matters of love, they were free and not judged. When the warrior tradition took power, women were demoted to a much lower and more controlled place in society. The anger in the masks worn by female characters well expressed their rage. Noh plays were often performed outdoors at shrines or other atmospheric places. In the deep night, with bonfires and torches, the masks must have taken on an even more mysterious appearance and portrayed vibrantly the negative side of the feminine psyche.

Noh plays often have female characters who are seeking a missing child, strongly desiring to meet again a son or daughter who was kidnapped or otherwise taken from them. Sometimes the play is a Hannyo and deals with romantic love between men and women. Perhaps a lower class street girl meets a nobleman and cannot forget him. She longs for him endlessly and becomes mad. She dances in front of Shimogamo Shrine, carrying the fan he had given her. In Japan, a fan is the symbol of union or togetherness. After many years, the nobleman happens to be passing in front of the shrine and sees the mad dancing woman. He would not have recognized her except for the fan she holds. It is not possible for them to be together in the real world, but they can find togetherness in the symbol of the fan that stands for their union. The girl, mad from her desire for the nobleman, embodies a fierce desire for the union of opposites and a quest for Totality.

In my work as an analyst, I usually meet the client in my consulting room. I am not certain, however, whom I am actually meeting. Sometimes it takes a long time before the real figure, the central core, of the person appears. Sometimes I see many more shallow masks before the true essence of that personality emerges. When it comes, it may appear in a positive or negative form. Whichever comes, I am glad to see what is true about that person. I am glad to meet the *shite* of that life. In Noh, there is the *mae* (before) *shite*, and the true *shite*. The true *shite*, a deeper representation of the personality, appears in a different form and costume from the *mae shite*. It emerges from a deeper psychic layer.

This visible difference in image is also helpful in understanding the dreams, stories, and art productions of the analysand.

MONOTONY AND INTEREST

When I first saw a Noh play, which can often go on for several hours, I felt a sense of monotony as the movement was so slow. I have experienced this same monotony in the consulting room. Things so often seem to move very slowly. In the beginning of analysis, the analysand is usually excited. Later, there is a slowing down in the process that is much like the vague meandering of the wandering monks. This slow pace is very important for our work in a world where things move so quickly and people want a quick fix and an easy answer to life's problems. Healing is naturally a slow process. It does not take place in ordinary time. In Noh, an actor may move a few steps on the stage and that movement may represent a journey of a thousand miles. Everything in Noh occurs outside ordinary time. Dreams also function in this kind of altered time and often have the atmosphere of ages past. Dream stories are of interest to oneself, and perhaps to the Self, and evoke our interest and pleasure in the activities of the soul.

BROKEN DREAMS

Among the many Noh plays, there is one called *Mugen Noh*. It is the oldest of the dramas. I find it especially interesting because, at the end of the play, a character says: "The dream is broken, morning is coming." This signifies that the entire drama has been a dream and now it has ended.

This story begins in the fall. A traveling monk appears and visits a famous well at Nata Temple. This well is famous because a handsome man once loved a daughter of King Aritsune, a noble king. Their marriage was held beside the well. As the monk stands there, a girl appears and offers him a cup of well water.

The monk asks her who she is. She says she is a girl from the village nearby but, actually, she is the *mae shite* for the king's daughter. She begins to tell her story of great regret and then disappears into the well. The real *shite* then appears onstage.

She dances, carrying a piece of clothing that had belonged to the handsome nobleman. This is the central part of the entire drama. She continues to dance, looking into the well. At first she sees her own reflection. Later, she sees the man's reflection through the power of the clothing she holds. In medieval times, noblemen and women each had their own special fragrance, created by incensing their garments with specially prepared combinations of scent. By holding his perfumed garment to her face, she can breathe in his scent and increase the vividness of his image. In this way, their separateness is lessened and the worlds of life and death, male and female, past and present come together on the Noh stage. Union occurs in the Noh play that is a dream. Morning, or consciousness, will come.

DEATH AND REBIRTH IN NOH

Noh began in the ancient dancing that took place in the courtyard of a Shinto shrine or Buddhist temple. Later, it came to be performed in the castles of the feudal lords. In its early stages, its purpose was ceremonial.

It asked blessings for the people and their crops, purified evil, and prayed for long life. There was a central character whose role was to cast out evil and invite happiness. The mask worn by this character is that of an old man. This image is important as it gives us a means to reset things old to things new. The old man character visited door-to-door and brought new life to every household in the form of his aged and happy face.

You may know the term *hängenbleiben*, which means to get hung up or fixated. Contrary to such a fixation, or lack of movement, the traveling monk figures of Noh bring change and then disappear from the scene. In medieval times, the philosophy among the aristocratic class bordered on nihilism. Death and its closeness permeated their thinking. This nothingness and its lack of resolution extended to the warrior class, a class that was in tune with Noh. Perhaps for this reason, it is notable that the endings of Noh plays very often do not solve the drama's central problem. Rather, they tell the story of the grudge or tragedy thoroughly and then the characters disappear from the world. This is quite a strong statement that all things are reset by death and then made new in rebirth.

NOH MASKS

I have many Noh masks in my consulting room. I would like to show you some of those I find most interesting. This is Hishimen, produced in the Kyoto district.

Figure 1 Hishimen

It is twisted and symbolizes a man with a severe problem. Many kinds of masks represent both positive and negative aspects of daily human life. Some are very old and have a unique name.

Figure 2 Drugemask

Figure 3 Old Man

It is interesting to note how many kinds of masks there are which represent the crone aspect of a woman's life.

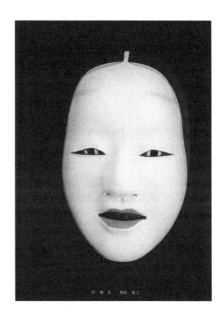

Figure 4 Young Woman   **Figure 5** Heavenly Maiden

TRAINING NOH ACTORS

As I have mentioned earlier, an actor's role as *shite* or *waki* is traditionally determined by his birth family. This tradition still exists but is not so strongly enforced in modern times. Today, even a man not born into a Noh family may go on to become a great Noh actor. An actor's training is of special interest.

In 1433, the famous actor Zeami wrote a book. He was seventy when he wrote the *Kadensho*, a secret account of the professional training of a Noh actor. He said that the training begins by age seven and requires that the trainee have a fairly good voice.

When the trainee is twelve or thirteen, as his voice changes, he must be able to carry a tune. At age seventeen or eighteen, he may have his preliminary first flowering. By twenty-three or twenty-four he reaches the border of his training and may have his first flowering. At age thirty-four or thirty-five, he reaches his peak. When he is forty-four or forty-five he can no longer imitate any other actor. When he reaches the age of fifty, he has produced his true blossom and continues blooming on into old age.

I am uncertain exactly what *shin no hana* (the true flower, or perhaps the flower of truth) means in essence. Clearly, it is seen as the peak attainment in an actor's career. The purpose of Noh is not just to perform beautifully in the traditional sense, but is a way of expressing beauty in developmental stages, which culminates in touching the deepest part of the Self. This Self-realization is represented by the stages of the blossoming of the flower of truth. When we compare these stages with the training and maturing process in an analyst's career, we must add some years to the stages of development. Yet, in both circumstances, the goal is a deeper union with Totality.

In conclusion, I quote from a famous Noh play that is known by every Japanese. This is spoken by Atsumori in the *Ko Waka Mai*, in a very old style of Noh. Atsumori loves to sing and dance and play just before facing his fateful wars. In it, Oda Nobunaga (an historical figure) speaks just prior to his death in battle. He says: "Life lasts only fifty years. Compared with the movement of heaven, it is like a dream. If one is once born in this world, he can never be diminished." Our dance of life is like a play, a poem, or a song. As analysts or analysands, we must choose our roles and play them with true intensity of heart. Perhaps then, the flower, be it the Western rose or the Eastern lotus, will bloom on into old age and beyond.

KAZUHIKO HIGUCHI, D. Min., is Ex-President of Kyoto Bunkyo University and the Association of Jungian Analysts, Japan, the Jung Club in Japan, and the Japanese Association of Sand Play Therapists, and continues as President of the Japan Life Line Telephone Service for Suicide Prevention. He is well known among the Japanese as one of the pioneers who helped bring Analytical Psychology to Japan. He is the author of *Jung shinrigakuno Sekai* (The World of Jungian Psychology).

PART FOUR

SPECIAL TOPICS

INTRODUCTION TO SPECIAL TOPICS
Murray Stein

It is not widely known that Jung's lectures at Clark University in 1909, when he and Sigmund Freud traveled there together, included a case report on the treatment of a three- or four-year old child suffering from a neurosis. This is one of the earliest reports on child analysis in psychoanalytic literature. Later Jung would famously say that he took little interest personally in early development and left that to the Freudians, and yet a number of his followers were actually well known child analysts, most importantly Michael Fordham. Erich Neumann, too, wrote an important work on early childhood development, *The Child*. In this section, Brigitte Allain-Dupré in her chapter "The Child's Side," presents the history and contemporary standing of child analysis among Jungian psychoanalysts. Gustav Bovensiepen, a much published author and international lecturer, offers a Jungian perspective on working analytically with a broad spectrum of adolescent patients.

Donald Kalsched, in his chapter, "Working with Trauma in Analysis," continues the discussion of unresolved early developmental issues and conflicts as they arise in the analysis of adults. Katrin Asper follows with her chapter "Psychotherapy and Congenital Physical Disability," which shows the early psychological traumatic roots of the suffering faced by analysands who were born with physical disabilities. Both of these articles illustrate ways in which contemporary Jungian psychoanalysts work with psychological problems and suffering that derive from early wounds, deficits, and damage to self esteem and functional capacities.

The relation between the psyche and the body is taken up further by Margaret Wilkinson in "Psyche and Brain," while Axel Capriles focuses on the psychosomatics and teleology of passion in "The Passions: Tactics of the Soul." These chapters represent two sides of a single coin, the endlessly fascinating and intriguing human psyche.

To speak of passion immediately raises the question of ethics: how should one conduct oneself in the midst of the passionate engagement with another that analysis often becomes? For the Jungian psychoanalyst this is a continuous concern since the work is conducted in emotional territories that are never easy to judge and often difficult to estimate and control. Hester Solomon, whose work on ethics and the self has received wide attention in the Jungian community, brings ethical considerations to bear on the conduct of analysis in her chapter "The Ethical Attitude in Analytical Practice." John Dourley, whose provocative books on a depth-psychological understanding of monotheistic theologies have found a wide readership, continues with a reflection on religion and psychological maturity in his chapter "Religion and Jungian Psychoanalysis."

Like all other forms of psychotherapy and psychoanalysis, Jungian psychoanalysis has been confronted with a demand to prove its value as a mode of treatment in the contemporary world. Jung's early laboratory research on the psyche, which resulted in the highly popular and clinically useful concept of the "complex," laid the groundwork for later Jungian research on a variety of topics, including most recently therapy outcome studies. Verena Kast, a leading Jungian exponent of the need for more research in the field of analytical psychology, provides the historical background of research in analytical psychology as well as a persuasive argument on the need for more and continuing efforts along these lines.

Finally, Helen Morgan presents a new application of dream work in her exposition, "The Social Dreaming Matrix." Building on the work of W. Gordon Lawrence at the Tavistock Clinic in London, Morgan and others have adapted the social dreaming matrix to Jungian understandings of the permeable psyche and social interconnectedness. This chapter, which concludes the section on Special Topics, considers the psyche's response in wider social settings and contexts.

24

THE CHILD'S SIDE: GENEALOGY OF THE SELF

Brigitte Allain-Dupré

Jung to Freud: Do you have experience with such young children?
Freud to Jung: Psychic work we do not yet have the slightest idea about!

CHILD ANALYSIS AND THE JUNGIAN WORLD

One might believe that the acknowledgment of child analysis dates back to the first IAAP congress in 1958, when five of the twenty presentations were devoted to this topic (Adler 1958). Child analysis would appear to be fully integrated into the Jungian world.

Yet the truth is not that simple: though Jungian organizations offer the field of child analysis explicit signs of legitimacy, in terms of an ongoing presence in publications and congresses, the Jungians have yet to integrate child analysis in their representations and identity. For example, the work of child analysts is rarely cited as such by analysts working with adults. In my opinion, this is due to gaps in the identification of its basic theoretical concepts.

Today, it is possible to fill these gaps because a significant corpus of research and coherent thought has accumulated over the past fifty years. I suggest that we go back to the origins of child analysis, in the basic assumptions described by Jung, and retrace the ground covered by Jungian child analysts since then. It will require that we describe the broadening of the *historic* Jungian concepts, pointing out those which gradually emerged as practice continued and those which provide theoretical foundations for today's practitioners.

FREUD AND JUNG DISCUSS THE CHILD AND THE INFANTILE

To understand fully the evolution, if not revolution, represented in the Jungian world by the legitimating of child analysis, we must go back to its genesis in the correspondence between Freud and Jung. At that time, childhood and the *infantile* were the subjects of a lively exchange.

The observations Freud and Jung made of the psychic and affective life of the children they were in contact with (Allain-Dupré 1996) prompted an exchange of metapsychological hypotheses. The first heroes were Little Hans, the son of one of Freud's Viennese friends, and Agathli, Jung's elder daughter. The case of Little Hans enabled Freud to conceive his Oedipus complex (McGuire 1974, 186–87). Jung's observations of his daughter when the family was expecting the birth of a new child enabled him to write "Psychic Conflicts in a Child" (Jung 1910/1916/1946).

Published in 1910, "Psychic Conflicts in a Child" is a psychological observation of a child grappling with the spurts of psychic growth, engaged in the process whereby she will attain a new step in her symbolic life. Unlike Freud, who emphasized castration anxiety as the source of Little Hans's phobia, Jung shows how his daughter's difficulties are signs of the natural activity of symbolic work, when the child tries to pierce the mysteries of procreation.

With the essays on "The Rumor" (Jung 1910) and "The Significance of the Father" (Jung 1909/1949), and one of the lectures given at Fordham University (to be discussed below), these are the only incursions Jung made into the specific world of childhood.

CARL GUSTAV'S STRAINED RELATIONSHIP WITH CHILDHOOD

In the first two chapters of *Memories, Dreams, Reflections,* one can note Jung's lively relationship to humanity's psychological substratum. His ability to recognize the power of the child's urge *to be* is particularly evident. Today, this urge can be interpreted as the pressure of the self, seeking integration in an ego open to the world of sameness and otherness. However, it is interesting to observe that the elderly Jung, reflecting upon his childhood, cannot relate it to a general approach to child psychology, which would have led to the idea that a child, as a subject, could benefit from a therapeutic space just like an adult. On the contrary, the distinctive characteristic of Jung's childhood is his solitude in relation to the depression of his mother (Bair 2004, 18).

This need for compensation is still present for Jung when, at age 33, returning to his childhood home, he recalls: "The world of my childhood in which I had just become absorbed was eternal, and I had been wrenched away from it and had fallen into a time that continued to roll onward, moving farther and farther away. The pull of that other world was so strong that I had to tear myself violently from the spot in order not to lose hold of my future" (Jung 1961, 20).

These archetypal fantasies provide us with an understanding of young Carl Gustav's first relations with himself, which clearly forms the basis for a theoretical hypothesis of the influence of the self as the principle that organizes and orients the subject's "realization of the unconscious" (Jung 1961, v).

Unlike Freud, who had fond memories of having been adored by his mother, Jung may have had a need to distance himself from childhood to avoid reopening old wounds. He nevertheless arrived at the unconscious aspects of the child by a much broader path, that of the archetype.

CHILD ANALYSIS IN A WORLD OF ADULT ANALYSTS

In "Child Development and Education," Jung asserted: "The prime psychological condition is one of fusion with the psychology of the parents, an individual psychology being only potentially present. Hence it is that the nervous and psychic disorders of children right up to school age depend very largely on disturbances in the psychic world of the parents. All parental difficulties reflect themselves without fail in the psyche of the child, sometimes with pathological results" (Jung 1923/1946, para. 106). Although this path is restrictive for the child, it has long been followed by many adult Jungian analysts.

Despite the fact that Jung seems to have shunned child analysis, the Jungian world is open enough to allow new positions to emerge. Children's psychotherapeutic needs have elicited pioneering positions as a means of alleviating what had been experienced as the lack of a metapsychological approach to the child's psyche.

BEYOND JUNG: THE CHILD'S INDIVIDUATION

Already in 1944 with the publication of *The Life of Childhood*, Michael Fordham announced: "Investigating the unconscious of children is to add stones to the foundations of a house which is in the process of construction. [...] Whatever originality this book may possess it draws its vitality from the genius of Professor C.G. Jung" (Fordham 1944, vi). Right in the introduction, Fordham writes: "a reproach which might be leveled with more justice at analytical psychology is its neglect of the psychology of childhood" (Fordham 1944, 4).

During World War II, Fordham's experience in the Therapeutic Hostels, caring for children who had been orphaned, enabled him to see: "they were evidence for my thesis that the self, in Jung's sense, was an active factor in child development, whereas Jungians thought it only became important in the second half of the life. [...] I was demolishing the idea that neurotic and psychotic children could only be treated indirectly, that is, through treatment of the parents. The case of the evacuated children became confirmation of my ideas: there were virtually no parents available anyway, so that parental influence in the present situation has ceased altogether" (Fordham 1993, 62, 85).

As Jung had done before him, Fordham adopted an empirical attitude, validating his theoretical intuitions with clinical experience. These intuitions would be evident to the generations of child analysts inspired by his ideas. Nevertheless, their innovative nature should be emphasized. They signify that, although Jung's initial writings on the child before 1912 are important, they are not necessarily the theoretical basis for contemporary Jungian child analysis. It would later be clear that the ideas Jung elaborated for the second half of life enable us to approach the products of the child's unconscious as well as those of the adult.

This amplification of Jungian concepts "from the child's side" is also a means of advancing Jung's work—with all due modesty—and linking it to the many contemporary discoveries about child psychology, be they from the research of various schools of psychoanalysis or from the fields of anthropology, sociology, and even education (Allain-Dupré 2006).

In institutional terms, child analysis was recognized to be a fully legitimate field of study at the 1983 IAAP Congress in Jerusalem (Report of the executive committee[1]). However, this legitimacy is still tentative. For example, in my opinion, Thomas Kirsch's book (Kirsch 2000) gives an insufficient presentation of the specificity of child analysis, considering the large number of practitioners and countries it concerns.

THE SELF: AXIS OF PSYCHIC GROWTH

Following this brief account of Fordhamian insights into the emergence of a concept of individuation starting at birth, we will now examine how Jungian analysts incorporated these insights into their work. Much more than a single article would be required to go into the meaning of the term *individuation* for Jungian authors writing about child analysis, as well as the definitions they attach to the word self. Let us nevertheless outline the question.

The self, classically defined by Jungian theory as "the archetypal center of the whole personality, conscious and unconscious" (Agnel 2005), is the "true axis for the growth of the psyche," as Elie Humbert stated it (Humbert 1977), the element bringing about the advent of the personality, a growth process that unfolds as long as a person is living.

The question is thus whether the same conception of the self is appropriate to describe the growth and adaptation taking place in childhood. Let us summarize what Jung means by "adaptation" by considering it to be the direct consequence of the fact that people are not *tabula rasa* at birth. "No man can change himself into anything from sheer reason; he only can change himself into what he potentially is" (Jung 1912/1952, para. 351).

Jung wants to explore the innate ability to form a relationship: the contemporary term for this is attunement, according to Daniel Stern (Stern 1985). In other

---

[1] Minutes of the Executive Committee, Zurich, October 1983, §9: "1st International Workshop of Analytical Psychology in Childhood and Adolescence. Mara Sidoli, a child analyst from London, had proposed at the Jerusalem Congress that more attention be given to analytic work with children and adolescents by the IAAP. A meeting had been arranged during the congress and attended by a good number of interested child analysts from different countries. The idea grew to form an International Group (but not a section of the IAAP) which would communicate ideas on analytic work with children and adolescents, and on training matter" (IAAP Archives). See the Workshop web site http://www.materia-prima.net/.

words, Jung sees the concept of childhood adaptation, which can be extended to the first half of life, as the maturational journey driven by the archetype of the self. For him, the psychic life of the subject takes place within the context of an ego originating in the self. This ego develops by forming relationships with others and with oneself, for the archetype is active and alive as such only when it is aroused in a relationship with an other (Agnel 2004, 30).

In Jung's writings on childhood (1906–1912), as in the descriptions of his own childhood in the first two chapters of *Memories* (Jung 1961), the psychic urge to reach consciousness, driven by the self in the ego, can be recognized in symbolic representations. Jung describes the conditions whereby an assumed subject was able to emerge in him as a youth, in particular in the possibility of gaining consciousness of his own shadow aspects, both collective and individual (Allain-Dupré 2007).

If we agree with the idea that "the objective self takes on its full meaning only in the accomplishment of the subject ego" (Agnel 2005), we must consider the period of infancy as starting this accomplishment. We need to consider what Jung calls "adaptation" in a much more creative meaning that its behaviorist echo could induce. The progress of the archetypal process driving this adaptive maturation must also be examined.

Jung's work compelled him continually to deepen his understanding of contents of a psyche that is not *tabula rasa* at the moment of birth. As a result, the emergence of an ego permitting the child to attain subjectivity, according to the human archetypal project, was taken for granted, as Fordham points out: "Thus the fact of the existence of the archetypes in childhood was neglected and, instead, their setting in the historical past was investigated. It is not strange that so fascinating a study should prove irresistible, but children should not on that account suffer neglect" (Fordham 1944, 4).

PIONEERING MOTHERS: MARIE MOLTZER AND
FRANCES WICKES

Despite the metapsychological gaps we have pointed out, child analysts appeared quite early alongside the thinkers, Jung and Freud. They were women. After Emma Fürst, who accompanied Jung in his first research with children (Fürst 1907), child analyst Marie Moltzer provided Jung with the clinical material he presented in 1912, in one of the lectures on psychoanalytic theory delivered at Fordham University, entitled "A Case of Neurosis in a Child" (Jung 1912/1949, para. 458).

The next Jungian child analyst of note was Frances G. Wickes. In 1927, she published *The Inner World of Childhood,* prefaced by Jung. From the outset, she emphasized the educational or rehabilitative approach adopted by any subject related to childhood. The concept of the self, absent from the edition of 1927, appears in the revised preface of 1988. It is mentioned in terms of the personification of the archetype: "The self—that sage who from the beginning lives in the psyche of the child and speaks the defining word in times of peril.[...] It is then that the long forgotten but still numinous experience comes to the aid of the perplexed traveler and shows him what he must now do if he would be free to continue on his way. Thus the self gives testimony to the Great Realities of the Soul" (Wickes 1927/1988, xv). Here, the concept of the self is applied with no reference to clinical practice. It is examined exclusively in terms of its positive and even moral influence.

Jung's preface to her book cites concepts which have since been largely explored by psychoanalytic writers on the mother-baby relationship. In light of the knowledge we have today, they seem insufficient, but at the time they were quite progressive. One might note, in particular, the idea of a psychic sharing between mother and embryo and later between mother and infant, based on *participation mystique*. This *participation* between mother and baby has been studied from the viewpoint of possession and the *mana* personality constellated between the two partners in the relationship (Allain-Dupré et al. 2005).

The writings of Frances Wickes are valuable in that they provide insight into how far Jungian child analysts had to travel from their starting point to construct the metapsychological corpus that is the foundation of their practice today.

MICHAEL FORDHAM AND ERICH NEUMANN, SECOND-GENERATION FOUNDING FATHERS

Michael Fordham (1905–1995)

In 1944, when he published *The Life of Childhood. A Contribution to Analytical Psychology*, Fordham had been working in Child Guidance Clinics and private practice for ten years (Fordham 1944). The fact that it was published in wartime is especially eloquent. In Fordham's eyes, development requires growth of consciousness, the basis for the individual's ability to distinguish right from wrong. Fordham establishes a relationship with the world of archetypes based on his experience with adult patients, in whom he can identify the energetic influence of the archetypes regardless of the parents' conscious or unconscious influence (Fordham 1944, 26). Research over the past few decades, like the links to neuroscience studied by Jean Knox (Knox 2003) and Margaret Wilkinson (Wilkinson 2006), have proven Fordham correct.

Fordham's examination of the concept of individuation led him to the groundbreaking discovery that the child psyche can draw upon psychological objectivity: "The child starts life with a psyche that is not known to him, but through which he grows and becomes conscious. It seems likely that he grows increasingly aware of his inner nature through the experience of archetypes, which we, as adults, recognize as parts of himself even though they are not at first realized as being so by the child" (Fordham 1944, 7).

Although they may seem self-evident today, childhood psychic autonomy and objectivity were the founding theories that had been missing from Jungian thought. However, Fordham had not yet made the application of Jung's theory of the self fully explicit. In 1957, Fordham continued exploring this terrain with the publication of *New Developments in Analytical Psychology* (Fordham 1957). As the preface announced, "The title is justified by the fact that a series of observations [...] have led me to something approaching a general view of child analysis and ego development: one consequence has been to emphasize the correctness of Jung's classical concept of individuation as a manifestation of the second half of life" (Fordham 1957, ix). Fordham had begun to find in Jung "an outline theory of ego development as well, though it is true that careful reading is needed to reveal it and it has never been set forth completely" (Fordham 1957, 104). Fordham had finally found the missing link between Jung's thinking and the theories which would underlie his own views on the subject of the analyzability of children.

In 1951, Fordham wrote the seminal article "Some Observations on the Self and the Ego in Childhood" (Fordham 1957, 131), in which he adapted Jungian theory of the integrative powers of the self to the psyche of the child. Fordham's observation of a one-year-old child scribbling blithely until she produced the "I" proved his hypothesis of a representation of the integrative function of the self, as evidenced in the *mandala*. He comments: "The relation in time between the discovery of the circle and the discovery of 'I' suggests that the circle represented the matrix of the self out of which the ego arose" (Fordham 1957, 134).

In 1955, Fordham wrote a related essay, "The Origins of the Ego in Childhood," in which he defined two new concepts, integration and deintegration, as a means of describing the results of the intervention of the self in the child psyche. "In comparing the self in childhood with the self in individuation we are also comparing the process of integration with another one for which I propose the term *deintegration*. This term is used for the *spontaneous* division of the self into parts—a manifest necessity if consciousness is ever to arise" (Fordham 1957, 117). Deintegration could further be characterized as a "readiness for experience, a readiness to perceive and act, but there is as yet no perception and no action. Both come into consciousness without distinction between subject and object" (Fordham 1957, 120). On the basis of deintegration, the self initiates a process whereby fragments of the ego are integrated and organized around a central ego. Infant observation according to Esther Bick's method then enabled Fordham to confirm the to-and-fro swing between deintegration and reintegration in the gradual emergence of the child's ego.

All these discoveries led Fordham to draft a more precise definition of how he believed child analysis could be structured, in a chapter entitled "Child Analysis" (Fordham 1957, 155). In 1969, he revised *The Life of Childhood* for a new edition, entitled *Children as Individuals*. It differed significantly from the earlier edition: "I have given much prominence to the self defined as the organized totality of conscious and unconscious systems. The conception applied to the child treats him as an entity in himself from which the maturational process can be derived. It does not include mother or the family" (Fordham 1976, 11).

In conclusion, I feel it is important to confirm that Fordham's early work had a profound influence on the community of Jungian child analysts. Later, Melanie Klein's influence would give a special tinge to the British Jungian child analysts and their followers. The Kleinian influence is a British cultural particularity, which is not necessarily shared by Jungian child analysts in other countries, although they do not deny it either. The writings of Mara Sidoli (Sidoli 1989, 2000) and Miranda Davies (Davies and Sidoli 1988), with Gustav Bovensiepen (Sidoli and Bovensiepen 1995), Barry Proner, and Jane Bunster attest to the specificity of the London School in the field of child analysis. Likewise, child analysts in France were influenced by the Lacanian Françoise Dolto and the Freudian Serge Lebovici. Their approach has left a perceptible mark on the epistemological substrate of the French Jungian child analysts (Vandenbroucke 2006).

Erich Neumann (1905–1960)

Neumann's approach (Vitolo 1990) differs fundamentally from Fordham's, in that it "depicts the conscious-unconscious dialectic in human psychology as a masterful mythological and symbolic fresco" (Lyard 1979). His thinking is more creative than metapsychological, in that it amplifies the idea of the archetype into an extremely precise and complex vision. His theory of the archetype reflects the one in *Symbols of Transformation*, as a *pattern of behavior*.

The Origins and the History of Consciousness (Neumann 1950) is the work in which Neumann lays the theoretical foundation for his understanding of the genesis of personality. Jung agreed to write an introduction to it, in which he asserted "the work grounded analytical psychology on a firm evolutionary base" (Young-Eisendrath 1997). Neumann's phylogenetic approach sparked much discussion (Fordham 1981, Shamdasani 2003, Hillman 1975, Vannoy-Adams 1997) that we shall not go into here.

However, Neumann's contribution to child psychology deserves consideration, even if it should be noted that he did not base his thinking on clinical practice with children. Like Fordham, he is convinced that an individuation process is at work from the moment life begins. This process is driven by the early presence of what he calls the ego-self axis. "The filiation of the ego means the establishment of the ego-self axis and a 'distancing' of the ego from the self which reaches its high point in the first half of life, when the systems divide and the ego is apparently autonomous" (Neumann 1966). Thus, the first moments of consciousness emerge from the unconscious, their seeds nourished by the primal relationship of child to mother. This is the concept at the heart of Neumann's posthumously published *The Child, Structure and Dynamics of the Nascent Personality* (Neumann 1973).

The child-mother relationship, specific to human development, is a "mythological reality, because it is inaccessible to experience, which is contingent upon some degree of consciousness. [. . .] Neumann chose the term *ouroboric* to describe the unity without tension of this psychic reality" (Lyard 1979, 15).

Amplification of this ouroboric unity postulated by Neumann leads him to consider that mother and child develop in a single, shared reality, undifferentiated by either: the psyche is so closely bound to the body and the world that no distinction can be made between body and world.

On the child's side, the archetypal organizer of this mother-child unity is what Neumann (also Fordham 1969, 100–101) calls the *primary self*. As the human embryo develops, the primary self contains the individual autonomous aspect of his personality. However, its development is part of "the foreign reality of the mother, who has a superordinate influence on the embryo. Only when the post-uterine embryonic phase is over can we demonstrate the full establishment of this authority called the individual self by analytic psychology" (Lyard 1979, 9).

Dynamics between the child's individual self and his mother create a specificity Neumann calls the *body-self*. Indeed, "in the embryonic phase, the mother's body is the world in which the child lives, not yet endowed with a controlling and perceiving consciousness and not yet ego-centered; moreover, the totality-regulation of the child's organism, which we designate by the symbol of the Body-Self, is, as it were, overlaid by the mother's Self" (Neumann 1988, 10).

Neumann coined the terms *centroversion* and *automorphism* to describe the mechanisms at work in the development of psychic life. "In the first part of life, centroversion leads above all to the formation of a center of consciousness, the use of which is gradually assumed by the ego complex. Automorphism is the specific and unique tendency of each individual to fulfill his potential, to accomplish his particular and constitutional nature within the community, or, if necessary, in opposition to or independently of it.[...] Automorphism and the relation to the other are inseparable, which seems to be characteristic of human development" (Lyard 1969, 10).

Whereas Fordham gained such a broad following that he is seen as the founder of the School of London, Neumann by comparison remained isolated. However, this does not mean that the Jungian community was impervious to his ideas. He is probably lesser known because his work as a theoretician rather than a clinician cut him off, to some degree, from young analysts in training. French child psychiatrist and Jungian analyst Denyse Lyard (Lyard 1998) has developed a profound knowledge of Neumann's theories, which she illustrates masterfully with her clinical experience, a foundation missing from Neumann's writings.

IS THERE SUCH A THING AS JUNGIAN CHILD ANALYSIS?

This is the question asked by Denyse Lyard, echoing the reflections presented here. She proceeds to establish an inventory of epistemological resources, placing the theory of the *primary self* in the foreground. Whether the concept is understood in the Fordhamian or Neumannian sense, the self functions, according to Denyse Lyard, "like an individual memory, recording the traces of unconscious experiences and capable of restoring them in a dream, in particular, or in the contents projected into the specific situation of analytic transference" (Lyard 1998, 79).

Therefore, both the Neumannian and Fordhamian approaches confirm that it is possible to analyze the child by recognizing the self's fertilizing effect on the individuation process, the source of the construction of the child's personality, in the dynamic of differentiation between ego and unconscious. It is interesting to note that when a single clinical case is considered in light of both approaches (Bosio Blotto and Nagliero 2005), the result is not contradictory, but complementary.

Nevertheless, the field of exploration and creation of Jung-inspired child analysts is not limited to these two thinkers. At gatherings like the annual International Workshop of Analytical Psychology in Childhood and Adolescence, founded in 1983 by Mara Sidoli and Gustav Bovensiepen, the depth of their exchanges is proof that the field is dynamic and thriving.

Now that the pioneers have opened the path with their scrutiny of the Jungian concept of the self, the challenge awaiting a new generation of child analysts is to further this exploration by seeking a more precise understanding of (a) the archetypal dynamic, (b) the psychic events that anticipate the child's gender identity based on the anima and animus, (c) the means whereby a sense of ethics is organized, between detachment from the parental superego and differentiation between right and wrong.

Let each adopt his or her own style, depending on his or her background. Carefully thought-out clinical practice will yield coherence, and each will contribute to this immense and never-ending project Jung began: the effort to bring the arcana of the human psyche to light.

REFERENCES

Adler, Gerhard. 1958. The First International Congress for Analytical Psychology. *Journal of Analytical Psychology* 4, 2: 187–89.

Agnel, Aimé. 2004. *Jung: La passion de l'autre,* Collection Les Essentiels. Toulouse: Milan.

Agnel, Aimé et al. 2005. *Le vocabulaire de Carl Gustav Jung.* Paris: Ellipses. Voice: Le soi.

Allain-Dupré, Brigitte, ed. 2005. Maria et le thérapeute. Une écoute plurielle. Collection "Confrontations." *Cahiers jungiens de psychanalyse*, ed. Brigitte Allain-Dupré.

———. 1996. Enfants de la clinique, clinique de l'enfant. *Cahiers jungiens de psychanalyse* 86: 67–81.

———. 2006. What do the child analysts bring to the Jungian thought? In *Proceedings of the 16th International Congress for Analytical Psychology*, ed. Lyn Cowan, 49–62. Einsiedeln: Daimon Verlag.

———. 2009. The ethics of the subject in child analysis: The Question of subjectivation. *Cape Town 2007.* Ed. Pramila Bennett. Einsiedeln: Daimon Verlag.

Bair, Deirdre. 2004. *Jung: A biography.* Boston: Little, Brown and Company.

Bosio Blotto, Wilma. 2005. Le paradis, retrouvailles et pertes. In *Maria et le thérapeute: Une écoute plurielle.* Collection "Confrontations," ed. Brigitte Allain-Dupré, 155–68. *Cahiers jungiens de psychanalyse.*

Douglas, Claire. 1997. The historical context of Analytical Psychology. In *The Cambridge companion to Jung*, eds. Polly Young-Eisendrat P. and Terence Dawson, 17–34. Cambridge: Cambridge University Press.

Davies, Miranda and Mara Sidoli, eds. 1988. *Jungian child psychotherapy: Individuation in Childhood*. London: Karnac Books.

Fordham, Michael.1944. *The life of childhood: a contribution to analytical psychology.* London: Kegan Paul, Trench, Trubner & Co.

———. 1957. *New developments in analytical psychology.* London: Routledge.

———. 1969. *Children as individuals.* London: Hodder and Stoughton.

———. 1976. *The self and autism.* London: Heineman.

———. 1981. Neumann and childhood. *Journal of Analytical Psychology* 26, 2: 99–122.

———. 1993. *The making of an analyst: A memoir.* Free Association Books.

Fürst, Emma. 1907. Statistical investigations on word associations and on familial agreement in reaction type among uneducated persons. Unpublished. See Jung, *Collected Works* 2 para. 886 n.13.

Hillman, James. 1975. *Re-visioning psychology.* New York: Harper & Row.

Humbert, Elie. 1977. *Vocabulaire des psychothérapies*, ed. André Virel, 274. Paris: Fayard. Voice: Le Soi.

Jung, Carl Gustav. 1909/1949. The significance of the father in the destiny of the individual. In CW 4.

———. 1910/1949. A contribution to the psychology of rumour. In CW 4.

———.1910/1916/1946. Psychic conflicts in a child. In CW 17.

———. 1912/1952. Symbols of the mother and of rebirth. In CW 5.

———. 1912/1949. A case of neurosis in a child. In CW 4.

———. 1923/1946. Child development and education. In CW 17.

———. 1961. *Memories, dreams, reflections.* Recorded by Aniela Jaffe. New York: Vintage Books.

Kirsch, Thomas. 2000. *The Jungians: A comparative and historical perspective.* London: Routledge.

Knox, Jean. 2003. *Archetype, attachment, analysis: Jungian psychology and the emergent mind.* London: Routledge.

Lyard, Denyse. 1979. Le modèle théorique d'Erich Neumann. *Cahiers de psychologiejungienne* 20: 1–50.

———. 1998. *Les analyses d'enfants: Une clinique jungienne.* Paris: Albin Michel.

McGuire, William, ed. 1974. *The Freud/Jung letters.* Princeton: Princeton University Press.

Nagliero, Gianni. 2005. Empathie et technique. In *Maria et le Thérapeute*, ed. Brigitte Allain-Dupré et al. Collection "Confrontations," ed. Brigitte Allain-Dupré, 77–89. *Cahiers jungiens de psychanalyse.*

Neumann, Erich. 1950. *The origins and history of consciousness.* Princeton: Princeton University Press.

———. 1966. Narcissism, normal self formation and the primary relationship to the mother. *Spring, an annual of Archetypal Psychology and Jungian Thought*, 81–106

———. 1973/1988. *The child, structure and dynamics of the nascent personality.* London: Maresfield Library.

Shamdasani, Sonu. 2003. *Jung and the making of modern psychology.* Cambridge: Cambridge University Press.

Sidoli, Mara. 1989. *The unfolding self.* Boston: Sigo Press.

————. 2000. *When the body speaks*. London: Routledge.

Sidoli, Mara, and Gustav Bovensiepen 1995. *Incest fantasies and self destructive acts*. London: Transaction Publishers.

Stern, Daniel. 1985. *The interpersonal world of the infant: A view from psychoanalysis and developmental psychology*. New York: Basic Books.

Vandenbroucke, Bernadette. 2006. On the experience of a group of child and adolescent analysts: Reinventing Jungian concepts. *Proceedings of the 16th International Congress for Analytical Psychology*, ed. Lyn Cowan. Einsiedeln: Daimon Verlag.

Vannoy-Adams, Michael. 1997. The archetypal school. In *The Cambridge Companion to Jung*, ed. Polly Young-Eisendrath & Terrance Dawson. Cambridge: Cambridge University Press.

Vitolo, Antonio. 1990. *Un esilio impossibile, Neumann, tra Freud e Jung*. Roma: Borla.

Wickes, Frances G. 1927/1955. *The inner world of childhood*. London: Appleton and Company.

Wilkinson, Margaret. 2006. *Coming into mind: The mind-brain relationship: A Jungian clinical perspective*. London: Routledge.

BRIGITTE ALLAIN-DUPRÉ, DESS, is a training analyst and supervisor with the Société Française de Psychologie Analytique and was co-Director of the Jung Institute where she was more specifically responsible for training child and adolescents psychotherapists. With Jungian psychoanalysts from Italy, Germany, and France, she published in French and Italian *Maria et le thérapeute, une écoute plurielle*. She is in private practice in Paris.

25

ADOLESCENCE—A DEVELOPMENTAL PERSPECTIVE

Gustav Bovensiepen

"I is someone else."

—A. RIMBAUD

Adolescence is often described as a transitional phase from childhood and family life to adulthood and the collective world in terms of ego development and social adaptation. However, individuation, the developing and unfolding of the self, takes place concurrently as an inner process.

To summarize some aspects of adolescent states of mind, I offer the following characterization.

Adolescent moods frequently alternate between high spirits and utter despair; typical is an abrupt change from anxiety and feelings of inadequacy to a form of grandiose certainty of omnipotence. Mindless states are common and lead sometimes to manic behavior, which can be interpreted by the parents (who are identified with the adolescent's projected superego) as the adolescent's complete refusal to take responsibility for his actions. At times, adolescents suffer also from intense feelings of shame resulting from the fantasized morbidity, ugliness, and insufficiency of their bodies; for the first time they become consciously aware of their own mortality.

Painful pricks of conscience are common when the adolescent simultaneously condemns and idolizes the parents, sustaining the faint hope of being completely understood and accepted by them. In psychodynamic terms, these complex and often confusing states of mind indicate the adolescent's task, which is to separate from mother and father and to leave the infantile relationship behind.

The large majority of adolescents manage to cope with these inner and outer conflicts without any serious signs of mental breakdown. Analytic psychology attributes this to the self forces that hold together the adolescent's inner world, a world threatened by *fragmentation*. Whether or not the self will be able to develop with sufficient strength and effectiveness to maintain cohesion depends in a person's early childhood experiences. The adolescent must succeed in maintaining an *inner continuity* in a phase of life during which many inward and outward changes are taking place.

According to Jung, there is interplay of regressive and progressive energy, an archetypal activity undertaken in the quest to reach wholeness: it is the dynamic function of the self. Psychically experienced as a rebirth, this process creates images derived from the child archetype. The child as an archetypal image contains the past, the present, and the future potentialities: the unity and the multiplicity of the psyche.

Two aspects are in my view of fundamental importance to understand adolescent development and to work with adolescents in therapy: (1) *Regression*, and (2) the *role of the body* in their psychic experience.

In *Symbols of Transformation,* Jung modifies Freud's understanding of the oedipal complex. He understands regression not only as a defense against genital tendencies, but also as a regression to the pregenital parental imagoes in the unconscious. This is a search for wholeness, the union of opposites, and rebirth. Jung considers incest as a metaphor to symbolize this regressive transformation of libido. Although he emphasizes the creative and regenerative nature of regression, he was quite aware of the danger inherent in the regression of libido, as the following quotation illustrates:

> Stripped of its incestuous covering, Nietzsche's "sacrilegious backward grasp" is only a metaphor for the reversion to the original passive state where the libido is arrested in the objects of childhood. This inertia, as La Rochefoucauld says, is also a passion . . . this dangerous passion is what lies hidden beneath the hazardous mask of incest. It confronts us in the guise of the Terrible Mother. (Jung 1911/12/1970, para. 253)

To illustrate his argument, Jung includes a plate showing a shaman's amulet depicting the devouring mother. The incest fantasy is treated by Jung as a special case of regression to a state of merging with the mother of infancy. This regressive tendency is unconsciously repeated in puberty, when the accompanying infantile anxieties are mixed up with sexual anxieties and unconscious incest fantasies. *The pre-oedipal parental images become sexualized.* To avoid the emotional experience of this mental state, some adolescents exhibit a strong defense (Jung's "inertia of libido"—ibid., para. 253) and fail to separate from their infantile ties. If the unconscious merger wish is too overwhelming, only a constricted ego can be salvaged from adolescence through pathological defences (e.g., pathological splitting, denial, projective identification). The result is symptom formation such as psychoses, eating disorders, borderline structures, and addictions. Adolescents in regression cannot develop a sufficiently stable self-representation for development. The archaic parental imagoes reactivated by puberty—for example, the devouring mother or the penetrating, raping father (as part objects)—cannot be integrated into the ego-complex. As a consequence, ego boundaries are not enlarged and the ego remains in fragile infantile dependence.

The second aspect being of central importance for the understanding and analytic treatment of adolescents is the *function of the body* in their psychic experience (for a detailed presentation of this conception including case studies, see Sidoli and Bovensiepen 1995). This follows from the particular significance of regression in adolescence. Pubescent adolescents *project their unconscious fantasies of a relationship with their internal parents into their own bodies and often unconsciously enact this relationship in their bodies*. The particular psychological significance of the body corresponds to the significance of the body in the psychopathology of adolescence. The psychic afflictions that typically occur during adolescence are essentially related to body experience: eating disorders, drugs, psychoses, self-injury, suicide, and the results of sexual abuse.

Besides its quality as a stage for the enactment of the relationship with the internal parents, the body is also used in such a way that adolescents take it as a container, a kind of container-object that helps them to cope with their overwhelming impulses, affects, anxieties and destructive fantasies (Bovensiepen 1991, 2008).

All this makes us understand why the body is so extremely narcissistically cathected in adolescence, a fact that should be considered with great attention in any psychoanalytic work with adolescents.

THE SUBPHASES OF ADOLESCENCE AND THE RELEVANT TREATMENT TECHNIQUES

By the end of the adolescent individuation process, some of the following *developmental goals* should be achieved:

1. The ability to accept and love one's own adult and sexually mature body
2. The capacity for nonincestuous object relationships and separation from the internal parents of childhood
3. Stabilization and differentiation of the ego-self relationship (identity)
4. Sacrifice of bisexual fantasies of grandiosity (adult sexuality)
5. The capability to contain internal opposites (deintegration and reintegration ability of the self)
6. The capability to take responsibility for one's own action in entering society (persona, ego-/ego-ideal development)

I suppose that psychoanalysts of different schools will agree with these items (and even more could be added). Point three and five in particular are central in the view of Analytic Psychology.

Adolescence, conceived as occurring from age 10 to 25, is a phase of life where essential internal and external physical, psychological, and social changes take place in rapid succession. Also in the psychological domain it is an extreme growth stage. During this period, the adolescent passes through various subphases in behavior and experience that require very different technical approaches. I distinguish five subphases that are presented according to five different criteria: *(1) instinct development, (2) anxiety level, (3) defenses, (4) complex dynamics / transference, (5) ego-self relationship.*

In this chapter I can, of course, just give a rough description of these subphases, based not only on clinical or "pathological" manifestations in adolescence, but rather more on the individuation process as a normal developmental process. The statements of age in this developmental overview should not be seen too schematically; they may serve just as a rough approximation.

A. Preadolescence (10–11/12 Years)

The *leitmotiv* of this age could be marked as regressive instinct activation versus ego control, The infantile ego must, as it were, develop heroic qualities to keep the terror at bay emanating from the pre-oedipal part-object "monsters." On a mythological level, figures like Hercules or Superman/Superwoman or virtual heroines like Lara Croft from *Tomb Rider* come to mind. Children in preadolescence often identify themselves with figures whose collective backgrounds are rooted in the archetypal images of the Vamp/Amazon for girls and the policeman/gangster for boys.

Instinctual development in this subphase is characterized by a still very unspecific and general rather than specifically sexual *instinct activation* and archaic (anal-oral) *instinct regression* like, for example, an increased urge to move around or toward sports ambitions. Many girls discover their love for horses ("Diana" complex) at this age. Boys rather experience their "thrill" with their play stations or computer games. Their fancy for teasing girls or telling dirty jokes is mostly exceeded only by their love of action movies. Computer games in particular are excellently suited to give them the experience of absolute control over the unconscious, often aggressive or sadistic fantasies and impulses that are triggered by certain games.

The *anxiety level* at this stage corresponds to the still unspecific instinct activation. The situation is dominated by rather diffuse instinct- and regression anxieties on a pre-oedipal level which may threaten the child's ego integrity. Sexual impulses in boys are somewhat defended by increased motor activity, whereas girls begin—sooner than boys do—to attend to their body as a whole and its outer appearance and spend much time in front of the mirror.

Defenses at this stage hamper analytic treatment by splitting, externalizing, and denial. Inner conflict is heavily denied, and the children use extremely rigid splitting, as in latency. Primitive anxieties are quickly warded off by manic overactivity, contraphobic behavior, hyperactivity, or schizoid aggressive behavior. Defenses in therapy can become manifest through rigid adherence to rule- or board games (superego resistance). Often it is difficult to get in contact with the children's fantasy life. Boys in particular have a distinct aversion to verbalization.

Despite the gradual resurgence of pre-oedipal anxieties, the *complex dynamics in the transference* are mostly oedipally affected and superego parts are copiously projected. That is, the therapist is easily turned into a strict teacher or authority whose rules need to be counteracted on the one hand, but on the other are unconsciously desired in order to put a stop to regressive impulses. The relationship with the peer group is very important; it strengthens contrasexual identification and differentiation from the other sex, and for both sexes the groups formed frequently bear the appearance of gangs.

Ego-self relationship: As in latency, the ego still feels relatively strong vis-à-vis the unconscious. Deintegration of the self triggered by instinct activation does not yet shake the child to a high degree as the ego-self axis is rather rigid and firm. In more deeply disturbed children, however, defenses of the self (Fordham 1985) like splitting, projective identification, and denial become dominant. This is one reason for the frequently strong resistance in an analytic therapy, where increased permeability to the unconscious is fostered.

Vignette: With a boy on the threshold from preadolescence to early adolescence (beginning puberty), it can be illustrated very clearly how threatening regression was experienced and how much his ego was afraid to lose control of the unconscious (for a detailed presentation of this treatment, see Bovensiepen 1986). The boy was a very imaginative and smart lad who suffered from various phobic anxieties. At the beginning of treatment, he completely and rigidly split off his anxieties and unconscious aggressive fantasies and projected them on to external persons, whom he then feared. When he reached puberty in the course of the treatment, the regressive impulses triggered by sexual maturation could not be controlled any more by his infantile ego. At night in bed, he often experienced massive panic attacks. In this situation he developed a contraphobic coping strategy: He sat down at the computer and wrote small ads, as for newspapers, with headings like "wanted" and "for sale." This activity brought him relief from his anxieties. The small funny ads were full of anal-aggressive and oral-aggressive allusions and swear words.

B. Early adolescence (12–13/14 Years)

The *leitmotiv* of this phase is a twofold regression: *ego regression* and *regression of the body-self*. Archetypical images like the mythologies of the mother/daughter or mother/son pair—Demeter/Kore (continuity) or Kybele/Attis (discontinuity)—form the background of the complex that is characteristic for this phase. Analytical treatment in this phase seems to be most difficult and often ends up in disruption. The differences between girls and boys become more and more distinct in this sub-phase.

Instinct development in this phase is largely dominated by sexuality, yet a strong mingling of oedipal and pre-oedipal fantasies and desires takes place as well. Masturbation fantasies may be homoerotically as well as heterosexually tinted. They are frequently connected with pre-oedipal, and at times quite bizarre, fantasies.

Vignette: An extreme form of this I saw in a boy's almost addicted fascination for so-called splatter movies, where in wild action sequences body parts fly through the air. This is a modern form of dismemberment fantasy. For him, the split off and fragmented parts of the self were "recovered" in the preoccupation with one's own body and were thus experienced alarmingly close to consciousness.

Anxiety levels are high in this phase. Instinctual anxieties, castration anxieties and pre-oedipal separation anxieties can be very much in the foreground. The alarming changes in the body are unconsciously answered by early anxieties of separation and loss (separation from the early mother's body). School- and other phobias as well as eating disorders preferably emerge in girls, while compulsive disorders and hypochondriac anxieties frequently occur in boys of this age for the first time. The fear of a homosexual relationship is much stronger in boys than in girls. While boys' anxieties are much more focused on the integrity of and worry about their virility and strength of their penis, girls experience their bodies in a more holistic and integrated way. Although interest is also strongly focused for girls on the developing secondary sexual characteristics, they more intensely include the whole body. At this age, splitting processes in the self and projection of parts of the self into particular body parts is much more developed in boys than in girls. Even later in adulthood women remain much more related to their bodies as a whole.

As for the *defenses*, boys now fight their anxieties preferably through grandiose thinking and omnipotent fantasies. The defensive cathexis to the maternal body of early childhood can be expressed in somatizing and psychosomatic symptoms. The ego is in a relatively weak position vis-à-vis the unconscious at this time. Therefore, the defenses aim at maintaining at least minimal continuity in the threatened infantile self. The boy's direct sexual interest in girls is not yet central, since anxiety prevails in this regard. Girls, however, become aware of their sexual identity and erotic impact on men earlier. Talking about boys among each other is much more frequent with girls than talking about girls is with boys.

Vignette: The following little incident may serve as an example of naïve play with already "adult" sexuality. A group of pubescent girlfriends had great fun in calling telephone sex numbers at night—the parents having gone out—and pretending to be adult women, hoping to get connected with men who were looking for chargeable telephone sex.

Boys at this age are more ambivalent about a sexual encounter with girls and seem to find them more frightening.

Vignette: A physically rather precocious 14-year-old boy came to see me for a first interview having been referred by a urologist whom he had consulted because he was afraid not to be potent enough to have sex with his 14-year-old girlfriend, which he absolutely wanted. Tired, depressed, and somewhat anxious, he sat in front of me, and suddenly (I could hardly believe my eyes) I noticed that he was playing all the time with a tampon. In our talk, it became clear that the tampon served as a symbol for his "too small" penis and also as a defense against his conscious wish to have sex with his girlfriend who "when she looked at boys just looked at their pants."

Complex dynamics / transference: The topic of separation and loss also becomes important, with the libidinal cathexis now being withdrawn from the inner parents of childhood. But then the adolescents are left alone with their parental complexes, as it were. These "objectless" void states may evoke depression or a lot of externalizing acting-out. The parents can be experienced in a highly ambivalent fashion just as they were during times of the toddler's maximum striving for autonomy. Joining peer groups is one way for adolescents to avoid potential conflict. In therapy the working alliance, rules, and agreements are experienced as restrictions of autonomy. Unconsciously, however, there is a strong need for ego control by the therapist. Transference resistance increases in the case of a positive parental transference because it induces incest anxiety.

Ego-self relationship: The deintegration of the self triggered by the adolescent's physical changes connects her/him with early objects. The process that Jung called a "division with oneself" (Jung 1931/1969, para. 757) reaches a first climax here. The fear of fragmentation can be responded to with strong splitting or merging tendencies of ego and self. An extreme oscillation of the sense of self and a labilization of the ego-self relationship may occur and lead to considerable clinical symptoms.

C. Middle Adolescence (15–17 Years)

This phase can be seen as peak of the adolescent individuation process. Here it becomes evident whether the reorganization of a flexible ego-self relationship (in the sense of a symbolic rebirth) will be achieved. If not, a psychotic development (fusion of ego and self) may occur or a neurotic procedure (cutting off of the ego from the self) may be launched. In the language of archetypical images, this situation can be symbolized by the "showdown" of the hero: the decisive battle of the hero/heroine (the ego) resulting in death or rebirth.

Instinct development clearly reaches a genital level now, and it has a—manifest sometimes, but latent for sure—bisexual coloring. Masturbation can take the function of sexual experimentation. The masturbatory activities and fantasies serve the development of the self (deintegration) and the maintenance of inner cohesion (reintegration). In general, adolescents at this age are sexually mature and try to integrate their sexuality into their personal relationships and friendships. The self-image is primarily measured against one's own supposed sexual attraction and strongly oriented along models in the media.

Anxiety level: Regression anxiety, in terms of unconscious incest fantasies, is still strong as annihilation and dissolution remain a threat (the hero / the ego in the belly of the whale-dragon) and the relationship between the ego and the self is at risk of getting lost. But now regression anxiety poses a real danger also at a nonsymbolic level, since the adolescents' unconscious incest fantasies now must confront their capacity for adult sexuality. If an increased libidinal withdrawal from the parent objects has already occurred, anxieties of loss and separation may be in the foreground as well as guilt and fear of imagined retaliation from the parents for being left.

Defenses: The central defensive fight is aimed against the regressive-incestuous trend (and thus against threatening early complex parts) and mostly has the character of archetypical defense (Kalsched 1996) and "defences of the self" as Fordham (1985) conceives it. Defences like pathological splitting, denial, and introjective and projective identification can temporarily determine the adolescent's entire experience. Diagnostically, it is often difficult to decide in the instance of an adolescent with a dramatic identity crisis whether a psychotic development looms or whether it is just a passing turbulence. Naturally, typical adolescent ego defenses like rationalizing, ascetism, and intellectualizing also evolve in this phase. The transference resistance in therapy can show as permanent devaluation and arrogance (as one witnesses, for instance, in the frequent and quite unconscious "arrogance" of the heroes/heroines in Greek mythology!) and in total thoughtlessness towards the therapist. At an unconscious level, this serves to affirm autonomy. Rapid mood swings within a single session and permanent oscillations between distrust and lack of distance can expose the therapist to a steady fire of stimuli, fantasies, and feelings. Under such strong pressure in the transference, the therapist often finds it difficult to realize what the adolescent actually wants to communicate and to maintain an attitude of containment and the ability to think.

At this age, the most frequent occurrence with girls is the beginning of an eating disorder, and the defense of her adult, sexually mature body can become manifest in an anorectic development.

Complex dynamics / transference: The withdrawal of libido from the internal parents and the cathexis of nonincestuous objects (male and female friends) are quite in the foreground. Now the peer group has the very important function (other than during pre- and early adolescence) to assimilate this released libido and give various forms of cathexis a try. The peer group can also operate as a container taking over the mother's "caring" and "holding" function, which is vehemently attacked in the personal mother but unconsciously still strongly desired. In analytic therapy it is important that an idealizing homoerotic transference (self-representative) will develop quite fast in order to create an internal space where the ego-self relationship can be reorganized. This often implies a radical devaluation or denigration of the personal parents, which can turn out to be a trap for the therapist should she or he fail to interpret it in the transference or deny negative transference manifestations. I think it is easily overlooked that in this phase particularly the adolescent's internal world needs a positive mother/father, even though the adolescent may behave as though she or he needs parents no longer at all.

From this angle, it is not surprising that adolescents at this age resist imagining their parents as a still sexually active couple. The archetypical fantasy of the *conjunctio,* the union of opposites, from which something new—the "child"— can evolve is an unconscious fantasy difficult to bear for adolescents in this developmental phase. On the other hand, the child motif can emerge, especially in periods of great change, and this is particularly active during adolescence. For the adolescent ego it implies a twofold threat: the regressive fear of actually becoming a child again on the one hand, and on the other the fear of being able to become a father or mother and have a child.

Ego-self relationship: There is still considerable vulnerability of the ego-self axis in this phase and a great narcissistic oversensitiveness. If nothing goes wrong, an ego-self differentiation is achieved and unconscious fantasies, omnipotent fantasies, and ideas of grandiosity can be better verbalized in the therapy than during early adolescence.

When the adolescent development at this age leads to a serious developmental crisis, it often manifests itself in how the individual deals with and experiences the body and sexuality. To what an extreme degree the body, as a psychic place of unconscious incestuous fantasies (in terms of my earlier explanation of the psychological function of the body as a container-object), may be treated and mistreated is illustrated in the following condensed vignette (a fuller presentation of this treatment is to be found in Sidoli und Bovensiepen 1995):

A., at first seriously anorectic, depressive, and often suicidal, developed a fierce bulimia with purgative abuse in the course of the long-term treatment. When this change of symptom occurred, A. had a very idealizing and increasingly erotic transference to me. In the analytical working-through, we found out that she had strong incestuous desires towards her elder brother and that before the outbreak of her bulimia she had occasionally listened at the door of her parents' bedroom and had heard them having sexual intercourse, which made her feel anxious and guilty. The symptomatic change to bulimia with its fierce purgative orgies made sense: In her unconscious imagination in the father-transference, she had the fantasy of having a child with me that had to be aborted as the forbidden fruit of incest. Often she stood in front of the mirror naked and filled with food, and with disgust she imagined how it would look to be pregnant. She had an unconscious oral procreation fantasy which is quite typical of children. At the same time, this incest fantasy helped her ward off the working-through of her infantile relationship with her mother and its woeful state.

D. Late Adolescence (17–20 Years)

The leitmotiv of this phase is the conclusion of the formation of psychosexual identity. The fascinating idea of bisexuality (as an unconscious fantasy, it represents the totality of the self) is given up in favor of a definite hetero- or homosexual orientation. The fantasy of bisexuality has to be sacrificed because at this age it is a defensive fantasy of grandiosity (identification of the ego with the self!). The archetypical background of this conflict can be characterized by the image of the hermaphrodite. This may partly explain the identification of many adolescents with figures in the media and pop culture whose looks and outfits are often quite androgynous.

Instinct development: Sexuality is now largely devoted to the service of exogamous (nonincestuous) relationships, and pregenital forms of satisfaction are no longer paramount.

Anxiety level: The fear of committing oneself to a determined psychosexual identification can impede giving up the fantasy of bisexuality. The finalization of a manifest homosexual development mostly occurs in this developmental phase. As a counterpart to the enhancement of the mental capacities and interests that are so typical of this age, fears about one's own creativity and power now emerge.

Defenses now have the character of ego defenses and no longer that of defenses of the self (Fordham 1985). Meltzer (1973) points out that the rigid splitting of latency should now be replaced by a more "resilient splitting" so as to give rise to the "gravitation centre" of a new proper personal identity. Splitting (as a normal, non-pathological process) should be resilient in order that various and changing identifications (through projective and introjective identification) can be tried out.

Resistance in therapy frequently refers to the defense of mourning for leaving the parents, for the sacrifice of the child's "paradise" and for the withdrawal of ideas of grandiosity. This was drastically demonstrated by an 18-year-old adolescent shuffling into the consulting room, plopping into the chair and saying: "Now I got it, I'm not the center of the world!" The therapeutic technique and resistances increasingly resemble those of adult treatment.

Complex dynamics / transference: With the stabilization of the separation from the internal parents of childhood, the adolescent manages to differentiate his/her internal parents as man and woman and as an adult couple and thus is able also to separate from the external parents. In the transference, this process goes together with a diminishment of reality distortions, and this helps the adolescent ego to establish less distorted relations with outer reality. The body loses its importance as the preferred place to project the relationship with the childhood parents. In dreams, figures with typical characteristics of animus and anima increasingly emerge. The ability for a positive, yet not so strongly idealizing, transference facilitates the analytic work at this age and allows a working alliance at the ego level.

Ego-self relationship: The deintegration phases of the self are experienced by the ego as less threatening. Given a favorable development, a relatively anxiety-free and permeable relationship of the ego with the unconscious has developed and can become operative in terms of adolescent creativity and activity.

E. Postadolescence: 20–25 Years

Without going into details, it can be said that this age is mainly marked by the stabilization of the psychosocial identity (the persona) and the rapprochement with the parents. Sexuality becomes devoted to procreation. When adolescence cannot be "finished" but is dragged on as a neurotic part of the personality, the personality features representing the negative sides of the *puer aeternus* (von Franz 1981) or the *puella aeterna* archetype may become locked into place: rigidity instead of self-renewal, overemphasis of the mental, unrelatedness, and restlessness as well as sexual promiscuity. Recently this developmental phase has been called "emerging adulthood" (Arnett 2000, 2007), and it has become evident that also in this developmental phase considerable disorders of identity and developmental breakdowns can occur (Bovensiepen 2009), even in young people who have coped with adolescence without major problems. Psychosocial data offers evidence that today people of this age (20–28 years) have more freedom and developmental opportunities than in any other period in their lives before or after (Seiffge-Krenke 2007, 70). Perhaps exactly these externally "boundless opportunities" are dangerous for an ego-self relationship that seems to have passed adolescence without problems, but possibly has reached only pseudo-maturity and then is at risk of breaking down.

CONCLUSION

From the viewpoint of developmental analytical psychology, a successful separation in adolescence presupposes an emotional and affective revival of the infant's early relationship to the mother, especially to the body of the mother. Adolescence as a phase of the individuation process offers a second chance for integration of those infantile parts (fantasies, emotions, and sensations) that could not be integrated during early development. This integration process cannot be separated from the development of the self. This concept is one of the most important areas of difference between analytical psychology and classical psychoanalysis. In psychoanalysis the conceptual emphasis is on the ego and its integration, in contrast to analytical psychology where the emphasis is placed on the self as a totality of the conscious and unconscious personality within which the ego is contained. In the latter theory, the self safeguards psychic cohesion, which is severely threatened during adolescence. If the course of individuation is successful, the ego becomes differentiated from the self. However, the intense psychic upheavals of adolescence activate deintegration of the self and this deintegration/reintegration of the self during this stage of life facilitates the differentiation of the ego from the self. Analytical psychology defines identity (the main development aim in adolescence) as a balanced relationship between ego and self.

REFERENCES

Arnett, Jeffrey J. 2000. Emerging adulthood. A theory of development from the late teens through the twenties. *American Psychologist* 55: 469–80.
———. 2007. *Adolescence and emerging adulthood: A cultural approach.* Englewood Cliffs: Prentice Hall.
Bovensiepen, Gustav. 1986. Die Funktion des Traumes für die Beziehung des Ich zum Unbewußten in der Analyse von Prä-Adoleszenten. *Kind und Umwelt* 51: 2–33.
———. 1991. Können Roboter lieben? Suizid, Selbstverletzung und die psychische Funktion des Körpers als "Container" bei Jugendlichen mit Frühstörungen. *Analytische Psychologie* 22: 273–94.

———. 2008. Mentalisierung und Containment. Kritische Anmerkungen zur Rezeption der Entwicklungs-und Bindungsforschung in der klinischen Praxis. *Analytische Kinder-und Jugendlichenpsychotherapie* 39, 137: 7–28.

———. 2010. Living in the soap bubble: The fertile couple and the standstill of the transcendent function in the treatment of an adolescent girl. *Journal of Analytical Psychology* 55, 2:189–203.

Fordham, Michael. 1985. Defences of the self. In *Explorations into the self*, 152–60. London: Academic Press.

Franz, Marie-Louise von. 1981. *Puer Aeternus*. Santa Monica, CA: Sigo Press.

Jung, C.G. 1911/1912/1970. *Symbols of transformation*. CW 5.

———. 1931/1969. The stages of life. In CW 8.

Kalsched, Donald. 1996. *The inner world of trauma: Archetypal defenses of the personal spirit*. London and New York: Routledge.

Meltzer, Donald. 1973. *Sexual states of mind*. Perthshire, Scotland: Clunie Press.

Seiffge-Krenke, Inge. 2007. *Psychoanalytische und tiefenpsychologisch fundierte Therapie mit Jugendlichen*. Stuttgart: Klett-Cotta.

Sidoli, Mara and Gustav Bovensiepen, eds. 1995. *Incest fantasies and self destructive acts: Jungian and post-Jungian psychotherapy in adolescence*. New Brunswick and London: Transaction Publishers.

GUSTAV BOVENSIEPEN, M.D., is co-editor of *Analytische Psychologie*. He is a training and supervising analyst at the Deutsche Gesellschaft für Analytische Psychologie and in private practice (adults, adolescents and children) in Cologne, Germany. He is the author of numerous clinical papers and he lectures in Europe and in the US.

26

WORKING WITH TRAUMA IN ANALYSIS

Donald E. Kalsched

There is a pain so utter
That it swallows substance up
Then covers the Abyss with Trance—
So Memory can step
Around—across—upon it
As one within a Swoon—
Goes safely—where an open eye
Would drop him—Bone by bone.

EMILY DICKINSON

Trauma is about pain so "utter" that it swallows up normal developmental processes, leaving an "abyss" or "basic fault" (Balint 1979, 18) between self and world outwardly and ego and Self (Edinger 1972, 40) inwardly. Fortunately, the story does not end with this cleavage because the human psyche has enormous self-curative powers. It "covers the abyss with trance" so that life can go on.

In what follows, I will explore this "trance" and how it emerges from the unconscious in the form of a sophisticated system of defenses that employs dissociation and splitting to compartmentalize intolerable aspects of experience. I call this defensive complex the *self-care system*, hereafter abbreviated SCS. It consists of an interlocking set of self and object-representations—usually an inner "child" and its protective or persecutory "guardian" (Kalsched, 1996). These inner personifications often appear in dreams when early trauma has been "triggered" by something in the patient's life or in the therapy relationship. Two case examples follow.

The SCS presents major difficulties in the analytic treatment of trauma because of the *resistance* it throws up to change. It is important that analysts understand this resistance and its paradoxical life-saving/life-limiting role in the patient's history. The SCS will not give up its control without the patient having an *experience* in which the lost "child," hiding in his/her inner world, is reached and helped. This, in turn, will not happen without special attention to the feeling-relationship between therapist and patient—specifically to the patient's sense of affective safety in the analytic situation.

For those familiar with attachment theory, the SCS can be thought of as a set of internal working models or schemas reflecting patterns of relationships that have been generalized and internalized (Stern 1985, Knox 2003, 104–37). These schemas provide a set of appraisals and expectancies about outer relationships that determine how the interpersonal world is interpreted and experienced. From a Jungian standpoint, however, the SCS is much more than an internalization of outer relationship-patterns. Its imagery and affects are amplified from within by the psyche's mythopoetic, archetypal dynamism, and the apparent "wisdom" with which it generates meaning, creates imaginative stories for the "child" and provides healing dreams, would seem to transcend what is often described as infantile illusion or defensive fantasy. More than one clinician has been deeply moved by the uncanny inner intelligence that seems to be mobilized under conditions of traumatic stress—to the point of suggesting that in its efforts to heal trauma, the psyche seems to have access to "higher," precognitive or trans-rational powers (Ferenczi 1988, 81, Jung 1912, 330, Bernstein, 2005).

However we visualize it, the SCS accomplishes a *partial* cure of trauma, enough so that life continues, despite dissociation and its effects in limiting a person's full potential. When people come for psychoanalysis *they often don't know that this partial cure is in place*, nor do they expect that their identities, informed for many years by "interpretations" from the SCS, will have to be "deconstructed" in the course of therapy. As Masud Khan (1974) reminds us, with these traumatically wounded individuals . . . "one is rarely dealing, at first, with the authentic illness of the patient. [Rather] . . . what is most difficult to resolve and cure is the patient's practice of self-cure. To cure a cure is the paradox that faces us in these patients . . ." (97).

THE NATURE OF SELF-SPLITTING

Imagine a very small child—say a little girl of three years—reaching out in love towards a parental figure—say her father. Imagine that this happens when the alcoholic father is drunk and that he exploits his little girl's affection by violating her body, further terrifying her with threats if she tells. At traumatic moments such as this, the child faces the potential annihilation of her very personhood—the destruction of her personal spirit—"soul murder" as Leonard Shengold (1989) called it. This catastrophic possibility must be avoided at all costs, and so, something quite extraordinary occurs. We tend to take this extraordinary thing for granted.

Suddenly "she" is on the ceiling, looking down at what is happening to her body which "she" has vacated. We call this dissociation. If you are in an unbearable situation and you are helpless to leave, a part of you leaves, and for this to happen the whole self must split in two in order to prevent the unthinkable anxiety from being fully experienced. The remarkable thing about this almost universal experience of traumatic splitting is that the "witnessing consciousness" seems to remain "present" but from another location, independent of the body! We have reason to think that the nature of this splitting is universal. Part of the little girl in our example "regresses" back to an embryonic stage of relative innocence and safety prior to the trauma. This regressed part will be buried deep in the body (somatic unconscious) and will be protected by amnesia barriers thrown up by the SCS (trance). On the other hand, a separate part of the little girl in our example "progresses," in other words, grows up very fast, *identifying with the aggressor and with the adult mind*, transcending the immediate unbearable pain with a precocious philosophical, rational, and sometimes "transcendent" understanding. The progressed part then "oversees" the regressed part. In its protective role, it provides soothing like a guardian angel. At other times, in order to keep the regressed part "inside," the progressed self may turn negative and persecutory. In rare cases, if the outer trauma continues unabated, and the person's essential core is in danger of annihilation, it becomes the SCS's task to organize the child's suicide (Ferenczi 1988, 10).

So a major purpose of the SCS is *to preserve and protect a sacred core of personality from immanent violation and destruction*. This "sacred core of personality," often presenting itself in dreams as the image of a "child," is referred to by D.W. Winnicott (1963, 187) as a "sacred incommunicado center" of the personality, or by Harry Guntrip (1971, 172) as the "lost heart of the personal self," or by spiritually oriented psychotherapist T. H. Almaas (1998, 76–82) as an ontological presence described simply as "essence," or in my previous book, as the "imperishable personal spirit" or "soul" (Kalsched 1996). This sacred center of the human person is not *equivalent* to the "child" in the system, but represents its divine inheritance, its generative innocence, and its life potential. Therefore, when this "child" comes into consciousness (see second case below) it sometimes appears with an aura of numinosity, that is, as a "divine" or archetypal child.

ORIGIN AND FUNCTION OF THE SELF CARE SYSTEM

To summarize, the SCS emerges out of a traumatic field of experience with others, especially early attachment figures and records a psychic split made necessary by the child's unbearable experience. This split is memorialized as an archetypal defense—a bipolar complex containing a progressed self (protective or persecutory guardian) and its regressed counterpart (child). The SCS performs the following functions:

- *Hermeneutic function*: Provides a "meaning" for the child's painful life when chaos and meaninglessness threaten. Interprets the child's subsequent experience in light of its "story," which is often that the child has caused the trauma, is therefore "bad," and must work continuously to become "good."

- *Interpersonal function*: Binds anxiety, regulates affect, and avoids retraumatization by inhibiting self expression and discouraging attachment, thereby regulating distance from the caregiver. Its favorite motto is "all by myself." Denies dependency, vulnerability or "weakness" (see first case below). Shapes the appraisals and expectations of the interpersonal world and fulfills its "agenda" through projective identification.

- *Self-regulatory function*: Oversees the dissociation of unbearably traumatic experience, separating sensation, affect, and image so that an impossible meaning is obliterated. Controls aggression and "bad" or shame-ridden self-states through dissociation. Controls the switching sequences in Dissociative Identity Disorder.

- *Self-preservative function*: Keeps the "innocent" pretraumatic child-part with its divine soul-spark, out of suffering, making sure that it is never violated. Provides self-hypnosis (trance) when necessary, including addictions. Recruits the mythopoetic resources of the psyche to provide "stories" for the devastated inner child, helps it to heal through the beauties of nature, love for animals, religious ritual, music, and so on. Keeps it company in the inner world, sometimes becoming rigid and ruthless in its disciplinary agenda. Organizes suicide when all else fails.

DIFFERENT TYPES OF TRAUMA

In Jung's autobiography (Jung 1965), he describes trauma as an "untold story."

> In many cases in psychiatry, the patient who comes to us has a story that is not told, and which as a rule no one knows of. To my mind, therapy only really begins after the investigation of that wholly personal story. It is the patient's secret, the rock against which he is shattered. (117)

When we use the word "trauma" we are referring to some acute or cumulative experience that "shatters" us. This shattering is both an outer event that shocks us and an inner event called dissociation. The traumatic shattering Jung refers to is one that eventually, with help, can be remembered as a coherent story. This is frequently the case with adult trauma where dissociation is limited to the traumatic event(s) leading to post-traumatic stress disorder with its characteristic symptoms. However, not all trauma can be remembered as a coherent story. Traumatic events in childhood may occur too early to be recovered in explicit memory. Here the shattering events occur when the child's ego is immature or still mostly unformed and perhaps deeply identified with abusive persons in the environment upon whom the child is dependent. With *early* trauma, dissociation is more far-reaching and systematic in its effects, actually affecting the right hemisphere of the brain which is most active during the first eighteen months of life, sometimes leaving enduring deficits in affect regulation (Schore 2003, 272).

Early childhood trauma involves a "shattering" that Jung did not contemplate when he described the secret story that remains untold. Such early trauma is a secret even from oneself and therefore *often will not be reported* as the patient enters psychoanalysis. This early, unremembered trauma presents a more complicated picture for the analytically informed psychotherapist and requires treatment approaches that go beyond the usual interpretive techniques of uncovering fantasy, modifying defenses, or relying upon spontaneous self-healing processes of the individuating psyche described by Jung.

HOW EARLY TRAUMA IS "REMEMBERED" IN THERAPY

The systematic effects of dissociation in early childhood permit life to go on but at the cost of a great severing within the inner world. A traumatized young child will not understand what has happened to him and will often not be able to report it to parents or others. Elements of the traumatic experience, such as sensations, affects, and images may be "encoded" in "state dependent" episodic memory in subcortical regions of the right brain and be unavailable to verbal processes including narrative memory (Van der Kolk and Fisler 1995). Whole pieces of the original experience may also be "stored" in the body, creating somatic symptoms without being available to consciousness (Van der Kolk 1994). This is part of the "trance" engineered by the SCS.

When shattered pieces of such unspeakable childhood events begin to emerge later in analytic therapy, they may threaten to destabilize the entire personality. The person having such experiences will not only feel "disturbed" by the intrusion of flashbacks, as in PTSD, but may feel "crazy," or "possessed." One's entire sense of identity may be shaken.

One trauma survivor just beginning therapy had intrusive flashbacks whenever she stopped presenting herself in her usual charming flurry of words. In a moment of silence, she suddenly heard a screen-door slam! Each time this happened it panicked her and convinced her that she was having a "breakdown." Slowly, and with careful attention to her feelings of safety in the moment, we pieced together a coherent memory. She was three years old. Her family lived in a trailer park. It was winter. Her mother, who was having an affair with an alcoholic man from a nearby trailer, shoved her out the door, telling her not to return for an hour. My patient wandered alone in the snow, lost and alone. Apparently this had happened repeatedly and was "remembered" only as a breakthrough sensation, devoid of affect, without visual imagery, and with a profoundly destabilizing effect. Such "kindling" responses (Wilkinson 2006, 79–81), in which the hyper-aroused state of the original trauma erupts later in the therapy situation, must be carefully managed by the therapist, whose main concern must be affect-regulation and restoration of safety and homeostatic balance.

In addition to flashbacks, unremembered childhood trauma may appear in the form of repetitious enactments with others that repeat relational patterns of the original situation, amplified by the internal working models that make up the

SCS. Trauma victims find themselves continually retraumatized as if caught in a self-fulfilling prophecy. In the early days of psychoanalysis, this seemingly self-destructive phenomenon was known as the repetition compulsion. Today, it is understood that such repetition will inevitably happen *inside the therapy relationship also*, and that while this is often experienced as a relational crisis, it provides an opportunity for the patient to live through the original traumatic breakdown-of-attachment in the transference—hopefully this time, toward a different outcome.

Finally, early trauma may return in the form of "archetypal memories" instead of personal ones. Early-trauma survivors often have vivid stories about past-life experiences, alien abductions, satanic ritual abuse, and so on (cf. Hedges 2000). Without questioning the validity of such "memories," the therapist must be aware that there is an archetypal filter through which early trauma reaches the ego, that is, the SCS. Thus, archetypal meaning is substituted for personal meaning. Such stories can provide a scaffolding of mythopoetic "other-life" meaning that holds the person in being until the more painful impact of interpersonal betrayal, neglect and abandonment *in this life* can be approached.

THE IMPORTANCE OF THE RELATIONSHIP IN THE HEALING OF TRAUMA

Over the last twenty years, clinicians working with early-trauma patients have made a painful discovery, namely, that the usual analytic situation, with its emphasis on words, its power differential between patient and analyst, and its tendency to "objectify" the patient through interpretation, often retraumatizes the very people that it was designed to help. It became clear that work with trauma survivors requires much greater mutuality, transparency, and affect-attunement in the analytic partnership, reminiscent of the early mother/child interaction. This discovery then led to a renewed interest in infant observation (Beebe and Lachman 1994) and attachment theory (Bowlby 1988), where it is clearly demonstrated that the earliest, bodily-based dyadic emotional communication between infant and mother is critical to the very formation of what Alan Schore (2003, 270) calls the "implicit self system" and the unconscious mind. Bowlby and his followers were able to show how easily interpersonal trauma can rupture this early *attachment relationship*, leading to an internalization of rigid, outdated, and maladaptive "schemas" or internal working models that replace the easy flow of negotiation with the object. These in turn lead to various forms of insecure or disorganized attachment which profoundly affect the trauma survivor's interpersonal relationships in later life and in analysis (Knox 2003, 115).

Analysts have begun to realize that *what has been broken relationally must be repaired relationally*. Early relational trauma inevitably enters the psychoanalytic relationship, and although this presents many potential pitfalls, it also offers unique opportunities for trauma's repair. If this is to occur, however, it calls for *affectively focused treatment*—what Schore (2003, 49) calls right-brain-to-right-brain communication. The analyst "tunes in" on an affect level to those dissociative "gaps" or places of derailment where the intimate feeling-connection with the patient threatens to come apart. The work of Philip Bromberg (2006) provides many examples of this delicate negotiation and how the analyst must become a full partner in the "dyadic regulation" of affect and co-creation of an entirely new intersubjective reality. Fortunately, in this process, what the analyst says or does will be less important than "how openly what does happen is processed with the analysand" (Mitchell 1988, x).

In addition to the increased monitoring of internal emotional states found in the "relational" approach, affective neuroscience, attachment theory, and infant observation have inspired a variety of new ways of working with trauma in the body. These methods understand that past trauma and its defenses will be embodied in present physiological states such as breath, gestures, muscular tension, movement, and so on, and seek to work directly with these, helping the patient become more aware of his/her internal sensations and perceptions. Among specifically Jungian contributions to this work should be mentioned the body-sensitive work of Marion Woodman (1984), the long-standing work of Joan Chodorow (1978, 1984), on "active imagination in movement," and the "authentic movement" work of Tina Stromsted (2001). Outside the Jungian area, Pat Ogden's (2006) articulation of a "Sensorimotor Approach" to psychotherapy provides many useful ways in which body-sensitive techniques can be incorporated into conventional psychoanalysis.

Other forms of the "expressive arts therapies" including various forms of art therapy and sandtray therapy (Pattis Zoja, this volume) are also especially effective in treating trauma because they bypass the left hemisphere and tap the mythopoetic resources of the psyche directly, opening otherwise dissociated affect in the body. The same could be said for Robert Bosnak's (2007) affect-focused work with dreams. The following two cases incorporate some of these new understandings.

CLINICAL EXAMPLE OF THE SELF CARE SYSTEM IN OPERATION

The following case is one of those rare situations where a breakthrough moment in a psychotherapy session, plus the dream that followed, unmasked the structure and function of the patient's SCS very clearly. The incident I wish to report occurred several months into the analytic treatment of a thirty-eight-year-old successful real estate broker who consulted me in crisis because things were not going well with a new man she was dating whom she hoped eventually to marry. He had complained that he really did not know her very well and felt she was "hiding herself" from him. This remark disturbed my patient enough to send her into therapy.

My patient was an only child, attractive, charming, and completely put-together on the outside with a very active life as a business woman and athlete, but with little access to her inner life or her feminine feeling-self. Her childhood, she claimed, had been uneventful—she had no real issues to work on—just the outer problem with the boyfriend who she decided (after looking it up on the internet) was "narcissistic" and having trouble with commitment.

One day she came in clearly hurt by some critical remarks about herself made by her best friend, who called her "shallow and superficial." My patient seemed undone by this, and although initially she deflected my gentle inquiries into her feelings and tried to cover them over with black humor, finally she was able (with my help) to stay with her hurt and sadness for a few moments. I asked her where this sadness was located in her body whereupon she pointed to her heart. At this moment, her eyes began to rim with tears. Taking advantage of this newfound affect, we were able to link the painful criticism of her girlfriend to a pattern of incessant shaming by her beloved father who, it turned out, had teased her relentlessly during grade school and junior high school about her "fat" body (she was slightly overweight as a child) and further ridiculed her about her "stupidity" in school.

As the shame-filled details of these experiences emerged in this session, she began to panic and have trouble breathing. A pattern of approach/avoidance regarding her feelings ensued. Her eyes would fill with tears, followed by a kind of restricted, spasmodic cry. After recovering she would make a joke about what a basket case she was—then sit nervously biting her knuckles until the tears came again. Each time I encouraged her to simply let the feelings come uncensored; to breathe into them and tell me more about what was coming to mind. But each time, she pinched them off involuntarily, apologizing for using my tissues, making some dark ironic joke, and then finally, to her great relief, the session was over.

I was moved by this difficult session, but as she walked from the waiting room and down the stairs my patient commented ironically that I "shouldn't worry". . . she would never bring the "puking, mewling, little one in here again" if she could help it! I was shocked to hear this statement from my patient who I thought would be as pleased as I was with the opening that had occurred in her feelings.

The next session she came in with the following dream.

I am captive with a group of young girls on a houseboat on some canal system. It is an inky dark night—very frightening. The Captain—dressed in black—keeps trying to kill us one by one. He's sinister and evil, like Hannibal Lechter in Silence of the Lambs. *I'm trying to escape with a young girl with whom I'm chained at the ankles but she is weak and can't keep up with me. She slips into the water and we can't go on so finally we are captured. The young girl lies in shallow water. I keep trying to pull her up with the chain so she can breathe, but she keeps falling back into the water. The Captain is watching this with pleasure. He comes over, gives me a gloating look, and with his boot on her throat pushes the girl under the water. I'm overcome with grief and rage as I watch her drown. I am helpless.*

My patient knew that this dream was somehow related to the session the previous day, but it seemed to her that the dream confirmed her worst fears about herself, in other words, that there was something basically wrong. "Who else," she insisted, "had sadistic dreams like this?"

What my patient did not realize (and I did not either) was how much an unknown part of her (the Captain) apparently hated her new-found feelings of vulnerability (the weak young girl to whom she is chained) and was trying to "kill" them, push them back into unconsciousness. In retrospect, I realized that her sarcastic comment upon leaving the previous session had come directly from this "Captain," from the persecutory side of the SCS with whom her ego was, at that moment, completely identified. The Captain must have also been present in the session as that unconscious inner factor that kept trying to cut off her feelings and move her out of her body and into her head.

In my patient's dream, her innocent pre-traumatic childhood self is represented by the weak young girl to whom she is chained. The dream ego keeps trying to pull her out of the water "so she can breathe," just as in the previous session she had struggled to express dissociated affect in her body as it emerged and was repeatedly "killed."

This dream and our mutual understanding of it helped my patient become more tolerant of her dependent inner childhood self, and as our work progressed she was able to risk more embodied affect, softening her armored defensive structure represented by the vigilant, destructive "Captain."

FINAL CASE: ARCHETYPAL CHILD AND DOLPHINS

A Wallstreet stockbroker in his late twenties consulted me for depression after his fiance broke their engagement and left him for another man. In response to her betrayal, my patient felt not only the usual feelings of grief, sadness, and anger, but began to feel desolate, unreal, "disconnected," and "dead inside." These feelings of depersonalization and derealization felt vaguely familiar. As I listened to his story, I wondered what early trauma might have been triggered by the current abandonment by his girlfriend. We soon found out what this early trauma was.

After an initial period of psychotherapy focusing on his lost relationship, we began to explore his personal history. He could not remember much from his childhood which had been "boringly normal, typically middle-class," except for one thing. He never felt he really belonged in his family, and the fantasy persisted that he must have been adopted. He felt there was something secret in his past . . . some dark "other life" he must have lived. He had even checked his birth records and confronted his parents with these ideas, but turned up nothing.

Several months into the analysis, and feeling especially depressed over his lost love-relationship, my patient remembered a repetitive nightmare he had had as a boy. In the dream he somehow ended up in the kitchen garbage can which was kept in the basement in a locked cupboard, a place to which he had been banished by his mother when he was "bad." This place was always terrifying to him. He said he would sometimes cry so hard in there that he would "go blank."

Hoping that this early dream would give us access to his inner world, I asked my patient to close his eyes and re-enter the dream, telling me what he saw and felt. At first he resisted, but I joked and reassured him and finally he let himself down into the image. The place he found himself in became a hall of horrors—a melange of distorted images of half-human beings and ghoulish apparitions. I asked him to stay with these images and tell me anything that came to him . . . especially what he felt in his body. He said he felt very small and scared—and then, when I added how discarded and unwanted he must have felt in his family— he burst into tears. With help, he allowed himself to surrender to these tears and not pinch them off. He left the session very shaken but strangely moved. That night he had the following dream:

I'm walking along a desolate sandy beach. I'm younger, I don't know how young. In the distance is a woman I've met before. She is wearing a white Terry-cloth robe with a hood. She looks ethereal, vaguely other-worldly. Not even her face is visible. A storm is brewing. We see a lump in the sand. She points to it, indicating she wants me to dig it up. I do, and discover the live body of a little boy. First I dig the sand out over his torso, so he can sit up. He is also wearing a long white robe and hood. His face is still under sand. I try to clear it, but the sand keeps falling back covering his eyes. Only his fore-head and chin are exposed. Finally I get him out and the three of us walk down the beach together. Suddenly we notice a sleek porpoise jumping in the water. Soon it doubles and becomes two, then four, then eight . . . until the ocean is alive with these animals. As we watch this sight from a lifeguard tower, a strong wind comes and blows us over backwards.

This exceptionally vivid dream seemed very strange to my patient, except he knew it had something to do with the prior session which, he said, had "blown him over." He felt that digging up the body of the boy must have something to do with digging up his past.

Not long afterward, my patient found out from an aunt that his now deceased mother had suffered a post-partum depression after his birth and had been hos-pitalized for six weeks. He had been sent to live with this aunt, who reported that she returned him to his mother gradually over a period of a year because his mother remained depressed and unable to cope. This information gave us a clue to the early trauma being repeated in my patient's life as his fiance left him. He had already been abandoned long ago, and in the process something inside him had been buried, remaining hooded and unavailable—faceless. We might think of this buried boy as a younger version of himself, the animated, pretraumatic "child" whose energy had left him (through dissociation) on the occasions of repeated terror in what he called his "punishment closet." As such, this hooded child represents the lost and now returning part of the patient's own whole ani-mated self.

As I pondered these possibilities, I happened upon a passage in Jung's (1959, 177) essay on the child archetype where he discusses the "divine child." Jung comments on the image of the "hooded one":

> Faust, after his death, is received as a boy into the "choir of blessed youths." I do not know whether Goethe was referring, with this peculiar idea, to the cupids on antique gravestones. It is not unthinkable. The figure of the cucallatus points to the hooded, that is, the invisible one, the genius of the departed, who reappears in the child-like frolics of a new life, surrounded by the sea-forms of dolphins and tritons.

This imagery corresponds almost exactly with the imagery of my patient's dream. A part of him, invisible until now—long since departed and buried—his "genius" or "daimon"—is made known again through the mediating attention of his "caretaker self" (hooded woman), an "other-worldly" defense with uncanny wisdom and a twinship connection to his buried spirit.

Our interpretation of this dream is further supported if we amplify the image of the dolphin. The mythic association of the dolphin with the dying and reborn "son" is very old. Pausanias reports that a part divine, part human child named Taras, son of Poseidon and Satyraea, was the dolphin-riding New Year Child of the Dorian city of Tarentum. From other evidence in Pausanias, Graves (1955, 291–92) finds it likely that the ritual advent of the New Year Child was dramatically presented at Corinth with the aid of a tame dolphin trained by the Sun-priests

This archetypal imagery gives us a glimpse of the life-saving function of the SCS. It preserves the lost heart of the self, invisible and hooded, until this innocent part with its "divine" cargo—heretofore kept out of the suffering of life—reenters the life-stream once again surrounded, in his dream, by leaping and playful animals which have always been associated with vitality, animation, and the return of light to the world.

My patient was not much interested in these mythological parallels. He was, however, deeply moved by a sense that he was somehow being reunited with a lost part of himself through the analytic exploration of his personal life history. His life no longer felt quite so desolate but somehow meaningfully stormy. He soon found a new girlfriend and left his therapy for a new life.

PSYCHOLOGY WITHOUT THE PSYCHE?

In the foregoing discussion, I have emphasized the mythopoetic, psychological, and "spiritual" functions of the SCS and have done this for a reason. On the one hand, recent revolutionary developments in neuroscience and brain studies (Schore, 2003a, 2003b) together with the discovery that even the development of the brain depends on the early relationship between child and mother (Gerhardt 2004) lead to an exciting convergence in the field. These two streams of thought come together to emphasize two heretofore neglected aspects of trauma and its treatment, namely, how trauma is encoded in the brain/body and healed through attention to the body and its *affects,* and secondly, how important the relationship is between therapist and patient for the repair of early trauma (Bromberg 1998, 2006).

I have personally been deeply informed by these new trends and have nothing but admiration for, and gratitude to, the men and women who have brought these realities into focus. I share their excitement. There is no question that in the past we have been too focused on verbal/interpretive forms of treatment in psycho-analysis and have neglected feelings, the body, and the therapeutic relationship. In the Jungian approach to trauma we have also been preoccupied with Melanie Klein's particular version of archetypal fantasy and how these images are them-selves traumatic. This has led to a relative neglect of trauma's outer reality, its prevalence in our lives, and its power to shape and distort the inner world.

However, the shadow side to all this enthusiasm for the brain and the interper-sonal is one that Jung warned about many years ago, namely, that we could end up with a "psychology without the psyche" (Jung 1933, 178). There is a tendency in much of what I read to turn away from the center of Jung's contribution—his discovery of that numinous spark of divinity in the inner world that he referenced as the Self. Much is made of the compatibility of Jung's thought with the new dis-coveries, his attention to affect, his relationality, and even his emphasis on self over ego. But there is also a reductionism that concerns me. No less a luminary in the field of trauma and its treatment than Peter Levine (1997) claims that "trauma is physiological, not psychological" (quoted in Taki-Reece 2004, 65). Margaret Wilkinson (2006), whose book has made a huge contribution to linking Jungian psychology with the new discoveries in neuroscience, presents two beau-tiful cases of trauma survivors who were literally saved by the mythopoetic psy-che—in one case by books and films—in another through drawing, a love of animals, and an imaginal inner figure who kept hope alive. Yet in summarizing her work, she says the cases demonstrate the childrens' "need to retreat from the dangerous world outside into the world of trauma-related pretend" (Wilkinson 2006, 51).

In my view, this minimizes the importance of the imagination, as if the "outer" world is where we "should" be living, free of inner world "pretend." Instead, as James Hillman (1975) reminds us, we live in the psyche like fish in the water, and trauma survivors sometimes live there more than the rest of us. Often they have a privileged view of that "other" world that comes to presence in our dreams and in those great moments of silence that even dissociation opens.

Object-relations theory and interpersonal theory provide the best understand-ing of how trauma develops but, missing a grasp of the self-curative capacities of the psyche's inner world, they do not adequately envision the healing of trauma that comes about through other than personal resources. The self-care system comes about as a result of acute or chronic failure by the relational environment to provide "good enough" attunement and empathic responsiveness for the grow-ing baby. Trauma occurs when this "failure" falls outside what Winnicott calls the "area of omnipotence," by which he means experience the baby can make sense of or "metabolize" within its own tolerance-limits or its own nascent symbolic capacity. Events that fall outside this area are "unbearable" or "unspeakable" and constitute nothing short of "madness," by which Winnicott means literally a "breakdown" of infancy that cannot be remembered and around which the growing child (with the aid of primitive defenses) must erect a false self, like a tree growing around an absent center hollowed out by a lightning strike.

This sobering and compelling story about the effects of early trauma represents a partial truth, but it is not the whole story. There is something essential that Winnicott leaves out of his completely interpersonal metapsychology, namely, the "nonhuman environment" outwardly (Searles, 1960), and the "prehuman environment" inwardly, in other words, the archetypal layer of the psyche (Jung). The child is not just in relationship to the mother, but to the "world" beyond and the "world" within—poised, as it were, between two great, beautiful and terrible mysteries. It is the mother's job to help mediate these Titanic realities. Without the mother's "good enough" mediation, the child will be exposed to these inner and outer beauties/terrors and this will inevitably lead to traumatic symptoms *in relationship*, for example, unresolved omnipotence and grandiosity, insecure/disorganized attachment, and so forth.

But the child will not necessarily be "mad." The SCS will come to its rescue, and this system will recruit the archetypal powers of inner and outer Nature in its "effort" to save the child's spirit—its core of health. The many myths that retell the story of children being abandoned and exposed but rescued by transpersonal powers or wild animals record this "saving" miracle by the SCS (Otto Rank). True, without an adequate human relationship to mediate "psyche and world" the traumatized child will have life-long difficulties in intimacy with others. Born of broken attachment bonds, its SCS will not allow it to trust a process of reattachment with others for fear of retraumatization. But the self that grows around these limitations will not necessarily be a "false" self and may in fact be more creative than mad, perhaps with a rich inner world, a privileged access to "nonordinary reality," a deep cultural life, and a huge passion for and capacity for life. In the language of Jerome Bernstein, these individuals will occupy a "Borderland" between the worlds rather than be "Borderline" personality disorders (Bernstein, 2005).

REFERENCES

Almaas, A. 1998. *Essence: The diamond approach to inner realization*. York Beach, ME: Samuel Weiser, Inc.

Balint, Michael. 1979. *The basic fault: Therapeutic aspects of regression*. Evanston, IL: Northwestern University Press.

Beebe, Beatrice, and Frank Lachmann. 1994. Representations and internalization in infancy: Three principles of salience. *Psychoanalytic Psychology* 11: 165.

Bernstein, Jerome. 2005. *Living in the borderland: The evolution of consciousness and the challenge of healing trauma*. London: Routledge.

Bosnak, Robert. 2007. *Embodiment: Creative imagination in medicine, art and travel*. London: Routledge.

Bowlby, John. 1988. *A secure base: Parent-child attachment and healthy human development*. New York: Basic Books.

Bromger, Philip. 1998. *Standing in the spaces: Essays in clinical process, trauma, and dissociation*. Hillsdale, NJ: The Analytic Press.

———. 2006. *Awakening the dreamer: Clinical journeys*. Mahway, NJ: The Analytic Press.

Chodorow, Joan. 1978. Dance therapy and the transcendent function. *American Journal of Dance Therapy* 2, 1: 16–23.

———. 1984. To move and be moved. *Quadrant* 17, 2: 39–48.

Edinger, Edward. 1972. *Ego and archetype*. New York: Penguin Books.

Ferenczi, Sandor. 1988. *The clinical diary of Sandor Ferenczi*. Ed. Judith Dupont. Cambridge, MA: Harvard University Press.

Gerhardt, Sue. 2004. *Why love matters: How affection shapes a baby's brain*. Hove and New York: Brunner-Routledge.

Graves, Robert. 1955. *The Greek myths*. London: Penguin.

Guntrip, Harry. 1971. *Psychoanalytic theory, therapy, and the self*. New York: Basic Books.

Hedges, Lawrence. 2000. *Terrifying transferences: Aftershocks of childhood trauma*. Northvale, NJ: Jason Aronson Inc.

Hillman, James. 1975. *Re-visioning psychology*. New York: Harper & Row

Jung, C.G. 1912/1970. *Symbols of transformation*. CW 5.

———. 1933. *Modern man in search of a soul*. New York: Harcourt Brace & Company.

———. 1940/1959. The psychology of the child archetype. In CW 9i.

———. 1963. *Memories, dreams, reflections*. New York: Random House.

Kalsched, Donald. 1996. *The inner world of trauma: Archetypal defenses of the personal spirit*. London: Routledge.

Khan, Masud. 1974. Towards an epistemology of cure. In *The privacy of the Self*, 93–98. New York: International Universities Press.

Knox, Jean. 2003. *Archetype, attachment, analysis: Jungian psychology and the emergent mind*. New York: Brunner-Routledge.

Levine, Peter. 1997. *Waking the tiger: Healing trauma*. Berkeley, CA: North Atlantic Books.

Mitchell, Steven. 1988. *Relational concepts in psychoanalysis*. Cambridge, MA: Harvard University Press.

Ogden, Pat, Kekuni Minton, and Clare Pain. 2006. *Trauma and the body: A sensorimotor approach to psychotherapy*. New York: W.W. Norton & Co.

Schore, Alan. 2003a. *Affect regulation and the repair of the self*. New York: W.W. Norton & Company.

———. 2003b. *Affect dysregulation and disorders of the self*. New York: W.W. Norton & Company

Shengold, Leonard. 1989. *Soul murder: The effects of childhood abuse and deprivation*. New York: Fawcett Columbine

Stern, Daniel. 1985. *The interpersonal world of the infant: A view from psychoanalysis and developmental psychology*. New York: Basic Books.

Stromsted, Tina. 2001. Re-inhabiting the female body: Authentic movement as a gateway to transformation. *The Arts in Psychotherapy* 28, 1: 39–55.

Taki-Reece, Sachiko. 2004. Sandplay after a catastrophic encounter: From traumatic experience to emergence of a new self. *Archives of Sandplay Therapy* 17, 2: 65–75.

Van der Kolk, Bessel.A. 1994. The body keeps the score: Memory and the evolving psychobiology of posttraumatic stress. *Harvard Review of Psychiatry* 1: 253–65.

Van der Kolk, B.A., and Ronald Fisler. 1995. Dissociation and the fragmentary nature of traumatic memories: Overview and exploratory study. *Journal of Traumatic Stress* 8, 4: 505–25.

Wilkinson, Margaret. 2006. *Coming into mind, the mind-brain relationship: A Jungian clinical perspective.* London: Routledge.

Winnicott, Donald. 1963/1965. Communicating and not communicating leading to a study of certain opposites. In *The maturational processes and the facilitating environment.* London: Hogarth Press.

Woodman, Marion. 1984. Psyche/Soma awareness. *Quadrant* 17, 2: 25–37.

DONALD KALSCHED, Ph.D., is a Clinical Psychologist and Jungian psychoanalyst who practices and teaches in Albuquerque, New Mexico. A training analyst with the Inter-Regional Society of Jungian Analysts, he lectures widely on the subject of early trauma and its treatment.

27

PSYCHOTHERAPY AND CONGENITAL PHYSICAL DISABILITY

Kathrin Asper

Psychotherapy and disability form a fallow gap in the landscape of psychology, medicine, and social pedagogics. There are few publications on the subject, and the topic appears in general specialist literature—if at all—usually only in footnotes. On the other hand, studies have increased in the past twenty years, although their effects are not as yet widespread. In addition, studies are most often quantitative and report only general tendencies while we as analysts see individuals, which require an individual approach. Nonetheless studies are important because they help clinicians to refine their concepts and empathy.

My comments here are restricted to physical disabilities of a congenital nature. The disabilities affect the quality of attachment and require medical attention and therapies of various kinds. Potentially they can have traumatic consequences in the long term. I am not therefore in this article going to be concerned with psychic and mental impairment nor with impairment to the senses and those occurring later in life.

The problem is complex since disability affects family life and brings into play the fields of medicine, physiotherapy, and psychotherapy and raises social, political, and life-view concerns, not to mention insurance issues. Disability is, moreover, bound up with culture and ethnology and with their religious and mythological underpinnings. Seen in an archetypal perspective, disability is one of the ubiquitous themes of the incapacitated god (Sas 1964). Think, for example, of the crippled Greek god, Hephaistos, also of the devil with his goat's foot. Adolf Guggenbühl was the first to write on the archetype of the invalid (Guggenbühl 1979), and he assigned the subject to the general theme of otherness.

People with disabilities experience a different kind of socialization in the family and in society, which requires them to live in "two worlds" if they participate in the world of normality. This means that they live with experiences that are different from those of the nondisabled. Living as a person with a disability in the other so-called normal world, and being and working socially interlinked with that world, represents a major challenge and effort. To live and exist in it without being continually disturbed by otherness means a constant stress and requires continuous psychic effort.

The road between these two worlds is full of hazards and pitfalls. It begins with the family where, in my experience, the disability is hardly discussed. This kind of silence and suspicion continues into adult life. Talking and dialogue are difficult from both sides.

Consider congenital disabilities like visceral inversion, cranio-facial malformations, cerebral palsy, or clubfoot, for example. The difficulties that people with congenital physical disability encounter later in life are the same as those of other persons when serious problems arise or a transition in life requires reorientation. It would be wrong to say that physical disability in itself gives rise to psychic difficulty, but the therapist must be aware of the different kinds of development involved and the special circumstances that each kind of disability may create. Intensive medical treatment and social and psycho-social hurdles can leave scars that break open and require the resources and special approaches that must be understood against the background of the particular disability in question. If this is not understood, a person with a disability is done less than justice and is damaged. The prospects of emotional difficulties arising from a psychic source must be broadened in the case of a disability since the disabled body, its treatment and visibility, have a profound effect on the psyche. It is therefore important to think somato-psychically—as from the body (Frank 1997, 40).

Congenital defects usually require early medical, physiotherapeutic, and speech-therapy treatments. These measures interrupt the child's relationship with maternal caretakers. These treatments with potentially traumatic effects often start at the sensitive bonding stage, and they have a major influence on the preverbal period of psychological and physical development. They mark the baby psychobiologically, therefore, and form the basis for feelings of abandonment, anxiety, and existential threat. In neurobiological terms, these early experiences—apart from genetic factors—condition neuronal associations that are stored in the implicit memory. They cannot be called up and cannot be represented in speech, but they influence future experience and the nature of psychological integration.

Certain events—e.g., medical treatment—may act as triggers later in life, recalling early experiences in the form of "acute post-traumatic stress disorder" (PTSD). In crises, numerous earlier positions may be revived, causing psychic stress and necessitating a reprocessing of early development. Long-term traumatic consequences in the form of a "complex post-traumatic stress disorder" (Herman 1993) may manifest, which must be recognised and treated with sensitivity and circumspection. The hitherto silent emotional experience of many years crosses the threshold into consciousness with a flood of chaotic emotions. Basic convictions wobble, future perspectives disappear. Those affected no longer comprehend themselves, are at risk of suicide, and develop psychic and somatic complaints. The disorientation and helplessness of those concerned and of their families and their caretakers are so profound because the thread of their personal history has snapped. There is also the risk of false associations.

Unfortunately, the late consequences of congenital physical disability receive far too little attention in education, research, and psychotherapy. This fact combines with the general neglect of physical disability in psychotherapy and theory-building (Olkin 1999). In addition, the demand for psychotherapy from those affected by congenital physical disability is small. This is because, among other reasons, the theories and approaches derived from working with persons without physical disability are simply transferred to those with this specific problem. The resulting interpretations and interventions can easily cause persons with a disability to feel ill and misunderstood and to be frightened away. Thanks to the change of paradigm promoted by "Disability Studies," persons with a disability are gaining a voice that is increasingly being heard. In the past, they were an object in the files of various specialists, and their experiences and knowledge were largely neglected (Frank 1997).

Added to this are discrimination and stigmatization (Goffman 1963) and the fact that disability is a permanent stress factor. Separation and autonomy are stages of development often delayed. Persons with a disability more rarely live independently, marry less and later, experience occupational restrictions, and are generally excluded from military service.

The remainder of this chapter will be devoted to discussing certain critical factors and issues that must be taken into consideration when dealing psychotherapeutically with adults in crisis who have lived with a congenital disability.

ATTACHMENT AND TRAUMA

A trauma is threatening, occasioning feelings of menace and helplessness beyond the processing ability of those affected. The experience of oneself and the world are shaken (Van der Kolk et al. 1996). Since the attachment phase is the matrix of structural growth, traumata during this period have particularly serious consequences if the dyadic regulating of the emotions is disrupted by traumatic events (Lieberman/Amaya-Jackson 2005). During this phase, the adaptive and nonadaptive systems become marked, influencing all subsequent relations with oneself, the world, and the trans-personal. Impairments at this stage influence the regulation of emotions, which forms the base of the growing structure needed to contain and process them later in life (Schore 2003, ch. 4).

Recognition of the importance of medical traumata has been slow in coming in trauma research. We now know that treatment for disease/disability can have serious traumatic consequences. Studies are available in particular for cancer, heart, and AIDS patients (Mundy/Baum 2004, 123–24.). We still have little precise knowledge as to how operations in the bonding phase of infancy influence the quality of attachment or mark neuronal facilitation and its later development (Landolt 2004, 68). On the other hand, present knowledge of factors that impair attachment (Brisch 1999, 77; Brisch/Hellbrügge 2003, 105ff.) and neuro-scientific findings (Schore 2005, ch. 2), case studies (Diepold, 1996), and the clinical experience of psychotherapists have led to the recognition that the treatment of congenital disabilities, in combination with other unfavorable factors, has a potentially traumatic effect and may have consequences in the long term (Bürgin 2007).

Relational experiences between mother/primary caretaker and child in the early years plays a decisive role in later development and is known as attachment. Small children introduce a relational range that in the most favorable instance is intrinsically meshed with that of the mother, whereupon the mother seeks empathic solutions to interpersonal and intra-psychic problems. If the attachment is relatively unimpaired, the basis is formed for feelings of security, trust, belonging, continuity, and the experience of consolation and being wanted. An "internal working model" is established, embedding subsequent expectations of trustful encounter (Bretherton 2001, 52). Disruption during the bonding phase may give rise to "insecure," "or "disorganized" attachment. The general attitude to life becomes one of uncertainty and lack of trust, and relational expectations are marked by anxiety, distrust, and ambivalence.

Impairment of the motor apparatus and cranio-facial malformations affect the quality of attachment. Movement or the intake of nourishment is obstructed and requires special measures such as physiotherapy and speech therapy. These disturb and interrupt eye contact, continuity, the presence of the mother, sounds, speech, and tactile contact (Egger 2006; Oster 2005, 276).

The nature of attachment undergoes no essential changes in the course of life, but its quality is capable of changing somewhat through new experience (cf. Gloger-Tippelt 2001). Disturbances in the bonding phase are responsible for comparatively greater anxiety and depression in later life (Brisch 1999, 234 et seq.; cf. Brisch/Hellbrügge 2003).

CO-TRAUMATIC PROCESSES

A child with a disability creates uncertainty in the parents and requires them to adapt to a usually unfamiliar situation (Stern/Bruschweiler 1998, ch. 9). Parents participate in the stresses and traumata of the children, and they in turn induce similar states in the parents, so we speak of co-traumatic processes (Pleyer 2004).

Expecting a child gives rise to idealistic fantasies in the prospective parents regarding the child and their future family life. In the head and heart of the mother and father, the imaginary baby is born prior to the real one. It will be a happy child because they want to give it everything! The imaginary child is incorporated in the archetypal representation of the divine child, which is to make everything new (Asper 1992; Jung/Kerényi 1969). This normal process enables parents to live towards the happy event with joy and confidence. However, the positive fantasies are also accompanied by more anxious ones, which may be summarized as: "if everything is all right, if the baby is really healthy and develops normally!" Fortunate indeed are the parents whose trust in the future is unimpaired; they are strengthened by a quality that has a positive effect as well on the future child.

Following the birth of the real baby, the parents must inevitably overcome a discrepancy between the imaginary baby and the real flesh-and-blood baby. When a birth defect exists, the step is all the greater.

The effect of a baby with a defect on the parents is primarily expressed in joy with the child, accompanied by devoting extra care to the child and an overwhelming feeling of wanting to do everything possible to facilitate a normal life for the child. In addition, fright, anxiety, fears, feelings of guilt and shame and, occasionally, self-blame are not uncommon. Added to this are such practical problems as difficulty with the baby's movements, its intake of food, and all the myriad of questions regarding the form and place of treatment and clarification about insurance coverage.

Not well known but with serious consequences for both members of the partnership is the revival of earlier injury and traumata in the mother. Pregnancy, birth, and babyhood are a vulnerable time for a young mother because they constitute a transition in her life. This activates earlier unconscious dynamics and contents that can prove stressful (Fraiberg 2003, 466). For example, a mother who was much discriminated against in childhood will have to distance herself from these feelings, and thereby she renders herself insensitive to discrimination her disabled child encounters. A medical trauma of their own may perhaps be put aside by becoming emotionally numb when the child undergoes surgery, gets treatment, and suffers pain. These defensive measures unfortunately result in the child's emotional neglect (Asper 1993, 147) because resonance and attunement to the child's needs become severely restricted and muted.

Organic speech impediment of cleft-palate children makes daily, repeated exercise with the mother and constant attention to speech and its correction necessary. Logopaedia and speech therapy kindergartens come later. The mother thereby becomes a co-therapist of the speech instructor. She concentrates on the correct pronunciation by the child, and this interrupts the child's spontaneous communications. This means that over time attention is placed on the child's phonetic formation of words and less on its emotional and intended communication. This affects the nature of communication and association at emotional and cognitive levels. The message is interrupted, which disrupts the child's trust in speech representation and also its ability to communicate. Unsecured attachment in the initial preverbal period continues. For the child, this means in the broadest sense not being heard or seen. The child may possibly lose confidence in its ability to express itself and begin to become silent. For mother and child, this means stress and unconscious enhancement of uncertainty on both sides. Obstructions in the kinetic apparatus, such as dysplasia, cerebral movement impairments, or clubfoot, for example, require surgery and intensive and continuous physiotherapy. This means an ongoing correction of spontaneous movement, which may well be accompanied by pain. Body limits are breached, and the body is occupied from the outside by the intrusive, foreign interventions in movement (Egger 2006). Dysplasia led in the past to the lower body and extremities being wrapped in plaster, which had to be replaced every few weeks in accordance with the body's growth. This meant hospitalization. These procedures continued formerly up to the third year of life. Not only was the small child's behavior thereby obstructed, but the child also lost visual and auditory contact with the mother since the mother could not carry a child in plaster around the house quite simply because of its weight. In the light of treatment and co-traumatic processes that start during the bonding period, the attempts by both mother and baby to form a secure dyad are impeded. For the child, this is an encroachment on its certainty of life and its trust, but it also means a loss for the mother who cannot live an unstressed dyad with the baby and sometimes develops a preoccupied attachment attitude (Gomille 2001, 201) and may tend to depression (Oster 2005, 276; Riecher-Rössler/Steiner 2005).

THERAPEUTIC APPROACH

Physical disability is not a disease. Nor does it necessarily mean either psychological problems or a predisposition to develop them. People with a physical disability may suffer from depression, anxiety symptoms, neuroses, and psychoses and so forth just like other people. As far as therapeutic approach is concerned, however, it is important to remember that persons with a disability have different psychosocial experiences and a history marked by surgery and long-term therapeutic measures that may possibly have been experienced as traumatic. This means that the therapist must obtain knowledge of the disability and its treatment and take account of this factor in designing treatment strategies and methods. Empathy amongst nondisabled therapists is often limited, and they must enlarge their imagination through reading or other sources such as narratives, literature on disability, interviews and films in order to familiarize themselves with the experiences of persons with a disability. Persons with congenital disability have preverbal experiences stored in implicit memory, but they cannot be recalled. They have their effects, however, and it is important that these emotions that sometimes flood into consciousness are put into order. Those affected often know surprisingly little about their early treatment, and only the therapist, who has taken the trouble of finding it out, can refer to it in the context of careful therapeutic handling. However, all psychic problems cannot be reduced to the disability, first because people are more than their disability and second because in certain cases the history would thereby be repeated. The history, in particular, is usually that the disabled child was already involved in a rehabilitation project within the family and her or his entire being is subsumed under this aspect. If this is repeated, the victim position is deepened and strengthened. Autonomy and being an individual thereby have fewer chances of development, and regression is promoted. From a diagnostic viewpoint, it is extremely important that the long-term effects of medical traumata are recognized. The complex post-traumatic stress disorder (C-PTSD) must be recognized and the patient approached accordingly. This diagnosis renders the diagnosis of co-morbidity largely superfluous,[1] unburdens the patient, and with appropriate treatment results in stabilization. This creates the prerequisite for a link between the "two worlds" in which children and later adults with disability are used to living. The usually silent and speechless world of disability and the early attachment experiences can now better approach the other, so-called normal world. The ego is gradually placed in a position of representing the two worlds of empirical and practical experience. A proper awareness of empirical experience associated with the disability is extraordinarily important so that wrong inferences are avoided. Where medical traumata exist and the child's personality is tied to the emotions surrounding these, emotional flooding appears that is not so easily put in place. The emotions—often tied to the body and finding expression here—require a length of time and intensive work until they are pictured in dreams and expressed in speech. In brief, the situation is sometimes quite unmanageable, occasioning helplessness in the patient and the therapist, and this creates a basis for fantasies that can be very destructive.

For example, a patient with complex posttraumatic stress disorder was depressive, anxious, and flooded with emotions for which he had no points of reference. He had a clubfoot and had received appropriate medical treatment and intensive physiotherapy. His physical limitations were finally overcome, but the treatment resulted in a personal feeling of being under extraneous control, an object of parental care, a case in the files of doctors and therapists with whom he had been in contact. This resulted in an inadequate development of the ability to achieve desired goals, to place limits, and to say no. He showed symptoms of abuse, which his therapist attributed to sexual abuse by his mother without knowing the history and disregarding the patient's somatic case history. The therapist considered this interpretation fitting for the clinical picture, and this put an end to her feeling of helplessness. The patient himself knew too little of his history and so he accepted that at last he had an explanation for his overwhelming nonspecific emotions, at last an explanation for the difficulties he had with the parents whom he had found highly stressful in early adolescence and in the course of separating from them. No one took into account that separation from the parents is very difficult with a disability. After all, the mother—usually—is the life-support system for many years, and loosening of the ties is therefore very difficult on both sides. Earlier emotional and interpersonal positions from childhood were misassociated here with sexual abuse, experiences showing similar symptoms as medical traumata. The consequence of this misinterpretation of the symptoms was highly destructive, creating massive feelings of guilt both among parents and patient, a breaking off of contact, inner loneliness, and enormous suffering. All this would have been avoided had the therapist bothered to dis-

---

[1] The diagnosis "complex post-traumatic stress disorder" replaces a long list of others, such as depression, anxiety disorder, dissociation, borderline aspects, personality disorder, etc. Often these clients received a diagnosis of co-morbidity, which was very detrimental and did not address the traumatic roots of their difficulties.

cover the history of treatment and the particular dynamics in families with a disabled child, learned the facts of the history of the patient, and strictly put aside the usual preconceptions from precisely this area, where, as we know there is little literature.

We must remember that with physical disability, patients are the specialists regarding their affliction, and it is they who have the experience, the knowledge of what this feels like, and what the effects are. Specialists are indispensable, but they must never forget that they do not have this experience and must therefore abandon preconceptions and assumptions even more than with people without physical disability.

A precise knowledge of the experience and medical-therapeutic biography has also proved fruitful in working with dreams. A man with crano-facial disability dreamed that another motorist was furious with him in a parking lot because he was aiming for the same parking space and was on the point of physically attacking him. The dreamer felt his anger rise and simultaneously wanted to put up his arm in defense. Halfway towards doing so his arm became numb. It would be easy to see here that the patient was aggression-inhibited. However, this patient's inhibition had a history that had to be known. His inhibition arose from a deep fear that his face could be damaged. This would have tremendous consequences, since the complicated bone and tooth rehabilitation that had cost him decades of his life could possibly have been destroyed. This in turn would have meant complex, laborious treatment with the uncertain outcome whether the result would be as good as on the first occasion. It is therefore not surprising that his arm becomes numb, that he thinks of his body and wants to protect it!

Family dynamics are also the subject of premature interpretation. Jungian psychoanalysts who like to hark back to mythological themes are often too quick to say about disability that the mother did not want the handicapped child and referred to the myth of Hephaistos, who as a baby was cast out from Olympus by his mother, Hera. It is a fact that the mother-child relationship is difficult if the child has a disability. Many factors account for this difficulty—the co-traumatic processes between mother and child, the early separations, the disruption in the bond, the way the handicap is integrated in the person concerned, who is often imbued with primary guilt feelings, reduced self-appreciation, anxiety, and lack of communication on the subject. Therapists should not forget that a disability affects both the child and the mother. In certain circumstances, not only does the child develop a negative mother complex, but the mother is also affected by this negative complex without her having caused it through her rejection. The negative mother at work is archetypal, as expressed in the myth. To pin responsibility to the personal mother is premature and destructive. Relationships and concrete situations are more complex. Persons without physical disability are often shocked at a child's handicap and project rejection on the mother, assuming that the mother has difficulties in accepting the child. However, mothers do not perceive it as such; precisely in the early baby period—which Winnicott referred to as a "normal illness" (Winnicott 1975, 305) because the mothering complex takes over guidance of personality—the provident, nurturing mother feature of personality takes on the central role, and the mother sees her child as particularly needy, a child with special needs. The rejection projected onto her is nonexistent; on the contrary, she is afflicted with fears regarding the child's future.

What must also be strongly stated with regard to the Jungian therapeutic approach is the sometimes misguided emphasis on symbolism. Handicaps are too quickly deemed symbolic. Of a person who cannot walk, it is said he cannot assume his own standpoint; of the blind, they must activate their inner perception. I have not invented these examples, but have heard them referred to in practice and by those affected. Such statements are simply inappropriate and repugnant.

The following are essential points to be considered where attachment problems are diagnosed and where the dyad has been disrupted as a result of medical traumata:

- Learning to understand one's own history .

- Gaining new affect-regulating experiences, which modify an insecure bond and develop the structure for emotional control.

- Working with available resources and replacing the pathogenetic approach by a salutogenetic approach (Antonovsky 1987). However, not doing so at the price of not observing or not appreciating the painful affective conditions, but taking due account of both.

- Working on the negative introjects (archaic super-ego, internal saboteur, protector-persecutor, traumatic introject).

- Working with available resources to develop special skills, insights and wisdom.

- Working on partial personalities—ego-state work, distinguishing the ego from the complex.

- Working on internal images, powers of representation through imagination.

All of this type of work must be approached psycho-dynamically and adapted to the trauma (Reddemann 2001). With insight turned cautiously, patiently and lovingly inwards, what a person has become is appreciated and gradually integrated with his resources and injuries (Asper 1993)—pursuing Paul Tillich's encouragement of "*acceptance of being accepted*" (Tillich 1962, 177), a patient can in the course of a therapeutic encounter put down new roots and open up the future to new possibilities for life.

REFERENCES

Antonovsky, Aaron. 1987. *Unravelling the mystery of health: How people manage stress and stay well.* San Francisco: Jossey–Bass Publishers.

Asper, Kathrin. 1993. *The abandoned child within: On losing and regaining self-worth.* New York: Fromm International Publishing Corporation.

———. 1992. *The inner child in dreams.* Boston: Shambhala Publications.

Bretherton, Inge. 1990. Communication patterns, internal working models, and the intergenerational transmission of attachment relationships. *Infant Mental Health Journal* 11:237–51.

Brisch, Karl-Heinz. 1999. *Bindungsstörungen.* Stuttgart: Klett-Cotta.

Brisch, Karl-Heinz, and Theodor Hellbrügge, eds. 2003. *Bindung und Trauma.* Stuttgart: Klett-Cotta.

Bürgin, Dieter. 2007. Potenziell traumatogene Faktoren in der Intensivmedizin. *Jahrbuch der Psychotraumatologie* 2007: 43–50. Kröning: Asanger.

Diepold, Barbara. 1996. Diese Wut hört niemals auf. *Analytische Kinder-und Jugendlichen Psychotherapie* 89: 73–85.

Egger, Patrizia. 2006. Die Besetzung des Körpers. In *Die Welt als Barriere— Deutschsprachige Beiträge zu den Disability Studies,* ed. Erich Otto Graf und Jan Weisser, 75–82. Rubigen/Bern: Edition Soziothek.

Fraiberg, Selma et al. 1975. Ghosts in the nursery. *Journal of American Academy of Child Psychiatry* 14: 387–421.

Frank, Arthur W. 1997. *The wounded storyteller.* Chicago/London: The University of Chicago Press.

Gloger-Tippelt, Gabriele, ed. 2001. *Bindung im Erwachsenenalter.* Bern: Verlag Hans Huber.

Gomille, Beate. 2001. Unsicher-präokkupierte mentale Bindungsmodelle. In *Bindung im Erwachsenenalter,* ed. by Gabriele Gloger Tippelt, 201–26. Bern: Verlag Hans Huber.

Goffman, Erving. 1963. *Stigma: Notes on the management of spoiled identity.* Englewood Cliffs, NJ: Prentice Hall.

Guggenbühl, Adolf . 1979. *Der Archetyp des Invaliden.* Gorgo: Zeitschrift für archetypische Psychologie und bildhaftes Denken 2.

Herman, Judith L. 1993. Sequelae of prolonged and repeated trauma: evidence for a complex postraumatic syndrome (DESNOS). In *Postraumatic stress disorder – DSM IV and beyond,* ed. J. R. Davidson and E. A. Foa, 213–28. Washington: American Psychiatric Press.

Jung, C. G., and Karl Kerenyi. 1969. *Essays on a science of mythology: The myth of the divine child and the Mysteries of Eleusis.* Bollingen Series XX. Princeton: Princeton University Press.

Kalland, Mirjam. 1995. *Psychosocial aspects of cleft lip and palate.* Helsinki: Yliopistopaino.

Landolt, Markus. 2004. *Psychotraumatologie des Kindesalters.* Göttingen: Hogrefe.

Lieberman, Alicia F., and Lisa Amaya-Jackson. 2005. Reciprocal influences of attachment and trauma. In *Enhancing early attachments. Theory, research, intervention, and policy,* ed. Lisa J. Berlin, Yair Ziv, Lisa Amaya-Jackson, and Mark T. Greenberg. New York/London: The Guilford Press.

Mundy, Elisabeth, and Baum Andrew. 2004. Medical disorders as a cause of psychological trauma and posttraumatic stress disorder. *Current Opinion in Psychiatry* 17, 2: 123–28.

Olkin, Rhoda. 1999. *What psychotherapists should know about disability.* New York/London: The Guilford Press.

Oster, Harriet. 2005. The repertoire of infant facial expression: An ontogenetic perspective. In *Emotional development, recent research advances,* ed. Jacquelin Nadel and Darwin Muir. Oxford/New York: University Press.

Pleyer, Karl-Heinz. 2004. Co-traumatische Prozesse in der Elter-Kind-Beziehung. *Systema* 2:132–49.

Reddemann, Luise. 2001. *Imagination als heilsame Kraft.* Stuttgart: Pfeiffer bei Klett-Cotta.

Riecher-Rössler, Anita, and Meir Steiner, eds. 2005. *Perinatal stress, mood and anxiety disorders.* Basel: Karger.

Sas, Stefan. 1964. *Der Hinkende als Symbol.* Studien aus dem C.G. Jung-Institut. Zürich: Rascher.

Schore, Allan. 2003. *Affect regulation and the repair of the self.* New York/London: W.W. Norton & Company.

Stern, Daniel N., and Nadia Bruschweiler-Stern. 1998. *The birth of a mother.* New York: Basic Books.

Tillich, Paul. 1962. *The courage to be.* New Haven/London: Yale University Press.

Van der Kolk, Bessel, Alexander McFarlane, and Lars Weisaeth, eds. 1996. *Traumatic Stress: The effects of overwhelming experience on mind, body and society.* New York/London: The Guilford Press.

Winnicott, Donald W. 1975. *Through paediatrics to psychoanalysis.* New York: Basic Books.

KATHRIN ASPER, Ph.D., is a training and supervising analyst at the International School of Analytical Psychology, Zurich. She is the author of many articles and several books and she lectures widely internationally. She conducts a practice in Meilen, near Zurich.

28

PSYCHE AND BRAIN

Margaret Wilkinson

Psyche embraces "the totality of all psychic processes, conscious as well as unconscious" (Jung 1921, para. 797). The development of psyche itself may be understood as emergent and relational, for it is formed in relation to another person, the primary caregiver. We may think of the individual human being as a unique mind-brain-body being that has emerged from the experience of the earliest and most fundamental experiences of relating. It is in the mother's eyes that the child first sees its unique self, and it is through the affect-regulating aspects of the relation to the mother that a child is able eventually to arrive at self-regulation of affect. Fuller development of the child is realized as the father comes to act as a bridge to the outside world, bringing experience that enables the child's arrival at full agency. For Jung, the transcendent function enables access to the self-regulating function of the psyche in adulthood, overcoming the distinction between conscious and unconscious and allowing the fullest experience of psychic wholeness for the individual who undertakes the journey which Jung termed individuation.

In working psychoanalytically with early relational trauma, early development is often mirrored in the quality of the transference relationship and then reworked in the course of the analysis. Increasingly, clinical practitioners have become aware that the relational aspect of therapy is primary. Research consistently demonstrates that the quality of the relationship with the therapist matters more than the theoretical orientation of the therapist. However, just as a child grows up and needs a father as bridge to the outside world, so our patients need interpretation to foster the fullest growth of mind. The question for the analyst must always be one of finding the fine balance between the two and then of appropriate timing of each in each phase of work with an individual patient. Balance and timing are key. In the countertransference, the analyst is able to develop a rich understanding of the relational issues for a particular patient and through interpretation to facilitate arrival at the capacity for adult separated attachment, characterized by connected autonomy (Orbach 2007, 9) that will enable the process of individuation.

The mystery of consciousness, of subjectivity, of psyche, is one that preoccupies many in the field of neuroscience. Edelman and Tononi comment

> No matter how accurate the description of physical processes underlying it, it is hard to conceive how the world of subjective experience—the seeing of blue and the feeling of warmth—springs out of mere physical events. And yet in an age in which brain imaging, general anesthesia, and neurosurgery are becoming commonplace, we are aware that the world of conscious experience depends all too closely on the delicate workings of the brain. (Edelman and Tononi 2000, 2)

THE EARLIEST DEVELOPMENT OF PSYCHE

Jung himself gave clues about the earliest development of psyche in his own reminiscences. In his eighties Jung recalled his earliest memory.

> I am lying in my pram, in the shadow of a tree. It is a fine, warm summer day, the sky blue, the golden sunlight darting through the green leaves. The hood of the pram has been left up. I have just awakened to the glorious beauty of the day, and have a sense of indescribable well-being. I see the sun glittering through the leaves and blossoms of the bushes. Everything is wholly wonderful, colorful and splendid. (Jung 1963, 21)

Jung also recounted a memory of sitting "perched in a high chair and spooning up milk with bits of broken bread in it. The milk has a pleasant taste and a characteristic smell" (Jung 1963, 21). In both remarks we see the linking of sensory experience with bodily sensation and emotional well-being in relation to his earliest experiences of care.

When the significance of the developmental perspective of psyche is fully appreciated, understanding of the significance of emotional neglect by the mother is born. Bromberg comments that developmental trauma matters so much because "it shapes the attachment patterns that establish what is to become a stable or unstable core self" (Bromberg 2006, 6). Sometimes modern theory has put too much responsibility for familial trauma at the door of the father without looking sufficiently carefully at early trauma and neglect in the maternal relationship. Perhaps this is because while betrayal of an infant by either parent may seem unthinkable, faithlessness by the mother is the most difficult for us to comprehend. Woodhead turns to neuroscience to ground her thinking about her work with traumatized mothers and babies (Woodhead 2004, 2005). She models an attitude, which the baby's mother has the opportunity to internalize sufficiently in order to "begin to be able to follow her baby's clues and meet her needs more empathically" (Wilkinson 2006, 41–42).

EMBODIED PSYCHE

Psyche is essentially embodied and can only be known in an embodied way. But how does psyche develop out of bodily experience? How does psyche become experienced and known? Where is the role of the brain in all this?

The integral nature of the mind-brain-body being came home very powerfully to me in a very personal way when recently I had a complete knee replacement. The day after the operation it seemed beyond the realm of possibility to lift my heel off the bed or to move my foot even an inch sideways as the physiotherapist required. My efforts to move my foot even a millimeter to the side remained fruitless. Suddenly, I found myself thinking about Knox's remarks about the earliest image schemas. Knox describes these as "probably the earliest products emerging from the self-organization of the human brain, a process that continues from birth and probably starts even *in utero*" (Knox 2004, 69). Such schemas develop directly in relation to earliest experience to the mother's body. Knox comments: "It is crucial to emphasize here the bodily basis of the image schema—*it is a mental Gestalt which develops out of bodily experience* and forms the basis for abstract meanings, both in the physical and in the world of imagination and metaphor" (Knox 2004, 69, italics mine). She comments that "the abstract pattern itself is never experienced directly" but "provides the invisible scaffolding for a whole range of metaphorical extensions that can be expressed in conscious imagery" (Knox 2003, 62). Knox explores Johnson's work in relation to the specific image schema "out," and the way in which such image schemas are metaphorically extended from the physical to the nonphysical realm (Knox 2004, 69–70, citing Johnson 1987, 34). As I willed my foot to move towards the edge of the bed, I sought to recruit this early image schema to help with my current dilemma. I said to myself "out," and sure enough what had previously seemed impossible happened as my brain was able to draw on something already deeply established in mind in the service of building the new neural pathway. "In" followed and enabled me to move my foot slightly back in again. From then on, as I sought to regain full movement I was able to use every bit of knowledge I had about neural pathways, building not only on the earliest schemas but also echoing the actions in the other side of my body, thus strengthening the messages as I exercised.

Knox has drawn our attention to the importance of image schemas or internal working models in the development of the capacity for imagination and reflective function, including the sense of psyche and the sense of self. In response to the earliest relational experience with the primary caregiver, developing psyche arises out of the developing brain. This in turn affects the brain's development as new neural connections are made as a result of interactions with significant others throughout life. A robust psyche may be thought of as a developmental achievement, for it develops out of a good enough relation to the earliest caregiver. Stein emphasizes that "the degree of richness of the matrix in this stage of containment is highly dependant upon the attitudes and resources that happen to be available to the adult care-givers" and is also "crucially dependent on their emotional stability and maturity" (Stein 2006, 201). In less fortunate circumstances, the psyche may be wounded at the deepest levels through the failure of the caregiver to reveal the lovability of the emergent infant psyche.

PSYCHE, SELF, AND NEUROSCIENCE

Both attachment theory and neuroscience have assigned fundamental importance to psyche, to self, just as Jung did in contrast to Freud's earlier emphasis on ego and ego function. Schore comments: "The centre of psychic life shifts from Freud's *ego*, which he located in the 'speech area on the left hand side' (Freud 1923) and the posterior areas of the verbal left hemisphere, to the highest levels of the right hemisphere, the locus of the bodily based *self* system" (Schore 2001, 77). Jung argued that: "The self is a quantity that is superordinate to the conscious ego. It embraces not only the conscious but the unconscious psyche, and is therefore, so to speak, a personality which we *also* are" (Jung 1953, para. 274).

A full exploration of the richness of the complexity of the relationship between self, psyche, and mind in Jung's thought is far beyond the scope of this chapter. Suffice it to say that the notion of the psyche is the area of an understanding where a Jungian perspective is perhaps most relevant to recent empirical studies in neuroscience. Jung's notion of the psyche that develops to the full over the life span through the process of individuation is congruent with the work of Damasio. Damasio suggested a "preconscious biological precedent," entirely outside of consciousness, which he termed the "protoself" (Damasio 1999, 153). By this he meant an essentially unconscious bodily-based foundation to the psyche, from which the core self, which we each become able to sense within, may develop. Stein explains that Jung's concept of individuation may be understood as "the process of becoming the personality that one innately is *potentially* from the beginning of life" (Stein 2006, 198).

Neuroscientists stress the importance of zones of convergence that receive and integrate inputs from many different brain areas. Particular areas of the upper brainstem that receive input from all the sensory modalities produce a "virtual map" of the skeletomuscular body. These areas are adjacent to the area where the mapping of inner visceral states takes place. The inferior colliculus (where the imprint of the mother's voice is thought to be stored) is also close to these areas, so our very sense of who we are may well be sculpted by our earliest experiences of our mother's voice. It is from these areas that an awareness of a coherent sense of self may ultimately emerge. Panksepp suggests that "basic affective states, which initially arise from the changing neurodynamics of a SELF-representation mechanism, may provide an essential psychic scaffolding for all other forms of consciousness" (Panksepp 1998, 309).

Schore has brought together a substantial body of research (EEG and neuro-imaging (fMRI), and positron emission topography (PET) data) that demonstrates that unconscious processing of emotion is associated with the right rather than the left hemisphere, and that the early developing right hemisphere is densely inter-connected with limbic regions and contains the major circuitry of emotion regulation. Research demonstrates that "the infant's psycho-biological reaction to trauma is comprised of two separate response patterns—hyperarousal and dissociation" (Schore 2007, 757). In the first phase, the mother who should be the source of safety becomes the source of threat, leading to somatic expressions of fear-terror; in the second phase, hopelessness and helplessness takes over, and the infant retreats into a cut-off, dissociated state as its whole system moves into playing dead as a last defense. Schore concludes that the massive psychobiological misattunement of such attachment trauma "sets the stage for the characterological use of right-brain pathological dissociation over all subsequent stages of human development" (Schore 2007, 759).

THE HEALING PROCESS

The birth of the personality in oneself has a therapeutic effect. It is as if a river that had run to waste in sluggish side-streams and marshes suddenly found its way back to its proper bed, or as if a stone lying on a germinating seed were lifted away so that the shoot could begin its natural growth. The inner voice is the voice of a fuller life, of a wider, more comprehensive consciousness. (Jung 1934 paras. 317–18)

The psyche can recruit a wide variety of experiences into the service of wholeness. One patient whom I will call Elly had very poor early experience. She came to a session and described a magical evening spent with friends, which she had experienced as helping to heal her psyche. Elly had been on holiday abroad, staying with a friend. One evening she was feeling off-color with a virus and was settled comfortably in the sitting-room. Jenny, her friend, was at home with her twelve-year-old daughter, Marie, while Jenny's husband was away on business. Jenny had begun to cook dinner when an extended power cut occurred, a commonplace in that particular country. Elly's friend was still able to cook dinner by gas while Marie lit every room with soft candlelight. Mother, daughter, and guest picnicked with the food laid out on the rich Indian carpet whose colors shone beautifully in the candlelight. It was a good experience for Elly. She saw mother and daughter enjoy each other's company in a way Elly had not known with her own mother. After dinner, Elly went to bed. She was staying in one of the children's rooms, which had a magical quality in the candlelight, especially for Elly who had experienced childhood illness in very different circumstances. She enjoyed the soft lilac pinks of the room and the silver moons on the drawn curtains. Above the child's desk were many happy family pictures taken over the years of the child's life. While Jenny went off to fetch an older child from an evening activity, Marie, who had confessed to being nervous of the dark, came into the room and sat down in the armchair saying: "Would you like me to read to you?" Elly realized she was empathically acting as her mother would have done with her when she was unwell, as well as finding a way to manage her fear of the dark. Both enjoyed the reading, first of poetry at Elly's request, and then the much-loved story of Mrs. Tiggy-Winkle by Beatrix Potter chosen by Marie. For Elly, the whole evening had a magical, soothing, healing quality that she somehow knew spoke to the hurt child in her in a special way.

This brief extract indicates something of the very different self-states that all of us can move through at different times. At one moment, we may be the grown-up friend that each of these women was to the other usually; at another, the dreamer with the capacity to imagine the magic or magical carpet; at yet another when the emergent feminine becomes revealed in the pre-pubescent girl as she tries on the role of mothering; or like Elly, as she allows herself to feel what it is to be a child again for a brief moment. In health we are able to move smoothly between different self-states while retaining a sense of "I," of a coherent identity. For some patients who have experienced early relational trauma, such transitions will certainly not be smooth. At one moment, the therapist may experience a relationship with a very self-controlled adult, with the adaptive self that has enabled the patient to manage life well enough, but then suddenly a very vulnerable aspect of the patient may emerge and both patient and therapist may be overwhelmed by the sudden transition to such a different self-state.

Jung's own struggles indicate that he understood these processes very well from quite an early age. In *Memories, Dreams, Reflections* he tells us of his lonely struggle at the age of twelve between an everyday self and an inner self who carried a sense of his deepest emotional truth for him. Jung comments: "to my intense confusion, it occurred to me that I was actually two different persons". . . "I felt confused and was full to the brim with heavy reflections" (Jung 1963, 50–51). Jung had a traumatic experience at the beginning of his twelfth year— bullying by another boy resulted in a fall that knocked him unconscious for a brief while. This was then followed by fainting spells. Jung understood even at that age that the secondary gain of such attacks was the chance to stay away from the school where he felt increasingly out of place. His growing self- awareness, which came with the onset of adolescence, emphasized to him only too plainly his otherness from his schoolmates. His initial conclusion that the second person "must be sheer nonsense" was something that he was to struggle with until much later in life, when as the result of a painful journey towards individuation he came to be more at ease with his self.

Bromberg warns that unintegrated affect from psychic trauma "threatens to disorganize the internal template on which one's experience of self-coherence, self-cohesiveness, and self-continuity depends. . . . The unprocessed 'not-me' experience held by a dissociated self-state as an affective memory without an autobiographical memory of its origin 'haunts' the self" (Bromberg 2003, 689).

Van der Hart et al. have highlighted the way in which dissociation may be used to maintain an effective defensive system in the face of overwhelming trauma. They highlight divisions between the apparently normal personality and other emotional aspects of personality. The "apparently normal personality" may be equated with the adaptive, coping, "false self," well known both in the consulting room and in the analytic literature as that part of the personality that manages everyday life. The emotional personality is reminiscent of Jung's traumatic complex. The writers understand the "emotional personality" to be stuck in the traumatic experience that persistently fails to become a coherent narrative memory.

The emotional personality may be characterized by vehement emotion, which is understood as overwhelming and nonadaptive. Such is the domain in which the emotional personality lives and which the therapist will encounter in the consulting-room. I am reminded of Jung's comment about the traumatic complex forcing "itself tyrannically upon the conscious mind. The explosion of affect is a complete invasion of the individual. It pounces upon him like an enemy or a wild animal" (Jung 1928, para. 267). The authors understand the apparently normal personality as "fixated in trying to go on with normal life . . . while avoiding traumatic memories" (Van der Hart et al, 2006, 5). They argue that each displays a different psychobiological response to trauma memories, which includes a different sense of self.

At the time when Jung began to struggle with his sense of a divided personality, he also was almost overwhelmed by a dreamlike experience that began in the same Cathedral Square where he had fallen as a result of a schoolmate's blow (Jung 1963, 52–59). Emergent metaphor in the form of dreams has long been one of the most powerful vehicles by which the psyche may achieve greater integration. Mancia suggests that the function of the dream is to create images that are "able to fill the void of nonrepresentation, representing symbolically experiences that were originally presymbolic" (Mancia 2005, 93). Dreams may be understood as metaphors that lead to the development of new neural pathways, thus enriching the mind-brain. Jung's dream terrified him but also moved him on, particularly in relation to his understanding of fathers in the broadest terms.

Analysis that seeks to process unintegrated affect needs to be like a double helix enabling left brain and right brain processes to interact. Teicher's research into the after-effects of trauma has shown impaired connections between the right and left hemispheres. In particular, the effective functioning of the fiber tract known as the corpus callosum, which is the major highway between the two hemispheres, may be reduced through the effects of trauma (Teicher 2000). While researchers pursue the exact nature of the way in which unintegrated affect may be integrated and unnecessary fear modulated, what is clear is that it will involve the circuitry of the right hemisphere. It is also clear that an understanding of the experience and the processing of the positive affect experienced in the consulting-room will involve the left.

CONCLUSION

As psyche is fundamentally associative and its development based on psychological identification, mechanisms such as transference and countertransference are rooted in the very earliest experience of mind. I work with many patients who have experienced early relational trauma. In its initial phases, the consulting room experience for these patients will need to explore early nurturing. However, as Stein points out, in the long term such work will be ineffective unless a transition occurs with the therapist changing to "another kind of person, a symbolic father" (Stein 2006, 209), who acts as a bridge to the outside world. Such an analysis mirrors the developmental steps that facilitate the full access to and expression of psyche and thus enables the process of "coming into mind" (Wilkinson 2006).

REFERENCES

Bromberg, Philip M. 2003. One need not be a house to be haunted. On enactment, disso-ciation, and the dread of "Not-Me"—A case study. *Psychoanalytic Dialogues* 13, 5: 689–709.
Bromberg, Philip M. 2006. *Awakening the dreamer: Clinical journeys.* New York: The Analytic Press.
Damasio, Antonio. 1999. *The feeling of what happens: Body, emotion and the making of consciousness.* London: Heinemann.
Edelman, Gerald M., and Guilio Tononi. 2000. *Consciousness: How matter becomes imagination.* London: Penguin.
Jung, C.G. 1921/1971. Definitions. In CW 6.
———. 1928/1966. The therapeutic value of abreaction. In CW 16.
———. 1934/1964. The development of personality. In CW 17.
———. 1953/1966. The function of the unconscious. In CW 7.
———. 1963. *Memories, dreams and reflections.* New York: Random House.
Johnson, Mark. 1987. *The body in the mind: The bodily basis of meaning, imagination and reason.* Chicago and London: University of Chicago Press.
Knox, Jean M. 2003. *Archetypes, attachment and analysis: Jungian psychology and the emergent mind.* London: Brunner-Routledge.
———. 2004. Developmental aspects of analytical psychology: New perspectives from cognitive science and attachment theory. Jung's model of the mind. In *Analytical Psychology: Contemporary perspectives in Jungian analysis,* ed. Joseph Cambray and Linda Carter, 56–82. Hove and New York: Brunner-Routledge.
Mancia, Mauro. 2005. Implicit memory and the early repressed unconscious. *International Journal of Psychoanalysis* 87:83–101.
Orbach, Susie. 2007. Separated attachments and sexual aliveness: How changing attach-ment patterns can enhance intimacy. *Attachment: New Directions in Psychotherapy and Relational Psychoanalysis* 1:1.
Panksepp, Jaak. 1998. *Affective neuroscience: The foundations of human and animal emo-tions.* New York and Oxford: Oxford University Press.
Schore, Allan N. 2001 The right brain as the neurobiological substratum of Freud's dynamic unconscious. In *The psychoanalytic century. Freud's legacy for the future,* ed. David Scharff. New York: Other Press.
———. 2007. Review of *Awakening the dreamer: Clinical journeys* by Philip Bromberg. *Psychoanalytic Dialogues* 1, 75: 753–67.
Stein, Murray. 2006. Individuation. In *The handbook of Jungian psychology,* ed. Renos K. Papodopoulos. Hove and New York: Routledge.
Teicher, Martin. 2000, Wounds time won't heal. *Cerebrum* 2, 4.
Van der Hart, Otto, Ellert R.S. Nijenhuis, and Kathy Steele. 2006. *The haunted self: Structural dissociation and the treatment of chronic traumatization.* New York and London: W.W. Norton & Company Inc.
Wilkinson, Margaret A. 2006. *Coming into mind: The mind-brain relationship: A Jungian clinical perspective.* Hove and New York: Brunner-Routledge.

————. 2007. Jung and neuroscience: The making of mind. In *Who owns Jung*, ed. Ann Casement. London: Karnac

Woodhead, Judith. 2004. "Dialectical process" and "constructive method"; micro-analysis of relational process in an example from parent-infant psychotherapy. *Journal of Analytical Psychology* 49, 2: 143–60.

————. 2005. Shifting triangles: Images of father in sequences from parent-infant psychotherapy. *International Journal of Infant Observation* 7, 2-3: 76–90.

MARGARET WILKINSON is a professional member of the Society of Analytical Psychology, London and a member of the editorial board of the *Journal of Analytical Psychology*. She lectures internationally on contemporary neuroscience and its relevance to clinical practice. She is in private practice in North Derbyshire, England.

29

THE PASSIONS: TACTICS OF THE SOUL

Axel Capriles

The Puerto Rican writer Luis Rafael Sánchez begins his novel, *The Importance of Being Daniel Santos*, with the historiography of the women of the famous Latin American singer. He comments that only mentioning the name of this popular Caribbean composer, a rigorous critic of reason and outstanding pupil of sensuality, produced a genital chaos. Daniel Santos had, indeed, a varied and intense erotic life. Apart from an immense number of short and casual relationships, he married ten times and had twelve children from twelve different women. However, more than a representation of Latin American macho, the turbulent life of Daniel Santos, his songs and dislocated voice, have become a myth, a symbol of passion in a broader sense. Rebellious and independent, he composed the song *Sierra Maestra* in 1957, dedicated to Fidel Castro, which later became the hymn of the Cuban Revolution. An alcoholic fully given to a dissipated and intense night life, he ended up in jail many times. The bolero, the musical genre he cultivated best and of which he became the most extraordinary exponent, is an ethic and an aesthetic of passion in the etymological sense of the word as affliction and suffering. The bolero is a hymn to what the French philosopher Claude-Adrian Helvétius thought to be to the soul what movement is to physics, a cult of intense emotions that opens us to the mystery and meaning of life. Daniel Santos shared with Helvétius, for one, the idea of the superiority of the passionate man over the wise and prudent one, and I imagine he also thought that the lack of passions makes us stupid (Helvétius 2007). Not many psychologists and thinkers in the history of Occidental thought have the same opinion. On the contrary, most of the Western intellectual tradition is the result of the discussion of the problems that passion presents to reason.

    C.G. Jung seems, at first glance, to be no different from that tradition. A hasty and inattentive review of his Collected Works and the writings of his most prominent followers noting the appearance of the term passion and the way it is most commonly used, will surely lead us astray into premature and mistaken conclusions about the limitations of Jungian psychology for the understanding of the complex world of affects, feelings, and emotions. The field not only lacks a differentiated terminology and uses various terms interchangeably with others, it has also not given rise to integrated and consistent formulations for a theory of affects. On the whole, the prevailing view within Jungian psychoanalysis seems to be biased and to follow what Robert Solomon (1993) calls the "Myth of the Passions," that is, the intellectual approach in which reason and emotion appear as antagonists, the ungrounded habit of thinking of the wide range of affectionate states as involuntary and inherently bodily reactions connected with instincts and rooted in the unconscious. There are plenty of reasons why a thoughtless overview can be misleading.

The first mention of the word passion in The Collected Works is found in *Symbols of Transformation (*1911-12/1970*)*, where Jung comes up with a simile, previously used by Immanuel Kant, to differentiate passions from emotions. Whereas Kant said that an affect is "like water breaking through a dam," violent and thoughtless, while "passion takes its time and reflects" (Kant 1974, 120), Jung however does not grant any reflexive capacity to passions and uses only the first part of Kant's simile in order to point out the abrupt and perturbing nature of affects ("like the sea breaking through its dykes") (Jung 1911-12/1970, para. 170). This view is conspicuous. In a much later work like *Synchronicity: An Acausal Connecting Principle*, the Swiss Psychiatrist still considers that "every emotional state produces an alteration of consciousness which Janet called *abaissement du niveau mental*; that is to say there is a certain narrowing of consciousness and a corresponding strengthening of the unconscious" (Jung 1952/1969, para. 856). He even associates passions with the psychology of primitive humans, "incapable of moral judgment" and other weakness, as we see in *Aion*, where Jung asserts that "affects occur usually where adaptation is weakest, and at the same time they reveal the reason for its weakness, namely a certain degree of inferiority and the existence of a lower level of personality" (Jung 1951/1968, para. 15). Many other authors in the different schools of analytical psychology have taken the same approach. Marie-Louise von Franz and Jolande Jacobi, both classical Jungians, consider that the shadow and the undeveloped and inferior parts of the personality manifest themselves in explosions of rage, cowardliness, envy, greediness, and all types of inadequate emotional moods. Erich Neumann, an evolutionist, writes that "emotions and affects are bound up with the lowest reaches of the psyche, those closest to the instincts" (Neumann 1973, 330), and Rafael López-Pedraza, an archetypalist, believes that emotions are irrational, non-cognitive, and imbedded in the body (López-Pedraza 2008).

With this perspective it is difficult to understand the psychology of a person like Edumdo Dantés, the main character of the novel of Alexandre Dumás, *Le Comte de Monte-Cristo,* who rationally and coldly planned his revenge over a time span of more than fifteen years. It also limits our understanding of culturally imprinted emotions, like the Japanese *Amae*, a complex behavior not only related to dependency needs and wanting to be loved or the desire to make an authority figure take care of us, but also to lean premeditatedly on a person and take advantage of his good will. In this sense, Jungian psychoanalysis is the heir to the strange intellectual process of psychological theorizing that took place during the eighteenth and nineteenth centuries in the European and North American mind that replaced the wide range of very differentiated categories like appetites, passions, affections, agitations, alterations, moral sentiments, feelings, or moods by an all inclusive and overarching secular concept: emotion (Dixon 2003). Even though the term emotion became interchangeable with other categories like affect or passion, it is not synonymous with the previous terms pathë, *pathos* or *páschein*, in Greek; *passio, affectus, affections,* or *cocitatio animi* in Latin. It lost the refined and distinctive meanings developed during many centuries of Occidental thought. Contrary to what is commonly believed, even in the Classical Christian teachings about the soul some types of affects were active and voluntary movements of the will. In such distant times as the ones of the *City of God,* Augustine, criticizing the Stoic negative vision of the passions, wrote about the virtuous, rational and voluntary affections of the soul (Augustine 2003).

The contemporary interpretation of passions as rational and intentional actions has not gained much acceptance within the Jungian community. Most classical Jungians are accustomed to seeing the passions as irrational and turbulent drives that blur our assessment of reality, as states of possession. We commonly describe them, as the ancients did, as obscure forces that take hold of our will without our consent, as the workings of powerful daemons or gods to whom we succumb—like the goddess Aphrodite who, infatuated and driven by desire was "compelled by Zeus to fall in love with the herdsman Anchises" (Kerenyi 1961, 77), recovered her true form after the pleasurable moment and felt ashamed for having slept with a mortal. Almost untouched since the most remote Antiquity, this notion and way of interpreting the experience of passion has found in Jungian psychology its modern paraphrase. It is the implicit model behind our scientific explanations of symptoms and affective reactions as the effect of partial personalities or emotionally charged complexes. It is the same narrative we use when we talk about the *numinous* epiphany of an archetype that takes control of the ego, or about someone possessed by the shadow or the anima, with the sole exception that the external causation was replaced by internal determination and the gods were renamed unconscious contents, archetypes or complexes. Not much new under the sun, so it seems. If we have a closer look at Jung's writings, however, and put aside the culturally biased opinions of the Swiss physician, we find that the theory of the complexes and the psychology of the archetypes offer an original and extraordinary contribution to a more contemporary understanding of passions and emotions. They not only help to differentiate the varieties of affect and to integrate the diverse aspects that build up an emotion (cognitions, judgments, values, motives, appetites, behaviors, ends), but they also bring us into a closer relationship with the mysteries and paradoxes of the passions.

At odds with the passages we quoted above, Jung defines feeling as a rational function, as "a process that takes place between the ego and a given content, a process, moreover, that imparts to the content a definite value in the sense of acceptance or rejection," while affect is the result of the increase of the intensity of feeling "accompanied by marked physical innervations" (Jung 1921/1971, paras. 724–25). This seemingly paradoxical statement, which lays a rational function (feeling) in the center of an irrational phenomenon (affect), is probably one of Jung's most enriching intuitions. Like Pascal's *logique du coeur,* or Max Scheler's formalism of ethical values, Jung's feeling function unveils the reason behind the unreasonable and provides the code to puzzle out the hidden language of passions as integrated forms of cognition, judgment, feelings, and purposeful action with which we assess, value and react to the inner and the outer world. The emotional charge of the feeling toned complexes has a logic of its own, which provides meaning and color to what is most intrinsically human. The hypothesis of the unconscious as multiple consciousnesses, of the existence of multiple luminosities and quasi-conscious unconscious contents, is, in addition, a powerful idea for the differentiation of emotions. The affect-laden representations, the images attached to our passions, reveal the different styles of consciousness and the purpose of the diverse tendencies that live within us and need expression.

Most present thinkers and researchers in the area of affectivity consider that emotions are important mechanisms of adaptation. Antonio Damasio signals, for example, that "emotions are curious adaptations that are part and parcel of the machinery with which organisms regulate survival" (Damasio 1999, 54). Textbooks of psychology define emotions as coherent schemas of organization or systems of synchronization that coordinate diverse aspects of organic and psychic functioning, which permit adaptive reactions to the environment. Common experience, however, shows us that most passions can be tremendously destructive and inadequate for adaptation. Examples abound: the uncontrolled rage that makes us lose a job; a loss of temper that makes us miss the target in a process of negotiation; a crazy erotic passion that tears down our marriage and ruins our political career; an envy that inhibits our attainments and deviates energy towards the destruction of others. Take the case of Othello whose jealousy leads him to the assassination of his highest value and love, Desdemona, and when he become aware of what he had done commits suicide. Or again, the life of Harpagón in the play *L'Avare* of Molière, whose miserly anxiety about losing his treasure made him live a miserable and isolated life, fearful even of his own children. Take the mythical and literary image of passionate and impossible love, born within prohibitions and obstacles, consumed by transgressions that end up in tragedy and death. Can we say that the passion of resentment guiding someone to an act of vengeance, which finally lands the person in jail, serves the function of adaptation or is "part of the bio-regulatory devices with which we come equipped to survive" (Damasio 1999, 53)? Is it really rational?

Contemporary authors criticize the Jamesian theory of emotions as feelings or sensations of physiological processes and understand the emotions as engagements with the world, as intelligent and complex processes that involve concepts and appraisals. They usually consider affects as reactions to the world, as acts of consciousness in which one evaluates persons, relationships, situations, things. Their rationality is one of adaptation, one that maximizes our well being. The judgment of the emotions takes into account the ambience, the social situation, and the people involved. The main limitation of these theories of affect that emphasize the intentionality and rationality of emotions and their function for adaptation is that they consider only the logic and purpose of emotions in relation to external objects and the external world. Faced with complex and destructive passions, however, their explanations fall short. They can only consider positive affects that serve the principle of life or support the system of consciousness. But, as Denis de Rougemont (1940) has very clearly illustrated in his studies of love in Western world, passion and death are closely interconnected. In order to clarify the many definitions and concepts of appetites, drives, feelings, and emotions, some researchers have established scales or levels of psychological organization of the affective life, from very simple proto-emotions or sensations of the internal status of the organism to third level emotions that become very complex symbolic processes. It is at this higher, complex level that we can properly talk about passions. It is in this stage of complexity, however, where we also find that passions are rarely connected with the functions of survival and adaptation of the organism. On the contrary, many times they work against it. Due to his unrequited love for Lotte, Werther kills himself. The cultural impact of Goethe's novel, *The Sorrows of Young Werther*, was so strong that it produced mimicry, an effect called *Werther-Fever,* suicides in some two thousand readers. The strange appeal of passion and death worried the German authorities and society so much that some writers thought it necessary to write an alternative novel with a more constructive and happy end. Sexuality serves the function of reproduction and preservation of the specie, but the impossible platonic love and courtly love do not. The essence of Arabic and Provencal eroticism is that unsatisfied love can only be expressed in the aspiration of death. The emotion of *orgé*, which for the Greeks was the essence of the heroic temperament, can lead to speedy death in battle. The classical hero, in fact, preferred a short and intense life in war to a balanced and long existence surrounded by a loving family of wife, children, and grandchildren. In addition, the common definition of passion as the dominance of one emotion over the whole personality tends to make us so one-sided that we lose the necessary flexibility for an efficient arrangement in social life. We have been witnesses of cases of extreme greed that not only freezes the love life of the person but even turns against the economic success of the businessman because it induces him to commit acts of corruption that bring about his downfall. If passions can be so negative and do not necessarily serve the function of adaptation, why after so many centuries of criticism against them have they been preserved by the process of evolution? Does not the main principle of Darwinian evolutionism establish that only those behaviors that contribute to the survival of the species will be preserved? If most passions cannot be understood in relation to the outside world, we should look at them from another angle and examine their purpose and meaning in relation to the soul. Jungian psychology's proposition of the existence of an inner world, a universe of archetypes as real and powerful as the external world, becomes an important contribution and an invitation to read the language of passions from another and more enriching perspective. If passions are forms of engagement, rational appraisal, and judgments of the world, they are, most of all, cognitions and valuations of the state of the soul, interactions with the internal psychic world through figures and situations of the outer world.

I have a very intelligent female friend who never finished university, married young, and in spite of her curiosity and restlessness dedicated most of her life to the well-being of her husband and children and the cultivation of conventional social relationships. Attracted by wit and eloquence and the scent of cosmopolitan intellectual circles, she nevertheless had to settle for a rather superficial and common life. She was in analysis for decades and never found remedy for her distress. At 42, she became caught up in a blind and passionate erotic relationship. One night at a cocktail party, she met an attractive young man ten years younger than herself and fell madly in love with him. She did not have to talk to him for a long time; she did not need to know more about him. She just felt a compelling urge to be with him. After this meeting, she started to have secret meetings with him, and after a few weeks she decided to run away with him, to escape and leave her family, and so she ended her twenty years of marriage. She had to go through hell to endure the conflict and gather the energy to come to her decision, but then one day she wrote a farewell letter to her husband and children revealing her secret and left. In addition to the pain and destruction to her family, the event became a scandal in the upper class social circles of Caracas and gave rise to all kinds of gossip. The passion, however, did not last long, and after a month or so, the magic gone, she was compelled to return and face her normal and profane reality again.

This story, so important and meaningful for my friend, is in fact quite a common event in the lives of many people. Similar experiences are reflected in myth and have been the inspiration of numerous novels and films. Such events often leave behind a trail of hurt feelings, mistrust, dismembered families, economical stress, even tragedy. Judged in terms of its effects in outer life, passion seems to be not too intelligent, in fact more destructive than constructive. If we follow, however, the classical Christian writers and understand the *perturbatio animi* as alterations or affections of the soul, that is, as autonomous movements and transformations of the psyche, we can read the passions as rituals and dances of the unconscious deities and personalities, as symbolic expressions of the process of individuation. This approach does not contradict the interpretation of emotion as goal-oriented behavior with formal and particular objectives. Instead of focusing our attention on the external objects and explaining the affects in terms of the situations that stimulated them or the persons to whom they are concretely directed, we must attend to their symbolic meaning and look for the internal objects, the partial personalities of the unconscious. This is not the old and typical excess of psychologization, which sees the entire world as a simple projection of internal needs or as exteriorizations of inward events. Emotions are not restricted to a realm inside of us. They are not just a private matter. They enter into the outer space, into the social atmosphere, and they create a field of interaction between the inner and the outer where meaning is derived from both. They are multidimensional judgments that includes the object as well as the subject, a state of consciousness through which we reconstitute the world according to our psychic state.

Far from original, my friend's experience follows an archetypal pattern well depicted in novels, movies, and myths. The sudden attraction, the taboo, the obstacles, the transgression, the secret encounters, the adversity, all belongs to this pattern. The object of passion, in this case the attractive young man, is indispensable, but he is basically a vehicle, the necessary instrument for the constellation of the whole pattern as the expression of soul. Once the infatuation was gone, my friend could not understand how it was possible that she had lost her head for this man. The occasion is determined by the inner needs, by the movements of the unconscious in their confluence with the social present. Following the title of Bryan Ferry´s song, used as the English title for the Chinese film of 2002 directed by Wong Kar-wai, my friend was "In the Mood for Love." A few months later, she was no more in that mood. Each part of the pattern is a psychic metaphor, an image that depicts the condition and intention of soul. The sudden attraction: the activation and projection of the animus. The prohibitions and obstacles: the inertia and habits that kept her in her common life and made it impossible for her to change. The transgression: the breaking of the persona, the jump into another level of existence. The destructive consequences: the havoc needed to redefine a life more faithful to her archetypal nature—all of this is part of the selfsame story told again and again across time and cultures. Very often, the concrete performance of the archetypal pattern in real life produces important insights and ignites a process of inner transformation. Sometimes it does not. After a period of intense inner discovery, the person feels fear of the abrupt changes he notices in him, and he performs what Jung called "the regressive restoration of the Persona" (Jung 1916/1953). The display of the pattern, however, leaves the scars of the process of individuation. In a sense, passions are calls for adjustments in the psyche. My friend finally started her much desired career as a writer. She published a book of erotic poems.

Contrary to Jean-Paul Sartre's idea that emotions are strategies we use to elude responsibility and avoid facing ourselves (Sartre 1999), we consider the passions the most coherent system for expressing our existential condition. Their language is, however, symbolic. In this sense, we can see envy as an alarm that recalls something missing in us, as a signal pointing out our inability to develop certain aspects of our personality, a failure of which the envied person becomes the evidence. It is not enough to compare ourselves with others or to perceive in someone something we wish but are unable to get. For a desire to become envy, the qualities or possessions of others must become symbols of our own incapacity and inferiority. That is the reason why the goal of rancorous envy is much more the destruction of the creative capacity of the other than the acquisition of his excellence and virtue. If we attend the call, however, we can work out the envy and transform it in emulation or competition, or it can help us at least to accept and understand the nature of our deficits and failures. It would be misleading to analyze the emotion just in terms of external objects, the money or the successful person. According to Murray Stein, envy is a "longing for the Self" (Stein 1996, 201), a "desire for direct access to the fountainhead of value" (200), which belongs "to the wellspring of creative energy" (203). This approach opens the door for a more positive valuation of the emotions. It allows us to see the teleology of passions, their hidden meaning and goal. As Murray Steins states: "In a Jungian theory of envy, we would think of it as a psychic symptom rather than as an expression of primary destructiveness . . . a signal of something going wrong, but it grows out of an otherwise benign hunger for full selfhood" (Stein 1996, 204).

In order to surpass the deceptive claim for basic emotions, Richard Shweder proposes that "emotion terms are names for particular interpretative schemes (e.g., "remorse", "guilt", "anger", "shame") of a particular story-like, script-like, or narrative kind" that people "make use of to give meaning and shape to their" experience (Shweder 1994, 32). Jungian psychoanalysis and the psychology of the archetypes deepen this metaphor by proposing myth-making as the primary activity of the psyche. The basic language of the archetypal patterns that mold our life is myth, stories of passionate gods and heroes that reveal the dominants of human experience. It is the *mundus imaginalis* as described by Henry Corbin, "a distinct field of imaginal realities" (Hillman 1988, 3), that provides values and form for the core scripts of the feeling toned complexes. Affects can be differentiated and reveal their meaning through the images of the story told. James Hillman, the Jungian analyst who has written most explicitly about emotions, says that "a mood descends, a passion strikes, an urge rises up," but the main question we have to ask about each emotional condition is: "what does the emotion want? What are its features, its characteristics? . . . How does it move through my body, what is its dance?" (Hillman 1992, xi). This is the work of analysis. If passions are irreducible movements of soul in synchrony with the outside world and thus strategies of the psyche, we have to understand their veiled intentions and comprehend their plan. It does not matter if they seem inappropriate, if they are alien to our will and ego. As psychic rituals, they disclose our archetypal nature, the divine images behind our apparent irrational behaviors, the rhythm of our individuation process.

REFERENCES

Augustine. 2003. *The city of God.* Trans. Henry Bettenson. Penguin Classics.
Damasio, Antonio. 1999. *The feeling of what happens.* San Diego: Harcourt.
Helvétius, Claude-Adrian. Del Espíritu. http://thales.cica.es/rd/Recursos/rd99/ed99-0257-01/bhelvet.html
Hillman, James. 1990. *Archetypal psychology: A brief account.* Dallas: Spring Publications, Inc.
———. 1992. *Emotion: A comprehensive phenomenology of theories and their meanings for therapy.* Evanston: Northwestern University Press.

324 *Axel Capriles*

Jung, C.G. 1911-12/1970. *Symbols of transformation.* CW 5.
———. 1916/1953. The relations between the ego and the unconscious. In CW 7.
———. 1921/1971. *Psychological types.* CW 6.
———. 1951/1968. *Aion.* CW 9i.
———. 1952/1969. Synchronicity: An acausal connecting principle. In CW 8.
Kant, Immanuel. 2006. *Anthropology from a pragmatic point of view.* Trans. and ed. Robert B. Louden. Cambridge: Cambridge University Press.
Kerényi, C. 1961. *The Gods of the Greeks.* London: Thames and Hudson.
López-Pedraza, Rafael. 2008. *Sobre emociones.* Caracas: Festina Lente.
Neumann, Erich. 1973. *The origins and history of consciousness.* Princeton: Princeton University Press.
Rougemont, Denis de. 1940. *Love in the western world.* New York: Harcout, Brace & Co.
Sánchez, Luis Rafael. 1989. *La importancia de llamarse Daniel Santos.* Hanover: Ediciones Norte.
Sartre, Jean-Paul. 1999. *Bosquejo de una teoría de las emociones.* Madrid: Alianza Editorial.
Shweder, Richard A. 1994. "You're not sick, you're just in love": Emotion as an interpretative system. In *The nature of emotion,* ed. Paul Ekman and Richard J. Davidson, 32–44. Oxford: Oxford University Press.
Stein, Murray. 1996. *Practicing wholeness.* New York: Continuum.
Solomon, Robert. 1993. *The passions: Emotion and the meaning of life.* Indianapolis: Hackett.

AXEL CAPRILES, Ph.D., is associate professor at the Catholic University, Caracas, Venezuela, where he founded the chair of Psychological Economics. He is director of the C.G. Jung Foundation of Caracas and past President of the Venezuelan Society of Jungian Analysts (SVAJ). He is a columnist of the main Venezuela newspaper, *El Universal.*

30

THE ETHICAL ATTITUDE IN ANALYTICAL PRACTICE

Hester McFarland Solomon

The provision for ongoing supervision during training as well as postqualification helps to ensure reliable access to ethical thinking in analytic practice, and is, in itself, an ethical act at the core of the analytic attitude. I am advocating that provision for regular supervision is a cornerstone of a professional analytic attitude. This position is based on theoretical and practical reasoning and is derived alike from developmental and archetypal perspectives.

Crucial to my argument is the view that the analytic attitude is in essence an ethical attitude, and that the achievement of the ethical attitude is tantamount to the achievement of a developmental position with archetypal sources. This developmental position reaches beyond what Klein and Bion had in mind when they referred to the paranoid-schizoid and depressive positions as stages in the developmental process. The ethical attitude, like the paranoid-schizoid and depressive positions, is not a once-and-for-all achievement, but rather is part of an internal human dynamic struggle that is experienced alongside and in relation to more primitive and sometimes more dangerous states of mind. Hence, just like the depressive position, the achievement of an ethical attitude requires mental effort, in particular, conscious effort, to sustain. It has its roots in archetypal sources and is not simply a matter of a set of rules that can be forgotten as long as ethical proscriptions are not contravened. This perspective suggests the importance of an ongoing supervisory relationship in the practitioner's clinical work as a place where that conscious effort is shared, explored, and reinforced.

The view that I set out in this chapter incorporates the role, developmentally and archetypally, of a "third space," or triangulation, and argues that it is essential to the hygiene of the analytic attitude and analytic practice, as it is essential for personal growth and development. The archetypal nature of the triangular relationship—represented here by the triad practitioner/ supervisor/patient—underpins the developmental achievement of the mental capacity for ethical thinking and behavior that is crucial professionally, as it is personally.

Achieving an Ethical Attitude: A Developmental Model with Archetypal Sources

It is a truism that it is not possible to be ethical in a vacuum. The ethical function is a relational function involving the assessment of subjective and intersubjective states. Throughout his many writings, Jung stressed the centrality of moral and ethical values in analytic treatment. He pointed out (1936/1964) that such values are ubiquitous and hence have a collective, archetypal foundation, while at the same time they are experienced most vividly at the personal level. John Beebe, in his important work, *Integrity in Depth*, also emphasizes the teleological aspects of integrity: the ethical stance lies at the source of wholeness and is the organizing principle of a human life (Beebe 1992, 75). But how does a capacity for ethical thinking and ethical action arise? From whence comes such a capacity, and what are the grounds for it to unfold from an archetypal potential through a developmental process?

In order to begin to address such fundamental questions, it is necessary to bear in mind the principles of symmetry and asymmetry that derive from our primordial genetic make-up, including the notion of endogenous and exogenous libido as the underlying bedrock matrix. This lay at the core of Jung's lifelong work, and it was one of the important areas in which he differed from Freud. Jung's view of psychic energy ("libido") was wider than Freud's and constituted an aspect of his schema of the psychic opposites: on the one hand, the impulse towards primordial fusional states, especially in relation to the Great Mother archetype; on the other hand, the capacity to leave the primary matrix and find sources of libidinal expression outside of it, in a third space, or third position. This capacity was based on the work of the rule of abstinence (incest taboo), which respects the differences between the generations and the sexes. If early provision of a good enough nurturing environment has been well established, the psyche is strong enough to undertake the task of finding its libidinal gratifications in exogenous situations. On this depends the health of the gene pool, family hygiene, and psychic hygiene. This is the source of the rule of abstinence in analytic work and, eventually the hygiene of our analytic institutions. What are the components of this early provision and its sources in our later professional lives?

In thinking in developmental terms about the conditions that foster an ethical capacity, I have suggested that these lie in the infant's or child's earliest experiences of devotion and reflection by the parental couple, who maintain an ethical attitude in relation to their infant or child. It is this parental attitude that is eventually internalized by the child and later activated as the self and ego develop in dynamic relation. This results in the formation of internal parents in the psyche (Solomon, 2000). The first stirrings of a nascent ethical capacity occur as the infant experiences being the recipient of the nontalionic responses of the parental couple in face of his or her various states of distress, including anxiety, depression, rage, and dread. Under the right conditions, the infant's experience of the parent's nontalionic responses is eventually internalized and identified with and becomes the basis for gratitude. The idea of the ordinarily devoted parent, mother or father, represents a deeply ethical mode in their devotion and thoughtfulness toward another, their infant, overcoming their talionic impulses, narcissistic needs, and frustrated rages, their shadow projections, and resisting by and large the impulse to skew their infant's development through requiring undue acquiescence.

The availability of the two complementary principles, thinking and devotion, evokes a notion that appears in various guises in psychoanalytic and Jungian analytic literature, that of the creative potential of the third, whether a third person, a third position, or a third dimension. The activation of this archetypal potential for eventual ethical behavior will be introduced through a series of good enough situations offered by caregivers capable of acts of thoughtful devotedness and of empathic thinking about their infant. This has a clear parallel with what happens in the consulting room, where the analyst's willingness to sacrifice narcissistic needs through the sustained activity of thoughtful devotedness to the patient, which we call the analytic attitude, protects the patient's development according to the needs of the self.

FROM DYAD TO TRIAD: THE EVENTUAL ACHIEVEMENT OF TRIANGULATION BEYOND THE DEPRESSIVE POSITION

I am conjecturing that the internalization of and identification with the agapaic function of the parental figures in their empathic holding as well as their thinking can trigger or catalyze a nascent ethical capacity in a young mind. The first steps include those primitive acts of discriminating good and bad that constitute the foundations of splitting and projection, which Samuels (1989, 199) calls original morality: the expulsion from the self of what is unwanted and felt to be bad into the other. This is a two-dimensional internal world, in which primitive psychic acts discriminate good from bad experience and split the bad from the psyche by projection into the caregivers—a first, primordial or prototypical moral discernment prior to the state where there is sufficient ego strength for anything resembling mature moral or ethical reflection to arise. This constitutes the condition for the creation of the personal shadow, which eventually will require a further ethical action of reintegration when the person has achieved an internal position of moral and ethical capacity.

To truly relate to another in their substantive subjectivity represents a transcendence of narcissistic ways of relating in which the other is appropriated for use in the internal world, denying the other's subjective reality. To live with the implications of this capacity to recognize and relate to the truth of the other is a step in psychic development beyond the depressive position. The depressive position is usually considered to contain acts of reparation based on guilt and the fear that the object may have been damaged and therefore may be unable to go on caring for the self (Hinshelwood 1989). As such, acts of reparation remain contingent on preserving the other for the benefit of the self. The ethical attitude envisaged here goes beyond this contingency and suggests a noncontingent realm of ethical behavior.

This represents a two-stage, dyad-to-triad process that reflects the two-stage developmental process in the infant, which is based on extensive neurophysiological evidence, in particular in the work of psychoneurobiologist Allan Schore (Schore 1994) and more recently elaborated by Jungian analyst Margaret Wilkinson (Wilkinson 2006). In this process, the neural development of the infant's brain must be matched by a parallel nurturing provision such that at first infant and mother are closely attuned (a "me/me" relationship) and later followed by complementary and compensatory discriminations (a "self/other" relationship), leading to the capacity for a "theory of mind" (Fonagy 1989). These researches show that the development *post partum* of the neural circuitry and structures of the infant's brain, which regulate the development of the higher human capacities (cognitive and socioaffective), is highly dependent on the quality of the early interactions between infant and caregiver. As the infant instinctively seeks to participate in activating the type, number, and timing of mutual exchanges, the infant, a proactive partner, is participating directly in the development of its own neural circuitry, in its own neural growth. These neural networks underpin the achievement of the higher psychological capacities, including that of ethical thinking and behavior. This suggests that there are grounds for considering that the ethical capacity is, at least in part, innate, derived from the earliest, instinctually based exchanges with its primary caregiver, and, at least in part, influenced by environmental factors. In other words, archetypal and developmental elements coexist and interact.

In this developmental framework, there evolves a gradual demarcation between self and other. This is the beginning of the capacity for triangulation. As philosopher and psychoanalyst Marcia Cavell has described: "the child needs not just one but two other persons, one of whom, at least in theory, might be only the child's idea of a third . . . the child must move from interacting with his mother to grasping the idea that both his perspective on the world and hers are *perspectives*; that there is a possible third point of view, more inclusive than theirs, from which both his mother's and his own can be seen and from which the interaction between them can be understood" (Cavell 1998, 459–60). Jungians would amplify this view by addressing the difficult but necessary work of withdrawing projections of a negative character, called shadow projections, through to a gradual capacity to view the self along with the other as separate but interrelated subjectivities with multivariate motivations, including shadow motivations. The withdrawal of shadow projections, predicated on the realization that the other is truly other and not assumed to be a function or aspect of the self, underpins and presupposes the ethical attitude. As such, it is a developmental achievement that derives from an innate potential, activated at birth and fostered by the continuous "good enough" experience of living in an ethical environment. These are acts *contra naturam*, foregoing insistence on the self's limited perspectives in order to encompass a wider view, including the recognition of that which is not ethical within the self. In Jungian terms, that recognition represents the integration of the shadow, a step toward incremental advances in the self's movement towards greater states of integration and wholeness. This is the individuation process, and it is predicated on a prospective view of the self in which the self's capacity for change, growth, and development are understood and experienced as being suffused with a sense of purpose and meaning.

TRIANGULATION: THE ARCHETYPAL THIRD

In 1916, Jung wrote two landmark works that can appear to be diametrically opposite in content and form: *Seven Sermons to the Dead* and "The Transcendent Function." The former was privately published and circulated at the time, while the latter was put away in a drawer and not published until 1958, only a few years before Jung's death in 1961. Both reflect, in different ways, the immediacy of Jung's distressing and threatening psychic experiences that arose following the difficult period of his differences with Freud and their subsequent painful and unsettling split. If the tone of the *Seven Sermons* was that of a quasi-Gnostic religious poem of his vivid psychic experiences at the time resulting from his "confrontation with the unconscious" (Jung 1961, 194ff.), that of "The Transcendent Function" was of a measured, scientific contribution to analytic theory building. Jung compared the latter to a "mathematical formula" (*1916/1969*, para. 131), and it could be interpreted as a dispassionate exteriorisation of his highly emotive internal state at the time, a kind of self supervision. In "The Transcendent Function," Jung set out an archetypal structural schema of triangulation in which he demonstrated that psychic change occurs through the emergence of a third position out of a conflictual internal or external situation. The characteristics of this third position cannot be predicted solely by those of the original dyad.

Whether or not he consciously drew on its philosophical origins, Jung's notion of the transcendent function is based on the idea of the dialectical and deep structural nature of all change in the living world expounded by Hegel in his great work, *The Phenomenology of the Spirit*. Hegel posited a tripartite schema as fundamental to all change, including psychic change, a situation in which an original oppositional pair, a dyad, which he called thesis and antithesis, struggle together until, under the right conditions, a third position, a synthesis, emerges. This third position heralds the transformation of the oppositional elements of the dyad into a position with new properties that could not have been known about before their encounter, the *tertium quid non datur* in Jung's terms. Hegel called this ubiquitous struggle dialectical, because it demonstrated how transformations in the natural world happen through the emergence from an oppositional struggle that can be understood to have symbolic meaning and purposefulness. This was a deep structural patterning of dynamic change that was archetypal by nature and developmental as a dynamic movement in time.

This archetypal schema can also be thought of as the basis of the tripartite Oedipal situation, where transformation from out of a primordial pair, mother and child, can be achieved through the third position afforded by the paternal function, whether this be a real father or a capacity of mind in the mother or in the child, or both. It is in this sense that we might speak of the emergence of the mind of the child, the child's identity, as separate from that of the mother, through the provision of a third perspective. For Jung, this would be thought of as the emergence of the self, through successive states of transformation and individuation via the transcendent function. In the context of the function of supervision, we could say that it is through the provision of the supervisory third that both patient and analyst are helped to emerge from out of the *massa confusa* of the analytic dyad. Both change as a result as individuation progresses.

In psychoanalytic theory, the importance of the negotiation of the Oedipal threesome, that archetypal triad *par excellence*, constitutes much of the psychoanalytic understanding of developmental achievement. Psychoanalyst Ron Britton evokes the notion of internal triangulation, which requires the toleration of an internal version of the Oedipal situation in order to resolve the lived Oedipal situation in the family. He describes "triangular psychic space" as "a *third* position in mental space . . . from which the *subjective self* can be observed having a relationship with an idea" (Britton 1998, 13). He concludes that "in all analyses the basic Oedipus situation exists whenever the analyst exercises his or her mind independently of the inter-subjective relationship of patient and analyst" (Britton 1998, 44). Evoking Jung's insistence on the importance of the passage from endogenous to exogenous libidinal experience, we can say that it is the working through of the Oedipal triangle in the family on which is predicated the passage from the endogenous to the exogenous position, crucial to the health, psychically and physically, of the individual, the family, the group, and the gene pool.

In developing Britton's idea of the Oedipal triangle as present through the internal events and relationships that occur in the analyst's mind, as links to an internal object or to psychoanalytic theory, I wish to reiterate that the external manifestation and facilitation of this internal triangular state is quintessentially present in the supervisory or consultative relationship. Here, two people, the analyst and the supervisor, are linked in relation to a third, the patient. Rose summarizes philosopher and psychoanalyst Marcia Cavell's notion of the third succinctly: "in order to know our own minds, we require an interaction with another mind in relation to what would be termed objective reality" (Rose 2000, 454). I hold that the provision of supervision, including the internal supervision that happens when the analyst thinks about aspects of the patient and the analytic relationship, is an important instance of "progressive triangulation" (Cavell 1998, 461). These are mental acts that counterbalance the instinctual longing for fusional states, where the self is lost in a hall of mirrors with another, and where projection, introjection, and projective identification reign supreme and are essential as ways of imaginatively identifying with the other. The provision of internal and external supervisory space allows for an ongoing interaction with another mind in relation to a third, the patient, who can be thought about because differentiated from the dyadic relating of the patient-analyst couple.

TRIANGULAR SPACE AND SUPERVISION IN ANALYTIC PRACTICE

The provision and function of supervision of analytic and psychotherapeutic work with individuals, children, couples, or families, creates a needed triangular space essential to the care and maintenance, the ongoing hygiene, of the dyadic relationships. I use the term "hygiene" in the sense that, through its provision, supervision keeps constantly activated the awareness of the analytic attitude, including its ethical component, in and through the presence of a third person (the supervisor), or a third position (the supervisory space), and that it acts as an aid in the restoration of the analytic and ethical attitudes when at times they might be lost in the maelstrom of clinical practice. Supervision is itself the representation of that attitude through the provision of a third area of reflection. The treatment, at profound levels, of the psyche in distress always involves a regressive and/or narcissistic pull back into endogenous, part object relating, those primitive either/or, dichotomous states of mind that are dominated by the various projective and identificatory processes that have to do with psychic survival. The provision of exogenous triangular space through internal or external supervision, or both, is essential to the maintenance of the analytic attitude in the face of the multitudinous forces and pressures at work within the analytic situation, arising from the conscious and unconscious dynamics within and between patient and analyst alike.

To the extent that this triangular space created by supervision is necessary to the hygiene of the analytic couple (just as the paternal, reflective principle is essential to the hygiene of the mother-infant dyad, providing the space for psychological growth to occur), supervision has an ethical as well as a clinical and didactic role to play in all analytic and therapeutic work, notwithstanding the years of experience of the practitioner. Whether supervision is provided in the same way as during training, with weekly meetings in a one-to-one situation with a senior practitioner, or in consultations with a senior practitioner at agreed intervals, or whether peer supervision in small groups is selected as the means of providing the triangular space, depends on the needs and inclination of the clinician.

In the case of the analysis and supervision of training candidates, there are particular ongoing boundary issues and other pressures inherent in the training situation that do not usually pertain in work with nontraining patients, such as the need to see a patient under regular supervision at a certain intensity over a certain minimum amount of time, determined by the training program. This will in turn foster in candidates their own ethical attitude, as they internalize the expectation that all analytic work, including the work of their own analysts and supervisors, is in turn supervised. The trainee will then know from the very outset of training that there is always a third space created in which he or she as a patient or as a supervisee will be thought about by another supervisor-practitioner pair.

Fostering the ethical-supervisory expectation is likely to engender a generationally based commitment to the analytic attitude within a training institution, as the tradition of good clinical practice is passed down across the analytic and therapeutic training generations. There is a longstanding assumption that the success of the candidate's progress through training is assessed according to whether he or she is judged to be ready to "work independently." Of course, the assessment of the trainee's capacity for independent judgment and a sense of viable autonomy is an important, indeed crucial, factor in the process of assessing whether someone is ready to qualify to practice as an analyst. I am arguing here that, included in this assessment should be a judgment about whether the candidate is aware of the need for and usefulness of the provision of a triangular space in which to discuss ongoing clinical practice, in order best to ensure against the risks inherent in working in such intimate and depth psychological ways, including the dangers of mutual identificatory states or the abuse of power.

My contention is that the full acceptance that the practitioner will have ongoing supervision or consultation of their clinical practice is a sign of maturation, both on the part of the practitioner as well as that of the training institution, as they assess their own and others' clinical competence. This is part of the assessment process that results in the authorisation to practice as members of the training institution. There is the added dimension that some members go on to become training analysts, supervisors, and clinical and theoretical seminar leaders, entrusted with the responsibility for training future generations of analysts. The expectation in the trainee of ongoing supervisory and consultative provision is modelled by the trainers, fostering the candidate's respect for and understanding of the conditions that create and sustain the analytic and ethical attitude. This includes attention to boundary issues that can arise within and through the intensity of the intersubjective dynamics within the analytic and therapeutic relationship. Gabbard and Lester (1995) provide a detailed discussion of the boundary issues in analytic practice. These intersubjective dynamics are inevitably released by the interpenetrative, projective, introjective and identificatory exchanges within the transference and countertransference.

The recommendation that members of analytic training institutions seek to establish an ongoing supervisory ethos to discuss their work, even if the provision is not systematically maintained, and that all training analysts and supervisors of the institutions have regular consultations regarding their training cases (including patients, supervisees, or training patients) represents a further development of those ubiquitous triads created by the training situation (the trainee-training analyst-supervisor; the trainee-training patient-supervisor; and the trainee-supervisor-Training Committee). The expectation of providing a space for reflection with another would benefit all parties concerned and at the same time increase clinical awareness. Without this benefit, we run the risk of identifying with narcissistic and other pathological processes and pressures, inevitable in analytic practice, as we are liable to treat those aspects in our patients that correspond and resonate with our own internal issues and personal histories. Hence I emphasize the importance of clinical "hygiene," of creating the third space of supervision that can help us to maintain our connection to genuine object relating and to staying alert to the pitfalls of intense dyadic relating.

REFERENCES

Beebe, John. 1992. *Integrity in depth*. College Station: Texas A & M University Press.

Britton, Ronald. 1998. *Belief and imagination: Explorations in psychoanalysis*. London: Routledge.

Cavell, Marcia. 1998. Triangulation, one's own mind and objectivity. *International Journal of Psychoanalysis* 79: 449–68.

Fonagy, Peter. 1989. On tolerating mental states: Theory of mind in borderline personality. *Bulletin of the Anna Freud Centre* 12: 91–115.

Gabbard, Glen and Eva Lester. 1995. *Boundaries and boundary violations in psychoanalysis*. New York: Basic Books.

Hegel, G. W. F. 1807/1977. *The phenomenology of spirit*. Oxford: Oxford University Press.

Hinshelwood, R. D. 1989. *A dictionary of Kleinian thought*. London: Free Association Books.

Jung, C.G. 1916/1961. Seven sermons to the dead. In *Memories, dreams, reflections*, 378–90. New York: Vintage Books.

———. 1916/1969. The transcendent function. In CW 8.

———. 1936/1964. Wotan. In CW 10.

———. 1961. *Memories, dreams, reflections*. New York: Vintage Books.

Rose, Gillian. 2000. Symbols and their function in managing the anxiety of change: An intersubjective approach. *International Journal of Psychoanalysis* 81:453–70.

Samuels, Andrew. 1989. *The plural psyche*. London: Routledge.

Schore, Alan. 1994. *Affect regulation and the origins of the self: The neurobiology of emotional development*. Hillsdale, NJ: Erlbaum.

Solomon, Hester McFarland. 2000. The ethical self. In *Jungian thought in the m o d e r n world*, eds. Elphis Christopher and Hester McFarland Solomon, 191–216. London: Free Association Books.

———. 2007. *The self in transformation*. London: Karnac Books.

Wilkinson, Margaret. 2006. *Coming into mind: The mind-brain relationship: A Jungian clinical perspective*. East Sussex: Routledge.

HESTER MCFARLAND SOLOMON is a training analyst and supervisor for the Jungian Analytic Section of the British Association of Psychotherapists, and has served as past Chair of the BAP's Council, its Jungian Analytic Training Committee, and Ethics Committee, and is a Fellow of the Association. She is currently President of the International Association for Analytical Psychology. She has published widely and is author and co-editor of several books.

31

RELIGION AND JUNGIAN PSYCHOANALYSIS

John Dourley

JUNG ON RELIGION

Jung's claim that he had discovered the "psychic origin of religious phenomena" allows of no exceptions (Jung 1968, 9). All religious experience and the religions such experience generates are expressions of this common provenance. What then is this origin? It is not an objective entity, personal or transpersonal. Rather, for Jung, the impact of the self and its archetypal impetus on consciousness is the operative psychodynamic of the common and universal origin of all religious experience and so of the religions such experience creates. This psychodynamic becomes the basis of Jung's "authentic religious function in the unconscious" (Jung 1969, 6). A sustained conscious engagement with the self in its major expressions, especially but not only when they attain the power of the numinous, constitutes the primary religious act for Jung and becomes the substance of religious practice itself. The "careful and scrupulous observation" of the manifestation of the self, with a priority given to the dream, is surely at the heart of Jungian analysis (Jung 1969, 7, 8). From Jung's broad perspective, then, every analysis is an ongoing religious event.

This understanding of religion greatly extends its boundaries. It would mean that the individual's nightly dream and the parade of gods, goddesses and their revelations throughout history proceed from the same single source, the archetypal unconscious and its mediator to consciousness, the self. It would also mean that the "careful consideration" of one's dreams as well as other possible manifestations of the unconscious would become the individual's personal revelation and the basis of one's unique and always developing myth (Jung 1969, 8). In this primary sense of religion the canon is never closed. In fact it is reopened with every new page in the individual's dream book. Religion, thus understood, forbids a religionless humanity, or a culture without religious bonding, since the power that grounds the religious impulse in the creation of the divinities and their societies is native to the psyche itself and accessible to anyone who turns to it.

Among the more important consequences of religion thus understood is the often painfully gained but immensely rewarding distance offered the individual from the collective myths into which one has been born through the ongoing discovery of one's own mythic truth most tellingly in the analytic process itself. As the self becomes incarnate in consciousness, it provides the only ultimate ground for the affirmation of one's deepest religious truth in relation to the overlay of mythic burden carried by one's native culture. Such affirmation provides a psychic place to stand in relation, for instance, to the religious, ethnic, political, familial, or any and every archetypal determinant affecting the individual's deeper self-understanding and behavior from the outset. Such a place puts the religious voyager in a position to respond in patterns ranging from a deepened appreciation to a total rejection of the symbol systems informing the culture of origin. Such a critical perspective is peculiarly able to gauge the impact of reigning myths on the emergence or repression of a deeper personal truth unique to its holder and enabling in its holder a more authentic relation to the All.

Cultivating religion in this primordial sense through experience of its universal source is always personal but never without social consequence. For Jung, the unconscious seeks always a more pervasive ingression into both individual and collective consciousness. Collectively, this urgency is recorded in the succession of epochs, periods and religions all in the interest of a more adequate realization of the unconscious in the history it makes through such manifestation. Those who cultivate the natural religiosity of the unconscious are often the bringers of a new mythology which meets the demand of the unconscious to overcome whatever constrictions the reigning myths might impose.

When examined in its details, Jung's myth urges a more inclusive sacralization through the current recovery of the divinity of the feminine, of the earthly and of the demonic largely excluded from Christian and monotheistic realms of the sacred. But Jung's myth also insists that this recovery, at least in the first instance, will result from the individual nurturing of an interiority sensitive to the limitations of currently presiding mythologies and to the current unconscious urgency for a broader, more embracing compassion, truly reflective of the totality of the psyche. Jung's emphasis on the priority of the inner life in the transformation of society and in the resistance to powers which would oppose it lie behind his statement, "Resistance to the organized mass can be effected only by the man who is as well organized in his individuality as the mass itself" (Jung 1964, 278). The citation presses to the question of what such organization in one's individuality would entail.

CONTAINMENT AND TRANSCENDENCE

The personal organization Jung is referring to as informing a contemporary religious attitude would demand nothing less that a radical revisioning of the relationship between the human and the divine or the transcendent. Jung will refer to the fecundity of the unconscious as, "of indefinite extent with no assignable limits" (Jung 1969b, 258). In so doing he calls up images of infinity which would visualize an infinite resource ever seeking a total expression in consciousness which individually, collectively, and historically can never be more than finite. In constructing this paradigm, Jung is effectively containing transcendence within the total psyche understood as the totality of its conscious and unconscious energies. His vision here forces the conclusion that the unconscious transcends consciousness infinitely but that nothing transcends the psyche itself. Transcendence becomes a totally intrapsychic experience. It describes the commerce between consciousness and its creator, the archetypal unconscious. The referent of the variety of revelations, including the three monotheistic variants, is not to one or other God beyond the psyche but to the movements of the archetypal psyche in relation to human consciousness, the only two agencies ultimately involved in the divine/human drama.

The consequences of this revisioning of the relation of humanity to divinity are far reaching. Jung characterizes the evolution of human religious consciousness as reaching a millennial culmination in the growing contemporary recognition that what is is holy (Jung 1969c, 402). In this context he naturally extends divinity to everyone. Jung's summation of the history of religion is one in which the many gods became one, the one God became man and, by extension, "the common man" (Jung 1969, 84). In a more daring passage he extends the hypostatic union, the Christian doctrine that in Christ two natures, divine and human, existed in one person, to everyone—at least as a developmental potential and demand (Jung 1969, 61). Maturation demands the conscious recovery of the individual's divinity. Such is the spiritual democracy Jung's archetypal theory affords.

These insights lie behind his assertion that the unconscious creates the gods as projections of its movements and that the evolution of religious consciousness has now reached the state where these projections be identified as such and withdrawn (Jung 1969, 85). This withdrawal in no way endorses an atheism or skepticism because the gods do not die when recalled to their source. Rather Jung would envision a direct dialogue with them in the safety of the containment of the psyche where they would be less likely to work the lethal communal divisions they do when they escape such containment (Jung 1968b, 23, 24).

These positions, foundational to Jung's thought on the psyche as religious, constitute the specific differentiation of his psychology from others. Obviously they raise the question of the existence of God or a number of them beyond the psyche. Theological jargon, useful here, describes such gods in terms of biblical or supernatural theism. Such theism defends the ontological objectivity of a personal, invariably male, divinity who creates nature and the human psyche, can arbitrarily address and interfere with then from a transcendent position beyond both, and remains indifferent to the outcome of worldly events and to their impact on Him because of an eternally achieved self-sufficiency. The fact that there are three such monotheistic gods all owing their geographical roots to the east end of the Mediterranean seems not to disturb the conflicting faiths of their constituencies even in the face of a suspicion, well founded on Jungian archetypal theory, that they are three variants of the same archetypal power whose main difference lies in their personal names. Martin Buber and Victor White held variants of such supernatural theism and Jung's intense and extended dialogue, especially with White, proved that such religious imagination is simply not compatible with his understanding of the psyche or the divine/human relation it supports (Dourley 1994, 2007). What then is?

THE RELATIVITY OF GOD AND JUNG'S MYTH

The myth endemic to Jung's understanding of the psyche, like all cosmogonic myths, contains a full blown ontology, epistemology, and philosophy of history's unfolding. It describes what is, how what is is known, and the direction history takes consequent to the answer to the problem of being and knowing. Jung's myth in the foregoing sense is most clearly evident in his extended discussion of the "relativity of the God concept" in his treatment of Meister Eckhart's experience (Jung 1971, 241–58) and in the elaboration of its consequences in his late work on Job (Jung 1969c). If the myth supporting Jung's conception of the "relativity of God" were to be put in a religious idiom it would describe the following drama. The creator, unable to unite its own opposites in eternal life, was compelled to create human consciousness as the only extant power in the universe capable of discerning the divine self-contradiction and cooperating with the divine imperative to unite in history the living antinomy that defied resolution in "preexistent" divine life itself.

In these passages Jung argues that the primordial experience of God is wholly from "one's own inner being" and so rules out direct commerce with divinity beyond the psyche (Jung 1971, 243). This cosmogony makes it obvious that human knowledge of the divine is based solely on the experience of the archetypal unconscious. Wholly other gods are wholly alien gods. Unless internalized, they can impede rather than enhance the experience of the divine native to the psyche. The joint inclusion of the ego and the unconscious in an all-encompassing organic unity, namely the psyche, lies behind Jung's description of the divine and the human as "functions" of each other engaged by the nature of the psyche in a dialectical exchange dating from the birth of consciousness itself (Jung 1971, 243).

Jung makes the nature of this dialectic explicit in his accurate account of Eckhart's mysticism based on key citations from Eckhart's sermons. In effect, Jung's appropriation of Eckhart constitutes one of the more impressive descriptions of the dynamics of individuation in his corpus. In a first movement, the projection of archetypal powers into objects beyond the individual—and this would include the divine itself—are withdrawn (Jung 1971, 245–46). In these passages, Jung mounts the most effective psychological counter imaginable to all forms of idolatry unavoidable when the gods escape their psychic origin. But as this energy returns to the psyche, it draws the soul into what Jung terms the "dynamis" or potentially consuming power of the unconscious (Jung 1971, 251, 255). This is a moment fraught with the danger of no return. In it, "God disappears as an object

and dwindles into a subject which is no longer distinguishable from the ego"
(Jung 1971, 255). Such radical regression recovers for the soul "the original state
of identity with God" (Jung 1971, 255). As the soul returns from this moment of
identity with its origin, it carries back to consciousness the energies borne by the
symbols which serve then to revivify life (Jung 1971, 251). Jung implies in these
passages that such cyclical renewal describes the rhythm of the individuating psyche itself and is as natural to it as the diastolic and systolic flow of blood through
the body (Jung 1971, 253). He could hardly be more explicit about the religious
nature of the cycle than when he writes, "*Individuation is the life in God*" (Jung
1976, 719; italics are Jung's).

Obviously a typical analysis would not extend to the point of a total dissolution of the ego in the abyss or nothingness of the Great Mother and so in a
moment of identity with divinity. Yet Jung did not understand Eckhart's experience to be somehow beyond that of the natural movement of the universal psyche. In some degree, it is present to everyone. Eckhart may have been peculiarly
gifted psychologically and so religiously, and Jung implies his experience anticipated the nineteenth century discovery of the unconscious by some six hundred
years (Jung 1968c, 302), but Eckhart's experience remains profoundly human
and so accessible to all. Recent appreciation of apophatic mysticism, the mysticism of immersion in the nothing, is evident in both theological and Jungian quarters (McGinn 1998, 2001; Ashton 2007, 2007b; Marlan 2005). With Jung this
cycle, so intimate to religious maturity, is also the cycle of individuation and so
would be operative in varying degrees in every analysis or sustained contact with
the unconscious when speaking in its native language, the symbolic. Religious
and psychological maturity thus becomes identified without residue.

BRINGING UP FATHER: JUNG ON THE EDUCATION OF GOD IN HISTORY

Jung's equation of religious with psychological maturation in the analytic
process of individuation extends to his understanding of what, in a religious
idiom, is termed "salvation" or "redemption" as such forces enter into and determine the movement of history itself. When he expands on his notion of the "relativity of God" in his work on Job, the intimate reciprocity he establishes between
the divine and the human engages each in the redemption of the other. Job as a
symbol of the ego comes to realize that he stands before a bipolar divinity, the raw
unconscious personified in Yaweh, whose pathologically labile nature was eventually driven to create humanity as the sole theater for its relief (Jung 1969c, 456).
This line of thought develops co-redemptive implications in the divine/human
relationship. Humanity redeems divinity when the conflict of divine opposites are
resolved in human historical consciousness at the insistence and with the assis-
tance of a divinely grounded urgency (Jung 1969c, 461). Reciprocally, divinity
redeems humanity through the synthesis of its opposites in a humanity enriched
by their union.

This process is far from an intellectual or spiritual exercise distanced from the suffering that alone can bring it about. Jung's most imposing image for the mutual redemption of the divine and the human as the base movement of history itself is that of the Christ figure dying in despair between implacable archetypal opposites (Jung 1969c, 408). For Jung the scene constitutes the substance of the answer to Job about the meaning of human suffering. The imagery means that humanity redeems itself and its source by suffering to the death the self-contradiction of that source toward the emergence of a consciousness in which the opposites that killed a conflicted consciousness are united in a third, namely, a more encompassing human compassion. The image of crucifixion between opposites toward a more inclusive sympathy also incorporates what Jung means by the "transcendent function," the only meaning of "transcendence" in his work and one that remains wholly intrapsychic (Jung, 1969d, 73, 87, 90).

It should be carefully noted that Jung not only depicts the death of the Christ figure between opposites as the answer to Job, he describes the image as both "psychological" and "eschatological" (Jung 1969c, 408). It is both because the movement of the psyche the symbol of crucifixion depicts is that of the reciprocal salvation of the divine and the human. The divine comes to "penetrate" the human through the human suffering of divine opposites toward a God made increasingly conscious and so incarnate in the resultant human consciousness (Jung 1976, 734). But the process is equally "eschatological" in that the meaning of history, driven by the psyche, is to bring God to ever greater consciousness in human historical consciousness, a process now understood as the basic telos or direction of history itself.

Again the highlighting of these cosmic motifs in Jung's understanding of the religious dimension of analysis seems to remove it from the realm of the more personal and earthy aspects encountered there. But do they really? Much of Jung's later work resulted from his efforts to bring psychological resolution to the karma he inherited from his father's religion and its questionable influence on his father, himself and his culture (Jung 1965, 215). His early dream of the phallus enthroned in the underground was a vocational dream calling on him to reconnect the Christian mind and culture severed from its life in the underground with its own roots there (Jung 1965, 11–14). In every analysis there is likely to be found such a severance from the balance and totality the unconscious offers and demands. The dreams almost infallibly lead to the unique form of that suffering in the individual. Jung would argue that God suffers in the suffering of truncated life. Such suffering made conscious in the interests of its resolution to whatever degree is the greatest contribution the individual can make to history and to God becoming conscious in it.

The suffering and alleviation of the divine self-contradiction in personal and collective life is at the heart of the experience of the only mystic more cited in Jung's corpus than Meister Eckhart—Jacob Boehm (1575–1624). Boehme's mystical experience has striking affinities with Jung's understanding of the psyche. With Eckhart, he too experienced a moment of identity with the One or the

Urgrund, but as he returned to the conscious world he discovered that the divine opposites were not united in an eternal harmony as the basis of a harmony into which the Spirit would lead created consciousness. Rather, the unity of the divine opposites could only happen in historical human consciousness (Dourley 2004, 60–64). Jung writes of humanity's long term "premonition" of "the idea of the creature that surpasses its creator by a small but decisive factor" (Jung 1965, 220). Probably Jung had in mind the experience of Job, but the premonition would be equally true of Boehme who gave it a more modern expression. With Boehme, the foundational religious presupposition in Jung's psychology attains a poetic but influential expression. Divinity creates consciousness to become conscious in it in the form of the union of its opposites. Boehme's religious experience was influential because it was taken up by Hegel who attempted to give it a more rational expression (Hegel 1825/1990, 119–25). Through Hegel it became foundational to Marx. With both, the underlying thrust is that divinity resolves its issues in humanity in the making of human history. Jung would give to this process a priority in the personal, Hegel and Marx in the collective. The process all three envisage is nowhere more dramatically stated than in the early Marx's claim that history itself moves to the unity of the individual with the species (Marx 1843/1972, 44–45). The individual would then act spontaneously on behalf of the totality. This is a form of microcosmic/macrocosmic mysticism externalized into history by Marx and Hegel, contained in the psyche by Jung.

Today the most challenging opposites that face humanity in its struggle to survive and thrive is the conflict bred between archetypally bonded communities in the form of religious or political faiths or in combinations of both. Jung's genius was apparent in his demonstration that the energies that had informed and bonded specifically religious communities morphed into political communities in the wake of the Enlightenment, the French Revolution, and the democracies (Dourley 2003, 135–36, 143–44). He calls such faith communities the "isms" and relates them to "mass psychosis" and "psychic epidemics" which have kept the body count high well after the religious wars which contributed so much to the reign of reason and so to the Enlightenment itself (Jung 1969e, 175). Jung is not unqualifiedly opposed to the necessary freeing of reason from religious and political constraint, though current reason, thus freed, now looks for its roots in a depth beyond itself which Western religions can no longer provide. On this presupposition, he sponsors a personal morality and religiosity whose primary demand is a consciousness reconnected with its own depth. Such consciousness works toward the liberation of the individual from new forms of collective unconsciousness not the least of which is the deification of uprooted reason. In effect, for many such liberation would mean the loss or moderation of current faith commitments either to reason or to religion toward a more acute critical sensitivity of archetypal agency and manipulation in the creation of mass-minded society most evident in conflicting religious and "rational" political communities.

Paradoxically, it is precisely in its moral demand to lose or lessen collective faith that the value of Jungian psychology can be questioned. In late correspondence with a UNESCO agency on processes that would foster peace, Jung freely confesses that his psychology works in the first instance with the individual. Its social hope he repeatedly grounds on the formation of a "leading minority" eventually able to influence authority at all levels (Jung 1976b, 610, 611, 612). The best way to undermine the next holocaust is apparently to dissuade one Nazi at a time. In the current atmosphere of greatly intensified conflict between unconscious communities bonded by their archetypal faiths, one must wonder if sufficient time remains for the Jungian enterprise to save humanity from its particular faiths in the interests of a more global compassion.

Jung himself seems not to have been too sure. Late in life he writes, "We are threatened with universal genocide if we cannot work out the way of salvation by a symbolic death" (Jung 1976, 735). In this context, a "symbolic death" would mean the death of the symbols, always religious in impact even when secular in form, which make current genocide possible and seemingly inevitable. The Spanish inquisition used to describe the killing of heretics as an "auto da fe," an "act of faith." The termination of the self-conscious stratum of evolution by conflicting faiths would be the final and global act of faith, the ecstasy that some already anticipate.

In certain key passages in his letters, Jung compares himself to Joachim di Fiore, the late-twelfth-century monk, who foresaw the very significant advances in the life of the Spirit made in the thirteenth. In these same passages Jung writes that the same Spirit which had constellated the Christian aeon now worked its invalidation (Jung, 1975, 138). The Spirit here would be the Spirit of the self working a new societal myth that might include but surpass in depth and compassionate inclusion the reigning conflicting myths now threatening humanity's future. Jung sensed that there was a new myth in the making and that a sensitive response to the current mythmaking powers of the unconscious was among the most effective ways to bring it into being.

CONCLUSION

In conclusion, Jung's thought on religion might be distilled into three propositions. Humanity cannot rid itself of its religious impulse because this is inherent to the psyche itself. Efforts to produce a religionless humanity are unconscious of this fact and so have failed. In their hands, religion has morphed into other forms of equally questionable value.

Religion universally is based on the impact of archetypal forces on consciousness and so can render those it possesses unconscious. Collectively and personally, the tighter the archetypal grip on mind or society, the less free is the individual or community who lose their moral responsibility in direct proportion to the degree of their possession or faith conviction.

Religion, collective or personal, has a history as collective or personal compensation. Such compensation always is toward a deeper personal integration in tandem with a more extended compassion. This unity of opposites is clearly evident in the culmination of the alchemical process Jung identifies in a consciousness resonant with "the eternal Ground of all empirical being" (Jung 1970, 534). Concurrently Jung contends that such consciousness would become a foundational element in a now emerging myth but would demand the widespread recovery of a human interiority long since removed from this common ground by historical processes described above.

These propositions describe the ontology and epistemology of religion universally and its current urgencies at least in Western society. Knowledge of the ultimate remains the experience of what is, namely the implacable urgency of the unconscious to become conscious, of God to become human. Having made all this so clear, Jung's challenge remains as true today as when he wrote, "Everything now depends on man" (Jung 1969c, 459).

REFERENCES

Ashton, Paul. 2007. *From the brink: Experiences of the void from a depth psychological perspective*. London: Karnac.

Ashton, Paul, ed. 2007. *Evocations of absence: Multidisciplinary perspectives on void states*. New Orleans: Spring.

Dourley, John P. 1994. In the Shadow of the Monotheisms: Jung's conversations with Buber and White. In *Jung and the Monotheisms, Judaism, Christianity, and Islam*, ed. J. Ryce-Menuhin, 125–45. London: Routledge.

———. 2003. Archetypal hatred as social bond: Strategies for its dissolution. In *Terror, violence and the impulse to destroy*, ed. John Beebe, 135–59. Einsiedeln: Daimon Verlag.

———. 2004. Jung, Mysticism and the double Quaternity: Jung and the psychic origin of religious and mystical experience. *Harvest* 50, 1: 47–74.

———. 2007. The Jung-White dialogue and why it couldn't work and won't go away. *Journal of Analytical Psychology* 53, 3: 275–95.

Hegel, G.W.F. 1825/1990. *Lectures on the history of philosophy: The lectures of 1825-1826*. Vol. 3, Medieval and Modern Philosophy, ed. and trans. R.F. Brown, Berkeley: University of California Press.

Jung, C.G. 1964. The undiscovered self. In CW 10.

———. 1965. *Memories, dreams, reflections*, ed. Aniela Jaffe. New York: Vintage.

———. 1968. Introduction to the religious and psychological problems of alchemy. In CW 12.

———. 1968b. *Archetypes of the collective unconscious*. CW 9i.

———. 1968c. Gnostic symbols of the self. In CW 9ii.

———. 1969. Psychology and religion. In CW 11.

———. 1969b. Transformation symbolism in the Mass. In CW 11.

———. 1969c. Answer to Job. In CW 11.

———. 1969d. The transcendent function. In CW 8.

———. 1969e. On the nature of the psyche. In CW 8.

———. 1970. *Mysterium Coniunctionis*. CW 14.

———. 1971. The Relativity of the God-concept in Meister Eckhart. In CW 6.

————. 1975/1953. *C.G. Jung letters, 2: 1951–1961*, ed. G. Adler, A. Jaffe. Princeton: Princeton University Press.

————. 1976. Jung and religious belief. In CW 18.

————. 1976b. Techniques of attitude change conducive to world peace. In CW 18.

Marlan, Stanton. 2005. *The black sun: The alchemy and art of darkness.* College Station: Texas A & M University Press.

Marx, Karl. 1843/1972. On the Jewish question. In *The Marx-Engels reader*, ed. R.C. Tucker, 24–51. New York: W. W. Norton.

McGinn, Bernard. 1998. *The flowering of mysticism: Men and women in the new mysticism 1200–1350.* New York: Crossroad.

————. 2001. *The mystical thought of Meister Eckhart.* New York: Crossroad.

JOHN DOURLEY, Ph.D., is a Jungian analyst and Professor Emeritus with the Religion Department, Carleton University, Ottawa, Canada. He is also a Catholic priest with a long-standing interest in the religious implications of Jungian psychology.

32

RESEARCH

Verena Kast

Working with the word association experiment at the Burghölzli, the famous psychiatric hospital in Zurich, Jung discovered the "emotional toned complexes." As we know, this was his first major scientific discovery. He was extremely proud to have shown with "empirical experiments"—that means, in a scientific way—the process of repression as described by Freud in his early writings on hysteria and dream interpretation.

Jung became internationally recognized because of his work on the association experiment, which he conducted with Franz Riklin who had brought the experiment to the Burghölzli from Germany. The important theory of complexes and the influence of emotion on dreams were connected to this research on mental associations. Jung started his career as an empirical psychologist, therefore, and he would most likely have turned into an outstanding researcher, as the famous German neuroscientist Manfred Spitzer has pointed out, had he continued along this line and not been so fascinated with the world of "spirits." For while Jung started his scientific career with the Association Experiment, at roughly the same time he completed his doctoral dissertation: "On the Psychology and the Pathology of So-Called Occult Phenomena." We should bear in mind, however, that at that time many people, including Jung's psychiatric mentor, Eugen Bleuler, were interested in "occult phenomena."

By pointing to these facts—the association experiment on one hand, and the studies of the occult and the mysterious aspect of the unconscious on the other—we capture the reality of Jung. This is our heritage as Jungian psychoanalysts. Jung wanted to be accepted as a scientific researcher on the one hand, and he wanted to study the unconscious on the other, even if this would damage his reputation as a scientist and result in people calling him a mystic. This is the heritage we have to deal with even today. We want to be a part of mainstream psychotherapy, and today this means being grounded in scientific results and research; and we also want to stay in contact also with the mystery of the unconscious.

ASSOCIATION EXPERIMENT AND DREAMS

The Association experiment has continued to this day to be a tool used for conducting scientific research in a number of fields: in linguistic studies, for exploring social prejudices, and in other areas of research. Currently it is also getting increased attention within the Jungian community. Leon Petchkovsky, an Australian Jungian psychoanalyst, is presently working with colleagues on a research project delineating the generic complex response using MRI technology. So far, the "very preliminary results suggest that a 'generic' complexed response involves some very similar pathways to those that sustain dream activity" (personal communication). It seems that Jung's statement that complexes are the architects of dreams is supported by the findings of Petchkovsky. The connection between complexes, the formation of complexes, and the regulation of emotions in dreams and through dreams is a connection Jungian clinicians have often experienced in their work with analysands. In fact, it is something we rely upon. Now the material basis for this can perhaps be established. In our age, many people will only accept "truth" that can be concretely and materially validated.

RESEARCH ON THE EFFECTIVENESS OF
JUNGIAN PSYCHOANALYSIS

In Switzerland, Jungian psychoanalysts are required to prove the effectiveness of their work, to show that practice is coherent with theory, and to demonstrate that effectiveness can be verified by disinterested others. (This is, of course, not only the case these days in Switzerland.) At the University of Basel, where only cognitive-behavioral psychotherapy is taught, students are often interested in Jungian psychoanalysis, but before really engaging with it they continually ask: What about research? Can you prove that your method is effective? Does it really help? They have been instructed that only cognitive-behavioral psychotherapy is strongly supported by research. And of course they believe this. For this younger generation—who will step into our shoes and eventually recruit the next generation of Jungian psychoanalysts—it is normal and expected to do research and to ask for proofs based on research data. This can give us reason to hope for the future.

The Swiss and German Jungian psychoanalysts Mattanza, Rudolf, and Keller conducted an outcome study on Jungian long-term practice in the years 1997 to 2003. The Swiss research project, which was sponsored by the Swiss Society for Analytical Psychology, the C.G. Jung Institute, and the IAAP, was completed in 2003. The results were excellent, in that Jungian treatment was shown to be effective in a study based on scientific criteria. For example, interpersonal problems decreased in a highly significant way (effect: o.76) (Mattanza et al., 167). On the other hand, there was no control group, and this was not a randomized study, so it cannot claim to be of "gold standard" quality in the strict scientific sense. It was a naturalistic study, based on what really happens in psychotherapy, and for research in psychotherapy this could be declared as a reasonable approach to a gold standard.

A second research project is now underway in Switzerland. All the different schools of psychotherapy are participating in an ongoing research project with outpatients (PAP´s: Praxisstudie ambulante Psychotherapie). Each school functions as a control group for the other schools. While this seems to be a very interesting and worthwhile project, the Swiss Jungians are not eager to cooperate. Since they have already participated in one study, they are not read to embark on another quite so soon. Moreover, the current study requires tape recordings of analytic sessions, and this creates a concern that the presence of a tape recorder might influence the analytical relationship. Taping sessions is not Jungian, some say. Research and psyche are uncomfortable partners and do not really fit together, they believe. Quite a lot of colleagues contend that we should stop doing research and simply be content to be "artists in Jungian psychology."

A CONSEQUENCE OF RESEARCH

In connection with the PAL study and conducted by German Jungians, there is a study titled "Differential effects of two forms of psychoanalytic therapy; Results of the Heidelberg-Berlin study." This study, financed by the health insurance system in Germany, compares two psychodynamic therapy approaches: psychodynamic therapy (PD), a focal therapy with a frequency of one to two hours per week, and psychoanalytic therapy (PA), which encourages regressive processes, requires more hours per week, and works more intensively with transference—countertransference dynamics. Both are long-term therapies. The findings: "The slightly better effects found here for the PA group would not in themselves suffice to justify the relatively high degree of effort they involve" (Grande et al., 482).

It is not only gratifying to have studies that prove that psychotherapy conducted on a Jungian basis is effective, and that Jungian psychoanalysts also belong to the mainstream of psychotherapy. There are also consequences to be drawn from these studies. Depth-psychologically oriented psychotherapy, or psychodynamic therapy (PD), is sought after and effective. With complex theory, Jungians have a consistent theory for conducting focal therapy by using the main complex clusters as foci on which to work with all the other Jungian tools and methods one has at one's command. In psychotherapy research, a table indicating changes in the structure of a focal point is described (Matanza 2006, 49). This can easily be transferred to the changes that take place in complexes.

In the various Jungian analytic training programs, training for psychodynamic psychotherapists is not generally offered. This might be instituted as a first step in the training of Jungian psychoanalysts. Candidates who would like to go further could then, in a second phase, train further to become Jungian psychoanalysts. Of course, most of us love analysis, and we believe in analysis, even if only few people can afford it and in spite of recognizing that in our everyday work we are dealing frequently with structural problems in people with personality disorders and with patients needing depth psychological oriented psychotherapy and not primarily analysis.

There is also other research being done in the Jungian world. Denis Ramos (Brazil) is, for example, conducting a project to show development and change in children using sandplay therapy. The main objective of her study is to develop a method that allows for the standardization of data from pictorial and verbal expressions as used by the patients during sandplay. It is a qualitative and a quantitative study.

I am sure there are more research projects underway in the Jungian community that I do not know about. It would be good to have a place where research projects and data would be collected, with low administration needs and open access for the interested public and other researchers.

THE DILEMMA

As Jungian psychoanalysts, we are faced with a dilemma: we need to participate in research, but at the same time we doubt the standards of the present level of the science that is applied to psychotherapy. A basic question is: what is the meaning of "scientific" when one considers the basis of psychotherapy? This is not only an academic question—it is a question of survival, a question of recognition and legitimation by the legal systems. Who should decide what "scientifically proven psychotherapy" should be? Cognitive-behavioral psychotherapists speak about gold standard research, and they feel that only their way has the right to be called scientific. Others, like Jürgen Kriz from humanistic psychology, argue for the acceptance of a plurality of methods and acceptable designs of research corresponding to the understanding of the human being and the various theories of the psyche. To pretend that only one school's so-called "gold standards" can be considered scientific is in itself highly unscientific. An exclusive claim to be entitled to the term scientific is not scientific at all. In fact, it may be fundamentalist and utterly lacking in the critical stance of true science.

What is needed is a discussion about "what is scientific psychotherapy?" And this should stand apart from "evidence based medicine," which is based on the gold standard of randomized controlled trials. There is as well "narrative based medicine," which follows the lines of phenomenological-hermeneutical methods of research. The ultimate touchstone for a scientific therapy is that it proves to be successful in clinical work.

Not only Jungian psychoanalysts have to deal with these problems, of course. It is the same for Freudians and for all psychodynamic psychotherapists.

NARRATIVE-BASED MEDICINE

The idea of "narrative-based medicine" could be of great interest and importance for Jungians. Qualitative methods of text analysis and interactions are based in the social sciences and cultural studies. Narratives allow access to the subjective experience of the storyteller (the narrator). The story can be a dream, a fantasy, or something from one's personal life history. Due to mirror neurons, the listener can identify with the narrator. The analysis of the narratives leads to cognitive-affective models of communicative interactions, or in Jungian terms to the influence of complex clusters and archetypal patterns on communication and behavior (Roesler 2006). Roesler shows a model for how, in personal narratives, one can find an archetypal pattern as nucleus. Using the methods of the narratology, one could compare the development of narratives in the course of an analytic process. Jungian psychoanalysts tend to be highly focused on narratives: personal life history narratives, dream narratives, active imagination narratives, and cultural and archetypal narratives like fairy tales and myths. Telling stories, and especially telling them in a friendly, benevolent, and supportive relationship, can change the narratives. If one is surrounded by a different emotional atmosphere, one may recall a story in a different way. One may be able to tell the old stories of wounding and trauma in a more positive way. How we tell the story of our life strongly influences the future. Analysts have a lot of experience in this field, and I think we should work out some of these ideas in more detail. The research undertaken from this angle would not be natural science but it could be social science.

CONCLUSION

Jungian psychoanalysts must build and maintain links to the mainstream of research in psychotherapy, but the methods for conducting relevant research must be more fitting to our basic theory. Today it is evident that we must fight vigorously for the reality of the inner world, but also for the connection between the inner and the outer world, between the consulting room and lived life. There is a great deal of conflict here, of course. The external world does not acknowledge subjectivity as valid. As professional analysts, we are struggling to find methods to make subjective experience "objective," so it can be shared with other people and serve as a basis for quantitative research.

There are many questions that must be addressed. Where are institutes doing research into Jungian psychoanalysis? How can researchers and practitioners work together? There need to be more sponsored professorships for Jungian psychoanalysts who are willing to work together with clinicians; there need to be clinicians who are willing to put time aside for contact with researchers. There need to be analysts who are willing to take part in the debate about what kind of psychotherapy research is needed today.

Basically, we need a change of mind. We need the conviction that research—several kinds of research—belongs to the profession of Jungian psychoanalysis. This should not be primarily because one has to do research in order to conform to state regulations, but because one is interested in what happens in analysis, in what helps best in which situation, in what is most effective as treatment. The motive should be that we want to become more and more truly professional. It is possible that the younger colleagues who are used to doing research during their training at university will be more willing to engage in this effort, but I doubt it. Those who come into the Jungian world are generally looking for imagination and for the inner world. But can we afford to concentrate not only on the inner world? Should we not also be willing to engage the outer world and to give to society what it needs and is asking for? Do we not understand the individuation process really as an interaction between the inner and the outer world?

The question boils down to: Do we as Jungian psychoanalysts really want to be professionals in the field of psychotherapy? Or, if not, what then?

EXPERIENTIAL RESEARCH

For clinicians, there is a kind of research that emerges out of the experiences in the consulting room. One might call it "experiential research." Out of clinical experiences with patients, one is constantly questioning one's psychological theories and reformulating one's convictions about what is effective. As a group, we are dealing with outcomes in psychotherapy and are trying to relate these results to our theories. The outcomes of psychotherapy research influence our clinical work and our supervision. Out of these experiences have grown a wealth of publications all across the world: How to work with symbols in painting, with active imagination, with dreams, with symbols, with transference-countertransference, and so on. What is lacking is a pool of colleagues interested in questions of theory.

My vision: to determine what aspects of our theories we should discuss, and on which aspects should research by academics be done (if we could find them!)? For example: Most Jungian psychoanalysts work with dreams and are convinced that they get good hints out of dreams, that dreams can change emotions, and so on. Clara E. Hill (not a Jungian) conducted a research project asking if people feel it is more helpful to talk about their own dreams, to talk about the dreams of other people, or to talk about personal conflicts. Talking about one's own dreams was rated the most helpful. I hope there are some people around who are interested in questions like this and have the opportunity to do this kind of research. Perhaps people can write dissertations on such themes.

ACADEMIC RESEARCH

Academics need not be clinicians in order to be interested in Jungian psychology. Their research is often more cultural, historical, and interdisciplinary—a broad field that makes Jungian psychology so interesting. The interaction with different fields of cultural science can provoke creative encounters and new developments. A lot of work has been done along these lines, also by clinicians. The question is, how can all this information be gathered and coordinated? And how does the scientific community and not only the Jungian community receive this data? This research can be very stimulating to our field. Why does this scientific exchange not really take place? Of course, there is the problem of languages. The research data published in German is in most cases not translated into English, and if it is it often seems not to be of interest to English-speaking readers. In the German-speaking area, we seem to be more interested in research data published in English . . .

WHY ARE WE NOT HEARD BY THE OTHERS?

How does the scientific psychotherapeutic community receive Jungian findings? Much of what has been discussed in psychodynamic therapies during the past few years are familiar "Jungian topics": the orientation to the resource-oriented perspective on psychopathology, and on clinical processes, creativity, and spirituality. The Jungian perspective is usually not mentioned but is rather used like a stone-pit filled with good material but not worth mentioning where it came from. Jungian psychotherapy has always been resource-oriented. Yet specifically Jungian concepts are rarely mentioned in recent articles about resource-oriented psychotherapy. Did we not express this clearly enough over the past years? Or do we have to prove scientifically what we refer to as resource-oriented therapy, and how it works? We are talking about creativity as being indispensable for the individuation process. It is expressed in thousands of article written by Jungian psychoanalysts. Spirituality, a perennial Jungian topic, is discussed even in relation to Freudian psychotherapy nowadays. Our contributions could be very helpful. And we have many contributions!

When we go and give lectures, when we are writing books about emotions, symbols, dreams, paintings, imagination, we often hear (especially from Freudian colleagues) that Jungians psychoanalysts are very creative, but a little bit wild, not very scientific, but stimulating. The books of some Jungians sell well, but they are not often quoted in the papers of the colleagues from universities. Analytical psychology has something to offer those people who are seeking meaning in their lives, who want to get in touch with the psyche, who want to become more conscious. Some institutes have "public programs" for such people, and these programs are very successful.

So—should we just leave it there and accept that we do not belong to the mainstream? Lack of research in the effectiveness of psychotherapy means that we risk not getting insurance to cover our services one day, but is this so bad? Are we ready to settle for being artists in Jungian psychology?

I personally would prefer that we seek to overcome the split between the inner world and the demands of the outer world. I believe that together we can do it.

REFERENCES

Grande, Tilman, et al. 2006. Differential effects of two forms of psychoanalytic therapy; Results of the Heidelberg-Berlin study. *Psychotherapy Research* 16, 4: 470–85.

Hill, Clara, Roberta Diemer, et.al. 1993. Are the effects of dream interpretation on session quality, insight and emotions due to the dream itself, to projection or to the interpretation process? *Dreaming* 3, 4: 269–80.

Kriz, J. 2007. Wie lässt sich die Wirksamkeit von Verfahren X wissenschaftlich begründen? *Psychotherapeutenjournal* 3: 258–61.

Mattanza G., I. Meier, and M. Schlegel, eds. 2006. *Seele und Forschung: Ein Brückenschlag in der Psychotherapie*. Basel: Karger.

Roesler, Christian. 2006. Narrative Biographieforschung und archetypische Geschichtenmuster. In *Seele und Forschung, Ein Brückenschlag in der Psychotherapie*, ed. Mattanza et al.

Spitzer, M. 2000. *Geist im Netz*. Heidelberg: Spektrum Akademischer Verlag.

DR. VERENA KAST is Professor of Psychology at the University of Zurich and training analyst and lecturer at the C.G. Jung Institute of Zurich. From 1995 to 1998 she was president of IAAP and is currently the president of the International Association of Depth Psychology and a member of the Board of Directors of the Lindauer Psychotherapiewochen. She lectures throughout the world, and is the author of numerous books on psychological issues.

33

THE SOCIAL DREAMING MATRIX

Helen Morgan

INTRODUCTION

Social dreaming is a pioneering methodology that seeks to explore the unconscious dimensions of the social world. It is based on the assumption that we dream not just for ourselves, but as a part of the larger context in which we live—an idea which has an ancient lineage. Long before Freud and Jung, dreams and dreaming had great significance to people in societies such as those of the Australian Aboriginals, Native Americans, Africans, and others. Dreams offered them a way of understanding the meaning of their lives and the world in which they lived. This perspective regards dreams as more than the private possession of the dreamer and suggests that, by exploration in a social context, the dream may help us widen our conscious, finite understanding further into the unconscious infinite.

HISTORY

Social dreaming was "discovered" and developed by W. Gordon Lawrence, a group analyst and organizational consultant at the Tavistock Institute of Human Relations in London. It was introduced into the formal life of the International Jungian community at the IAAP Congress in 1995 in Zurich, where a Matrix was convened every morning by myself and Peter Tatham, and has been a part of the IAAP Congresses ever since. It is now used in a wide variety of settings by Jungians all over the world. Social dreaming fits well within the Jungian context as it assumes the reality of a collective unconscious from which the dream may emerge to speak of the collective rather than only to the individual.

By the early 1980s Lawrence had become increasingly interested in the nature of the dream from his own personal analysis and from his work, his reading and his travels. For many years he held in mind not only the interest in the individual dream as developed in psychoanalysis, but also its place in traditional societies outside of the West as a respected expression of the tribal or societal present and history as well as a predictor of the future. Throughout the history of Western society, the dream has always been held as significant in certain corners, but in modern times it was Freud and then Jung who first formulated a means by which the dream could find credibility in mainstream society. Lawrence noted the way in which this reverence for the dream took on a populist aspect but questioned whether the linkage of the dream with a model of the psyche that is discrete and individualistic meant that this interest had come to feed narcissistic preoccupations and thus serves further to cut us off each from the other.

It was his discovery of the book *The Third Reich of Dreams: The Nightmares of a Nation* written by Charlotte Beradt that helped Lawrence make the connection between the dream as an individual and as a social phenomenon. Between 1933 and 1939, Beradt collected 300 dreams by Germans that she noted in code and hid in the spines of the books in her library. Subsequently, she was able to send them to different addresses abroad where they were kept till she herself left Germany for America. It was some years later that she came to evaluate her material, when there was a large body of historical facts on the Nazi regime available through documents and research. Beradt makes the point that these dreams were not the products of unresolved inner personal conflicts but arose from and spoke about the political atmosphere in which the dreamers lived.

The ideas in this book led Lawrence to wonder what we might learn about our own society by attending to and collecting dreams as a mass observation. Not just of society *as such*—its historic and present processes—but of society in a process of becoming. The methodology he saw as required to allow this emergent nature to surface turned away from Freud's reductive, deductive analysis and towards a more Jungian perspective that honours the dream in its own right and seeks to unravel and decode its symbolism through association and amplification.

As an experiment, Lawrence and his colleagues set up an eight-week program in 1982 at the Tavistock Institute of Human Relations. The program consisted of 90-minute sessions entitled "A Project in Social Dreaming and Creativity." It was then they decided to call the gathering a 'Matrix' rather than a "Group." "Matrix" is the Latin for uterus and means "the place out of which something grows." To further remove the concept from that of group work, they also placed the chairs in a spiral rather than a circle. This was an attempt to underline the focus of the event on the dream rather than the individual and a way of lessening the transferential dynamics that occur in the more usual group setting.

Following this initial experiment, nothing more was done for six years. At that time, Lawrence was asked to organise a teaching conference in Israel on "Leadership and Innovation." Asked to provide a structure that was itself innovative, Lawrence formulated a program consisting of dialogue groups, mutual consultancy sets, and twice daily social dreaming matrices. A fuller report of this experiment is in Lawrence's book, *Social Dreaming @ Work* (Lawrence 1998). The success of the venture led Lawrence and others to run similar events throughout the world.

THE SOCIAL DREAMING MATRIX

The social dreaming matrix is a special kind of container that is set up and maintained in a manner that maximizes free association to and amplification of the images offered by the dreams. The focus of attention is the dream and not the dreamer, and the primary aim is the transformation of thinking. The intention is to take away the emphasis on the individual ego and to allow a letting go of the need to perform and of the problems of persona. By "losing" the ego in the matrix, proper attention can be paid to the dreams and hence to the unconscious of the group. Thus a deeper, more democratic dynamic can emerge.

In the matrix, chairs are arranged in a spiral or a series of snowflakes so that, unlike a group sitting in a circle, the space is filled and participants are not necessarily facing each other. The convenors open and close the matrix, which is usually of 60 to 90 minutes duration, at the beginning of which the task of the matrix is stated. This task is *"to associate to the dreams made available to the matrix in order to make links and find connections between individual thought and social meaning."* The convenors' role is to keep participants to the task of association and amplification and *not* interpretation, and usually to record the dreams. When a series of matrices are held over a number of days, such as at the IAAP Congresses, the matrix is always open to any participant of the Congress. Participants do not need to attend each day, nor do they need to have themselves had a dream to attend. In these cases, the language of the matrix is English, although it is often the case in such a multicultural environment that dreams are related in other languages and the participants work together on translation. In other instances where the conference is bilingual, interpreters have been used so the matrix may use both languages.

SOCIAL DREAMING

We exist within a web of emotions and thinking, which is present in every social relationship. The web is infinite, mostly unacknowledged, and unconscious. The dream arises from this web of infinity, and a fragment comes within the grasp of our finite, conscious, knowing mind. The social dreaming matrix offers a way of receiving the dream so that we might push the finitude of our conscious understanding towards the infinity of the unconscious through the medium of the dream and the associative thoughts it may give rise to.

The central hypothesis behind the matrix is that we dream not just for ourselves but also as part of the larger context in which we live. To explore that context, we need to approach the dream from a different angle and in a different setting from that of the analytic dyad. In the latter case, the interest is in the associations of the dreamer and, possibly, of the analyst in the countertransference. The dream is regarded as a communication from that individual's particular psyche within that particular transference. How the dream may be interpreted will be viewed differently depending on one's theoretical framework, but on the whole the dream will be perceived as essentially belonging to the dreamer.

In social dreaming a different approach is taken. Any dream that is spoken of within the matrix then belongs to the matrix. It harks back to a time when dreaming was part of the discourse of daily life and where its meaning might be publicly owned rather than being seen as a private, secret business for the individual.The personal relevance and meaning for the person who brings the dream may be explored and interpreted privately elsewhere, but in the matrix these personal implications are avoided. Instead, the dream is taken up as belonging to all and played with, associated to, and thought about as such.

The matrix is established as a different container from individual analysis, but is also set up deliberately to differ from a group in which analysis is taking place. In an analytic group, the focus is on the relationship among the participants and in particular on the relationship with the group facilitator through the transference. Any material that emerges within the group, including dreams, will be considered and interpreted in light of these relationships. In the social dreaming matrix there are no such interpretations—either concerning relations among participants or with the convenors.

In the matrix, one dream is part of a whole sequence of dreams. The task is to explore the pattern that connects the dreams, and this requires a combination of analytic and synthetic thinking. The approach leaves aside the personal, atomistic focus and emphasizes the systemic, holistic quality of dreams so that individuals who take part are relieved of the need to defend their private inner worlds, and instead engage in a co-operative venture to better understand the social milieu.

The central point is that individual analysis offers one sort of container for the dream and is worked with from one set of assumptions. The social dreaming matrix offers another sort of container and works from a different set. The question arises as to whether, if the container changes, different dreams are dreamt. Lawrence maintains:

> To take the same thought processes as are used in psychoanalysis into a social dreaming matrix is not valid because, it is my hypothesis, a different version or even type of dream is evoked. More particularly, if the container system for receiving the dream is changed, the dream-contained will change. . . . What I think the social dreaming matrix questions is the ideology that dreams belong to a person and are to be interpreted as such. This is not to devalue that kind of work—so important for myself in my own psychoanalysis. All I am saying is that the matrix produces different kinds of dreams through dreamers. The context is different, that is all. (Lawrence 1998, 31, 33)

SOCIAL DREAMING IN CONTEXT

Social dreaming, as described above, can be used within the conference setting as a way of exploring the theme of the conference as well as the themes of the wider social setting. It also can be used as a means of shedding light on organizational shadows. Our view of organizations often is constrained by the observable, logical, and rational. It frequently relies on theories and strategies designed to maintain control over outcomes—even in the midst of turbulence, complexity, and unpredictability. Despite this, the dynamics hidden in the shadows typically present the most challenge for those working with and in organizations. An exploration of what is unspoken, tacit, and presumably unknown, can reveal shared fears, fantasies, and conflicts and thereby provide a deeper understanding of organizational reality.

No organization can operate without the conscious ego activities concerning policy making, management, representing, negotiating, and decision making. These belong to the realm of ego functioning, but all risk clashes of personality, power struggles, inflation, matters of kudos, and so on. The social dreaming matrix can provide a very different sort of space where the same personnel can engage with each other in a very different context, which promotes collaboration in exploring uncertainty and paradox. As we know from individual analysis, the dream presents us with what *is,* rather than what "ought to be" and therefore offers the expression of shadow material within a framework which is not restricted by morality, judgment, or superego.

There is insufficient space to give examples of the content of such matrices in this article. The books listed in References (below) contain examples of the application of social dreaming in a variety of settings, including a write-up of some of the social dreaming matrices held at IAAP Congresses over the years since the first one in 1995. It is almost impossible to give much more than a taste of any such event. Each individual exists during the life of the matrix as a nodal point in a net that works with the dream images in a flux of associations. Where you are located in this net, literally and metaphorically, determines what experience you have and what you remember. Some dreams will be heard better than others, some comments will not be heard at all. All dreams change slightly in the telling and yet more so in the hearing. It is the coming together of individual differences that make the container, and each person will take away a different perception of what has happened. What emerges is a web of meanings, and there will be as many impressions and associations as there were participants.

SUMMARY

Social dreaming seeks to explore what the dream may be communicating about the social and political context of the dreamer. There is a sharing of dreams, and then meaning is expanded and developed through association, amplification, and systemic thinking in an attempt to give voice to the echoes of thought that exist in the space between individual minds and the shared environment. The focus shifts from the dreamer to the dream, and since the dreams are not related to the social status of the dreamer it is an entirely democratic environment. Those taking part are encouraged to surrender themselves to trains of thought without monitoring for importance, relevance, or whether they are nonsense or disagreeable. Thus linear thought processes are broken up, and because one idea will lead to another, this can generate thinking that is surprising and synchronous. There are no conclusions, and the thinking remains full of paradox, contradictions, doubt and uncertainty leading to what Lawrence refers to as a "multi-verse" rather than a "uni-verse" of meanings.

REFERENCES

Beradt, Charlotte. 1985. *The third Reich of dreams: The nightmares of a nation 1933–1939.* Northamptonshire, UK: The Aquarian Press.
Lawrence, W. Gordon, ed. 1998. *Social dreaming @ work.* London: Karnac.
———. 2005. *Introduction to social dreaming: Transforming thinking.* London: Karnac.
———, ed. 2007. *Infinite possibilities of social dreaming.* London: Karnac.
Morgan, Helen, and Peter Tatham. 2003. Social dreaming at Cambridge. In *Proceedings of the 15th International Congress for Analytical Psychology.* Einsiedeln: Daimon Verlag.

HELEN MORGAN is a senior member, training analyst, and supervisor for the Jungian Analytic Section of the British Association of Psychotherapists, of which she has recently been president. Her background is in therapeutic communities, and she now works mainly in private practice in London. Besides a number of articles on social dreaming, her published work includes papers on the application of Jungian analytic thinking to the new physics, modern Western society, and race and racism in psychotherapy.

PART FIVE

TRAINING

Introduction to TRAINING
Murray Stein

The training of the next generation of Jungian psychoanalysts is a concern for all professional Jungian groups and one that occupies a good deal of time and attention in all Jungian societies. In most societies, it is the central and most labor intensive activity undertaken by the membership. Worldwide there are several variations on the basic model of training, as Ann Casement's research shows in her chapter on "Training Programs." Casement also compares the Jungian trainings of the IAAP to the three models in the International Psychoanalytic Association. The basic structure of Jungian training, which descends from the psychoanalytic model designed originally by Karl Abraham and his Freudian colleagues in Berlin in the 1920s, revolves around three basic elements: didactic seminars, personal analysis, and supervision of analytic cases. How the requirements are organized and distributed varies from country to country and training institute to institute. Nevertheless, all these requirements are covered in one fashion or another.

The most fundamental feature of Jungian training has been, since Jung himself was in charge of what passed as training in Zurich before WWII, the personal training analysis. Dyane Sherwood in her chapter "Training Analysis" gives a highly personal account of what it is like to endure the trials of undergoing analysis while passing through the rigors of a training program. Catherine Crowther discusses the current understanding of supervision and the delicate role the supervisor of analytic cases plays within the context of the training program. Both articles vividly depict the intricacies and complications of these aspects of training.

In the end, the hoped for product of training is a mature personality and a competent Jungian psychoanalyst who is a lifelong learner.

34

TRAINING PROGRAMS

Ann Casement

For the purposes of this chapter it seems appropriate to give a summary of my background specifically in the area of training at the International Association for Analytical Psychology (IAAP) and elsewhere as follows: Chair of Training for four years at the Association of Jungian Analysts (AJA) until the late 1990s; Chair of the United Kingdom Council for Psychotherapy (UKCP) from January 1998 to September 2001, playing an active role in every aspect of the organization including its Training Standards Committee; Chair of the Society Applications Sub-Committee of the IAAP Executive Committee from 2001 to 2007, part of whose task is the assessing of training programs of groups applying for training status as Societies of the IAAP; member of the IAAP Executive Committee's Study Group for Training and Governance, which evolved into the Study Group for Professional Organization and Development; contributed a paper as a member of a plenary panel on training at *The Journal of Analytical Psychology*'s (JAP) fiftieth anniversary conference in Oxford in 2005, which was subsequently published in the JAP.

The Study Group for Training and Governance came into being as a result of Murray Stein's presidential address to the IAAP Delegates Meeting in Barcelona 2004 in which he stated with his customary prescience: "As the burning topic of professional ethics occupied our association in the late nineties and resulted in an Ethics Committee . . . so the issue of governance and training standards will, I believe, be central of the agendas of the coming years." The Ethics Committee was a long time in the making as it required much consultation and thoughtful discussion, and, no doubt, the addressing of issues to do with governance and training standards will take time to evolve.

A discussion on training standards at the IAAP was initiated by an item entitled Training Standards at the Executive Committee, Council of Societies, and IAAP Delegates Meetings at the 2007 Cape Town Congress. This called for the establishing of an IAAP Training Standards Sub-Committee (TSS-C) to develop minimum standards and duration of training. This was presented by Deborah Egger, President of the Association of Graduate Analytical Psychologists

(AGAP), and me but was put together and supported by Members and Training Societies of the IAAP. A TSS-C is needed to support the IAAP in upholding one of the aims spelt out in its Constitution as follows: Art. 2, Point 3: To require the maintenance of high standards of training, practice, and ethical conduct. The Delegates Meeting agreed with the recommendation that the next administration set up a working party to gather information from the Group Members around the world on the question of training standards.

It is important to note that the IAAP, as is the case with similar umbrella bodies, has to hold the tension between evolving into a regulatory body and maintaining its status quo as a loosely federated organization of organizations. The UKCP was in a similar position but, at the time of my chairmanship, had put in place a Training Standards Committee producing training requirements for its constituent member organizations, including a minimum four-year part-time training. Both the IAAP and UKCP have specific structural issues they have to contend with: in the case of UKCP, its innate disparity results from the fact that it encompasses several different modalities of psychotherapy; the IAAP, on the other hand, represents one modality spread globally across diverse languages and cultures.

A central task for the IAAP is that of identifying and representing bona fide Jungian analytic groups and individuals who may apply to it for membership. The core identity of Jungian psychoanalysts is formed through a lengthy immersion in the ethos of an IAAP designated training society. This allows for the deeper aspects of psyche to be reached, in other words, the spiritual and archetypal, which enable the individual to move into living a life that is open to the nonrational realms of the symbolic in a consistent way that facilitates ego-development so that it is relegated to being in service of the Self. As Jung says: "while I am only a passing phenomenon . . . the 'Other' in me (is) the timeless, imperishable stone" (Jung 1963, 59).

In some parts of the world where there is no IAAP registered Training Society available that can offer the necessary in-depth training, there is in existence a Routers Program leading to Individual Membership of the IAAP. Briefly, the idea for this Program grew out of the Developing Groups and was voted for at the Delegates Meeting in Florence in 1998. The criteria for the Routers Program include academic qualification, personal analysis, clinical supervision, personal development, examinations, all of which have to be satisfactorily completed before an application may be made to become an Individual Member of the IAAP. Every individual member is required to abide by the IAAP Code of Ethics.

By way of contrast, I thought it would be interesting to garner information on the International Psychoanalytical Association's (IPA) training specifications and contacted Professor Shmuel Erlich, Chair of its Education Committee. He has been most helpful in preparing a summary of the IPA's extensive documentation for inclusion in this chapter.

In the course of our correspondence, Professor Erlich sent me the Requirements for Qualification and Admission to Membership. Briefly, it sets out three models of training that will in due course be accredited and regulated by the

IPA. These are the Eitingon, French, and Uruguayan models, which were approved by the Board in March 2007. The names of the three should not be interpreted as implying a geographic location. Some features of these models are as follows. Under the Uruguayan model, analysis requirements consist of "considerable immersion" in analysis prior to candidate admission and five more years concurrent with the duration of training. The Institute is organized into groups responsible for the various didactic functions—personal analysis, curriculum and supervision—thus minimizing the traditional training analyst role. Under the Eitingon model, the didactic curriculum is a scheduled series of seminars over a period of four or five years or a minimum of 450 hours and at least 150 hours of supervision on at least two analytic cases. In the Eitingon model, the personal analysis is concurrent with the training, whereas in the French model it takes place largely before admission to training. The duration of training under the three models varies from a minimum of four years to much more extensive periods.

COMPARATIVE STUDY OF IAAP TRAINING PROGRAMS

As part of the source material for this chapter, I have turned to Denise Ramos's excellent Comparative Study of Training Programs, hereinafter referred to as the Study, which she presented at the Barcelona Congress in 2004. The data in this extensive Study was obtained from Societies' training programs and requirements, as well as a short, easy-to-complete questionnaire. There were responses from twenty-one training programs from a possible total of thirty-two IAAP societies with training status, or approximately 65.62 percent of all IAAP training programs. The distribution by region was well balanced, including North America, South America, Europe, Israel, and Australia and New Zealand. The criteria included were as follows: eligibility, time requirements, evaluation stages, and curricula. The focus in this chapter is on curricula as there seemed little point in reproducing the Study, but a brief mention of the other criteria surveyed in the Study demonstrates that it takes into account the age eligibility for candidates, professional requirements, personal analysis, licensing, and the number of hours of clinical practice required during training. The Study shows a great deal of homogeneity in all these areas, and candidates end their training having completed between 301 to 500 hours of analysis. The minimum duration of training broke down as follows: 52 percent have four years, 19 percent have five years, 24 percent have six years, and 5 percent have eight years.

With regard to curricula, I set forth below what the Study shows to be a substantial degree of homogeneity in the basic subjects related to analytical psychology. These are:

- History of Analytical Psychology
- Fundamentals of Analytical Psychology
- Association Experiment
- Complex Theory

- Psychological Types
- Theory of Archetypes
- Persona and Shadow
- Anima and Animus
- Defenses of the Self
- Projective Identification/Participation Mystique
- Individuation Process and its Symbols
- Psychology of Dreams

It is worth noting at the outset that the societies whose training programs appear in this chapter are all different from the ones consulted for the Study apart from the Brazilian Society for Analytical Psychology (SBrPA). The other five are: C.G. Jung Institut Berlin; C.G. Jung Institute of Korea, Korean Association of Jungian Analysts (KAJA); Jungian Psychoanalytic Association (JPA); The C.G. Jung Institute of San Francisco (CGJISF); The Society of Analytical Psychology (SAP). Some of these training societies are long-standing members of the IAAP whilst others are of more recent origin. The diversity represented by these trainings worldwide is complemented by the fact that there is a degree of uniformity in some areas, particularly in requiring minimum four-year duration for training. All the societies involved have been sent a draft for their comments, and I am grateful to them for their generous help in the formation of this chapter. I have received a great deal of extensive and in-depth material from each of them, but constraints of space prohibit including all of it. In view of this, I have selected certain areas to concentrate on, including, in some instances, details of personal analysis, though it goes without saying that this is a requirement throughout training in each of the models. The lengthier SBrPa entry is an exemplar of the depth and caliber of all six training programs.

1. C.G. JUNG INSTITUT BERLIN

The training program I was sent by the C.G. Jung Institut in Berlin, formed in 1947, is for the Winter Semester 2007-2008, which includes an extensive literature list. I will first summarize the General Study Plan for the Diploma Programs, which gives an outline of the three programs that may be pursued at that organization. The Psychoanalyst course is a minimum five-year part-time study program to be done while working. The Child and Adolescent Analytical Psychotherapists study program is also a minimum five-year part-time one to be done while working. The Depth Psychology–based Psychotherapy study program is a minimum three-year full-time one.

The general outline of studies includes what is covered in each of the three trainings, including the following: Theory and Treatment of Trauma, Introduction to Theory of Dreams, Ethics and Professional Issues, Basic Medicine, Theory and Practice of Group Therapy, Neuropsychology. The seminars listed give descriptions of their content as follows:

- Fundamentals of four-hour psychoanalytic treatment. This seminar covers the formal requirements within and without the frame of third-party payment, with special attention paid to treatment indication, technique and psychoanalytic process. It will also look at the difference between three and four hour per week treatment.
- Psychotherapy of psychotic illness.
- Introduction to classic psychoanalytic developmental psychology. Theorists covered are: Anna Freud, Melanie Klein, D.W. Winnicott, C.G. Jung, E. Neumann, M. Fordham.
- Concepts of psychopathology from the view of analytical psychology. Paranoid Schizophrenia, Borderline Disorder, Depression, Anxiety Neurosis, Psychiatric Emergency including suicidality, Criteria of "Mentalisierungsstörung" compared with Jungian Psychoanalytic concepts.
- Psychosomatic II. Skin (Neurodermititis), Asthma, Heart Neurosis, pain syndromes, psychotherapy with chronic and incurable illness.
- Separation in psychoanalysis. The implications in the analytic process of Freud and Melanie Klein's theories of early childhood separation issues.
- First Hour—technical seminar on taking an anamnesis.
- Comparative Psychotherapy.
- Colloquium on relevant psychoanalytic literature.
- Freud Seminar: Psychoanalysis of love.
- Psychopathology and Understanding Neurosis from the view of Analytical Psychology: Compulsive Disorder.
- Analytic Psychotherapy with severe trauma patients.
- The history of Psychoanalysis with emphasis on psychoanalysis and nationalism.
- Treatment techniques. Freud's technical works, especially "Zur Einleitung der Behandlung"; Kernberg's Transference focussed psychotherapy; Transference/Countertransference; Interpretation and other Interventions; Dream work and the function of dreams.
- Psychoanalytic Developmental Psychology and Gender Differentiation.
- Pregnancy and Birth; Abuse of Girls and Boys; Socialization differences related to Gender.
- Technical Seminar on Analytic Psychotherapy. Frame and setting, treatment plan, end of treatment in context of transference/countertransference.
- Dream Seminar. Besides the Jungian position, modern dream research will be presented and practice casuistic material.
- Psychoanalytic Developmental Psychology.
- Ethno-psychoanalysis and Intercultural Psychotherapy.

- Analytical Psychology under contract with medical doctors.
- Psychopathological Results. The meaning of differential diagnosis, therapy indication and psychodynamic history of psychoanalysis.
- Introduction to Child and Adolescent Psychiatry.
- Important psychoanalysts in the Kleinian tradition: Hanna Segal, Joan Riviere, Edna O'Shaughnessy, Irma Brenman-Pick.
- Concepts of depth psychology based psychotherapy.
- Ego Psychology and Object Relations Theory and psychoanalysis.
- The theory of neurosis from Schultz-Henckes.
- Concepts in Analytical Psychology: Typology.
- Concepts in Analytical Psychology: Complex theory and its development.
- Concepts in Analytical Psychology in the clinical context: Theory of Dreams, basics of neurobiology, archetypal structures.
- Family neurogenetic patterns.
- Psychoanalytic Dream Theory—Literature Seminar (Authors: C.G. Jung, M. Freeman, S. Menzos, U. Moser, A. Springer, A. Hamburger).
- Psychodynamic Organizational Counselling: supervision, coaching, etc.
- Theory of Family Therapy.
- Introduction to Infant Observation.
- History of Analytical Psychology from E. Neumann's "Depth Psychology and the new Ethic."
- Introduction to theory and methods of behavioral therapy.
- Psychotherapy in comparison with Gestalt Therapy.
- The symbolic attitude as analytic position between "mentalizing" and container/contained.

2. BRAZILIAN SOCIETY FOR ANALYTICAL PSYCHOLOGY

The Analyst Training Course of São Paulo includes:

- 8 semesters of seminars
- 8 semesters of individual and group supervision
- 1 year following the conclusion of the theoretical and practical program for the preparation and presentation of a course conclusion dissertation.

The curriculum is comprised of four discussion areas and in-depth theoretical and practical training:

- The analytical psychology field (1st and 2nd semesters).

- The development of personality (3rd and 4th semesters).
- Psychopathology (5th and 6th semesters).
- The Opus (7th and 8th semesters).

The analytical psychology module aims to introduce the main lines of Jungian thought, defining its fundamental framework from a historical, philosophical, and epistemological perspective. It focuses on the cultural ethos in which Jung's theories were generated, initially within the Freudian psychological field and after with the background of his own ideas and values, which define a particular conceptual and practical field. The basic elements of structure and dynamics of the psyche are presented in this module.

The personality development module covers the various theories about development according to C.G. Jung's concepts and his followers, ranging from childhood to maturity and old age cycles, passing through the periods of transformation. The meaning of each life stage is understood within the "individuation" process, pointing to the archetypes manifested in each cycle and how these interact during the course of life. During this module candidates study the theories of complexes with the archetypal roots and the dominant complexes during development.

The concepts of psychopathology are reviewed within the analytical psychology theory. This module studies the pathologies relevant to clinical practice such as: obsessive-compulsive disorder, hysteria, anorexia, addictions, psychosomatic disorders, narcissism, personality disorders, psychosis, and psychopathic disorders. The understanding of such disorders is deepened through the symbolic comprehension of its expressions, analysis of dreams and fantasies, mythical "amplification" and their parallels in culture.

The opus forms the full meaning of the individuation process, of the search for psychic integration through the analyst's understanding and experience. It reconciles theory and practice providing teachings which are at the same time both strictly personal and universal. The work of Jung is focused as a whole and shows the development of fundamental concepts and the route to individuation. Texts studies include: alchemy, synchronicity, philosophical and religious traditions, symbolism in dreams, art, literature and mythology, levels of evolutions of consciousness, and practical clinical subjects related to these topics.

- 1st year—1st semester seminars include: The History of Dynamic Psychiatry, the social and cultural context of the 19th century and new systems; Philosophical Foundations; Jung's Life and Work; The Freud/Jung Letters; Theory of Complexes; Psychic Energy; Instinct and Unconscious; General Aspects of Dream Psychology; The Transcendent Function; Theoretical Considerations on the Nature of the Psyche.

- 1st year—2nd semester: Genesis of Symbols of Transformation; The Archetypes and the Collective Unconscious; Symbols of Transformation;

Personal Unconscious and Complex; Ego and Consciousness; Persona; Shadow; The Ego between Shadow and Persona; The Archetypes of Anima and Animus; Self; Psychology and Poetry.

- 2nd year—1st semester: Myth of the Great Mother; Psychological Aspects of the Maternal Archetype; Primal Relationship Disorders; Consciousness, Unconsciousness and Individuation; Psychology of the Child Archetype; The Primal Relationship and the Ego-Self; From Matriarchal to Patriarchal; The Myth of the Father; The Importance of the Father in the Destiny of the Individual; Memories, Dreams, Reflections; Primal Identity and Projection; The Patriarchy; Life Stages; Abandoning the Child; Michael Fordham—Historic Localization: Author and Work; Individuation in the First Half of Life: The Conceptual Model of Michael Fordham; Implications of Michael Fordham's Conceptual Model in Clinical Work.

- 2nd year—2nd semester: The "Observed" Newborn of Contemporary Theories; Fantasy in Childhood: The Symbolic Function; The family as a Symbolic Dimension of the Self; Oedipus: Archetypes and Roles; Adolescence; Psychology and Alchemy; Psychological Types; Psychology of Transference; The Archetypal Image of the Wounded Healer; Abuse of Power in Psychotherapy; Mythology.

- 3rd year—1st semester: Attachment Theory; Narcissism; Echoism and Narcissism as Creative and Defensive Structural Functions; Echo, Narcissus, and the Coniunctio; Borderline Disorder; Narcissism and Echoism in the Transference; Depression; Panic; Hysteria; The Roles of Will and Power in Perversions—the Psychodynamic of Masochism; Masochism—a Form of Psychic Elaboration; Masochism and Psychic Pain; The Psyche of the Body; Addictions; Eating Disorders; Autism: Conceptualism, Epidemiology. Aetiology: current hypotheses. The Mind Theory; Mythology; Clinical Practice.

- 3rd year—2nd semester: Psychiatry and Symbolic Psychopathology: The Matriarchal (sensualist), Patriarchal (control), Alterity (encounter), and Totality (contemplation) Spectra; The Creative and Defensive Structural Function of Envy—Salieri's Neurotic, Psychopathic, Borderline and Psychotic Defenses; Psychopathic Defense; The Psychopathology of the Structural Function of Love; Concepts and postulates of analytical psychology applied to conjugal dynamic and couples' theory; Narcissist-borderline complementarities in wedlock; Couples and Family Psychotherapy; Psychopathology from the archetypal psychology point of view; Dreams; Techniques of Imagination; Transference/Countertransference; Historical Summary on Children's Psychotherapy; Symbolic Language and Expressive Techniques; Psychopathology: Development Disorders; The Wounded Healer Archetype; Oriental Mythology Course; Mythology.

- 4th year—1st semester: Sandplay; The Psychic Structure of Fairy Tales; The Process of Humanization and the Archetypal Theory of History; The Dissociation of Subject-Object in Western Culture. The Exclusion of Intuition, Feeling, Ethics, Introversion and the Loss of Totality in Culture; Symbolic Amplification; The Psychic Structure of Fairy Tales; Psychology and Religion; Religion, Mysticism and Alchemy; Study of an Individuation Process; Taoism; The Secret of the Golden Flower; Creativity and Art; Psychological Creativity; The Creative Process Nature in the Analysis and Identity of the Analyst; The Usefulness of Research in Psychotherapy.

- 4th year—2nd semester: The Components of Coniunctio and Conjunction; The Sense of the Alchemical Process; Content and Meaning in the Two First Degrees of Conjunction; Synchronicity, Archetype, Psychoid Archetype, Encounter of Psyche and Matter, The Relationship between Pauli and Jung; The Therapeutic Value of Alchemical Language and The Seduction of Black; The Silver and the White Earth; Rubedo; The Human Conflict of Good and Evil and the Myth of Meaning; Encounter with the Self; Rescue of the Feminine in Individuation; Ethics and Rituals in Present Times; The Ethic Issue in Individuation; Reflections on Ethics in Present Times.

3. JUNGIAN PSYCHOANALYTIC ASSOCIATION, NEW YORK

The Jungian Psychoanalytic Association (JPA), which became an IAAP Training Society in 2004, is a learning community, a model that shifts emphasis from training in a hierarchical structure to learning by participating in a community of ongoing professional development. As such, the primary endeavor is to allow clinical and personal encounter with the unconscious, and to support and model the attitudes and methods for such an encounter. A learning community acknowledges asymmetry between teachers and students, analysts and analysts-in-training, but it does not rely on the exercise of power in its model of education.

An examination is part of the process, yet it is different for each candidate; each candidate is expected to consider carefully, with a group of three analysts, what it means (personally, professionally, and theoretically) to be an analyst and how that is to be acquired and manifested. Second, all evaluations are done in a point-of-contact manner, meaning face-to-face with the teacher or supervisor, rather than through review committees. There is also support for the candidate to evaluate the training itself and the ability of instructors to communicate and contribute to the candidate's learning. This results in an ethos of mutual risk-taking and high level of candidate contribution. Finally, the personal growth of the candidate is respected as belonging to the individual's analytic process.

The JPA utilizes various learning modalities to engage different learning styles and expand on the many ways the psyche can be engaged. Weekly classes are supplemented with day-long dream practica, candidate-organized individual reading tutorials with faculty members, weekend colloquia that allow extended topical interaction and discourse among and between analysts and candidates, and finally a graduation project that encourages creative and multidisciplinary integration.

Finally, the JPA is working towards Eranos-style presentations from a spectrum of disciplines and analytic approaches to encourage a general psychology of relevance to the practice of analytical psychology in contemporary culture.

Curriculum:

1. Symptom and Symbol Formation
   - Psychopathology: Causation and Telos.
   - Teleology in Jungian Analysis and Psychic Process: Source Works in Contemporary Literature.
   - Numinosity and Creativity in Analytic and Developmental Traditions: Relative Uses of Illusion, Fiction, and Image.

2. Fields of Psychological Process
   - The Intrapsychic: Complexes, Dreams, Defenses, Character Structures, the Interpersonal; Transferential, Community/Group/ Culture; Transpersonal.
   - Jung's Clinical Vignettes: From the Collected and Uncollected Works Dissolve and Coagulate: Complexes, Dissociability, Organization, and Dissociation.
   - The Archetype: Historical, Classical, Dynamic, and Contemporary Interpretation.
   - The Cultural Unconscious.
   - Jungian Hermeneutics and Semiotics.
   - Four Years of Dream Practicum—Which covers dream theory, applications of various approaches to dreams, hermeneutics, active imagination and other imaginal techniques, field theory, symbol formation, mythopoesis, as well as aspects of relevant neuroscientific and psychological literature.
   - Four Years of Case Seminar.
   - Ongoing Clinical Supervision.

3. Transformational Systems: Images and Applications
   - Alchemy and Mysterium, Gnosticism.
   - Creation and Dissolution of Consciousness.
   - From Africa to Alchemy: Egyptian States of Mind.
   - Contemporary Jungian Discourse.
   - Psychic Reality and States of Mind: Interpretive Modes of Imagination.

4. Mythopoesis and Mythologems
   - Mythologems and Their Psychodynamic Applications.

- Creation of Consciousness: Personality Structures and Contemporary •
  Psychoanalytic Theories as Modern Mythologems.

5. Psyche-Soma Conjunctions
   - Neuroscientific Literature on the Nature of Mind and Psyche.
   - Individuation and Its Manifestation: The Various Relationships to
     Psyche's Objectivity; Art and Creativity in Analysis.
   - Symbol/Psyche/Body.

6. Analytic Attitude and Technique
   - The Depth Dimension of Analytic Ethics.
   - Amplification and Active Imagination.
   - The Question of Technique in Jungian Psychoanalysis.
   - Amplification, Interpretation, and the Transferential Field.
   - Survey of Techniques in Jung's Collected Works.

4. KOREAN ASSOCIATION OF JUNGIAN ANALYSTS

The Korean Association of Jungian Analysts (KAJA) was voted in as an IAAP
Training Society in August 2007. The minimum duration of training to become
a Jungian analyst is seven years part-time. In August 2004, KAJA was voted in
as an IAAP nontraining society of the IAAP. Prior to this, the C.G. Jung Institute
of Korea was founded in October 1997 and became an Institute for Training in
Research in Analytical Psychology in 1998. This was formed by Jungian members of the IAAP and members of the Executive Committee of the Korean
Society for Analytical Psychology which had been founded in 1978. Now, the
C.G. Jung Institute of Korea implements KAJA's training program accompanied
by an extensive reading list, including references from psychoanalysis, psychiatry, and cultural anthropology. The training has two steps: the Propaedeuticum
and the Diploma course and examinations are required for graduation at the end
of each step.

1. The Propaedeuticum is a preparatory step for the Diploma course wherein
the training candidate learns basic theory of analytical psychology and related
schools of psychotherapy. The candidate should also be well equipped with the
basic attitude of realizing their own unconscious in the Jungian way through personal analysis. The theoretical studies part of this step include the following subjects: Fundamentals of Analytical Psychology; Psychology of Dreams; Theory of
Complex and Association Experiment; Comparative Theories of 'Neuroses';
Fundamentals of Psychopathology (for nonpsychiatrist candidates); Comparative
History of Religion; Primitive Psychology; Psychology of Myth and Fairy Tales;
Ethics in Analytical Practice.

This step also includes 150 hours of personal analysis, a minimum of six
semesters study, the submission of two seminar reports one on the association
experiment and the other on the archetypal symbols, and a minimum of 300 hours

within 6 months psychiatric placement (for nonpsychiatrist candidates) at recognized clinics.

2. The next step is the Diploma Course which is based on the fundamentals of analytical psychology and which requires the capacity to apply it in practice in order to achieve an understanding of the unconscious. This step includes personal analysis, supervision by authorized control analysts, group supervision for control cases, seminars, workshops, special lectures and research in analytical psychology. The theoretical studies include the following: Theory and Practice of Analytical Psychology (Symbols of Individuation, Development of Personality, Transference/Countertransference); Interpretation of Dreams; Psychological Interpretation of Myth and Fairy Tales; Understanding of Symbolic Expression of the Unconscious (in Paintings); Clinical Psychiatry (Diagnosis, Differential Diagnosis, Psychiatric Treatment for Nonpsychiatrists Only); Studies of Analytical Cases; Research in the Field of Analytical Psychology.

The Conditions for Applying for the Diploma Examination are as follows:

- A total of 300 hours of analysis (minimum 150 hours after graduating from the Propaedeuticum).
- Over 500 hours of analysis with patients under the supervision of a control analyst, including over 100 hours of individual supervision by a control analyst. A report from the control analyst.
- More than 6 semesters study at the Institute.
- Essays on the psychological interpretation of myth and fairy tales.
- Additional 300 hours of psychiatric clerkship (for nonpsychiatrist candidates) after graduation from the Propaedeuticum.
- Report of 3 cases of analysis.
- Minimum of 40 sessions of group supervision for the control case.
- Diploma thesis under the instruction of an analyst assigned by the Training's Executive Committee of the Institute.
- Report of the Assessment Committee of the Institute after the investigations of the cases of candidates.
- Final decision by the Training's Executive Committee referring to the report of the Assessment Committee.

5. The C.G. Jung Institute of San Francisco

Thomas Kirsch sent a personal communication to clarify the position between the Society of Jungian Analysts (SJA), which was formed in San Francisco in 1950, and the C.G. Jung Institute, which was formed in July 1964. The Society is the professional arm while the Institute maintains the training program and the relationship to the public. As the membership was the same in both bodies, the Society was amalgamated into the Institute in the 1980s in an effort to have only one legal identity and all activities take place under the aegis of the Institute.

The training curriculum consists of four years of weekly seminars taught mostly by Institute members. The first two years cover basic theoretical and clinical matters such as: complexes; archetypes; mythology; symbolism; typology; developmental theory; general psychodynamics; psychopathology; analytic techniques including dream interpretation, active imagination, and sand play; transference/countertransference. Experiential and didactic group process sessions are scheduled for first- and second-year candidates.

The third- and fourth-year curricula are planned jointly by the Curriculum Committee and the candidates to include advanced topics as well as specialized subject. In addition to the seminars, regular attendance at a 39-hour continuous case conference is required which must be completed prior to advancement to control analysis.

The Institute's Analytic Training Program states that an applicant must have completed no fewer than 200 hours of personal analysis prior to submitting an application form. This must be with a qualified Jungian analyst from among the following associations: Association of Graduate Analytical Psychologists (Zurich); C.G. Jung Analysts Association (Washington); C.G. Jung Institute of Los Angeles; The C.G. Jung Institute of San Francisco; The C.G. Jung Study Center of Southern California; Chicago Society of Jungian Analysts; Dallas Society of Jungian Analysts; Georgia Association of Jungian Analysts; Inter-Regional Society of Jungian Analysts; Jungian Psychoanalytic Association; New England Society of Jungian Analysts; New Mexico Society of Jungian Analysts; New York Association for Analytical Psychology; North Carolina Society of Jungian Analysts; Ohio Valley Association of Jungian Analysts; North Pacific Institute of Analytical psychology; Pacific Northwest Society of Jungian Analysts; Pittsburgh Society of Jungian Analysts; Philadelphia Association of Jungian Analysts; Society of Jungian Analysts of San Diego.

A candidate in training is expected to continue with personal analysis during the entire training period.

Analytic training is divided into three stages:

A. Preliminary (this is a trial period of mutual evaluation between candidate and Institute which lasts one year or longer, according to the needs of the individual candidate).
B. Candidacy.
C. Advanced (includes control analysis with at least two training analysts).

The First and Second Year Curriculum for 2007-2008 includes seminars on the following: History of the IAAP and the C.G. Jung Institute; Before Jung met Freud; Archetypal Images; Complex Theory; the Ethical Attitude; Myths and Fairytales; Masculine and Feminine; The Self; The Religious Function of the Psyche.

The Third and Fourth Year Curriculum for 2007-2008 includes seminars on the following: Symbols of Transformation; Two Essays on Analytical Psychology; Dreams; Early States, Transference; Fairy Tales; Experiencing and Reflecting upon the Analytic Space; Transference/Countertransference; Fordham; Alchemy; Mysterium Coniunctionis; Getting a Grip on the Grip of the Field; Freud and Jung; Jung, Energy, and Kundalini.

A candidate is certified as having completed training as a Jungian analyst when they have successfully completed the seminars, control analysis, and a paper on a control case that is deemed satisfactory by the Certifying Committee and one or more qualified external Jungian analysts.

6. THE SOCIETY OF ANALYTICAL PSYCHOLOGY, LONDON

The Society of Analytical Psychology (SAP) was established in 1936 but was not incorporated until 1946 due to the intervening war years. For the purposes of this chapter, the Training Committee has sent the Training Program for 2006/07 which is a four-year course of seminars. There is insufficient space to do justice to it here and a partial representation will have to suffice. The seminar lists below are accompanied by extensive readings lists. Case presentations and workshops are interspersed with the seminars.

The First Year of seminars includes:

- Jung in Context, including seminars on Jung's Roots in Psychiatry and Psychology; Jung and Freud; Jung and Science; Jung and Philosophy.
- Freud: The Interpretation of Dreams; Sexuality; The Unconscious; Dreams, Hysteria and the beginnings of transference; Infantile Sexuality and The Oedipus Complex; Pleasure Principle vs. the Reality Principle; The Ego in Freud's Structural Theory; The Ego in Relation with the Superego; The Creation of Illness; Freud's Archetypal Vision.
- C.G. Jung: Development of Theory; Discussion of Freud and Jung. Fordham's Model of Development; The Primary Self and Deintegration. Introduction to Object Relations.

The Second/Third Year of seminars includes:

- Aims of Analysis.
- Transference: History and Development.
- Countertransference.
- "On Not Knowing Beforehand."
- Interpretation.
- Personality of the Analyst.
- Active Imagination and Amplification.
- Symbols and the Transcendent Function.
- Working with Dreams.
  Psychology and Spirituality.

Fourth Year of seminars includes:

- Assessment and Diagnosis.
- Working with Trauma.
- Perversions.
- Eating Disorders
- Ethics
- Jung and the Academy.
- Research.

The SAP considers that the training candidate's personal analysis with a senior member of the Society at a frequency of four times per week is at the heart of the training and has to predate an application to train by at least a year. This continues at four times per week throughout the training until the candidate is elected to membership of the SAP. Alongside the personal analysis and theoretical seminars, the other pillar of the training is weekly supervision of four times per week analytic work with two (one male and one female) long-term cases by two training analysts. The Training Committee and the Director of Training meet monthly to oversee the training curriculum and each candidate's progress, aiming to integrate all three types of learning, with the help of a personal tutor for each candidate and a year group facilitator to attend to the candidate group dynamics. After four years of seminars and at least two years of work with analytic patients, and when their supervisors agree, a clinical paper about analysis of a patient with a theoretical commentary is submitted by each candidate as part of the final assessment of their readiness to join the Society.

CONCLUSION

There is limited space in this chapter to do a comparison of the six Jungian training programs and the three IPA models (Eitingon, French, Uruguayan) referred to in the introduction of this chapter. Suffice to say there is a degree of overlap in the structure of training between them, which the following few examples serve to underline: the five-year part-time Psychoanalyst course study program run by the C.G. Jung Institut Berlin equals the five-year duration in the Uruguayan model; and the Jungian Psychoanalytic Association's emphasis on a learning community rather than a hierarchical structure is akin to the French model's doing away with the title "training analyst." The French model states: "Supervision is regarded as the process that makes the candidate an analyst. Emphasis is on deep analytic listening—to patient material, and that of the candidate." (IPA 2007:5). This principle applies to training offered by the six Jungian Societies as does the following statement from the Eitingon model: "Analysis is an integral component of training . . ." (IPA 2007:5). Above all there is a *minimum* duration of four years for all the trainings referred to in this piece—the reality being that they all last considerably longer.

ACKNOWLEDGMENTS

I am indebted to the six IAAP Training Societies who have generously contributed to the making of this chapter. They are: SbrPA—Brazilian Society for Analytical Psychology; C.G. Jung Institut Berlin; Jungian Psychoanlaytic Association; C.G. Jung Institute of Korea, Korean Association of Jungian Analysts; The C.G. Jung Institute of San Francisco; The Society of Analytical Psychology.

I would like to thank Professor Shmuel Erlich, Chair of the Education Committee of the International Psychoanalytical Association, for his contribution to this chapter.

I would also like to thank Deborah Egger for help with the German translation and Adriana Oppenheim with the Brazilian Portuguese.

REFERENCES

Jung, C.G. 1963. *Memories, dreams, reflections*. London: Routledge & Kegan Paul.

Ramos, Denise. 2004. *Comparative study of training societies*. International Association for Analytical Psychology.

Training Programs of the following IAAP Training Societies: SbrPA—Brazilian Society for Analytical Psychology; C.G. Jung Institut Berlin; Jungian Psychoanalytic Association; C.G. Jung Institute of Korea, Korean Association of Jungian Analysts; The C.G. Jung Institute of San Francisco; The Society of Analytical Psychology.

ANN CASEMENT, LP, is a Senior Member of The British Association of Psychotherapists, a Member of the Jungian Psychoanalytic Association, and a New York State Licensed Psychoanalyst. She served on the Executive Committee of the International Association for Analytical Psychology from 2001 to 2007 and is currently the Honorary Secretary of its Ethics Committee.

35

TRAINING ANALYSIS

Dyane N. Sherwood

A training analysis is the heart and soul of analytic training, because a good enough analysis is essential for the future analyst to find a unique personal identity and way of working analytically, a healthy and realistic relationship to the Jungian community, and an ongoing commitment to self-examination and consultation when facing the many challenges of an analytic practice. Jung was the first to recognize the necessity of a training analysis (Kirsch 1995, 437), yet there is a dearth of clinical articles on this topic, no doubt due to the delicacy of writing about clinical work with someone in the same, small analytic community, even should permission be granted.

The importance of undergoing therapy as a part of training for psychotherapy professionals is not the norm in the United States, where symptom-focused treatment using pharmacological and cognitive-behavioral approaches is dominant. In contrast, the psychoanalytic schools view symptoms as unconscious communication and recognize the central role of transference. Much of our analytic literature addresses the power of transference and countertransference, especially ways in which the analyst may conceptualize and work with these intermeshed phenomena. Jungians also emphasize the importance of the symbolic function as a bridge between the conscious and unconscious. Whether we refer to the healing of the soul, psyche, or psyche-soma, we recognize that analysis requires more than technique, education, or insight.

Because of the limitations of writing in any detail about the training analyses of others, I will write about my own experience, which begins with finding my way to Jungian analysis. As a young person, my attitude was rational and analytic, in harmony with the collective *Zeitgeist*. Then, while doing postdoctoral work in neuroscience, I began to remember my dreams. On a holiday in the Engaden, I read *Memories, Dreams, Reflections* (Jung 1961). It was a life-altering experience for me, as for so many. Nevertheless, when I made the long-contemplated move from neuroscience research to clinical training, I believed that the only serious and responsible course was to enter a classical Freudian program. Fortunately for me, a lone Jungian analyst taught the introductory clinical process class. I learned for the first time about typology when he remarked that I was intuitive and asked how I had managed to do the precise and technical intracellular recording required by my research! I began to realize that I had been working in a sensation-thinking field because of my fear of the unconscious. Only later did I see that my decision to study in a very traditional psychoanalytic program had preserved this defense.

What became my Jungian training analysis began seven years prior to beginning analytic training at the C.G. Jung Institute in San Francisco, after a dream led to my ending a Freudian psychoanalysis and letting go of any plans to become a Freudian psychoanalyst. In the dream,

> *I was lunching at a mountain restaurant in the Swiss Engaden. I ordered a fresh trout, which would be prepared from trout kept live in a tank. It was brought to me whole on my plate, and to my horror it began to wriggle. My first thought was that I knew exactly how to end its agony by taking my knife and pithing it at the base of its brain. Instead I became hysterical and jumped up, crying loudly, "It's alive! It's alive!" I did not know what to do! A man nearby turned the spoon in his cup upside down and said, "It is over."*

I believe that only the hysteria of my dream ego could have gotten me off the couch! I ended my psychoanalysis, with great respect for the analyst and recognition that his approach was not the right match for me. After this dream, which signaled that my unconscious was alive—not to be only *analyzed*, cut up—my inner life burst forth in ways that were exciting, bewildering, and at times overwhelming. My former Jungian teacher referred me to a seasoned Jungian analyst, who was a wonderful match for me: a feeling type who brought great empathy and depth to the work. She was strong in just the areas where I needed so much help.

Until I became an analyst myself, I could never have begun to imagine the complexities that my analyst *may* have experienced, not only because of my hard-edged thinking but also because of my wish to enter analytic training. I recall an explicit interchange several years into the work, when I brought up the question of my readiness to apply to the analytic training program. My analyst's tone became firm, and she told me that it was not yet time. When I asked why, she said that I might be accepted on intellectual grounds but that my dreams indicated that I was not ready. She could not explain this to me. Not long after, I had a dream in which various people from the Institute were walking through her consulting room disrupting my session, and I knew that in addition to my not being inwardly ready I was not prepared for the potential intrusions of the life of the Institute into my analytic space. Several years later, I *knew* I was ready to apply, and I would have fought with my analyst had she said otherwise!

Perhaps this is a good point to describe the San Francisco training program, since each program is a product of its founders and the surrounding cultural and professional context (Kirsch 2001; Horne 2007; Kelly 2007). In California, there are no unlicensed analysts: one must have a professional license granted by the state. This requires a graduate degree in medicine, psychology, social work, nursing, or a master's level counseling program, as well as two to three years of supervised clinical work (usually in a clinic or hospital setting) and written examinations as to general professional knowledge, diagnosis, and ethics. Many train as psychotherapists after pursuing a first career rather than directly after an undergraduate degree. In the early years of our Institute, candidates were accepted in their last year of residency or shortly after being licensed, but the trend over the years has been to admit people only after they have had considerable analysis beyond the 200 requisite hours and when they are already experienced practitioners. Some apply after their children have grown and they have been in practice for thirty years! Therefore, in San Francisco most training analyses now take place during the second half of life.

In the San Francisco Institute, there is no special category of training analyst, and the candidate is free to choose any analyst member of the institute. This means that there is no need to disrupt an analysis at the beginning of training because the analyst in question is not a training analyst. In fact, it is generally agreed that an applicant will benefit from a well-established analysis with a strong working alliance in order to contain and process complexes stimulated by the evaluative, personal, and group stresses of training. Our policy contrasts to that of our local Freudian psychoanalytic institutes, which require the training analyst to be chosen from a select group of analysts. Some institutes also permit an earlier analysis with a training analyst to fulfill the analytic requirement, but most often the training analysis may begin at the same time as training. I have psychoanalytic colleagues who have waited years to apply in the hopes that their analyst would become a training analyst so that they would not need to change analysts or undergo a second analysis.

A Jungian training analysis in San Francisco, then, takes place while the candidate is practicing and leading a full adult life, perhaps raising a family or caring for elderly parents. The candidate attends four years of seminars, a clinical case conference, and group process, and undergoes a period of intensive supervision of analytic work culminating in a paper and a meeting with a board. The time to complete the program ranges from six to more than fifteen years, and during this entire time the candidate is expected to remain in individual analysis. The candidate may work sequentially or concurrently (rare) with more than one analyst, in addition to analysts who consult about the candidate's clinical work.

Special consideration is sometimes given to candidates who have a spouse who is already an analyst or candidate, allowing them to see an analyst from outside our institute. Presumably, this protects the candidate from contamination caused by projections (positive and negative) onto the spouse or his/her reluctance to discuss the spousal relationship because the spouse is a colleague or student of the personal analyst. While the incest archetype is a part any analysis, if it is too concretely present it can be iatrogenic.

This brings me to mention the intensification of incestuous and narcissistic complexes that accompany a training analysis. In our institute, the training analysis is considered sacrosanct and entirely confidential, a sealed alembic, and the analyst is not allowed to give training committees any input whatsoever regarding the analysand. Of course, this does not mean that the training will not contaminate or present special challenges to the analysis. The analysand and analyst in a training analysis are part of a larger community in which the analyst is already a full member and the analysand is aspiring to become a member. This can activate authority complexes in both.

Moreover, the analyst has her own opinions, reactions, and projections with regard to the institute, its various members, and its training program. How are these managed? At times, a small digression from an analytic stance in the form of a carefully phrased question or comment or a raised eyebrow can, in my opinion, be helpful. The danger is that such an intervention can short-circuit an exploration leading to the candidate's developing confidence in her capacity to make judgments and navigate the complex views and relationships within the group.

Some analysts openly share their disdain or admiration for certain colleagues, for certain ways of doing analysis, and for the institute itself. This can foster collusion between analyst and analysand of being the inflated outsider, or the consummate insider, who sits in judgment. The analysand is in a position of either joining with the analyst or risking confrontation and rejection; it also deprives the analysand—and the analyst—of facing potential shadow or idealization issues that are being carried by the group or by some individuals or ways of doing analysis. Defensive splitting can protect the pathological narcissism of both, which no doubt would encounter painful challenges should genuine engagement with the group be attempted. This recalls Guggenbühl-Craig's commentary on the analyst-as-sorcerer:

> sorcerers . . . are unwilling to tolerate any colleagues or competitors. … Fascinated by this inner figure, the average analyst would like all those in need of help to turn exclusively to him. . . . [T]he fantasy that he is the best and most powerful of sorcerers, makes it impossible for him willingly to send cases to colleagues of equal status, . . . [A] devilish little sorcerer within him lays claim to being the only one . . . who really understands anything about analysis. (1971, 39–40)

> Training analyses in particular are subject to this danger. The trainee may remain an "apprentice" for the rest of his life, that is, an admirer and imitator of his training analyst. Or he may try to become a master sorcerer himself, which leads to bitter recriminations between old master and former apprentice; the younger analyst harbors deep resentments against his older colleague, while the latter feels himself betrayed. The two can no longer work well together. (1971, 40)

It should be added that analysts may consciously or unconsciously try to "convert" their candidate-analysands into apprentices or apostles, to the "true" or "right" way of working, thus violating the analysand's need to discover her own unique potential as a human being and as an analyst. This can be a particular problem if the analyst identifies strongly with the analysand.

If a parental transference/countertransference remains unresolved, some training analyses can last for the lifetime of the analyst or analysand, but not because it has remained a valuable interchange in service of the analysand's individuation. I have seen some analysts come into their own only after the death of an analyst-mentor. Another scenario is that the analysand may assume, unconsciously or consciously, a caretaking role toward an aging or ill analyst—in order to meet the analyst's needs for relationship, validation, and/or income—at a point in time when the analyst should have retired from practice. (I am aware of a startling number of analysts who had hidden worsening disabilities or terminal illnesses, which denied their analysands the opportunity of a related ending to the work.)

How does an analyst provide a safe and reliable analytic container while dealing with issues of personal, physical, financial—and most important—analytic vulnerabilities and limitations? These questions become even more crucial during a training analysis. Once an analysand has entered a training program, she is in a position to learn more about the analyst—whether fact, projection, or gossip. Likewise, the analyst may hear others discuss the analysand. Hopefully, the analyst is capable of holding and processing the material, but will the analysand feel able or willing to bring up negative information about the analyst? Will positive opinions or projections onto the analyst by colleagues and candidates inhibit the need for the analysand to address real and projected inadequacies and failures on the part of the analyst? The analysand may become aware of events and situations, private or professional, that are highly charged and painful for the analyst (such as death of a family member, marital infidelity, divorce, hostility from colleagues, and so on), requiring careful attention to countertransference reactions that interfere with the analysis of the candidate's material.

Joseph Henderson, who entered an intensive analysis with Jung in 1929 at the age of twenty-six, has given an account of the way his personal complexes fixed upon the well-known break between Jung and Freud:

> At that time it was generally supposed that the rupture of their relationship was due to a father-son conflict, Freud being the father and Jung the son. . . . [I]t was natural that the father-son aspect of the Freud-Jung relationship mobilized my own ambivalence toward the father. In the light of my early transference to Jung, I was inclined to see him as the misunderstood son of an authoritarian father; but then, since Jung was a father figure, too, I found plenty of room for considerable resistance to him. In such a state of resistance, I felt that Jung was the bad (or at least unsympathetic) father and Freud the good (or, shall we say, misunderstood) father. And then it all turned around, and Jung became the good father again.
>
> I soon realized that the Freud-Jung controversy was inhibiting the process of separation from, or repair of, my own parent images and, if allowed to go on, could become itself a kind of false parent. Jung was very good about understanding this problem and

helping me to disidentify with what was in the projection of my father image. But in spite of his help, a certain problem remained, because I felt that some of the personal suffering that C.G. and Emma Jung experienced following the break with Freud still existed. (Henderson 1982, 3–4)

Henderson later came to his own understanding of the break between Freud and Jung through the study of historical materials, having remained on good terms with Jung after his analysis came to a completion in 1939.

In a training analysis, the analyst and analysand may attend conferences and meetings and observe one another interacting with others. These situations are presumably handled on a very individual basis, with the analyst taking into account the state of the transference at that point in time. When I was a new candidate, I mentioned to my analyst that I was going to attend a small group lecture at the Institute. At the meeting, people seemed surprised that she was not present. When I brought this up at my next analytic hour, she told me that she chose not to come after finding out I would attend. I was very moved by the sacrifice she had made when, unknowingly, I was participating in a small group which she had attended for many years. Some years later, we both became aware that we were comfortable attending a small, nonclinical professional meeting. Other situations may involve larger events where the analyst and analysand may observe one another interacting with colleagues or speaking. It is important that the analysand feel free to bring up any reactions.

Joseph Henderson described to me a similar shift in his transference to Jung. Sometime in the early part of his work, Jung happened to be driving from his house into town immediately after Joe's analytic session, and he offered Joe a ride. Joe accepted, but sat stiffly, not knowing what to say when he found himself in this strange situation outside the consulting room. He was relieved when the ride was over, and the situation was never repeated. Some time later, however, he was invited to a formal dinner, which Jung also attended. He felt perfectly himself in this situation. Later, after his analysis had ended, he described what he called a resolution of the transference into a "symbolic friendship." He believed—and I agree—that, having been analyst and analysand, it is not possible to move to the mutual intimacy of an ordinary friendship. Yet, another kind of warm and mutually respectful relationship sometimes develops of its own course.

Issues of love and hate, competition and envy, anger and fear, shaming and humiliation, wounding and being wounded, joy and sadness are present in every deep human encounter. In a training analysis, these can be complicated or exacerbated. How will the eros be expressed? If the analysis includes a period in which the patient, analyst, or both fall in love, the pain of not being able to act upon this feeling can be intensified or mitigated if they cross paths outside analysis, especially when a partner or spouse is present.

Sibling rivalry and also feelings of kinship may develop when an analysand discovers that a fellow trainee is also seeing the same analyst. I recall dreaming that I entered a beautiful cathedral, entirely alone, and saw my analyst sitting next to a candidate analysand whom I considered to be much more mature, interesting, and well-related than myself. It was a terribly painful dream, as I truly believed that my analyst much preferred working with her and would never share a deep connection to the numinous (represented by the cathedral) with me, as she surely did with my sister trainee. My analytic work then involved an exploration of these feelings and my coming to a greater acceptance of my own shortcomings but with fewer feelings of inferiority, as well as a new appreciation of my unique relationship with my analyst—not through reassurances but through her caring attention to our work.

On the other hand, as an analyst I frequently feels pangs or jabs of envy when an analysand tells me of the wonderful help that a consultant gave her or expresses admiration for the unique abilities of the consultant or of another analyst. At times, this can get in the way of my reflecting on the meaning of that communication at that time. Is my envy projective identification or my personal complex? It is a delicate balance to watch for counter-therapeutic splitting, acting out, and dilution of the transference or countertransference, while avoiding the inflation of believing that the analysis is not only central but all-important. I am frequently reminded that if I am a good enough analyst the analysand will need to find additional symbolic and interpersonal avenues for development. Each candidate will require multiple mentors to develop a unique way of working and an analytic flexibility in order to engage with different patients. Every analysand, in a sense, needs to outgrow, or grow beyond, the training analyst.

This leads to the issue of "termination," the ending of a training analysis. I recall from my courses taught by traditional Freudians that the "termination" of an analysis precludes future contact, in order that the analysand work through issues of loss and mourning. Although this view is no longer stringently held, I can appreciate its value, especially the value it could hold in facing existential issues. This structure also avoided concretizing the question of what kind of relationship might *actually* develop after "termination," leaving the pair more open to exploring fantasy material. In a training analysis, this lack contact is not possible, as both will remain in a small community, possibly for the rest of their lives. In a large institute, analyst and analysand may have minimal contact and avoid serving together on committees. In smaller institutes, this may be much more difficult.

A bad ending can affect an analyst's or analysand's comfort in attending institute events. Since a bad ending usually involves highly charged and unresolved complexes and the failure of a capacity to symbolize, the hate may last a lifetime. The analyst may feel especially vulnerable, since the analysand is free to talk about the analysis to colleagues, perhaps with significant distortions, and some analysts have had their practices affected adversely by such talk, to which they are prohibited from responding because of confidentiality. On the other hand, the analysand may feel vulnerable because he feels he has lost the esteem of a respected or powerful analyst; or he may feel contempt or disgust because such a disappointing analyst is still a member of the institute. At best, it may take many years for the analysand (and also the analyst) to begin to understand what happened and to initiate some kind of meeting or resolution; at worst, the analysand finds another analyst who colludes with projections onto the previous analyst. (In recent years, some analysts from within and outside our institute have done specialized impasse consultation to both analyst and analysand, with very helpful results.)

My own training analysis ended in a very natural way, several years after I completed my analytic training. I had become deeply engaged in research on alchemical imagery and symbolism, which came to hold the same powerful cathexis for me that my analysis had held for so long. The image that comes to mind as symbolic of this shift in my psyche is that of a woman gracefully riding a fish or dolphin, found on the ancient Celtic Gundestrup Cauldron.

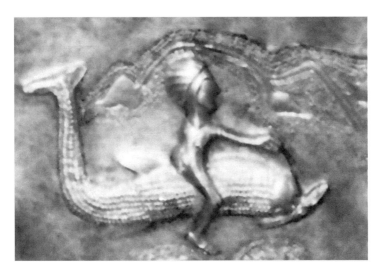

Detail of the ancient Celtic Gundestrup Cauldron
(National Museum of Denmark)

The analytic process has a life of its own now, continuing as I learn from my patients, from my colleagues, from nature, and from what my Lakota friend Pansy Hawkwing calls *Wakan Tanka*, "The Great Mystery."

My training analysis was not a cure, nor did it make me whole or complete. It did completely change my experience of being alive, helping me to accept human limitations and to discover possibilities. I am grateful for my analyst's depth of understanding, kindness, and calm empathy. Most essential were her integrity and her carefully focused analytic attitude.

REFERENCES

Guggenbühl-Craig, Adolf. 1971. *Power in the helping professions*. Dallas, TX: Spring Publications.

Henderson, Joseph L. 1982/1995. Reflections on the history and practice of Jungian analysis. In *Jungian analysis*, ed. Murray Stein, 3–28. Chicago: Open Court.

Horne, Michael. 2007. There is no 'truth' outside a context: Implications for the teaching of analytical psychology in the 21st century. *Journal of Analytical Psychology* 52, 2: 127–42.

Jung, C.G., with Aniela Jaffé. 1961. *Memories, dreams, reflections*. New York: Random House.

Kelly, Tom. 2007. The making of an analyst: From 'ideal' to 'good-enough. *Journal of Analytical Psychology* 52, 2: 157–69.

Kirsch, Thomas B. 1982/1995. Training analysis. In *Jungian analysis*, ed. Murray Stein, 437–50. Chicago and LaSalle, IL: Open Court.

———. 2001. *The Jungians: A comparative and historical perspective*. London: Routledge.

DYANE N. SHERWOOD, Ph.D., is a member and on the teaching faculty of the C.G. Jung Institute of San Francisco. She is co-author, with Joseph L. Henderson, of *Transformation of the Psyche: The Symbolic Alchemy of the Splendor Solis* and the editor of *Jung Journal*.

36

SUPERVISION OF THE APPRENTICE

Catherine Crowther

Becoming an analyst is essentially a long extended period of apprenticeship and of internalization of one's mentors, with all the ambivalence that entails. The various schools of Jungian training differ in the importance they place on intellectual scholarship and the learning of theory, but all agree that great emphasis should be given to enabling and appraising a trainee's personal "readiness" and self-awareness. That means the capacity to experience deeply and honestly one's interior processes of mind in relationship with others. How in practice is this achieved? The personal analysis clearly carries this as a prime objective. Yet perhaps the second most potent influence on the trainee is supervision. The supervisors' function is to provide an arena that will help the deintegration/ reintegration process of forming a professional identity as an analyst (Fordham 1957). Supervision helps to gather in and make "operational" in the consulting room all the accumulated life experience, theoretical knowledge, instinct, empathy, intuition, and authenticity of the novices in their encounters with their own and their patients' unconscious processes, as well as resonating with archetypal collective images with each individual patient. Analysts retain throughout their professional lives strong transferences to the figures of significant supervisors and are often seen as belonging to a lineage of supervisors within a training institute.

From the outset I want to declare my enjoyment of both supervising and being supervised. Notwithstanding the important consideration of the supervisor's position of relative power and authority, the creative purpose of supervision is to foster mutual curiosity about relationships, to open up mental and emotional experiences for the purpose of exploring whatever geological layers of unconscious meaning can be mined in the personal and collective psyche. This is interesting and stimulating work, sometimes painfully honest, at other times frustratingly uncertain, at still others enjoyably revelatory. Ambivalent attitudes toward supervision are rife. There is little space for learning if supervision is felt as persecutory or rivalrous, yet these are common reactions. Analytic work, involving as it must the whole personality of the analyst, lends itself to painful feelings of narcissistic exposure in supervision, unlike the supervision of other skills. Is the implication of the awkward term "supervisee" that the object of supervision is the person rather than the work of the therapy? As Hopwood (2005) notes: "Supervisees may easily feel criticised for the people they are, rather than merely for what they do." And yet if trust and curiosity can be established, supervision stops feeling like monitoring of standards and is sought after as a "space for thinking."

The unique gift of our psychoanalytic tradition to the helping professions is the idea that supervision is a valuable life-long tool for continuing to learn. It is not only for the untrained and inexperienced, but it is a necessary component of our ongoing professional and creative development. However, this chapter will deal only with those aspects of supervising that relate to training new psychotherapists and analysts, and it also draws on my experience of supervising in a different culture, Russia, where psychoanalysis is resurgent after half a century of being banned.

The debate continues about how to balance the ingredients of the various professional functions of the supervisor—teacher, mentor, facilitator, boundary keeper, judge, container, or auxiliary analyst? Obviously aspects of all these roles are significant, some overt, some in the shadow. Jung's attitude of respect for his patients, his recognition that the analyst is equally immersed in the process, and his dislike of dogma have laid down the foundations for a tradition of Jungian supervision that aims to enable, facilitate, and empower. The supervisees grow into and develop their individual analytic abilities and learn to become themselves with decreasing anxiety as they are shown "the art, the craft and the method of analysis" (Hubback 1995, 98).

AUTHORITY AND ETHICS

Although creativity, mutuality, play, trust, and enjoyment are acknowledged as vital qualities of supervision, the fact of the supervisor's overseeing role cannot be denied, as well as its archetypal life as part of a projected superego complex. The power dynamic is never far away, and may turn in reality or fantasy to persecution. In training institutes, it is largely the supervisor who reports on and makes judgments about the quality of the trainee's analytic work. At worst this inflames the trainee's paranoia and the supervisor's inflation. The exercise of authority and power is also encountered in these days of increasing public concern about standards of mental healthcare provision, the rights of patients, and the regulation of psychotherapy, where supervision cannot be divided from the function of protection of the patient and monitoring standards of practice. Regular, ongoing supervision or consultation with colleagues about our work is now officially enshrined in Britain as a requirement for annual renewal of registration as a psychotherapist. We work within an ethical framework in which the welfare of the patient is axiomatic. What is the authority of the supervisor in an institution—is it by role, profession, or personal qualities? What is the supervisor's responsibility if she finds herself presiding over work that she considers a poor standard or is even harmful? How does responsibility conflict with confidentiality when violence, crime, or child abuse are reported? I raise these as ongoing concerns, without clear or obvious answers. We help our supervisees to understand the vital purpose of enabling sexual and aggressive fantasies, suicidal and other self-harming attitudes to be aired, but supervisors also have to make judgments about whether and when there is a need to act outside the analytic framework to protect the patient, supervisee, or others from harm. Holding the tension between the opposing functions of authority and imagination is one that Jungians respect. As Shearer says: "Jung's psychology is uniquely suited, in that it takes the paradoxical nature of psyche as its starting point, and the union rather than the annihilation of psyche's manifold opposites as its goal" (Shearer 2003, 209).

TRAINING AND APPRENTICESHIP

While the apprentice blacksmith or plumber works alongside his teacher, with his work visible to scrutiny and guidance, this sort of supervision would destroy the very essence of the analytic method. Zinkin calls it the impossible profession and asserts that it is impossible for the supervisee to "tell" or the supervisor to "know" what is occurring in the reported session. "A supervised analysis is not an analysis, which is a private two-person affair, but something else. The supervisor is, all the time, both present and not present—which is impossible" (Zinkin 1995, 244). Having acknowledged this contradiction, Zinkin suggests that supervisor and supervisee are in effect sharing a fantasy of a patient in analysis. He confirms his enjoyment of supervision as a worthwhile joint imaginative venture, and speaks of enormous learning and profit for both parties, let alone the presumed benefit to the patient.

Many analysts have questioned the appropriateness of the term *supervision*, with its overtones of loftiness, authority, judgment, and managerial function in the subtle facilitation of the emergence and growth of a new analyst. They prefer ideas such as mutual learning (Astor 2003), space for thinking (Mollon 1997), education (Wharton 2003), shared dream space (Shapley 2007), and play (Perry 2003). Hopwood (2005) invokes the supervisor as midwife, while the images of the labyrinth, the matrix (Perry 2003), and the prism (Wiener 2007) have all been suggested to convey some of the complexity of supervising. This brings us to consider how much supervision should be seen as didactic, or rather as facilitation of learning, and to remind ourselves of the Latin roots of the word *education*, *e-ducere*, to lead out, with the implication for our profession of bringing to consciousness what is already (unconsciously) formed.

The supervisory like the analytic relationship is not symmetrical—one party is more senior, experienced, and knowledgeable than the other. Yet it differs in that the relationship takes place at an adult level that does not encourage regression nor explore transferences, although both are likely to occur and may be acknowledged. Infantile transferences to the supervisor may be reinforced by an infantilizing atmosphere towards trainees within the training institute as a whole.

On the other hand, some supervisors actively work to exclude regression by treating trainees with the respect due to a junior colleague, as indeed they will become when they join the society in a few years time.

NOT KNOWING VS. TECHNIQUE

Famously Jung repudiated theorizing and technique:

> Since every individual is a new and unique combination of psychic elements, the investigation of truth must begin afresh with each case, for each 'case' is individual and not derivable from any preconceived formula. . . . We miss the meaning of the individual psyche if we interpret it on the basis of any fixed theory, however fond of it we may be. (Jung 1946/1966, para. 173)

Yet if the task of every analyst is to use the self in the service of understanding our patients, this cannot be done without learning something of the analytic traditions, techniques, timings, boundaries, ethics, and styles of the working method. Supervisors try to teach the art of analysis by creating an atmosphere in which experiential and emotional learning can take place, and creative, playful conjecturing can emerge. The goal is to enable each trainee to develop organically in their own individual style of being an analyst. The supervisor's evaluative role in training inevitably inhibits the trainee's freedom to be himself or herself, but usually over time the trainee's initial impatient anxiety about trying to "get it right" turns to trust in the reflective process, and toward openness to ambivalence, honesty about confusion or lack of understanding, and learning from "mistakes" as part of the normal currency of supervision. The supervisor aids this process by demonstrating an open-minded attentiveness to the patient's material and a respect for the trainee's point of view, avoiding dogmatism by "emphasising that there are no correct conclusions to be reached, only hypotheses to be tested" (Wharton 2003, 86). The supervisor presents a model, and the trainee gradually learns through identification with both supervisor and personal analyst the analytic attitude of listening with a third ear to unconscious and symbolic contents, of waiting in a state of curiosity and not knowing, of not imposing a premature meaning until the material has revealed a potential shape.

Nonetheless some discipline is required in the learning process. There is a risk that exaggerated reliance on "not knowing" can be a pretext for woolly thinking and avoidance of needful challenge to the patient's status quo. Some supervisors find the use of verbatim notes essential in exploring the fine grain of a session and for uncovering so called "blind spots" in the trainee's ability to process a neurotic countertransference. Certainly, remembering as much detail as possible of the minute-to-minute sequences of sessions can be valuable in helping trainees to look at their wording and timing and to notice later what escaped their attention in the heat of the session. Others find that such verbatim written reporting deadens the emotional spirit of the analyst-patient exchanges by too consciously processing the themes, motifs, and interactions in supervision. One of my supervisees has an ingenious method of writing her notes in interlocking circular bubbles that spread out across the page in a sort of reverie, rather than record in a linear cause and effect model. Perry is concerned that verbatim notes can

> exclude the exploration of the myriad events of a session such as the apperception of a mood, the non-verbal language created by the participants, and the 'unmentionable' associations and responses of the supervisee. These latter generally coagulate around anxieties about physical contact, erotic longings, increased availability through extra sessions, writing letters, telephone contact, the activation of a sado-masochistic complex, the use of tokens, the acceptance of gifts, succumbing to pressure to reduce fees, 'non-analytic' interventions or inexplicable failures in empathy. Talking about these in supervision is often shame-ridden but can lead to growth and the development of individual style. (Perry 2003, 194)

In the early days of psychoanalysis, personal analysis and supervision were not at first separated, and because they share so much of the same necessary attentiveness to countertransferences and psychological atmosphere, there are sometimes confusions as to where the appropriate dividing line between the two functions should be. Supervisors often notice that particular patients present issues such as aggression, separation, eroticisation, intimacy, which activate a corresponding preoccupation or else a "blind spot" of denial in the supervisee's neurotic countertransference, effectively preventing the supervisee from hearing the patient in an attuned way. Opinion is divided about how this should be addressed with the supervisee, some making a direct suggestion to the supervisee that it is a matter for their personal analysis, others feeling strongly that this would constitute a gross interference in the supervisee's analysis. I hold with Astor's humorous yet serious comment:

> I disagree with those supervisors who tell their supervisees to take such and such a feeling to their analyst. We are analysts, so let us proceed analytically rather than as traffic policemen. Apart from anything else this comment usually indicates some rivalry or unexpressed hostility towards the supervisee's analyst, as if the problem would not have arisen if the analyst had done a better job. (Astor 2003, 55)

Proceeding analytically means patiently and repeatedly drawing the supervisee's attention to the problem *as it affects their work* and trusting their readiness to recognize it as fruitful personal material. Thus supervision is often a powerful spur to aid a supervisee's psychological growth. The long duration of analytic trainings is essential to allow this acceptance of complexes and the reintegration of what belongs to the supervisee but was experienced in projection onto the patient. If the supervisee proves unable *over time* to respond to the spotlight shed on the problem area during supervision as a source of enlightenment, but feels it as a persecution, this helps to reveal a problem in the supervisee's analytic capacity, which hopefully it is possible then to acknowledge together in supervision. But it is not within the supervisor's remit to force the pace of the supervisee's analysis, merely to slow down (or in rare cases to terminate) the supervisee's progress towards qualification.

SUPERVISION AS CONTAINMENT

The ideal of the analytic pair contained safely in the confidentiality of the *vas bene clausum* cannot remain a literal form when the supervisor is admitted as a third party, bringing in the dynamics of a triangular relationship. Despite breaking the seal on the sacred vessel, paradoxically the presence of the third can augment the reliability and durability of the analytic container. The analogy is with the role of father or grandparent in protecting the intimacy of mother and infant, enabling their relationship to weather storms and thus deepen. A trainee—akin to a new mother—may be overwhelmed by the destructive power of infantile emotions evoked in the transference, and needs my grandparental support not to despair nor to accept at face value a patient's disparaging attack on the unhelpfulness of the sessions. Supervisors, like grandparents and fathers, are sometimes tempted to take over and become directive if they see the trainee not coping very well, and certainly supervisees sometimes have the fantasy that a different analytic "mother" would be better for their patient. Instead, the supervisor is needed to keep the twosome together. Discussion of the supervisee's collusion with the projected sense of failure, of the patient's powerful use of projective identification to convey the despair, hurt, and neediness that cannot be borne but are turned into attack or acting out, can become a window of insight. The supervisor allows the full venting of the supervisee's fierce emotional countertransference reactions, which—without understanding—could otherwise have threatened the patient, even the continuation of the analysis. The supervisor's intense psychic involvement combined with a thinking function untrammelled by passion allows enough emotional distance to act as the benign third. What is being fostered is an attitude of curiosity and enquiry, not judgment, about how the trainee comes to be dominated by the patient's primitive state, so that a space for consciousness and differentiation is opened up.

This has been conceptualized as a containing oedipal triangle (Britton 1998). I have found this idea helpful particularly when supervising in Russia. The long political history of abrupt disappearances, the forced break-up of relationships, the betrayals of trust, and the official policies that encouraged termination of unwanted pregnancy seem to have predisposed some Russian supervisees to anticipate unconsciously that conflict, tension, and disagreement with their patients will lead inevitably to the destruction of the analytic relationship. This can sometimes lead to the supervisee's passive (killed off) resignation to a patient's premature departure, or else an appeasing accommodation to the patient's demands, in a clinging attempt not to lose them. Supervision can question these polarized attitudes by helping the supervisee to acknowledge the deadly impulses on both sides and to start to challenge, interpret and work with, rather than simply to accept, the patient's departure by looking with interest and curiosity at all the potential *meanings* of the rejection. The presence of the third opens up space to think and fosters a new experience of the power of symbolic understanding to restore confidence in the patient that both the personal and cultural shadows are accepted, need not be destructive, and thus can actually strengthen the robustness of the analytic twosome.

TRIANGLES AND PARALLEL PROCESS

Mattinson's (1981) discussion of the triangular relationships within supervision draws attention to the ever shifting focus among the patient-analyst pair, the analyst-supervisor pair, and the supervisor-patient pair, and to the hazard that one corner of the oedipal triangle may at any time become either neglected or overemphasized. There are also other relationships molding and impinging on the supervisory relationship in training. The fantasy of rivalry in a triangle with the trainee's analyst is present at many levels, with the trainee having to compare styles of analyzing and to deal with divided loyalties, while both the supervisor and the analyst of the trainee speculate on each other's efficacy, alerting them to primitive feelings of shame and embarrassment, triumph and superiority. Shearer (2003) comments on the "painful energies of alliances and exclusions that ricochet around figures of three. . . .Yet trinities are sacred too across time, place and culture, and three is nothing if not a moving number" (Shearer 2003, 208). Because the training institution, indeed the whole edifice of psychoanalysis, attracts transferences and identifications, Perry thinks in terms of "a series of permeable concentric circles rippling out from the patient, containing all participants" (Perry 2003, 195).

Although the ostensible focus of thinking in the supervision triangle is on the analytic couple, the other two relationships require attention. Most supervisors—especially in training settings—also attend to the quality of the trainee-supervisor relationship. Supervisors are interested in the manner in which the supervisee brings the patient into supervision and in the whole atmosphere of the supervision session. Just as we try to encourage trainees to listen with empathy and to observe their patients with the whole body, not just with their ears, attending to their physical and mental countertransference reactions, so supervisors also model this attitude. Supervisors attend to their supervisees' body language and tone of voice, scan for hints of anxiety or inflation, tune into the psychosomatic effect the supervisee is having on them, while trying to attain sufficient distance to think about the multilayered potential meaning of their reactions.

"Parallel process" (Ekstein and Wallerstein 1958) describes a phenomenon frequently observed in supervision, particularly group supervision, whereby the supervisee's presentation of the patient has a marked emotional effect on the supervisor or the group as a whole. This countertransference at a distance is treated as psychological information, as an echo of whatever affect or dynamic interaction had been current, probably unconsciously, in the transference between patient and supervisee during the analytic session. Here is an example from my supervisory practice:

> *A supervisee was unaware of her masochism in tolerating the covert aggression of a patient, but seemed to act out a parallel attack by politely dismissing her colleagues in the supervision group who tried to point out the patient's undermining effects on her. She sweetly insisted on "proving" to them her different view of the patient's behavior. The group members were uncomfortably submissive to her theory, until one person eventually voiced the feeling of masochism at the tone of the discussion and admitted to rising anger at being covertly "bullied" to agree. This emotional honesty about the parallel dynamics of the present situation had a more persuasive effect on the supervisee than any previous reasoning about the dynamics between herself and the patient, and she became open to considering the sado-masochism she had been avoiding.*

One of Ogden's (1999) hallmarks as a clinician is his detailed use of his own reverie as a source of self-analysis and self-supervision. He asks his supervisees not only to write process notes of the verbal exchanges in the sessions but also to include every moment-to-moment thought, fantasy, feeling, and physical sensation, even including sessions that the patient does not attend. He does not try to make simple one-to-one correspondences between the supervisee's reverie and the patient's thoughts and feelings but plays with them associatively and lets them "reverberate" within the supervisory discussion, gathering them in as "analytic objects" whose meaning may emerge. His own reverie about the characteristics of the supervisee's presentation and manner is equally part of the enquiry, to be shared in the discussion. However, Sedlak (2003) sounds a warning note against too heavy a reliance on countertransference to the detriment of listening closely to the patient's material. He quotes Pontalis who questions "the fashion of delighting in the display of one's countertransference, as if to say that one is seeing with one's blind spots, listening to what one is deaf to, and conscious of one's unconscious" (Pontalis 1975, quoted in Duparc 2001, 161). We do well to remind ourselves that these intuitions cannot be taken as established facts, however striking (and helpful) the parallels are. But we have all had occasion to marvel that following a tentative or free-associative uncovering of an as yet unexplored aspect of the analytic relationship in supervision the patient in the very next session spontaneously addresses exactly the same subject. The concept of an objective psyche speaks of the communicative power of a shared unconscious process among all three parties, where all are learning.

The third pairing in the supervisory triangle is that of the patient-supervisor. Whether or not patients are told of a supervisor's existence, they often seem to be aware of their presence, sometimes unconsciously sensing or dreaming of either the reassuring, or else the interfering, presence of a third figure. They may consciously use the fantasized supervisor to undermine the analyst ("Very clever! I see you've been to supervision yesterday!"). There is no doubt that the supervisor has her own distinct attitudes and reactions towards the patient as reported by the supervisee. It is important that the supervisor's opinion is not imposed upon an acquiescent supervisee. Learning will be only by imitation if the supervisor responds directly to the patient with a proposed interpretation, and the supervisee merely echoes it. Often last week's theory does not relate directly to this week's sessions, and so supervisees need encouragement to trust that their own internalised sense of theory will reappear when required.

LEARNING ABOUT BOUNDARIES

Perry's "unmentionables" listed in the quote above relate to the frame of the analytic session and are illustrative of the intensity of feelings generated around boundaries. It is a vital part of the apprenticeship to learn not merely to handle but to examine challenges to the "rules" about time keeping, the analyst's non-self-disclosure, breaks, etc., by recognizing what patients are unconsciously communicating by acting out to test them. To do this, it is vital that trainees find their own internalized, personal psychological boundary, which is strong yet flexible and which they value, rather than reproducing a notion of external "rules" that they merely enforce and hide behind. The "rules" constitute the scaffolding that helps to stabilize the building up of an experience of boundaried inner space, where creativity, self-discovery, and relationship with the other can grow. Supervisors model a formality in the frame, time keeping, and boundaries of supervisory sessions.

Supervising in another culture, Russia, has required renewed thinking about my conventional boundaries, to declare what I feel is essential and irreducible about the frame and what can be more flexible. Russian psychotherapists do not work in a tradition of charging patients for taking holidays and are often willing to change session times on demand. The resumption of work after the long Russian summer break does not have a date but is often dependent on the patient phoning the analyst. The mobile phone and email are always the means of communication because letters are not reliably delivered, and it may even be seen as intrusive to ask the patient for an address. My feeling has often been that it is the analyst who is intruded upon by the frequency of mobile phone calls outside of session times. Discussions with Russian supervisees have often elicited relief to be able to acknowledge widespread countertransference feelings of resentment, avoidance or fear of patients' demands. This has prompted a richer awareness of the *meaning* and purpose of the boundaries, in particular how analyst and patient are both deprived of necessary engagement with the negative transference if a robust frame is not in place.

Martin (2003) notes that according to Money-Kyrle, the secure frame of the analytic session enables the patient to face "the recognition of the inevitability of time and ultimately death" (Money-Kyrle 1978, 443), and so there are bound to be attacks on it as a defense against dependency, separation, and death anxieties. However, being caught off guard by a patient's unexpected personal question on the threshold of the consulting room can throw novices into a loss of their symbolizing capacity. They may respond at a concrete literal level, or else become defensive and forbidding. The space for thinking in supervision can help to right the boat again in subsequent sessions when the incident can be returned to more thoughtfully.

BECOMING A SUPERVISOR

The vital position of supervision in our profession cannot be emphasized enough. Yet it is a skill imparted almost by osmosis. It used to be assumed that a good analyst would automatically become a good supervisor over time and possess an inborn ability to communicate and teach apprentices the skills of the trade. Zinkin (1995) points out how difficult it is to assess what makes a good supervisor, while affirming the responsibility of training institutions to attempt to do so. When Zinkin wrote about this in 1995 there was no training available in supervision. There was only the memory of one's own supervisors, implying on the one hand the legacy of inspirational supervision, on the other the dead hand of orthodoxy and imitation (or alternatively retaliatory reaction against) passing down the generations. Since then, courses in supervision for experienced practitioners have been developed in Britain and elsewhere. Usually these courses acknowledge that supervision cannot be "taught" any more than analysis can. The courses are not didactic but are rather designed to provide a terrain for the exchange of ideas and questions, encouraging reflective practice to develop through the "supervision of supervision." In turn, the course organizers and supervisors meet for discussion to "co-supervise" their supervision of the novice supervisors. The hunger for more space for thinking is evidently aroused by supervising.

Most of the existing analytic training supervisors, however, have attended no formal courses as supervisors themselves, but reflect on their supervisory methods by reading and writing about them and may participate in peer discussion groups where supervisory issues are drawn out. It is notable that many recent books about supervision are compilations of essays from various perspectives and are the product of collaboration (Kugler 1995; Martindale et al. 1997; Hughes and Pengelly 1997; Driver and Martin 2002; Wiener et al. 2003; Petts and Shapley 2007). It appears that collegial discussion is a vital ingredient of developing the art of supervising. New supervisors, by virtue of their membership on training committees, undertake another version of informal apprenticeship. There they absorb and digest the values and attitudes of senior supervisors, listening and then contributing to the careful assessing procedures of the various training bodies they serve, as they consider the readiness of supervisees to qualify to practice. This affords a measure of valuable "learning on the job." McGlashan (2003) uses the phrase "the individuating supervisor" to emphasize how personal growth and self awareness need to develop in the person supervising as much as in the one being supervised.

The archetypal involvement in the master-apprentice pair inevitably brings its own shadow side. Our analytic "nonjudgmental" attitude can turn to the other pole. Alongside our wish to enable and facilitate the growth of our supervisees is of course its opposite, to use our power malignly to undermine the rightful authority of the apprentice. At the same time that we encourage disagreement and challenge of the supervisor's view, we may dislike the loosening of the idealizing transference to us, as the novice finds his own ideas and voice. We are well advised "to be aware of the envious need to clip the wings of our supervisees, as their potential and growing expertise threaten us" (Shapley 2007, 14). It is important that supervisors listen with humility and doubt ("dubium"—to be of two minds) (Perry 2003), encouraging discussion of difficulties within the supervisory relationship, in order to avoid becoming entrapped without realizing it by the shadow aspects of our own personalities.

CONCLUSION

There is no doubt that my own clinical practice is enhanced and sharpened by being a supervisor, as well as by receiving supervision. I have found supervising in a different culture enlightening in the multifaceted learning it has afforded me, and have been struck by both the universality and uniqueness of what is presented. The enjoyment of shared learning, of watching supervisees grow and experiment with their talents, is very real. I believe in the importance of the supervisor allowing and containing unconsciousness and fantasy, while at the same time holding the essential third position, which stands for differentiation, consciousness and perception. The encouragement of supervisees to use their imagination and thinking is not only for their own sake and their patients' but also in the interests of the continuation and expansion of analytic theory for future generations.

REFERENCES

Astor, James. 2003. Empathy in the use of countertransference between supervisor and supervisee. In *Supervising and being supervised: A practice in search of a theory*, ed. Jan Wiener, Richard Mizen, and Jenny Duckham, 49–64. London: Palgrave Macmillan

Britton, Ronald. 1998. *Belief and imagination*. London and New York: Routledge.

Driver, Christine, and Edward Martin. 2002. *Supervising psychotherapy*. London: SAGE Publications.

Duparc, Francois. 2001. The countertransference scene in France. *International Journal of Psychoanalysis* 82, 1: 151–69

Ekstein, Rudolph, and Robert S. Wallerstein. 1958. *The teaching and learning of psychotherapy*. New York: Basic Books

Fordham, Michael. 1957. Notes on the transference. In *New developments in analytical psychology*. London: Routledge and Kegan Paul

Hopwood, Ann. 2005. Is there a Jungian approach to supervision? Unpublished talk given to supervision course, Society of Analytical Psychology.

Hubback, Judith. 1995. Styles of supervision. In *Jungian perspectives on clinical supervision*, ed. Paul Kugler, 96–99. Einsiedeln: Daimon Verlag.

Hughes, Lynette, and Paul Pengelly. 1997. *Staff supervision in a turbulent environment: Managing process and task in front-line services*. London; Bristol, PA: Jessica Kingsley Publishers.

Jung, C.G. 1946/1966. Analytical psychology and education. In CW 16.

Kugler, Paul, ed. 1995. *Jungian perspectives on clinical supervision*. Einsiedeln: Daimon Verlag.

Martin, Edward. 2003. Problems and ethical issues in supervision. In *Supervising and being supervised: A practice in search of a theory*, ed. Jan Wiener, Richard Mizen, and Jenny Duckham, 135–50. London: Palgrave Macmillan

Martindale, Brian, ed. 1997. *Supervision and its vicissitudes*. London: Karnac Books.

Mattinson, Janet. 1981. The deadly equal triangle. In *Change and renewal in psychodynamic social work: British and American developments in practice and education for services to families and children*. MA: Smith College School of Social Work.

McGlashan, Robin. 2003. The individuating supervisor. In *Supervising and being supervised: A practice in search of a theory*, ed. Jan Wiener, Richard Mizen, and Jenny Duckham, 19–33. London: Palgrave Macmillan.

Mollon, Phil. 1997. Supervision as a space for thinking. In *Supervision of psychotherapy and counselling*, ed. Geraldine Shipton, 24–34. Buckingham; Philadelphia: Open University Press.

Money-Kyrle, Roger E. 1978. *The aim of psychoanalysis: The collected papers of Roger Money-Kyrle*. Perth, Scotland: Clunie Press

Ogden, Thomas. 1999. *Reverie and interpretation: Sensing something human*. London: Karnac Books.

Perry, Christopher. 2003. Into the labyrinth: A developing approach to supervision. In *Supervising and being supervised: A practice in search of a theory*, ed. Jan Wiener, Richard Mizen, and Jenny Duckham, 187–206. London: Palgrave Macmillan.

Petts, Ann, and Bernard Shapley. 2007. *On supervision: Psychoanalytic and Jungian analytic perspectives*. London: Karnac Books.

Pontalis, J.-B. 1975. A partir du contre-transfert. Le mort et le vif entrelacés. *Revue Français. Psychanalysis* 12: 73–88.

Sedlak, Vic. 2003. The patient's material as an aid to the disciplined working through of the countertransference and supervision. *International Journal of Psychoanalysis* 84, 6: 1487–1500.

Shapley, Bernard. 2007. On supervision. *Karnac Review*. London: Karnac Books.

Shearer, Ann. 2003. Learning about supervision. In *Supervising and being supervised: A practice in search of a theory*, ed. Jan Wiener, Richard Mizen, and Jenny Duckham, 207–23. London: Palgrave Macmillan.

Wharton, Barbara. 2003. Supervision in analytic training. In *Supervising and being supervised: A practice in search of a theory*, ed. Jan Wiener, Richard Mizen, and Jenny Duckham, 82–99. London: Palgrave Macmillan.

Wiener, Jan, Richard Mizen, and Jenny Duckham, eds. 2003. *Supervising and being supervised: A practice in search of a theory*. London. Palgrave Macmillan

Wiener, Jan. 2007. The analyst's countertransference when supervising: Friend or foe? Journal of Analytical Psychology 52, 1: 51 – 69.

Zinkin, Louis. 1995. Supervision: The impossible profession. In *Jungian perspectives on clinical supervision*, ed. Paul Kugler, 240–39[??]. Einsiedeln. Daimon Verlag.

CATHERINE CROWTHER is a Professional Member of the Society of Analytical Psychology, in private practice in London. She is past chair of the SAP training committee and co-convener and supervisor for the IAAP program in Russia.

INDEX

Abraham, Karl, 361
active imagination, 118, 122, 123, 172
  and alchemy, 118
  panaceas of, 125–26
  poisons of, 124–25
  and postmodernism, 118, 128–29,
    131–32
  and psyche, 128
  and psychopathology, 124
  and quintessence, 119
  stages of, 120–21
  and subjectivity/objectivity, 120
  as subversive, 128
Adler, Gerhard, x, xv, 38
Adler, Hella, x
adolescence, 269–70
  developmental goals in, 271
  and fragmentation, 269
  integration in, 279
  regression in, 271, 275
  and role of body, 271
  subphases in, 271–72
affect regulation, 190–91
  and countertransference, 190–91
a-imaginal, 11–12
Almaas, T. H., 283
Altmeyer, Martin, 184
Amae, 317
amplification, 109, 111, 122, 123
  as a bridge, 112
analysis, co-creation in, 207
analytical attitude, as ethical attitude, 325

analytical psychology, xv, 82
  debates in, 86
  in Eastern Europe, xii–xiii
  history of, ix
  lay analysis in, xvi
  national associations in, xiii
  shifts of influence in, xii
  spread of, xi–xiii, xviii–xiv
analytical dyad, 206, 207
analytic practice, supervision in, 325,
    331–32
analytic process
  beginnings/endings in, 164–67
  container in, 174–76
  frame in, 169–72
  holding in, 172–74
  as reductive and synthetic, 159
  reverie in, 171
  as spiral, 164–65
  void and meaning in, 165–66
analytic psychology, 279
analytic relationship, tasks of, 197–98
analytic third, 171–72, 174, 203
Anchises, 318
Andrews, Julie, 76
Aphrodite, 318
archetypes, 30
Armstrong, Karen, 64
Astor, James, 391
Athena, 43
Atsumori, 252
attachment, in children, 299

399